Arthur Penrhyn Stanley, Rowland E. Prothero

Letters and Verses of Arthur Penrhyn Stanley, D.D.

Between the Years 1829 and 1881

Arthur Penrhyn Stanley, Rowland E. Prothero

Letters and Verses of Arthur Penrhyn Stanley, D.D.
Between the Years 1829 and 1881

ISBN/EAN: 9783337107642

Printed in Europe, USA, Canada, Australia, Japan

Cover: Foto ©ninafisch / pixelio.de

More available books at **www.hansebooks.com**

LETTERS AND VERSES

OF

ARTHUR PENRHYN STANLEY, D.D.

BETWEEN THE YEARS 1829 AND 1881

EDITED BY

ROWLAND E. PROTHERO, M.A.

BARRISTER-AT-LAW

LATE FELLOW OF ALL SOULS COLLEGE, OXFORD

AUTHOR OF 'THE LIFE AND LETTERS OF DEAN STANLEY'

LONDON

JOHN MURRAY, ALBEMARLE STREET

1895

PREFACE.

THE material from which this selection of Dean Stanley's letters has been made is abundant. But the choice has been restricted by several considerations.

From their private nature a large number of the letters are unsuitable for publication ; a still larger number refer to matters which would be of little interest to the general public ; others have been already used in the ' Life of Dean Stanley,' or were incorporated in his writings with little or no change ; others turn upon theological controversies which have, perhaps, occupied too large a space in the recently published biography of their writer, and are therefore excluded from these pages.

The letters given here have been chosen, as far as possible, for their general interest, or for the light which they throw upon the character, tastes, and habits of mind of the late Dean Stanley, and upon the moral and intellectual influences by which he was most powerfully affected. None of the letters have been published before in their present shape,

and none of them touch on theological controversies.

In date most of the letters belong to the early
or middle portions of Stanley's life.   It is not difficult to explain this preponderance. After his mother's
death in 1862, he found, as he told his cousin, the
Hon. Louisa Stanley, that, even on his foreign travels, he could 'no more write as heretofore.'   'A
blight has fallen on my powers of writing, at least of
writing letters, against which I cannot contend,' he
writes to Mrs. Arnold in 1863.   His marriage, the
pressure of literary work, and the discharge of his
duties at Westminster checked the flow of his
correspondence from 1864 to 1876.   After his wife's
death in the latter year, the old feeling of loss of
power returned in an intensified form.   Before his
own death in 1881 he lost the two correspondents
to whom some of his best letters were addressed.
His cousin, the Hon. Louisa Stanley, died in 1877,
and his sister, Mary, in 1879.

To the letters have been added, at the dates
when they were written, his Oxford Prize Poem
'The Gypsies,' and several minor pieces of verse
which, whatever opinion may be formed of their
merits, were eminently characteristic of the man.

Wherever it was thought to be necessary or
found to be possible, a brief introduction is prefixed
to each letter, explaining the allusions it contains
and the circumstances in which it was written.   It
is difficult to draw the line between an excess and a

deficiency in annotation. The object aimed at has been to supply such information as will enable the letters to be read with greater ease and pleasure. The form of introductions has been adopted, in order that the reader may neither have his attention distracted from the letters by foot-notes, nor find explanations, which he may think superfluous, forced upon his notice by references inserted in the text.

Letters LXXX, CVI, CVII, CVIII, CIX, and CX are published by the gracious permission of Her Majesty the Queen.

The Editor wishes finally to express his gratitude to those who have assisted him in deciphering the letters, explaining the allusions they contain, or preparing them for publication, and especially to Mrs. Charles Stanley, the Hon. Maude Stanley, the Dean of Westminster, Sir George Grove, and Mr. G. H. Holden, Assistant Librarian at All Souls' College, Oxford.

LETTERS AND VERSES

OF

DEAN STANLEY.

—◦◦◦—

I.

A. P. S. to his Sister, Mary Stanley.

SEAFORTH SCHOOL.

[Arthur Penrhyn Stanley, born December 13, 1815, went to a small preparatory school at Seaforth, kept by Mr. Rawson, in September 1824. The poem with which the following letter begins celebrates the birth of the son of Captain (afterwards Sir Edward) Parry, the Arctic navigator, who, in 1826, married Stanley's first cousin, Isabella, the fourth daughter of Sir John Stanley, Bart. (created in 1839 Lord Stanley of Alderley). See 'Life of A. P. Stanley,' vol. i. ch. ii.]

Seaforth : November 17, 1829.

Dear Mary,—And so the dear little boy is come at last. I had been expecting him so long. I was so delighted when I heard of it, that I must write a little ode to him :

> Hail, thou lovely little stranger,
>   Thou, whose smile, so bright and sweet,
>   Shall thy noble father greet
> Now escap'd from ev'ry danger ;
>   Him, whose brave undaunted soul
>   Dar'd explore the Northern pole,
> Storm and ice and snow defying ;

B

Him who, with ecstatic joy,
Kisses now his lovely boy,
In the lowly cradle lying.
    Not upon a sunny day,
    In the reign of flow'ry May,
Didst thou first behold the light ;
    Not beneath the azure sky
    Giv'n to June or hot July,
Did'st thou bless thy parent's sight !
    No ! but gloomy, sullen, sad,
    In a robe of vapour clad,
Dark November saw thy birth ;
    Tempests all around thee growl'd,
    Raging winds about thee howl'd,
Rain that deluged weeping earth ;
    And thy entrance into life
    Was 'mid elemental strife,
'Mid the terror of the storm.
    Yet November, fierce and dread,[1]
    For a while his fury stay'd
To admire thy beauteous form.
    May thy breast with ardour glow
    Hostile to thy country's foe !
May'st thou burn with gen'rous fire !
    May'st thou fearlessly oppose
    Piercing cold and frozen snows,
Worthy of thy noble sire !
    May thy future conduct prove
    That thy high-born mother's love
Is not ill bestowed on thee !
    May thy mirth her sorrow cheer,
    May'st thou dry her falling tear,
Playing with an infant's glee !

---

[1] This alludes to the rain stopping when he was born. Perhaps I have made the day rather too stormy ; but never mind.—[A. P. S.]

As thy swelling charms arise—
Rosy cheeks and sparkling eyes,[2]
To thy parent thou'rt a treasure.
May thy lively looks and voice
Soon the souls of all rejoice,
To the world around a pleasure!

I hope Master Edward will like this. What a contrast you will have—a grave owl and a merry parrot! It has been raining a great deal lately, and filled the common, roads, &c., with puddles and streams, and overflowed the brook, and now it is so miserably cold I must go and warm myself. Well, now I am warm and so I go on. I will send some more poetry to you when I have time.

I have been to another meeting at Liverpool; but it was not at all entertaining. There was no noise or riot or anything of the kind. There were only two good speakers, Mr. Burnet and Mr. *Dillon* (not Theobald). There was one poor old gentleman, an Irishman, who could not quite make out whether he was a bachelor or a widower twenty years. We then had dinner in Liverpool and went about the town—Mr. Rawson and Mrs. Rawson and we four separate. We had just come out of a shop when we saw a gig without a driver galloping away down the street; it ran over a poor woman and broke her backbone: then dashed between two carts and was shattered to pieces— such crowds of people, such running after scattered pears, such groans of the poor woman, such screams of her children, such inquiring about the gig, there were. I bought a new purse and a knife. I find I have more room than I thought I should have, so here is a little ode of Anacreon's.

---

[2] Perhaps I have made the child too beautiful. If his cheeks are not rosy, you may call them 'laughing,' and, if that won't do, put 'cherry lips.' If you don't like 'sparkling eyes,' call them 'sweet blue' if they are, or 'dark black' if they are. But if they are any other colour, I cannot remedy it except 'rolling.'—[A. P. S.]

To bulls has Nature granted horns,
With hoofs the courser she adorns,
Swiftness to hares by terror driven,
To lions ravenous mouths are given,
On fishes fins she has bestowed,
And wings to flying birds allowed,
And man with valour is endowed.

For woman—none of these were left ;
But Beauty was her only gift,
To which all warlike spears must yield,
Preferr'd to ev'ry ample shield ;
And she on whom this gift is pour'd
Can always conquer fire and sword.

Give my love to all at home.

I remain,

Your affectionate

A. P. STANLEY.

II.

A. P. S. to Mary Stanley.

RUGBY SCHOOL.

[This letter was written from Rugby School at the time of the agitation caused by the Reform Bill. Stanley, who went to Rugby, then under Dr. Arnold, in February 1829, was at Mr. Anstey's house. He was promoted into the sixth form in August 1831. See 'Life,' vol. i. ch. iv.]

Rugby : Thursday, October 20, 1831.

My dear Mai,—I trembled as I opened your letter, for after I had sent my letter the thought suddenly struck me that I had not put 'M.P.;' but I comforted myself by thinking I could not possibly have been so foolish. I was aware of the crime of not inclosing the letter, but I was in such a hurry that I really had not time. All the same, I am very much obliged to you for your frank. *We* have not been quite so quiet as you. I don't know whether it was any way connected with the Bill; but, the next day after the news, a barn was burnt down not two miles off, and also came a shocking story of an old woman who was murdered in the same place. The first is true; the old woman, however, is supposed to have slipped into a pond, and been drowned. Well then, a night or two ago there was another cry of fire; the school engines were sent for, and we all tried to catch a glimpse of it through our barred windows, but in vain! However, a fire there was, only two fields out of the town, and a barn was burnt, but a haystack saved. This is the last we have had. It has not made much commotion. Our housekeeper was rather alarmed, as she said that Mr. Anstey was 'a known anti-reformer;' but some of the boys comforted her by telling her he was only a moderate Whig. It was said that the last fire originated from some of the 'gentlemen of the school' lighting their cigars there (don't you suspect me strongly ?); but this we don't allow at all.

I have had my week of especial Præpostorship, in reading one of the lessons in chapel, in calling over, and in parading the schools to keep order. The first of these I got through successfully, except that I gave out the chapter before I had found the place; the second also, except that I mispronounced one or two names of the boys; the third was the most disagreeable. I had put off learning some lines I had to say till then, hoping to have time in the quarter of an hour of walking the school; this was quite impossible, not that the boys were riotous and rebellious—quite the contrary, but the continued murmur which was not loud

enough to reprimand was quite distracting, and the sudden
change from that to the deep silence of our own school just
before we began the lesson was something quite stupefying.
I managed to get through without setting any punishments.

As for my additional *protégés*, the Glazbrookes (you
were right in your spelling), they are substantial fellows,
who can, I think, make their own way. I have not taken
any particular notice of them yet.

We have fires in our studies now, which is in the morn-
ings a great luxury, but afterwards it is rather too hot.
Do you know I think I am becoming hotter? We (the
sixth) have been playing our annual match at football with
all the rest of the school, *i.e.* twenty-eight against two hundred and seventy. In former times it was an easy conquest
for the sixth ; but this time, so great was the degeneracy of
the stock that we had very little chance. I and one or
two more of the most useless incumbrances stood in goal,
i.e. waited to catch the ball whenever the opposite side kicked
it in. This is a very idle station for the superior side,
as the actual players keep the ball away ; but this time it
was very hard work ; and we, the goalers, were in a state
of great responsibility. However, I got a great share of
glory by falling full length on the ball at the feet of one of
the fiercest of our adversaries, and also, as Sarah [3] would
have remarked, with great remnants of my feat on my
trousers. For once in my life I was interested in the game ;
but the conclusion of it was that Dr. Arnold was so much
alarmed at the inequality of the numbers, and the great
exertion we should put ourselves to, that he stopped it.
Mind and tell me if ever you hear anything of his going to
leave. Not that I at all think he is ; but such is a report,
and people about here seem to have got it into their heads

[3] Sarah Burgess, his nurse and faithful friend. For an account of her
death see *Life*, vol. i. pp. 470–1.

he is to be made a bishop. I don't believe a word of it. Ah! we had an archbishop here some few Sundays ago—Dr. Whately; he preached in the chapel, and the next day, I think it was, he heard he was Archbishop of Dublin. I should dread hearing Dr. A.'s last sermon here. The other Sunday he preached a common sermon—I mean nothing particular to affect him—but a very good one, and towards the end he became so animated that it was all he could do to get through it. His voice failed him, or rather was so altered that it seemed quite different ; in short, I never saw anything that gave me more an idea of an inspired man ; and, after the sermon was over, he bent down his head in the pulpit, and, as far as we could judge, he sobbed like a child. He is certainly the very best preacher I ever heard, the very best I could ever wish to hear. What would he do in his last sermon !

Good-bye, dear Mai.   Yours affectionately,
                 A. P. STANLEY.

III.

A. P. S. to Mary Stanley.

RUGBY SCHOOL :
THE ESSAY PRIZE AND THE ENGLISH VERSE PRIZE.

[Stanley, who had been joined at Rugby School in February 1832 by his brother Charles, gained the English Essay and the English Verse Prizes, the subjects being respectively 'Novels and Novelists' and 'Charles Martel.' See 'Life,' vol. i. ch. iv.]

Rugby : Saturday, April 14, 1832.

My dear Mai,—I am fated to answer your letters instantly. I should have written yesterday, but that I was not sure whether you were come back. I have got the English Verse ! I sent in, as I told you last Monday, 192 lines. On Thursday reports were disseminated of the extraordinary goodness of one copy—particularly one master, who told his pupils that it was the best school exercise (the sentence has undergone several gradations, so that I cannot tell which is the correct version) ever shown up, or that he had ever seen, or the best ever done at Rugby. Another master (Sir Stephen's friend), to whom Charley goes for private mathematics, said to him (he had questioned him on our names before, and is very merry to the boys), ' Well, Mr. Charley, does Arthur intend to get the English Verse ? What will papa say if he does ? ' This tickled Charley's fancy very much. Well, of course, with all this there was little doubt of what would happen. So on Friday I went off to school earlier than usual, knowing that it would come out that day ; but before I had got into the quadrangle, the shout went out for Stanley ! So I had to run breathless into the school, where it was given out accordingly. There were no second prizes given to the other competitors. Dr. A. then said that as my verses were so ' exceedingly good,' he should give a half holiday for them, especially after the disappointment of the year before, when the English Verse had not been good enough to get a prize. All this was very satisfactory, was it not ? So now I have got two ; and I forget whether I told you in my last letter that I had got the third prize for the Latin verse. The English I shall have to speak regularly.

I have got my essay back from Dr. A., but I shall not be able to send you a copy just yet. I went to have it looked over with him, and he praised it very much, and said there was no part that wanted cutting out ; but that it was so long that it would require abridging for reading it, and accordingly suggested some places for shortening it. He was looking at something about Smollett, and said that ' Humphrey Clinker' was not thought enough of generally, and, upon my telling him I had never read it, ' Oh ! you must read

" Humphrey Clinker " ! If you have not, I must lend it you.
It is not too much to say that I have read it through fifty
times,' and accordingly he jumped up and got it down for
me.   It is very difficult work abridging it, and sacrificing
one sentence after another ; but, however, I shall improve
it in some respects, and you shall have both copies.   Likewise ' Charles Martel,' when I can get him copied out.   But
really I shall have so many copies of both one and the
other claimed that it is rather a bad job. Tell papa I speak,
and the grand day is on the Wednesday after Easter
Sunday.

I have been pondering over a new coat, but I have at
last come to the determination that the one I had at the
ball will do.   The only objection is that when, in speaking
the English verse, I stretch forth my hand in action, the
sleeves, being rather short, come down ; but I can remedy
that by a long shirt-sleeve, and perhaps my forefinger
turned down upon the rebellious coat-sleeve.   Charley bids
me not forget to tell you that I was sitting in my study
rather absent, and, wanting him, I called out as loud as I
could, ' Charley,' then, immediately perceiving my blunder,
I called as usual ' Young Stanley ! ' Luckily the first call
was unintelligible to all but him, and he came running in
so surprised ; but I can always call him ' Young Stanley '
now with great ease.

The other night some of us dined with Dr. Arnold.
He said that when he was travelling last holidays to the
Lakes by Brereton Green with all his train of fry, servants,
&c., when they had got to Knutsford the fry began to
lament that some char they had brought for dinner had
gone back to Brereton in the return chaise ; but they
thought no more about it till, when they came back this
half, they found it here.   The people had not only had the
honesty to keep it, but the sense to send it here (knowing

who Dr. Arnold was) by one of the Cheshire boys. He used, when he had more time, to keep a journal of the weather like papa, and could tell for many years together on what day of what month the weather changed, &c. When Mrs. Arnold asked him in joke what kind of April it was this time ten, fourteen &c. years ago, ' Oh, the 18th it cleared up, on the 19th I bathed, on the 12th our almond tree budded, &c.' I certainly was very much astonished at Mdlle.'s resolution. I had often heard her talk about it, and had a dispute with her last holidays where the East Indies were. I was very much pleased with Owen's letter. When do you write again ? Now goodbye, my dear Mai.

Your affectionate

A. P. STANLEY.

How does Sarah go on now ? Charley shall not be ruined by fishing. Will you please suggest to me a sound that we heard on the Venasque night, besides the owl ? I am much distrest for the sake of the rhyme after ' the owl's lament,' ' the eagle's yell.' ' Yell' in itself is bad ; but I shield myself under Scott's ' when the eagle was yelling ;' but I am afraid they never yell or anything at night. For I have begun by saying that the watchfire on the Pyrenees is the beacon, not the hunter's ; the sounds are the clash of arms, not the owl.

The mumps are the prevailing illness now ; perhaps I shall have them

IV.

A. P. S. to Mary Stanley.

RUGBY SCHOOL.

[This and the following letter refer to the recitation of his prize-essay and prize-poem at the Speech Day in Easter week, 1832. See ' Life,' vol. i. ch. iv.]

Thursday, April 19, 1832.

Dear Mai,—I have just got the mumps! not *very badly*, however, and I shall probably come in in time to speak. However, if I don't, I must comfort myself that I might be dreadfully bothered by speaking, and that I shall gain more fame from the singularity of the case, which I suppose has never happened before at Rugby. Really copies are in such request that I think I must have one or both printed ; the two English generally are, and if I can make any compact with the booksellers here, I think I shall ; however, I will send you a written copy of the abridged essay first and afterwards of the original one. It is rather a hard job, because in the abridged one I have improved the order of the last part, but at the same time left out a good deal which you would like to see, and which, as I said before, Dr. Arnold liked very well.

Tell mamma that I have finished ' Humphrey Clinker' and have been very much amused with it, though I should perhaps not have gone steadily through it without the Doctor's recommendation. I should think it would be a nice book to travel through England and Scotland with, and see how the descriptions then, which seem very clear, agree with the different places now. I have had my English verse looked over the other day ; he corrected only one ambiguous word, and left out two lines. I said, in the description of the Moors passing the Pyrenees, that before them

Lay the green vines, and sea-like plains of France.

Dr. Arnold said he was sure, when he read that line, it was written by somebody who had been through France.

We have just had a new regulation on Sundays, that, whereas before we had only one lesson, improperly called *lecture*, of some chapters in the Bible, there is now another properly called lecture given by each master to his form on religious subjects without anything for the boys to prepare. Accordingly Dr. Arnold lectured us for about half an hour. It was quite perfect. It was on Genesis, beginning at the first chapter, and the exceeding clearness and truth and newness of what he said were delightful. Of all the new rules he has made, there is none perhaps which would have excited more disturbance some years ago, and none which is now more perfectly acquiesced in. I don't think there was any boy in the sixth who was not pleased with his lecture ; and in general, with the other masters, though probably not so good, I believe the lectures were liked. They were all on different subjects, and not only am I very glad of it on my own account, but I think it will be a very good thing in general. Whether the interest in it will wear off with the novelty, I cannot say ; but at present it certainly is not unpopular. I heard likewise of the Reform Bill on Saturday evening at about six o'clock—was told by an anti-reformer as 'Have you heard the dreadful news ?' Some boys had been at Dunchurch, when the seven o'clock express that passes through went by, and came back on the coach that comes from Dunchurch to Rugby. They were anti-reformers, and a man on the coach said : ' Of course you young gentlemen will have an illumination to-night ?'

My mumps are better this evening; the chief inconvenience has been a great headache, which is now subsiding. Indeed they are not the proper mumps altogether, only an inferior degree. Will you please send a box of pills by papa, as the people in this town have not got them ? Tell Catherine that if I get in to speak the English Verse, I shall be far too frightened to laugh ; however, I will try and open my mouth.   Your affectionate

A. P. STANLEY.

Charley wants his 'Isaac Walton' by papa; he thinks 'Walton' may not be sufficient to make you comprehend.

V.

CHARLES MARTEL: A PRIZE POEM.

[The following are the opening lines of the prize-poem on 'Charles Martel,' which Stanley recited in Rugby school-room on Wednesday, April 25, 1832. The poem, together with the prize-essay on 'Novels and Novelists,' was published by Rowell and Son, of Rugby, in 1832.]

Why gleam the watch-fires on the mountain's breast?
The hunter takes not there his midnight rest.—
'Tis not the owl from wood and cliff that calls,
'Tis not the rushing avalanche that falls!
The fatal hour is come—the beacon's glare,
The clash of arms proclaims the Moor is there!
In fruitless strength your guardian peaks ye rear,
Proud mountain-barriers! 'gainst their wild career.
Onward they come—like thousand streams that flow
Through thousand gorges from the eternal snow.
In all the magic pomp of eastern war,—
The turban's snowy folds, the flashing scimetar,—
A nation—not an army—swept along;
Such and so numerous was the mighty throng.
Thirsting for blood, and fresh in strength and fame,
Chief of the host rode princely Abderame;
And far and wide, beneath his eagle glance,
Lay the green vines, and sea-like plains of France.
On those fair lands the morrow's sun arose—
Gone was that virgin bloom, that rich repose.
There blackened tracks, and smoking ruins spread;
The heathen triumph'd, and the Christian fled.

A cry went up among the sons of France :
The minstrel's song hath ceas'd, the merry dance.
From land to land an awful shudder ran,
And nation gazed on nation, man on man.
The valiant trembled, and the wicked pray'd—
The feud of chiefs, the war of kings was stay'd ;
All felt, or thought they felt, the avenging rod,
And Europe, awe-struck, own'd the Truce of God !
'The Moor ! the Moor ! The man of endless war,
'Who comes on eagle's pinions from afar ; [4]—
'Whose tongue we know not, and whose gods we hate—
'Dreadful as death—invincible as fate !'
And who shall save ?

VI.

A. P. S. to Mary Stanley.

RUGBY SCHOOL.

Rugby : Thursday, April 26, 1832.

My dear Mai,—As you have by this time got my poem
and essay, I may perhaps be allowed to quote. ' The fight
is o'er, the victory won !' [5] It is over at last. My mumps
recovered so as to let me in again for Sunday : and I re-
hearsed for the first time on Monday ; was enjoined to
speak louder, which I did on Tuesday, and I believe made
myself quite audible. On Wednesday morning I went
down the town, and, as I expected, just met papa coming
in. We and another family who had come for their son's
Latin prize poem breakfasted with Mr. Anstey. I then
took papa to Mr. Price, and then 'within my study sate
alone,' and then came 'the tedious time of dread suspense

---

[4] Deut. xxviii. 49.—[A. P. S.]
[5] A quotation from the prize-poem on 'Charles Martel.'

&c.' till 12, during which I kept saying my poem. I washed my head very properly, and made it quite decent, I think, without the help of artificial curls : took two glasses of wine, and 'then rushed abroad to meet the dreadful hour.' The day had luckily cleared up, so that I had not the splashing through mud and wet as I had expected, and I arrived safe at the school with nothing forgotten, with my prize-essay to read ; my two poems were neatly rolled up, and tied with three blue ribbons (by the housekeeper), and one to prompt from.

The people now began to flock in, and as Dr. Wool and Mrs. Wool came in (the late master, you know) there was a thundering peal of clapping. But, however, this was nothing to me, and when the people were settled, the first speaker (*i.e.* Latin poet) began to speak. I was all this time not in a very great fright, not near so much as in my fifth-form essay, but still in a very great tremor. I spoke second ; so as soon as the first boy had done, I got up with my roll in my hand, and, trying to look at no one, I set off as loud as ever I could, and did not feel very much alarmed, except when I forgot it every now and then ; but my prompter prompted very loud — too loud for all but me — and so I got on without many blunders.

Perhaps you will like to hear particulars. The first place where I used any distinct action was the 'sea-like plains of France,' where I waved about my arms over the plains ; the most vehement part was ' On, Christians, on.' Then it had been suggested to me that, if the old opposition master, Mr. Moor, was present, I should point at him as ' The Moor, the Moor ; ' and there he was when I got up, just opposite me, but I dared not use the action. I was very near leaving out four lines beginning with ' perchance above &c.' but I just remembered in time ; and I said ' the *unknown* ocean, and the *boundless* shore ; ' and, lastly, I forgot my

first bow before I walked up for the prize (which was two
large folios, 'Diodorus Siculus,' a fine edition of a Greek
book ; and though not very useful now, yet a good and
venerable book to have), which it was all I could do to carry
back.   Then there intervened the Latin essay, and then I
was again quite comfortable for the essay.   I think it could
scarcely have been that ; but, just as I was beginning, I felt
such a queer sensation at the top of my head, just as if my
hair was standing on end : but it very soon went down, and
I went on in a strenuous tone to the end, and then, as I
went up to get the last prize, there rose from all sides a
tremendous peal of clapping.   Those few moments certainly
gave me as much pleasure as I have ever had, I think.
And it fully repaid me for all the trouble I had had.   My
essay prize was a very venerable old folio, bound in vellum,
'Chroniques de Monstrelet' of 1603.   After the speeches
came the dinner ; and as the Latin poem boy was not there,
I had to sit at the head of the table, which in one point
proved fortunate, as I sate before veal, and had not a single
slice to carve.   Afterwards I had to propose the customary
toasts, all of which I cut very short, without bestowing any
praise on the persons proposed.   And then the day was
over : to quote again, ' it leaves a blank upon the mind, like
that depression of spirits which so frequently follows vehement mirth.' [6]   I have not seen papa again to-day, as it is
rather early, and such a miserable rainy day ; we are both
waiting, he at the inn, I fear, but I shall go down soon.   I
have sent my poem and essay to the printers, and shall
have it done about Monday.   I will take plenty of copies
to myself, and leave the rest to defray the expenses.   I am
become quite experienced now.   Will you please tell me
exactly how much may go in a frank ? as I can then perhaps send copies by driblets to you if they will go.   I had

---

[6] A quotation from his prize-essay.

a congratulatory letter from Uncle Penrhyn, who had read them on their way. I shall write to him to-day. How am I to get my prizes home ?

Yours ever,
A. P. S.

Arthur has now left me a little room to write to you ; I have not been very well this week, for I was rather mumpy, but I am much better now. Tell Catherine that Arthur does his exercise with his arms every night in our bedroom, and I think he can reach nearer his toes than he could. It was a great pity that, though I was at the speeches, yet I was in such a place that I could not see Arthur at all : but I could hear every word he said, for he spoke very plainly and very loud.

I remain, your affec.
CHARLIE.

VII.

A. P. S. to Mary Stanley.

RUGBY SCHOOL AND THE INFLUENCE OF DR. ARNOLD.

October 9, 1832.

My dear Mai,—We were both much amused with our packet. Charley wants to know the colour and more particulars of Picnic.[7] His former attack is not quite well (the doctor said it was from stomach), but he has been staying out (Charley observed the other day that some of the masters called it 'stopping out') these two or three days for rheumatism, which has been going up and down all over him and made him very miserable ; but he is getting better now. I gave him 'Kenilworth'—choosing

---

[7] The new pony at Alderley.

it as having been read by Catherine. I hope, when he has done with this, he will have no more of anything. At the end of this week comes the examination, which I shall be most heartily glad to have got over. I shall just see how it is, but otherwise it is a great bore, not having entered sincerely into it with any more definite object. I am also rather melancholy this week, as some of the boys who are going are those whom I have known the best and longest in the school, and some who will be a great loss to the school generally. I should think Dr. Arnold would feel it a great deal, as this is the first set which have gone out wholly from him, and some of them he is very fond of—almost so as to consider them as friends. The other day he thanked the form for the way they had done their work, especially this half year, and said, with tears in his eyes almost, that the time he passed in the library with us was a delight and amusement to him. I am glad he thinks so; it is more than I should think. There has been something so affectionate in his last sermons, that I can see that they are meant very much for those who are going, especially for one whom he is anxious about. Whatever happens in the week to diminish my respect for him, it always comes back on the Sunday when I hear him preaching. The other night, when some of the sixth were dining with them, he showed them various odd things of his, such as a great collection of prose, poetry, squibs of Charles the First's time, &c. &c. made by him, and a newspaper scrap-book like papa's, and his childish drawings, on which Bunch observed, 'Why, papa, how well you drawed when you was a little boy!'

I suppose you mean me to get you a 'Christian Year'? Well, perhaps I may. The weather is turned cold, so we are looking forward to fires with great eagerness.

I have had such an odd secret correspondence lately

with Captain Phipps Hornby, who wanted to know about his son, so I had to write a long letter to tell him all I knew. I had to do an English theme afterwards; of the two, I think the letter was the hardest, and then I had to put it under cover to Lord Digby, so that you may imagine with what awe I folded it up, but I think it was decent enough. However, I suppose it is all a profound secret. It made me half laugh, half be melancholy, to be called 'a young man,' and be written to as such—the first time I ever was so I think.

We have been having two candidates here, both of whom I went to hear; the first was moderate enough, but the next, oh! such a radical. I think he would have driven you mad—vote by ballot, no seats for bishops, &c. &c. However, it was very amusing, and, at every grievance he spoke of, a dirty old man near me said, 'Oh dear! Oh dear!' in such a ridiculously pitiful tone. While he was abusing the Church vehemently, one of the mob got up; and so a pause ensued, and the man said, 'I think the gentleman's sentiment is true. A clergyman certainly has more than his due!'

Now love to all and good bye.

Yours ever,

A. P. STANLEY.

VIII.

A. P. S. to Mary Stanley.

VISIT TO LONDON.

[In November 1833 Stanley gained a scholarship at Balliol College, Oxford. In the following July he left Rugby ('Life,' vol. i. ch. iv.). The interval from August to October 1834 was spent at Hurstmonceux with Julius Hare. John Sterling, whose life has been written by both Julius Hare and Thomas Carlyle, and who was the close friend of F. D. Maurice, was then curate at Hurstmonceux.

The following letter describes his journey from Alderley to London, his first impressions of the capital, and a visit to his mother's brother (who had assumed the name of Penrhyn in addition to that of Leycester) at East Sheen. In the early stage of the journey his companion was C. J. Vaughan, now Dean of Llandaff, his schoolfellow, future brother-in-law, and lifelong friend. In London he was joined by his brother Charles, who was by this time at Woolwich Academy. Edward John Stanley, afterwards the second Lord Stanley of Alderley, the 'Edward' and 'Edward John' of this letter, was then acting as the Whig Whip.

The 'Bull and Mouth,' a famous London coach-office, stood on part of the site now occupied by the General Post Office in St. Martin's-le-Grand. 'The Salopian' was an inn at Charing Cross, 'much frequented,' says Sir Richard Phillips in 1804, 'by gentlemen of the army.' The Colosseum in Regent's Park contained, among other sights, a panorama of London from the top of St. Paul's. It was pulled down in 1873.

The article in the ' Quarterly Review,' on ' Eton School —Education in England ' (August 1834), was written by Dean Milman.]

The Cedars [East Sheen] : Monday, August 25, 1834.

My dear Mai,—I write as soon as I can, so you must not grumble. We got our two inside places, in which we came all the way, as the outside was full ; our fellow passengers were as usual very uninteresting. What a fine and large church it is at Ashbourne ! It seemed like coming among the shadows of departed years, when, after the hilly, heathy country of Derbyshire and what Dr. Arnold calls 'the fat green surface ' of Leicestershire, we came in sight of the Charnwood Forest hills, where, with Vaughan's explanations, I recognised all the places I knew so well from my old friend Rose at Seaforth. We reached Leicester about seven, where Vaughan found a note begging him to bring me with him to stay there that night. However, this was, of course, out of the question, and so I continued my journey alone, a beautiful moonlight night, and I slept pretty well. We came into London by way of Islington, but had no view of the great place before, both as it was misty and I was inside. I got out at the 'Bull and Mouth,' and called for a cab, which came without any trouble, and, having first ascertained the fare, which was eighteenpence, and the number, I had a very pleasant drive through the City, under St. Paul's, and I was quite sorry to reach the 'Salopian.' There was no attempt to make off with the luggage! It was about seven; so I went to bed and had a doze for two hours. I was rather stupefied, but nothing else, with my journey. When the bar was opened, Charley's letter was brought, saying he could get leave, and at a quarter to nine he came in. We had such a happy breakfast together, then set off for the office, where we found Edward could not be till twelve. Went to Westminster Bridge; saw the House of Lords, which Charley had not seen and which I was glad to see, as it will give me an idea of how things look in the debates, and explained one or two stories connected with it: then went into the Poet's Corner and the part of the Abbey which was visible while the service went on; but as it was going on, we could not see the rest then. I rather wish we had waited; but I think this was the only part of the day we mismanaged, and our excuse must be that we knew we had a good deal to see and we only had one day before us. However, what we did see was very striking. I then had my hair cut, and we took a cab with our luggage to the White Horse Cellar, where we left it, and then set off walking for the Zoological Gardens by Regent Street; called on Justice Vaughan on the way, as his nephew had told me to do, and, as he was not in, left my card.

As we were going up Queen's Arcade, we met Edward going down to the office. He was rather surprised, but

had very confused ideas about us, settling that I had come
from Rugby and that it was Charley's vacation ; and said
that he was coming to Sheen that day, or when he could.
I am rather proud of having been the one to see him, as
neither Charley nor he would have stopped but for me.

Regent Street seemed quite interminable ; but the
length of the walk was quite made up for by its magnificence. If it had not been for the hatchments here and there,
I should have thought all those houses after the circus had
been great public buildings. There were not many carriages.
We went all round the Zoological Gardens, where Charley
says the beasts were duller than usual, but easier to see,
as there was no crowd. You may imagine us walking
about ; I felt how dull it would have been without him ;
as it was, he knew just where to take me and so to econo-
mise time, and we could observe who the monkeys were
like, &c. &c. What I liked the best were the brown bears,
both on the pole, and one in a cage that was the very image
of the one in the German stories fiddling. And those
crested sort of peacocks that hopped so exactly like exceedingly silly people ; the monkeys were rather quiet, but
the way in which they picked the fleas off each other was
capital, one so very earnest and the other so very submis-
sive. The vultures are certainly the very perfection of
loathsomeness. We want to know if the road goes over
the arch, and whether the suicide of the white bear is
true.

As we came back we thought we might as well see the
Colosseum. I never saw anything so like a great baby-
house. At some parts, such as the Swiss cottage and grotto,
we sate down and laughed in fits ; it looked so very absurd,
with the mixture of truth and falsehood so jumbled that
we could not tell what was sham and what not. However,
the panorama of London was very curious, only it seemed

rather inconvenient to have the parts one knew best furthest off. We next called at Queen Anne Street; the servant asked us who we were; I gave my card, and so we were shown up. And Lady Louisa came in. She was much what I might have fancied; we stayed for about twenty minutes, chiefly talking alternately of Rugby and Woolwich. As we were coming back through New Bond Street, Charley suggested going in to see the great microscope; so then we had all the monsters magnified millions of times. They reminded me of the pictures you see in 'Paradise Lost' of the beasts beginning to hunt and eat each other. There was one show of snakes which looked so exactly like a Fury's head.

We got to the White Horse Cellar just in time to catch a Sheen coach, which took us over Putney, not Hammersmith, bridge. The river was very high and looked magnificent in the bright evening sun. Charley explained all the places, and pointed out Mrs. C. Page's. The first sound we heard on opening the upper gate was Lion and the dogs barking, and the next, the little boys calling out, 'Cousin Arthur and Cousin Charley.' We were just in time for dinner. Just after the first course, in walked Edward John; he was very talkative; he told stories of his work, how troublesome it was to have people coming to see him every moment when he was at work (which made me rather glad he had been away); how Lady Glengall had come for a warrant to search all the State papers for one hundred years back, and had at last gone with a letter for the Recorder, in which he begged him to explain to her the reason she could not see them; how a clergyman had sent a petition to the king, begging for a preferment on the plea that they were both descended from the same great progenitor, viz. William the Conqueror—with pedigree affixed; how another had appealed on being turned out

of his curacy by the Rev. Marcus Beresford after having in
vain appealed to the Bishop and Archbishop, who were
both Beresfords too. Phipps Hornby arrived late.

I went to bed at eleven and slept soundly. Eddy and
Oswy come to call me in the morning and try to shut me
up while I am washing. I am in the store room. What
has most struck me hitherto has been Regent Street, the
Thames at Putney, and Westminster Bridge. Have you
read the article in the 'Quarterly' on public schools? I
think it is very fair, all things considered, but there were
one or two places where I longed to make a note. Yesterday I thought so of their all being at Rugby again. I
think I have told you all. I am not quite satisfied with
our arrangements in London ; but we were as happy as
possible, and saw a good deal. I stay till Friday and
nothing seems likely to keep me longer. So with dear love,
and kisses to the children, and telling Emmy how I want
some one to tell me all the trees on the lawn.

Believe me, yours ever,

A. P. STANLEY.

IX.

A. P. S. to Mary Stanley.

FIRST IMPRESSIONS OF OXFORD.

[In October 1834, Stanley went into residence as a
scholar of Balliol College, Oxford. The following letter
was written a few days after the destruction of the Houses
of Parliament on October 16, 1834. Its interest lies in the
contrast of the religious atmosphere of Rugby and Hurstmonceux with that of Oxford in the early days of the
Tractarian Movement. A sketch of the Master of Balliol
(Dr. Jenkyns) and the Fellows of the College, including
Frederic Oakeley, J. M. Chapman, and A. C. Tait, was
written by Benjamin Jowett, and will be found in the 'Life
of W. G. Ward,' pp. 114–16. In Dean Burgon's 'Twelve

Good Men' (vol. i. pp. 296–373), Charles Marriott is described as 'the man of saintly life.']

Balliol College, Oxford : October 25, 1834.

My dear Mai,—I fear I was too much wrapped up in other matters and too much secluded from papers to sympathise fully with the fall of the two Houses. It certainly must have been a fearful thing for the Hall and Abbey; and, if the Abbey had been burnt, I should indeed have mourned over it. But to work. Tuesday: Breakfasted at Christ Church with E. Egerton, meeting Lord A. Loftus, Faber, and one or two more. It was cut short, however, by Lord A. and myself having to come away at half-past nine to hear, with the other freshmen, Jenkyns read the College Statutes in chapel. They were in Latin and took an hour and a half—a curious specimen of writing, certainly, consisting of an elaborate comparison between a college and a man's body, in which, for instance, the two priests were compared to the lungs as dealing with 'spiritual things;' we scholars are the calves of the legs; the chief part was taken up with attributes of the Master, which he read with becoming pomp, and self-complacency.

I unpacked &c. in the morning, and went out calling in the evening on sundry Rugbeians who had called on me. You need not be alarmed that I should cultivate their acquaintance too much. I am very circumspect. I was called upon—amongst others—by Dr. Duncombe while I was out, by another brother of the tutor of Dr. Arnold's children; in short, my acquaintance seems very large. Wined—*i.e.* took dessert—with Highton at Queen's.

Wednesday: Breakfasted with Mr. Churton, where I met Marriott, a tutor or fellow of Oriel and a friend of Price's and Newman's, and therefore rather a curious person to know. They discussed Pusey's sermon and

Newman's, which was very interesting as a specimen of Oxford divinity. About the first they both agreed, admiring it very much, and rather scandalised at my very humble dissent from it. Poor Mr. Sterling! what would he have said at the sermon, or still more at the comments on it? I thought it most prudent and decorous to hold my tongue altogether after my first protest. Marriott said that it (the sermon) was quite an era in their history, and supposed that I had not been in the way of hearing the errors it was directed against,—the errors being the whole system of Mr. Sterling's sermons. About Newman they split, Mr. Churton being an Evangelical, and then too I had to keep my mouth fast to prevent breaking out with Arnold's sermon on St. James. Marriott looked on Newman's sermons just as I do on Arnold's, and I agreed mostly with what he said. Wednesday night, wined with Holden, my predecessor in these rooms, and a scholar of Shrewsbury. He seemed clever, an excellent scholar, and has the most good-humoured face I ever saw, and, in spite of his beginning with a most furious attack on Arnold's theological ideas, I like him very well. This day I began upon Herodotus.

Thursday: Breakfasted with Palmer of Magdalen, to whom Arnold had given me a recommendation. Except Highton, who was there, they were all Balliol men, most of whom I knew before, the most noted being Wickens, an Etonian, of whom Holden told me that he was very clever. Came back too late for my mathematical lecture, for which I apologised on the score of the breakfast. At twelve went to my first lecture to Oakeley—in Livy. We construed in the old way, word for word, in turn, with one or two unimportant remarks from him. I certainly was rather astounded when he said at the beginning 'that there were reasons for supposing that the first part of Livy was not quite authentic, and the best dissertation on it was in Hooke!' I don't know whether he has heard that there is such a book as Niebuhr, but it would seem not; and, if so, it is rather disgraceful, I think. However, he is not a good tutor, and so not a good specimen of Oxford. Moberly's lecture I shall be very glad to hear. Marriott called in the afternoon and expressed his deep veneration for Newman, which grew the more he knew of him. I could not muster courage to say a word against him. On Wednesday, by the way, I went to call on the younger Churton, and while I was there, Newman came to the door to speak to him. I ran to the window and just caught a glimpse of him. I feel a great interest about him, partly from his relation to Arnold, partly from his being so strange a man—as he must be. I called too on Dr. Duncombe.

Thursday, I went on some calls, read the lessons in chapel, and went to the Debating Society, which was dull. Friday: Breakfasted with a Rugby man of this college, and went to Moberly to St. Mark lecture, which was pretty good, and to Herodotus lecture. I returned a call which Dr. Gilbert of Brasenose had made while I was out, and saw Miss Lander, who was very well and told me of Lord Derby's death. On Wednesday I dined with the Warden of New College. I went out to walk with Lonsdale the other day and found him very agreeable, though not, I think, so clever as I had imagined. Most of the men at lectures construe well, and are better than I should have expected from a promiscuous set (though I suppose we are less promiscuous than other colleges) such as we have. Tell Catherine I am much obliged to her for her slippers, which I often wear, in spite of the warning of an old woman on the 'Tally-ho,' who told me that they would infallibly spoil my feet; poor woman! I have two pairs of sheets and two table-cloths.

Yours ever,
A. P. S.

A. P. S. to Mrs. Stanley.

THE NEWDIGATE PRIZE POEM.

April 2 [1837], Oxford.

My dear Mama,—All is over! The poem went in at a quarter to twelve last night, and I think Brodie's, in point of real poetical power, is much superior to it—though (I think also) inferior in point of arrangement and richness of ideas. His end is the least good, as being obscure and not sufficiently pointed. The length is 270 lines.

The two poems are so totally different that it is hard to compare them. On the one hand, my plan is more complete and more varied, and my end is much better. My verses too are much stronger, and more antithetical and pointed. On the other hand, I have no one idea so poetical as the one which pervades his poem, and which is as beautiful in the expression as it is in the conception. His motto explains his plan :

> The Youth, who daily farther from the East
> Must travel, still is Nature's Priest,
> And by the vision splendid
> Is on his way attended :
> At length the Man perceives it die away,
> And fade into the light of common day.

The description of the child at the beginning is very fine indeed, and there is no comparison between my bald, forced, and monosyllabic lines and his profusion of imagery, and most absolute command of language, and most harmonious and unbroken versification. I think there can be no doubt that his is really the best, though, at the same time,

it is so unlike a prize poem that I think it more than doubtful whether it will succeed.

I think the fairest thing would be to say that mine is
the best *poem*, and his the best *poetry*. The last, I think,
is certain : the first, of course, is doubtful, but still is what
hopes may be built upon.

Yours ever,

A. P. STANLEY.

XI.

THE GYPSIES : A PRIZE POEM.

[Stanley's poem won the Newdigate Prize, and was
recited by him in the Sheldonian Theatre at Oxford on
June 7, 1837. The notes are by him.]

How sweet the scene—a shrine of deep repose,
And solemn calm amid a world of woes ;
The forest-skirts, along whose leafy maze
And tall grey stems the green light gently plays ;
The quiet lane, to whose wild hawthorn bowers
The infant Spring entrusts her earliest flowers ;
The rose-clad cottages that-cluster round,
Each with gay porch and plot of flowery ground ;
The patch of russet moor—the joyous scene
Of children sporting on the heathy green—
Is there a spot where Earth's dim daylight falls,
That with such power all evil thought appalls ;
Where shade, air, waters—all beneath the dome
Of the blue sky, so speaks, so breathes of Home ?

Fond dreamer, pause ! Why floats the silvery wreath
Of light thin smoke from yonder bank of heath ?
What forms are those, beneath the shaggy trees,
In tattered tent, scarce sheltered from the breeze ?

The hoary father and the ancient dame,
The squalid children, cowering o'er the flame ?
These were not born by English hearths to dwell,
Or heed the carols of the village bell ;
Those swarthy lineaments, that wild attire—
Those stranger tones, bespeak an Eastern sire ;
Bid us in Home's most favoured precincts trace
The houseless children of a homeless race ;
And, as in warning vision, seem to show
That man's best joys are dimmed by shades of woe.

Pilgrims of Earth ! who hath not owned the spell
That ever seems around your tents to dwell,
Solemn and thrilling as the nameless dread
That guards the chambers of the silent Dead?
The sportive child, if near your camp he stray,
Stands tranced with fear, and heeds no more his play ;
To gain your magic aid, the love-sick swain
With hasty footstep threads the dusky lane ;
The passing traveller lingers, half in sport
And half in awe, beside your savage court,
While the weird hags explore his palm to spell
What varied fates those mystic lines foretell.

Where be the Spirits that attend your will ?
Where your dread ministers for good and ill ?
The mighty storms your funeral dirges sing ;
The gladsome flowers to greet your footsteps spring ;
The murmuring streams your minstrel songs supply ;
The moss your couch, the oak your canopy ;
The sun awakes you as with trumpet-call—
Lightly ye spring from slumber's gentle thrall ;
Eve draws her curtain o'er the burning West —
Like forest birds ye sink at once to rest :

The busy world, with all its glittering show
Of outward grandeur and of inward woe,
Mars not with morning cloud or noonday glare
The ethereal freshness of your brighter air ;
Free as the winds that through the forest rush—
Wild as the flowers that by the wayside blush—
Children of Nature, wandering to and fro,
Man knows not whence ye come, nor where ye go—
Like foreign weeds cast up on Western strands,
Which stormy waves have borne from unknown lands ;
Like murmuring shells to Fancy's ears that tell [8]
The mystic secrets of their ocean cell.

Drear was the scene—[9] a dark and troublous time—
The Heaven all gloom, the wearied Earth all crime ;
Men deemed they saw the unshackled Powers of ill
Rage in that storm, and work their perfect will :
Then, like a traveller, when the wild wind blows,
And black night flickers with the driving snows,
A stranger people 'mid that murky gloom
Knocked at the gates of awe-struck Christendom !
No clang of arms, no din of battle roared,
Round the still march of that mysterious horde ;
Weary and sad, arrayed in pilgrim guise,[1]
They stood and prayed, nor raised their suppliant eyes ;

[8] '. . . . . Applying to his ear
The convolutions of a smooth-lipped shell—
. . . . . murmurings from within
Were heard, sonorous cadences—whereby,
To his belief, the monitor expressed
Mysterious union with its native sea.'
Wordsworth's ' Excursion.'

[9] The Gypsies first appeared in Europe about the commencement of the fifteenth century (*Hoyland*, p. 12), a period of such universal misery in Christendom as to give rise to a popular opinion that it was the season in which Satan was loosed.

[1] When they first made their appearance in Europe, they pretended to be pilgrims.—*Hoyland*, p. 13.

At once to Europe's hundred shores they came,
In voice, in feature, and in garb the same ;
Mother, and babe, and youth, and hoary age,
The haughty chieftain,[2] and the wizard sage :
At once in every land went up the cry,
' Oh ! fear us not—receive us—or we die ! '
No lust of wealth, nor scent of distant war,
Nor wisdom's glory lures them from afar ;
'Tis not for these the Children of the night
Have burst at once on realms of life and light ;
'Tis the dread Curse—behind them and before—
That goads them on, till time shall be no more ;
They claim no thrones—they only ask to share
The common liberty of earth and air—
Ask but for room to wander on alone
Amid Earth's tribes unnoticed and unknown !

Few were their words, and broken was their tale,[3]
Mixed with wild tears and penitential wail ;
A tale of dark unexpiated crime,
Of some dread Vision in the dim old time ;
They spake of lovely spots in Eastern lands,
An isle of palms, amid a waste of sands—
Of white tents pitched beside a crystal well,
Where in past days their fathers loved to dwell ;
To that sweet islet came at day's decline
A Virgin Mother with her Babe Divine ;[4]

---

[2] Thus, at Paris, they were led by twelve dukes.

[3] Their account of themselves, amidst much variety, seems to have agreed in this—that they were performing penance for past sin. Thus, in France, they gave out that they were condemned to a seven years' wandering for apostasy from the Christian faith.—*Hoyland*, p. 18.

[4] 'Aventinus delivereth, that they pretend for their vagabond course a judgment of God upon their forefathers, who refused to entertain the Virgin Mary and Jesus, when she fled into their country.'—*Sir T. Browne, Vulgar Errors*, book vi. c. 13.

She asked for shelter from the chill night breeze,
She prayed for rest beneath those stately trees ;
She asked in vain—what though was blended there
A maiden's meekness with a mother's care ;
What though the light of hidden Godhead smiled
In the bright features of that blessèd Child,
She asked in vain—they heard, and heeded not,
And rudely drove her from the sheltering spot.
Then fell the Voice of Judgment from above,
'Who shut Love out, shall be shut out from Love ;[5]
'Who drive the houseless wanderer from their door,
'Themselves shall wander houseless evermore ;
'Till He, whom now they spurn, again shall come,
'Amid the clouds of Heaven to speak their final doom.'

Scorn not the tale—for well might Fancy trace
The hand of God upon that sinful race ;
Cities have fallen and empires passed away,
Earth's giant forms waxed hoary with decay,
Since the lone people 'mid our moors and glades
Looked heedless round, as on a world of shades !
By German streams, through England's good green woods,
In Spain's deep vales, by India's ocean floods,
By desert moor, huge cliff, or willow grey,[6]
Still the dark Wanderers meet us on our way ;
Amid glad homes for ever doomed to roam
In lonely woe, themselves without a home !

The Negro slave returns, in troubled dreams,
To moonlight dances by his palmy streams ;

[5] 'And he that shuts Love out, in turn shall be 'Shut out from Love.'
[6] 'In Germany and Spain they shelter themselves under forests shaded by rocks ; and are partial to willows, under which they erect their sleeping-places.'—*Hoyland.*

D

The Scythian hails, amid the solemn glooms
Of dim ancestral groves, his fathers' tombs ;[7]
The wandering Israelite from year to year
Sees the Redeemer's conquering wheels draw near ;
Still dwells in thought, beneath the meteor light [8]
Of Syrian skies by Zion's towery height ;
Still loves on lonely Lebanon to gaze,
Or track old Jordan through his thicket maze :[9]
On these alone no solitary star
Of ancient joy beams kindly from afar ;
No altar-hearth is theirs ; no common shrine,
The central birthplace of a mighty line ;
No blazoned ancestry of hero sires
In lowly hearts to waken high desires ;
No lay, no legend of a glorious past,
Its living light 'mid present shades to cast ;
No blessèd Isles, no rest beyond the grave ;
No future King, omnipotent to save ;
Even Nature's self, beneath whose constant eye
They live and roam, in whose kind arms they die,
In vain to them, with all a mother's love,
Unfolds her charms around them and above ;
The changeful smiles, the living face of light—
The steady gaze of the still solemn night—
Earth—with her treasure-house of beauteous forms—
Air—with her vast array of calms and storms—
Bright lakes, the glistening eyes of solitude,
Girt with grey cliffs and folds of mighty wood—
All these are theirs—but still from year to year
To Nature's voice they turn a dull deaf ear ;

[7] See Herodotus, iv. 127.

[8] 'The morning rays of the East are not, as in Europe, a vague and confused light—but dart like arrows of fire of many colours from the common centre whence they all issue.'—*Lamartine's Pilgrimage*, vol. ii. p. 2.

[9] The Jordan is almost concealed by the thick covering of wood along its banks.—*Ibid.* ii. pp. 62, 64.

Spring's joyous burst, and Summer's golden prime,
Float o'er their senses like a drowsy chime ;
Autumn's wan leaves and Winter's death-like snows
To them alone no solemn truths disclose ;
No hymn[1] of praise with Morn's bright incense blends,
Through Eve's deep calm no wonted prayer ascends ;
That sullen scowl, that wild and wanton leer
Ne'er smiles in peace, nor softens into fear ;
Yea, God and Man, the Future and the Past,
Are but to them a chaos dark and vast—
One gloomy Present, one unchanged To-day,
Stirred by no storm, and brightened by no ray.

Speak, ye wild winds from Scythian [2] plains that blow,
And tell this fearful mystery of woe !
Speak, glorious Ganges,[3] from the snowy cell
Of thy pure fountains—speak, if thou canst tell !
Fled they of yore, as some would fondly deem,
From the dank groves that veil thy sea-like stream,
What time stern Timur, with his savage band,
Burst like a storm o'er Brahma's shrinking land ?
Heard they the nations heave their long, last groans
Amid the crash of Asia's thousand thrones ?
Speak, ye dead Forms, for countless ages hid
By storied Sphinx or ancient Pyramid—
If early bards their tale aright have told—
Speak, for ye know this wandering race of old,
Speak the dead secret of your children's fall,
And from the mist of years their golden times recall !

Say, can it be, that while this world was young,
While yet Heaven's glory round her childhood hung—

---

[1] For the absence of religion among the Gypsies, see *Hoyland*, pp. 44, 45.
[2] Alluding to the theory which derives them from the Sigynnæ (Herodot. v. 9.) or from Tartary.
[3] Alluding to the theory deriving them from India.

In lonely splendour walked upon the earth
The swarthy sires whence these derive their birth—
Of giant power—of eagle's piercing ken—
Wisest and mightiest of the sons of men ?
What if in yonder chief of tattered vest
Glows the same blood that warmed a Pharaoh's breast ?
If in the fiery eye, the haughty mien,
The tawny hue of yonder Gypsy Queen,
Still dwells the light of Cleopatra's charms,
The winning grace that roused the world to arms,
That called Rome's legions to a watery grave,
And bound Earth's lord to be a woman's slave ?
Lo, Mizraim's king-craft, of its glory reft,
Is shrunk to petty deeds of midnight theft !
Lo, Egypt's wisdom only lives to pry
Through the dark arts of paltry palmistry !
The salt that lacked all savour from above,
The daring pride that knew no humble love,
The priestly lore that worshipped all save God,
Beneath the foot of man must evermore be trod !

Remnant of Ages—from thy glory cast—
Dread link between the Present and the Past—
Where are the tribes that bowed beneath thy might,
That drank from thee as from a fount of light ?
One only race of all thy great compeers
Still moves with thee along this vale of tears ;
Long since ye parted by the Red Sea strand ;
Now face to face ye meet in every land ;
Alone, amid a new-born world, ye dwell—
Egypt's lorn people, outcast Israel !
Like the Two Forms [4] in sackcloth garb arrayed,
By the rapt Seer from Patmos' shores surveyed—

[4] Rev. xi. 3.

Prophets of ill, that stand in speechless woe
On Earth's highway to bid the nations know—
How fallen they, who shone so bright of yore,
One skilled in human, one in holier lore—
How dark their fate, who turn to uses base
Earth's highest wisdom—Heaven's divinest grace!

Wanderers, farewell! 'Tis not for erring man
The mystic rule of God's decree to scan:
Dark is the past; yet still in clear expanse
The Future spreads to Hope's imploring glance;
It cannot be—so drear, so dark a spot
God's glorious Universe for aye should blot;
'It cannot be'—at once with awful cry
The thousand kindreds of His earth reply:
'We, too, are fallen—we too in deserts stray,
'With bliss in sight—with home beside our way:
'We, too, are deaf to messages of love,
'Angels unheeded round our footsteps move:
'This is a solemn world—a "dreadful"[5] spot—
'The gate of Heaven—and yet we know it not!'

Oh! weary days of promise long delayed—
O glorious gifts with thankless scorn repaid—
When will ye end? Oh, when shall man's lost race
Among God's angels take its ancient place?
When shall this vagrant tribe of unknown birth
Regain her rank among the realms of Earth?
When shall lost Israel seek his Father's throne,
And hail a holier Zion than his own?
When shall God's Church her final rest attain,
Pure from all blemish, washed from every stain?

[5] Genesis xxviii. 16. 'He said, Surely the Lord is in this place; and I knew it not. And he was afraid, and said, How dreadful is this place! this is none other but the house of God, and this is the gate of heaven.'

Peace—faithless murmurers! Like the tranquil sky,
Behind Earth's clouds, unseen, yet ever nigh,
Though to and fro Man's restless hopes be driven,
Still round us broods the changeless calm of Heaven;
Still He who knew not where His head to lay,
Who wearied sat beside the noontide way,
He still would bid the lowering tempests cease
That mar the vision of that perfect peace—
With spell divine would lull the troubled breast,
And call the wayworn Wanderers to His rest!
There the lost pilgrim shall no longer roam,
There the lorn outcast find a lasting home!

XII.

A. P. S. to C. J. Vaughan.

WILLIAM PALMER AND POLITICS IN 1837.

[From Oxford Stanley had paid a visit of one day to C. J. Vaughan at Cambridge. William Palmer, whom Stanley elsewhere describes as 'on a level with Newman in his opinions,' was a Fellow and Tutor of Magdalen College, Oxford. After vain efforts to unite the Anglican and Greek Churches, he joined the Roman Church in 1856.]

Oxford : Sunday [July 1837].

My dear Vaughan,—I had a very pleasant journey back and am almost well in consequence. For about twenty miles of the way I had W. Palmer, returning from the examination at Rugby. He had been exceedingly delighted with Arnold individually; thought that his sermon on Sunday was excellent, but his intellectual opinions were monstrous; thought also that he had been led into them not, as most by malice from without, but, through a political theory, by charity from within.

There was a Northamptonshire clergyman—an ordinary political High Churchman of the old school—sitting in the coach. He fired up on hearing Arnold mentioned, and thereupon ensued a most amusing conversation, displaying in vivid contrast two opposite phases of the opinions :

' Do you indeed think Dr. Arnold amiable ? ' ' Certainly. His errors, fearful as they are, have sprung from charity.' ' Charity may be in excess. People make charity a cloak for all sorts of evil.' ' Charity can never be in excess. So far as it is charity, it is wholly pure and good.'

The man, thinking that here they should agree, and stamping vehemently on the floor : ' I think Dissent a *horrible* thing—making a rent in the body of Christ, &c.' ' Yes. But lifeless orthodoxy is little better, &c.'

Then a little politics. ' Do you not think, sir, that the Church is adverse to democracy ? ' ' The Church is independent of forms of Civil Government, sir. She bows to all, whether the tyrant be one or many.' ' The present Ministry will heathenise the country. They don't care for the Bible.' ' They have a great respect for the Bible ; they believe the acceptance of the Bible to be synonymous with Christianity.' ' I am convinced that the Conservatives will come in next election to keep the Whigs out for twenty-five years ! ' ' Convictions are pleasant till they are frustrated by events. O'Connell has a principle. Roebuck has a principle. The Conservatives have no principles whatever.' ' You do not think that the principles of the present Ministry are permanent ? ' ' In one sense nothing on earth is permanent. But I believe they will outlast the present century.' ' We shall have a bloody revolution.' ' Blood is accidental. We may be revolutionised without blood.' ' The Universities will be annihilated.' ' They may be annihilated without blood.'

Thoroughly puzzled, he took a different tack. 'Pray, sir, are there many disciples of Newman, Pusey, &c. at Oxford?' 'In one sense I trust that there are at Oxford no disciples of any man living. In another, I believe that every clergyman in the Church of England holds the principles which those gentlemen have brought prominently forward, though not always quite judiciously.'

It was very amusing indeed, and at last the man ceased in thorough amazement.

On Saturday I dined with your cousin[6] at Oriel, and there met Newman, who was exceeding affable and agreeable. I had never been in company with him before, and so was highly pleased.

I look back with great pleasure to my solitary, I mean single, day at Cambridge, and have not at all repented of the expedition. And now believe me

Yours ever,

A. P. STANLEY.

XIII.

A. P. S. to Mrs. Stanley.

OXFORD—W. G. WARD AND NEWMAN.

[This letter was written on the eve of Stanley's final examination for his degree at Oxford. The examination, which began on November 12, resulted in his obtaining a first class. W. G. Ward, who had been elected to a Fellowship at Balliol in 1834 and was Mathematical Lecturer at the College, was ordained deacon in 1837, priest in 1839. At this time, as a follower of Arnold, he denied the necessity of the Apostolical succession. For this reason Oakeley declined to sign his testimonials for deacon's orders. When he was ordained priest in 1839, he signed the Articles in the sense in which Newman interpreted them.]

[6] Henry Halford Vaughan.

Rugby : September 30 [1837].

My dear Mamma,—I am exceedingly well, and hope that this will quite set me up. The air has always agreed with me, and the talking and walking will be doubly useful. How I do look forward to my final deliverance ! For the first time, I think, for six years I do feel thoroughly home-sick ; not that I was not always glad to come home, or that I now find my work less interesting, but I feel more than ever that home is different, not only in degree but in kind. By the end of November all will be quite over.

Your account of the ordination reminds me of Ward's business, which I think will end in Oakeley's not signing, but doing it so quietly as to produce no trouble. He (Oakeley) wrote (without mentioning names) to ask the advice of the Bishops of London and Chester and of Keble. The two Bishops, characteristically, have returned no answer ; Keble, an answer extremely dubious, saying that he thinks the succession is sanctioned by the Church of England, but at the same time, as if to deter Oakeley from what he thought a rash step, quoting authorities the other way, which seem to me to prove exactly the reverse. He also asked Newman's advice, who thereupon had a long interview with Ward, urging him to defer his ordination, listening to all that Ward said most candidly, and ending by bursting into tears, saying that he had never been so much interested and that he was too much overcome to continue the dialogue.

It appears that there had been a delusion abroad, in which Newman shared but is now undeceived, that all the Balliol Low Churchmen, and especially myself, had been converted by Oxford. I was not a little amused to find myself dining with him at Palmer's the day after he had discovered his mistake. His manner at first, I think, was very different from what it had been the last time I saw him ; afterwards he seemed to repent, and talked very kindly again about conversion, &c. The delusion shows, at any rate, that I have been discreet. At the same time I have now no doubt that, supposing (of which there seems every possibility) that I keep my present opinions, I shall have sooner or later a stormy time in Oxford. All that I have heard during these discussions has more than ever convinced me that the doctrines which the Newmanists wish to be inferred from the famous words in the ordination service, are certainly not sanctioned, but rather contradicted, by every other formulary of the Church of England. The Reformers must, I think, have meant it to include High Churchmen, and at the same time to be really (as Shepherd on the Common Prayer explains it) an application of our Lord's words to a ceremony where the more natural mode of expression would have been a prayer.

Arnold found that Bishop Otter quite coincided in his views of the London University, but wished to put him (Dr. Arnold) in the front of the battle against the anti-religious party, which is prudent. Dr. Arnold says he shall now lose his character as completely with the Radicals as he has already with the Tories. He is chiefly full of his views about education and of his Roman History at present.   Yours ever,

                              A. P. STANLEY.

XIV.

A. P. S. to C. J. Vaughan.

THE INFLUENCE OF NEWMAN.

[Stanley had always hoped to be elected to a Fellow-ship at Balliol. His openly expressed sympathy with the opinions of Dr. Arnold, however, rendered his election improbable. In this uncertainty he at one time thought of standing at Oriel, and was encouraged to do so by Henry Halford Vaughan, who was then a Fellow of that college, and afterwards Regius Professor of Modern History. See ' Life,' vol. i. ch. vii.]

Oxford: Feb. 27, 1838.

My dear Vaughan,—I am quite ashamed of not writing before ; but I thought you were so busy that you would hardly care to hear, and for these last days I had put it off, expecting to hear of the Tripos. I sympathise with your deliverance from experience, and with your anxieties from probabilities. I do hope it may all turn out well. I am getting on well with my essay, and hope to have finished the rough copy by the middle of next week, and I have also been tolerably well.

I forget in what state my Fellowship prospects were when I last wrote. I think, however, it is since then that I had a very encouraging letter as to Oriel from your cousin, and an interview with the Master, remarkable only for the unfathomable mystery which he displayed, and with Chapman, who spoke more decidedly as to voting against me, if I persevered in my opinions, from which he first, then and there, made an ineffectual attempt to convert me. Oakeley also I conversed with, and he of course was staunch in his opposition. But Tait has quite come round, and in fact I have no doubt that at this moment I should be elected if it came to the point. The question, therefore, now is, whether it is prudent to run the risk and to bring the whole question to an issue, as I think I might in November, before the University and the country, if they persevered in rejecting me on those grounds, and so get in ; or whether this would be rash, and whether the advantages of Oriel coming first are a counterpoise.

Your letter about my turning Newmanist came

strangely in accordance with my own state of mind about
it now.   Not that I am turned or turning Newmanist, but
that I do feel that the crisis in my opinions is coming on,
and that the difficulties I find in my present views are
greater than I thought they were, and that here I am in
the presence of a magnificent and consistent system shooting up on every side, whilst all that I see against it is
weak and grovelling.   At the same time my impression
that the voice of St. Paul's Epistles is strongly against it
remains very deep, and I feel that to become a Newmanist
would be a shock to my whole existence, that it would
subvert every relation of life in which I have stood or
hoped to stand hereafter.   I dread to think of it even
as a possibility, and I dread also the possibility of a long
and dreary halting between two opinions, which will mar
the pleasure of every opinion I hold for an indefinite
period.   With this feeling you may be sure I shall not
join it without a desperate fight, within and without, that
I will leave no stone unturned which may enable me to
keep in that line of life to which I had thought God had
called me, and from which a conversion to Newmanism
would lead me away into a path utterly unknown to me.

I know of no system to which I can hold except
Arnold's ; and, if that breaks down under me, I know not
where I can look.   But, whatever happens, I trust that
God will help me to make up my mind for the best ; and
pray do not you do anything hastily because I do it.
Remember, I look to you as one of my great supports
and strongholds against Newmanism, and I shall not
come into it until you have given me your fair leave so to
do.   I will not trouble you with my peculiar perplexities
till you have got through your work ; but meantime do
not be unnecessarily alarmed about me, and do not tell
any one of this, because I am particularly anxious that my

case should not be exaggerated on the one side or the other. Pray for me that I may come into the truth, and

Believe me ever yours,
A. P. STANLEY.

XV.

A. P. S. to C. J. Vaughan.

NEWMAN'S INFLUENCE.

[C. J. Vaughan was bracketed Senior Classic with Lord Lyttelton in 1838.]

Oxford : March 4, 1838.

My dear Vaughan,—I hope that your not holding your primacy alone is not so great an evil as to make the primacy itself not a subject of congratulation. I long to hear particulars, as otherwise I am in ignorance of what to think of it.

I am much more at peace about Newmanism than when I last wrote. The opposition which it seems to meet from the Canonical Scriptures seems so very strong, that I am content to lay the question on the shelf for a time, and not to read the Fathers till I have possessed myself as much as possible with the spirit of the New Testament.

Believe me now, yours ever,
A. P. STANLEY.

XVI.

A. P. S. to C. J. Vaughan.

ORDINATION.

[Stanley, then a Fellow of University College, Oxford, was ordained Deacon in December 1839 by the Bishop of Oxford, Dr. Bagot. To his Fellowship was attached the obligation of taking Holy Orders. The following letter was written from the house of his father, the Bishop of

Norwich. For an account of Stanley's interview with Archdeacon Clarke and his difficulty in accepting the damnatory clauses of the Athanasian Creed see 'Life,' vol. i. pp. 225-29.]

Norwich : January 12, 1840.

My dear Pagan,—I calculate on your being extremely kind to me the next time we meet, as I am in the very lowest spirits that I have yet attained, and therefore deserving of every attention from the hands of those who had a share in thrusting me there. Nothing important occurred at Oxford after the celebrated dialogue with the Archdeacon. I have not even any notion whether he told the Bishop or not. The Bishop merely appeared on the stage at the very close of the scene, delivered a weak charge with considerable dignity, and, on the next day, the ordination took place. It was very imposing—more so than the Norwich ones, from there being twice as many, thirty of each order. The most pleasing thing to me was to hear, from time to time, the kind though stiff tones of the Archdeacon's voice breaking in throughout the service— the same voice whose sanction of the lax subscription still resounded in my ears. With the sermon I happily agreed in every particular ; indeed it was in some respects very appropriate to me. But it was to me then, and has been ever since in my recollection, more like a solemn and unnatural dream than a real fact. I should say also that on the day before, I received a letter from Arnold, which added whatever could be added of solemnity to the ordination, and softened whatever could be softened of the bitterness of subscription.

Since I came here I have performed every service peculiar to the Diaconate, except that of marrying. I have read prayers, administered the Communon, preached, and buried. I am glad to have had it over. The preaching is supposed to have been better than could be expected. It seemed very unnatural and strange, a sort of being oneself and not oneself. I preached nominally on Isa. lxi. 9, but really on Matthew v. 2-9. I somehow don't think I shall ever rise above a deacon—at any rate, not till I have clearer views both about subscription and the presbyterate ; but sufficient for the day is the evil thereof. I expect the whole thing will have the effect either of making me a great Newmanite or a great Radical. At present I incline to the latter. This seems contrary to your late advice ; but I seem as if I were come to a standstill, and must get out of it by a violent plunge. By the way, penny post having commenced, I continue here. The question is, whether I shall adhere to Ward or Brodie, whether I shall be nothing whatever, except an obedient, quiet, and so far happy, follower in the train of Newmanism, or whether I shall be a great agitator in the cause of (some sort of) Reformation. I am in somewhat better spirits, but still in a horrid confused state. Perhaps, however, all this may subside when I get quietly back to Oxford. One favour, my dear Pagan, I must ask, which is that, if between this and Easter you have an occasion, you will explain and justify the proceeding to your Oriel cousin—*i.e.* if an occasion occurs, when you could do it without intrusion—not that any of my proceedings are of importance to him or any one else ; but as I had touched on the question with him, and as he might guess my own opinions, I cannot bear that any one like him should think that I had rushed headlong on, without doubt, scruple, or protest, for the sake of 250*l.* And it is so extremely awkward having to talk about one's own conscience &c. &c., that, if possible, I should like it to be done by a third person—and who better than yourself ?

Ever yours,

A. P. STANLEY.

XVII

A. P. S. to Mrs. Augustus Hare.

CARLYLE : ORDINATION.

Oxford : Feb. 15, 1840.

My dear Auntie,—I am glad you have got Carlyle's Essays to read ; those on Goethe I have not seen. The three which throw most light on his religious opinions are, I think, those on Voltaire, Diderot, and Johnson. I have heard it so strongly suggested by two or three people that there is a resemblance between his and Strauss's notion of Christianity that I am afraid there must be some truth in it.

Still I cannot help hoping that, whether designedly or not, he may become the means of reviving a true Christian feeling, or at least of preparing the way for it in those branches of literature and of action, from which Englishmen latterly seem almost to have banished it, and that he may make people feel that what he calls the worship of Sorrow is, in the highest possible sense, far above the worship of Genius. Such at least seem to me truths which may be suggested by his writings, however strangely some of his doctrines seem to clash with them.

I have never properly thanked you for your letter about my ordination, which I assure you, however, I have not the less valued, or shall be the less anxious to try, as far as in me lies, to observe. It is perhaps an unfortunate thing for me, though as far as I see unavoidable, that the overwhelming considerations immediately at the time of ordination were not difficulties of practice, but of subscription. And the effect has been that I would always rather look back to what I felt to be my duty before that cloud came on, than to the time itself. Practically, however, I trust it will in the end make no difference. The real thing which long ago moved me to wish to go into orders, and which, had I not gone into orders, I should have acted on as well as I could without orders, was the fact that God seemed to have given me gifts more fitting me for orders, and for that particular line of clerical duty which I have chosen, than for any other. It is perhaps as well to say that, until I see a calling to other clerical work as distinct as that by which I feel called to my present work, I should not think it right to engage in any other; but I hope I shall always feel, though I am afraid I cannot be too constantly reminded, that, in whatever work I am engaged now or hereafter, my great end ought always to be the good of the souls of others, and my great support, the good which God will give to my own soul.

Ever yours affectionately,
A. P. STANLEY.

I do know Newman, and shall be very happy to give the sermon to him.

XVIII.

A. P. S. to Mary Stanley.

SCHLEGEL.

[This letter was written from Bonn in 1839, where Stanley, then a Fellow of University College, Oxford, was staying with A. C. Tait, the future Archbishop. August Wilhelm von Schlegel was appointed Professor of Literature in the University of Bonn in 1818, and held the chair till his death in 1845. His famous 'Lectures on Dramatic Art and Literature' were delivered at Vienna in 1808. His translations of foreign masters of literature, especially his version of Shakespeare, and his critical writings in 'Das Athenäum' and the 'Charakteristiken

und Kritiken,' made him one of the recognised leaders of
the Romantic movement in Germany. Stanley's description of his private life differs from Heine's sketch of his
public appearances as a lecturer, wearing kid gloves,
dressed in the latest Parisian fashion, scented with *eau de
mille fleurs*, with his servant, dressed in the livery of the
noble house of Schlegel, standing behind him to snuff the
wax candles and administer the glass of sugared water.
See ' Life,' vol. i. ch. vii.]

Bonn : Sept. 1839.

My dear M.,—Having heard that Schlegel did not object
to be called upon, or, as Mrs. Brandis said, ' liked to be
famous,' we went, sent up our cards, and were shown into
two rooms, much neater than any other German rooms I
have seen. One was hung round with English pictures of
India and a bust of himself; the other with a sort of
tapestry and a bust of Niebuhr. In ten minutes he came
in, a very little man with a neat, brown, curly wig, a coat
between a frock coat and a great coat, no neckcloth, and a
reddish face with a long nose.

He began about indifferent subjects—J. C. Hare,
Georgiana Hare ; thence to a deaf professor who gave
lectures still, which were often unintelligible from his
straining his voice too much ; then about the review at
Coblentz ; the magnificence of Ehrenbreitstein ; the
absence of such fortresses in England. From this we led
him on to the constitution of the Army, which he described at great length, especially the Landwehr. When
we asked him about the Government, he seemed a little on
his guard. He praised it extremely ; said that its benefits
were so well appreciated that the education of the people
would never give them any revolutionary ideas. ' In the
twenty years that I have lived here, I have seen the vast
difference between the French and Prussian Governments.
When Bonn was a part, first of the Republic, and then of

the Empire, the weeds grew in the streets : the roads, which now extend from one end of the Monarchy to the other, did not exist ; the vineyards on this side the Rhine could not sell their produce in France, which had wines of its own, and the other side could not receive them ; now, of course, they are sent all over the Monarchy ; and thus it is not to be expected that a man will rather have his horses tired by the bad roads and sticking in the mud, in order to hear the declamations about liberty in the Assembly. The Constitutions of Reason that sprang up in the French courts are good for nothing; a regular administration is the great thing.' We asked whether there was any perceptible effect from the education. ' Oh yes ! When I first came to Bonn very few of the mechanics, labourers, &c. could write at all, none well, and the carpenter used to bring in his bills written so badly that I could hardly read them. But in ten years after, there was a considerable improvement in the writing. " How is this ? " said I. " Oh, it is my son who has written it out." ' We asked whether it had raised their tastes, made them drink or smoke less than before. ' Oh no ! Do you think that reading and writing will effect that ? '—and then alluded to our Temperance Societies excluding beer &c., but allowing wine.

We then described to him our tea-total system. This amused him extremely. He got up, repeated the word, and exclaimed, on hearing what it meant, ' Why, you will all die of dropsy,' and thence he went off, something after the manner of Sydney Smith, expatiating on the nature and effects of tea drinking, during which his Oriental and Shakespearian knowledge displayed itself amusingly. ' Why, you have not drunk tea long ; it was not in use in Shakespeare's time. An English breakfast was roasted eggs and heated wine ; it was first used as a

E 2

luxury by the higher classes, and thus it was that Pope
speaks of it in the " Rape of the Lock ; " and from them it
has gradually crept through all classes. Oh ! what there is
in habit! Here you begin the day by pouring down two
cups of this liquid, with boiled eggs and toast and muffins,
and then do you take it again in the evening ? Why, there
is a sort of superstition about it. Beer is, like it, a decoction
of an herb, and beer can do no harm, for Tacitus speaks
of it as being used in the heroic times of Germany. We
have a specimen of what a nation becomes by drinking
tea ; there are the Chinese, who have drunk it for 1,600
years, and now they are so effeminate that they never
go out for fear of catching cold, and all their soldiers are
packed in cotton wool.   This is what you will become
by drinking tea. And then your habit is so strong that
you never leave it off. My friend, the president of the
Gardens at Calcutta, said to the English there, " Of course
you don't drink tea here ? "   " Oh, yes, twice a day."   It
is well enough in cold climates, but in India one would
expect to drink nothing but sherbet &c.   The inhabitants
of the Northern climates know better ; the Dutch drink
tea ; they cannot have had it long, as their trade did not
extend to China till the sixteenth century, but the French
drink only a little.   In Italy and Spain they drink
chocolate ; tea is never heard of. Chocolate and coffee
have some nourishment, and here you drink this liquor in
such abundance, of which the only nourishing part is the
milk and sugar.   And then China is the only country
where tea is grown. The Emperor of China might, by
shutting up his harbours, make you the most unhappy
people in the world.   And, after all, you have not the best
tea. The Russians have the best, and they (as if to
contradict what I just said) are planting tea in Siberia.
I hear too that it has been tried in India, and in America

it will be tried, and the whole world will become one great tea plantation. No! you must drink beer.' ' But do not people get drunk on beer?' He seemed surprised at the question. ' And then there are whisky and gin, and to get drunk on them does not produce an amiable drunkenness. I heard a story the other day of a whisky cask thrown on the coast of Ireland in a shipwreck, which the Irish, who were left in charge, drank, &c. &c. But, seriously, you must leave off drinking tea ; it will not do for your farmers ; they require something more nourishing ; they must have beer.' In this way he ran on quite uninterruptedly ; two or three times he used a word or phrase not exactly applicable, but in general his English was perfect, and sometimes flowed on for some minutes without even a foreign accent. As we were in a hurry, it was necessary to get up in the middle of his discourse ; but still he went on to the door with us, declaiming against tea till the very last moment when we were on the threshold, and he sent his compliments to the Hares.

As instances of his neatness, the first thing that caught his eye when he came into the room was one of the sketch-books on the sofa, which he immediately caught up, thinking it was something left about in the room ; and, in the midst of his conversation, he suddenly saw some dust on the sofa, which he carefully stooped down and blew away.

Ever yours,
A. P. STANLEY.

XIX.

A. P. S. to Mary Stanley.

TIRYNS; MYCENÆ; ARGOS; CORINTH; THE SARONIC BAY.

[In 1840–1 Stanley, accompanied by his younger brother Charles, then a lieutenant in the Royal Engineers

and quartered at Corfu, and E. M. Goulburn, afterwards
Dean of Norwich, made a tour through Greece. For de-
scriptions of Delphi, Athens, Marathon, and Olympia, see
' Life,' vol. i. pp. 268–79.

Stanley's visit to Tiryns was, of course, made before
the excavations of Schliemann and Dörpfeld (1876–84)
had revealed the palace. The allusion to the fortifications
of Tiryns occurs in the Iliad (ii. 559). Mycenæ, probably
an offshoot of the older Tiryns, was traditionally founded
by Perseus, son of Zeus and Danaë, who killed his grandfather Acrisius, as the oracle had foretold. Here, also,
recent excavations by Schliemann and the Greek Archæo-
logical Society have opened many new points of interest.
The so-called ' Treasury of Atreus,' now regarded as a
grave, is the largest of the ' beehive ' tombs discovered at
Mycenæ.]

Athens : November 9, 1840.

My dear M.,—I write in haste to catch the post. We
started on November 3 in a boat from Piræus, and with a
fair wind reached Ægina. The temple there, though
beautifully situated, is on the whole the least interesting
point I have seen. From Ægina we sailed to Epidaurus,
the interest of the voyage being enhanced by a race with
another boat containing three bearded Englishmen, whom
we wished to anticipate in the choice of horses and rooms.
In food we were independent of them. ' They have,' said
the illustrious Giorgio,[7] who had examined their stores,
' bread and eggs. But where are their beefsteaks ? where
are their grapes ? where their roast turkeys ? where is their
porter ? where their wine ? ' We beat them by half an
hour, and made ourselves masters of all the horses in the
place. They, however, got some from the country, and the
next day we formed as harmonious a party as the emula-
tion of the previous night and the natural antipathy to
beards would allow.

The great sight of the day was the sacred inclosure of

[7] The courier.

Æsculapius. It is interesting from the great beauty of the road thither, which redeems Greece from its character of barrenness—intense luxuriance of clematis, pines, arbutus, oleander in full pink blossom. The sanctuary itself is a large open plain, surrounded by hills, its surface scattered with ruins of temples. In one side is a theatre—the most perfect (but one) in Greece—all the seats of white marble, only so far different from their original beauty that they are now partly overgrown with shrubs. The great facility of hearing even the lowest pitch of voice was very remarkable.

Thence we rode over a plain, heavy with wild thyme, between mountains of absolute sterility, to Napoli, which we reached at 7 P.M. Here we were moved by compassion to share our plenteous provisions with the Beards, and the next day started in a carriage round the plain of Argolis by Tiryns, Mycenæ and Argos.

Of these the first is very interesting to an antiquary, being the very oldest known remains in Greece and described by Homer. The last is interesting from its great name, but for little else. But Mycenæ I thought—after Delphi—the most striking place I had ever seen. You advance to the utmost extremity of the dead yellow flat of the plain, where a bold irregular cluster of mountains closes it. On the northern slope is the site of the famous temple of Juno, to which Cleobis and Biton dragged their aged mother from Argos in default of oxen (as Charley proposed that we should drag ours when she came there groaning under asthma). Into the bosom of these mountains, and beneath one, which frowned under a dark cloud, itself as black as coal, like the very fiend itself of the accursed house of Atreus, run two low hills, between two descending torrents, distinguished from the surrounding plain by a clothing of that hoary thyme which so well accords with the aged spot.

In the face of the first and lowest of these hills, you suddenly turn from the midst of the most absolute desolation into the presence of a huge chamber, under the hill, with two compartments, and entirely formed of perfect massive blocks of stone. What this was no one knows. But whether it is the treasury of Atreus or the tomb of Agamemnon, it certainly is as old as either. In like manner, on the face of the farther hill, are the walls of that ancient city, into which one can quite imagine that Perseus withdrew from the murder of his grandfather as far back as he could, consistently with his still looking out over that wide plain, with its insular hills and glittering bay. In the ascent of the hill, you suddenly come before the ancient gate—the gate of the citadel of that mysterious family of Pelopidæ—the gate which is the scene of the most famous tragedies of Æschylus—the gate where the most ancient kings of Greece sat in justice. It is still perfect, and, what is inexpressibly striking amidst the death-like desolation around, over it is a block of green basalt, with the forms of two lions, perfect all but their heads, on each side of a pillar carved with the utmost distinctness.

The whole scene carries one back to the antiquity, not of Greece only, but of the world, not of classical, but of primeval mythological times. No account of it, nothing but imagining to oneself the scene that would best suit the close of the play of Agamemnon, can give any notion of it.

The next day we rode to Corinth, forming a cavalcade of twelve horses. The great variety was very striking. First there was the dead plain of Argos, then a narrow gorge, literally choked with bowers of myrtle and oleander. It is now November, and in the whole tour I saw not one leafless tree ; the whole vegetation is evergreen. Then came an open heathy table-land ; then a lonely plain, sunk deep

into the heart of the hills, with the three columns of the
temple of the Nemean Jupiter still standing.   For so small
a ruin it is the most impressive I ever saw.   Then we descended through the most singular mixture of green bushes
with white clayey ravines, like the bleaching bones of the
ancient kingdom of Sicyon, through which we were passing,
and so down by moonlight upon the plain of Corinth with
its towering citadel.   Here we stayed for half a day, going
up the Acrocorinthus, where I cannot say that I was particularly struck with the view, but the day was cloudy.

We slept at Calamachi on the way to Megara.   The
next morning we set out on a short day's journey to Megara
by the passage of the Saronian rocks, which, on the whole,
must be the most magnificent in the world—the boldest
precipices, clothed partially with pines of emerald green,
looking out on the Saronic Bay—a sea of glittering blue,
land-locked by mountains of the most delicate and fairy
outline that can be conceived.   A second short day, by
Eleusis, which I have not time to describe, brought us back
to Athens, where we found Goulburn well.

What we shall next do is not quite settled.   Charlie
goes back to-morrow.   Nothing could have been more
pleasant than he has been, or more useful.   Many things
he has observed which I should have overlooked.   Whatever conjectures of mine he allows, I consider as certain.

Ever yours,
A. P. STANLEY.

XX.

A. P. S. to Miss Emily Wodehouse.

FOXES IN GREECE.

[On his return from Greece, Stanley was detained
for five days in the quarantine at Malta. ('Life,' vol. i.

pp. 278-9.) There the following letter was written. It is
addressed to Miss Emily Wodehouse, aged eleven years,
the daughter of the Rev. C. N. Wodehouse, Rector of
Morningthorpe and Canon of Norwich. ('Life,' vol. i.
pp. 244–5.) Stanley always called his little friend by the
name of 'Goupil,' the old French word for a fox, because
of the colour of her hair.

'Goupil' or 'Golpil' is said to be derived from the
Latin 'vulpeculus,' and was in ordinary use till it was
superseded by 'Renard,' the name given to the wily animal
in the famous epic.]

Malta : Feb. 3, 1841.

My dear Goupil,—I have been writing letter after
letter to my learned friends, and have been saying how one
of the greatest pleasures of travelling in Greece was that it
reminded me of them so often. 'What then,' at last I
exclaimed, 'and did it never remind me of the Goupil?'
Yes—Goupil—twice ; and you shall hear how, though you
may be shivering in the east wind and snow at Norwich,
and though I am scorched up by the burning sun at Malta.
Listen, then, Goupil, and wonder.

1st. It was on a dark night in November that we were
riding along the banks of a great marsh, which, if you look
in the map for Bœotia, you will find called the Copaic lake.
The sun set as we passed an old majestic rock, at whose
foot the blind old prophet Tiresias, when he was being
carried away captive after the fall of his country, stopped
to rest under its shade, and drink of a spring which rises
beneath it ; and there, in the bosom of the green hills of
Mount Helicon, looking out on the still waters of the lake,
and on the Mountain of the Sphinx overhanging his native
city in the distance, he died. The night became darker
and darker—the cold wind whistled through the feathery
reeds from which in ancient days Bœotian singers made
their pipes ; the white mist rose out of the marsh ; the
road became worse and worse ; the guides more and more

ignorant of the way; the mountains grew darker and darker on the starless sky; when on a sudden, from the midst of the desolate marsh, there arose a long, wild, piteous cry, as if the ghost of Tiresias was wailing still over the evils of his long and melancholy life. 'What is that?' said Goulburn to me. 'What is that?' said I to Mr. Daniell. 'What is that?' said Mr. Daniell to Georgio. And what do you think Georgio answered? 'Oh! it is the *wild foxes.*' Yes, Goupil, it was the cry of the Greek jackals. This was the first time.

2nd. It was a stormy day in December when three horsemen were seen galloping over the plain of Marathon. A gleam of sunshine passed over the yellow plain and blue sea, as they approached the large mound in the middle of the flat fields, which Aristides the Just raised, twenty hundred years ago, over the bodies of the 292 Athenians who fell fighting against the Persians on that very spot, when from the top of the mound there appeared a living creature, which looked round about him, and then, as the three horsemen came nearer, jumped up, ran down the side of the mound, and escaped into the mountains. And what do you think, Goupil, was the living creature that now inhabits the most famous mound of earth that can be found in the whole world? It was a large red *fox.* And what was the consequence? It was that when the three horsemen rode to the top of the mound, one of them thought, not only of Miltiades and the flying Persian army, but also of the red-haired Goupil in the Cloisters of Norwich Cathedral.

Ever yours,

A. P. STANLEY.

XXI

A. P. S. to Mary Stanley.

ÆTNA.

[On his way back from Greece, Stanley, accompanied by Hugh Pearson (see note to XXV.), made a short tour through Sicily.

J. H. Newman was in Sicily in February 1833.]

Messina : March 10, 1841.

My dear M.,—The rainy weather at Palermo settled on the third day into a perfect deluge, and, when in the evening we embarked for Messina, we were in despair. As if to cast the last damp upon our expedition, a man, who had just made the tour of Sicily, filled us with alarming stories of swollen rivers, and dreadful inns, and indefatigable banditti, so that when we landed at Messina, we were at the lowest ebb. From this moment, however, our star began to recover its ascendency. I went to consult bankers and consuls, who pronounced our tour to be perfectly feasible, and accordingly, on the following morning, Pearson and I started at 7 A.M. for Taormina on our way to Syracuse.

When we started, heavy clouds hung over the hills; but by the time we reached Taormina, everything was clear except Ætna itself. Before we had been there half an hour, the veil drew off and out came the great mountain—in most unexpected colours certainly, for instead of the mass of white which I had seen before on the voyage, it was, from the shadows of the sun setting behind it, entirely black as night. We were very fortunate, and saw it again the next morning in its natural aspect of whiteness. The view is very magnificent, but does not come up to my

notions of the finest view in the world.   The great beauty
of it consists in the extraordinary combination of the most
picturesque rocks, town, promontories, the seas and coasts
of Italy and Sicily, and the huge pyramid of Ætna, round
the ruins of the ancient Theatre of Tauromenium, which
certainly, for any one building, is in the most striking
situation of any that I ever saw.

The next day brought us to Catania, a very interesting
drive, literally death in life and life in death.   On the one
hand, the road passes through streams of lava, descending
straight from Ætna into the sea, sometimes huge blocks
like the Chaos in the Pyrenees, sometimes black fields of
desolation like the neighbourhood of Wolverhampton.   On
the other hand, a most glorious day succeeding to the rains
had brought out in all its power the first burst of the Sicilian
spring, so that one could really see with one's eyes, how—

> Rising like the ocean tide
> In flow'd the joyous year.

It was indeed like a mighty flood, which seemed to rush
along so fast that one could hardly keep pace with it ; far
and near, through every crevice of the lava rocks, there
seemed to come a torrent of luxuriant vegetation, flowers
of every colour, golden lichens, trees bursting into bud
and blossom, corn of emerald green, and gigantic cactus
and Indian figs which seemed the natural produce of so
fantastic a soil.

It was also mythologically interesting from being the
scene of the landing of Ulysses, and of the death of
Acis, the last recalling the well-known picture in the
drawing-room at Alderley, which is not so unlike the real
scene as such pictures usually are.   Catania itself is chiefly
remarkable as being a most stately city rising out of a bed
of lava, and in the most awful proximity to Ætna.

The third day I seemed to be in Greece again—a day of twelve hours on mules to Syracuse. We passed over plains and rivers and hills, of which the great feature is the most splendid view of Ætna—from this side, beyond all question the finest mountain I ever saw, rising almost immediately from the sea with no rival far or near, snow-white, all but the very top where the snow has melted from the fire, and shooting up into the blue sky really like the pillar of heaven.

At Syracuse we remained Saturday and Sunday. It is not worth seeing for any beauty of situation ; but historically, and especially to anyone who knows Thucydides—and fortunately I had one with me—it is one of the most interesting places I have seen out of Greece. From being built among rocks, all the localities remain as at Athens, though every vestige of the town itself (the largest, I believe, of all antiquity) is vanished. There are also some of the most curious remains of ancient Christianity in the Church of the First Bishop of Syracuse, that I have yet seen.

On Monday we returned to Catania in a large cavalcade, consisting of ourselves, the servant of the inn, and a Capuchin monk—just like the Canterbury pilgrimage. On Tuesday we posted with most incredible speed from Catania to Messina, a mountainous journey of seventy miles, between 7.30 A.M. and 6 P.M.

We really ought to be thankful. Whenever it was important for us, the weather was not only good, but so good as to be absolutely delicious—a warm sun tempered by a breeze so fresh that one seemed to inhale health at every breath, and the two long rides, even with all the inconveniences of galloping on kicking mules, were really agreeable. The rivers were perfectly passable, though, to be sure, we had to turn the mouth of one of them by the rather odd process of riding through the sea. But what was perhaps most deserving of notice is the extraordinary attention to us as English. What *have* the English done in Sicily? Not once, nor twice, but again and again, we really seemed to travel like princes merely for our country's sake. The English language, too, was spoken where least expected—far more than in our own possessions of Corfu and Malta.

We had great fun in ransacking the Livres des Voyageurs. Among other entries was 'Newman,' suffering from 'a very fatiguing journey.' Excuse my writing at the end. The steamer is the cause.

Ever yours,
A. P. STANLEY.

XXII.

A. P. S. to the Rev. J. N. Simpkinson.

ARNOLD AS REGIUS PROFESSOR OF MODERN HISTORY ;
A. H. CLOUGH.

[The Rev. J. N. Simpkinson, who had been Curate to the Rev. Julius Hare at Hurstmonceux, was a Rugbeian and an intimate friend of Stanley's. Subsequently Rector of North Creake, Fakenham, he died in 1894. Dr. Arnold succeeded Professor Nares as Regius Professor of Modern History in 1841. He delivered his Inaugural Lecture at Oxford on Dec. 2, 1841. A. H. Clough, then a scholar of Balliol, failed to obtain a First Class in the summer of 1841, and unsuccessfully tried for a Fellowship at Balliol in the autumn of the same year. In the spring of 1842 he was elected to a Fellowship at Oriel.]

Rugby : December 4, [1841].

My dear Simpkinson,—Two things induce me to write. *First.* Every one who loves Arnold ought to have been present at the august scene of his Inaugural

Lecture last Thursday, and as you were not there in
the body, I feel bound, so far as in me lies, to make you
so in mind.

The usual place is a small room in the Clarendon
Buildings ; but fortunately we had so far anticipated the
amount of the audience as to secure the Sheldonian
Theatre. But the numbers were far more than any one could
have expected, far more than any professor has addressed
in Oxford since the Middle Ages.

Imagine that beautiful building with the whole of the
area and the whole of the lower gallery completely filled ;
the Vice-Chancellor in state ; the Professor himself distinguished from the rest by his full red Doctorial robes. It
was certainly one of the most glorious days of my life ; to
listen once more to that clear, manly voice in the relation
of a pupil to a teacher, to feel that one of the most important Professorships was filled by a man with genius and
energy capable of discharging its duties, to see him standing
in his proper place at last and receiving the homage of the
assembled University, was most striking and most touching. The lecture lasted just an hour. It was listened to
with the deepest attention, and began and closed with a
burst of general applause. I will not describe it because it
is to be printed ; but everyone seemed perfectly satisfied.
The most cautious man in Oxford was heard to break into
an enthusiastic declaration that the two ideas which the
sight of Arnold always, and especially on that day,
suggested, were the ideas of truth and power. He came
and returned the same day. Mrs. Arnold and Jane were
with him, he looking over examination papers all the way.
It seemed like the infusion of new blood into the veins
of the University. Whatever objections may be found to
details, I felt there was a freshness and vigour in his
words that reminded me of his own description of the

renovation of the worn-out generations of the Empire by the energy of the German race.

Secondly. Clough's reverse at Balliol. Perhaps you do not need consolation. But to me, partly for his sake, partly for the sake of Balliol, it seemed so great a misfortune that I cannot help venting my lamentations over it. But there is this great comfort. Some of his papers were done so splendidly as fully to show that the spring of genius has not yet been dried up within him, and therefore I hope he will get in at Oriel. Not that I ever thought that the genius was gone; but I feared that the power of expressing it to the world was gone. What a singular person he is! I, of course, never having been intimate with him, can only reverence him at a respectful distance. But the little I do know of him has always made me think and maintain that he is the profoundest man of his years that I ever saw, or that Rugby ever sent forth. His very misfortunes invest him with a kind of sacredness, for, academically speaking, who ever was so unfortunate—so able, so laborious, and yet so unaccountably failing? How singular a contrast with my fortunate career, and yet with no apparent reason! But I am full of hopes for him. It may be superstitious, but I cannot help thinking that so remarkable a concatenation of disasters has not been without some great end. But I forbear.　　　　　　Ever yours,

　　　　　　　　　　　　　　　A. P. STANLEY.

XXIII.

A. P. S. to Mary Stanley.

DEATH OF DR. ARNOLD.

[In this and the following letter, Stanley describes the sudden death of Dr. Arnold, which took place at Rugby on the morning of Sunday, June 12, 1842.]

June 14, 1842.

My dear M.,—Oh the bitterness of waking this morning
to the sight of this place with the thought that he who was
its light and life is gone !

I got here last night at 8.30, and met Lee, the former
under-master of Rugby and now head-master of Birming-
ham, who gave me the general outline.   I found the Prices [8]
were at the school house, and went there for them.   I met
the nurse Roland on the stairs, who burst into an agony of
grief on seeing me.   Then Matt came and took me into
the study, where I found all the children, except the two
youngest who come to-day, the Prices and Lake. [9]

Alas ! I was too late for what I had most hoped to see.
They say that immediately after death the face was fixed
with a painful expression ; but that it gradually changed
till it settled into the most heavenly smile, which lasted till
corruption came on.

Mrs. Arnold could not see me last night, having seen
so many in the course of the day, but will this morning.
She told Mrs. Price that mamma's letter, which I sent up
to her, was the greatest comfort she had yet received.   She
had been in frantic grief at first, could not think that there
was no hope, but gradually calmed, and is now composed.
Price thinks that, instead of sinking, as I thought she
would from having so entirely leant upon him, she has that
in her which will rise and appear, now for the first time, to
support her in the hour of need !

I have seen her.

For the week previous he had been unusually bright
and cheerful.   On Saturday he felt a slight pain in his
chest, but did not tell Mrs. Arnold lest she should prevent
his bathing, and went, as usual, and bathed with Lake in

[8] Mr. and Mrs. Bonamy Price.
[9] W. C. Lake, afterwards Dean of Durham.

the afternoon, talked as usual in the evening, and went to
bed at twelve. On Sunday morning he felt a violent pain
in his chest, at 6 A.M. The doctor was sent for, gave him
something which abated it, learnt from him that his father
had died of a complaint in the heart; then, on another
pain shooting through the left arm, saw that it was hopeless; told Mrs. Arnold, who had just before called Tom
up. A few minutes more, and the rattle in his throat
announced that he was gone. This was at 8 A.M.

This is the substance of the medical part. Now for the
wonderful comfort which must remain to us all about him
as long as we live. You remember our observing how the
last half-year of his life seemed to have come upon him like
the calm sunset of a stormy day. This seemed to have
gathered intensity as it drew to its close. From the time
of that fatal rupture, there seems to have been a halo
of gentleness and holiness about him, which every one
observed before, and which every one now recalls distinctly.
I was much struck with the beginning of it, the last time I
saw him, and all the masters speak of it as most remarkable. Mrs. Arnold says that now, on looking back, she
can recall an awful kind of anxiety about him, unlike anything she ever observed before, and, from various little
things which he said or did, he—though without the
slightest knowledge of any disease like that which killed
him—seems to have unconsciously felt a presentiment of
some great change.

One of the days when he was ill of his feverish attack,
he called Mrs. Arnold to his bedside, and said: 'Mary, I
feel that God has been very good in sending me this
chastisement. I have felt such a rush of love towards God
in my heart for the last two or three days.' He then told
her that he had never kept any diary, but that he had been
thinking how many good men had done so, and that it

F 2

seemed a want of humility in him not to do anything of the kind. Accordingly, beginning on Trinity Sunday, from time to time, before going to bed, he wrote short prayers and meditations in a private book. Of these all are remarkable (she said parts of them to me) as breathing such deep devotion to God and Christ ; one praying for himself and his dear wife to be strengthened, particularly for that greatest calamity of one being taken before the other.

But the most remarkable of all is one written on the Saturday evening at 12 P.M., which Mrs. Arnold only found on coming down to the study on Sunday morning after he was dead. The substance was as follows :

Saturday, June 11.—The day after to-morrow, if I am permitted to live so long, will be the birthday of my 47th year. How large a portion of life is gone! In one sense I may say already, 'Vixi.' I thank God that I believe all ambition has been mortified fully in my heart, and that I feel ready now, not to advance from my present position into higher stations, but gently to withdraw from it into humbler occupations. I pray that God will make me more zealous and humble, more gentle and patient. I have much work left to do, particularly that great work which I have most at heart, for the night cometh when no man can work. But I pray also that God will make me ready to let it be performed by others, if that be His will.

This was the substance : but it was expressed with an energy and clearness that I cannot in memory fully represent. This must have been written without any further presentiment of death than that general sense of awe which I spoke of as impressed upon him and Mrs. Arnold during his last month on earth.

But to return. On Saturday afternoon, for the first time since he came to Rugby, he wound up all the affairs of the school on Saturday instead of postponing it to Monday morning. In the evening he walked backwards and forwards with Lake on the grass plot in the garden, talking about the different doctrines on the Eucharist—Lake taking the Tractarian side. Lake says that the gentleness and kindness with which he spoke were wonderful—not a word of harshness, and expressions of the deepest devotion and love. He then went in, looked over papers (I think); at twelve, wrote the journal.

When the pain came on in the morning, which seems to have been very great, he said once or twice with great fervour, 'Thank God for me.' 'For what?' they said. 'I feel that this pain is good for me.' He also clasped his hands fervently, as if in thanksgiving. Then he said, 'If you have no chastisement, then are ye bastards and not sons.' Then he told Mrs. Arnold to read the 51st Psalm, and repeated after her the 12th verse. Then she read the exhortation in the Visitation for the Sick, and again, at every sentence, he said 'Yes! yes!' most fervently, and again repeated, 'Then are ye bastards and not sons.' (This verse also, with reflections on the same subject, occurred in the journal.) Also he looked up and said: 'Jesus said unto Thomas, Because thou hast seen Me, thou hast believed: blessed are they that have not seen, and yet have believed.' He appears to have been aware that he was dying, during the second hour of his illness. But he had no notion that he had this disease, and, when the pain first came on, would hardly let Mrs. Arnold get up and call the doctor.

The funeral is at twelve on Friday. No one will be *invited* except those in the house. But any one who wishes may attend the procession, such as myself for example.   Ever yours,

                                   A. P. STANLEY.

XXIV

A. P. S. to Mary Stanley.

DEATH OF DR. ARNOLD.

[William Winstanley Hull, of Lincoln's Inn, formerly Fellow of Brasenose College, Oxford, first knew Dr. Arnold at Oxford and became one of his most intimate friends. He and his brother, the Rev. John Hull, were associated with Stanley in his efforts to procure some explanation or relaxation of the subscription to the Articles which was demanded from candidates for Holy Orders. At the age of eighty-four he travelled to Oxford to vote for Stanley when his nomination as Select Preacher was opposed in 1872 (see also XC.). John Philip Gell was appointed in 1839, on the recommendation of Dr. Arnold (see Arnold's ' Life,' letter cxciii.), Head Master of the then newly-founded College in the north of Van Diemen's Land. His letter to Mrs. Arnold on the death of her husband is quoted in full at the end of the tenth chapter of Arnold's ' Life.']

Rugby : June 15, 1842.

My dear M.,—My account yesterday was, I am afraid, broken and indistinct, but it is difficult to collect one's thoughts sufficiently to write a long letter. Did I mention that in his journal, as also in those thanksgivings during the fatal attack, he expressed very strongly the feeling that ' I have had a life full of blessing ; I have received so much good from God ; shall I not also receive evil ? ' and ' I have never had pain before ; how good it is of God to send it to me now ! ' Also the verse, ' Blessed are they that have not seen,' &c. had taken a deep possession of his mind for some time before. He was always very fond of dwelling on the confession of Thomas, and, within the last month, he selected it as the subject for the last painted window in the chapel, with that verse to be inscribed underneath it.

A little while before his death Willy was looking at the beginning of his MS. volume of sermons, where, according to his invariable custom, was written at the beginning, 'February' (or whatever the month might be), '1842 to ——,' and said, 'Papa, why do you always leave this blank?' and he answered, 'Ah! Willy, it is very difficult for us to feel as much as we ought to do. It is one of the most solemn things I do—to write that and remember that I may not live to finish it.'

One of the instances of his thoughtful kindness was that the two examiners who were here for the examination (that examination at which I had fully hoped next year to be examiner), had sate perfectly silent at dinner on Friday and fell out of the general conversation, which Tom noticed to his mother afterwards, and accordingly on Saturday his father particularly addressed himself to them and did everything he could to bring them forward. One of the things which he prays in his journal to be guarded against is the use of vehement language about persons and opinions, and especially that he may be kept from it of himself without the suggestion of others.

Whilst speaking of the journal, I may as well say that Mrs. Arnold does not allow anyone to copy any part except, I believe, the passage written on Saturday night. *That* therefore may, and I think ought to, be shown to people; the others you may use at your discretion. The more I think of it, the more remarkable it seems. When I am inclined to see nothing but inexplicable darkness and confusion, I fall back upon those passages with such unspeakable comfort. I hope I am not presumptuous; you know I shrink from everything expressing anxiety on these matters, but it does look as if they had been expressly provided as a proof that he was being ripened and prepared in a most solemn way for his departure, and that his character needed this last trial of chastisement in order to subdue its harsher features and absorb them into that abyss of tenderness and love which, to any one who knew him, was always evidently at the root of all his qualities, but which never till this last month seems so entirely to have engrossed his whole nature.

The result of the examination of the body is that it was *angina pectoris*, produced by attenuation of the heart ; in every other respect the most perfect health. It is most exceedingly rare for the first attack of this disorder to be fatal ; yet in him it certainly seems to have been so. Neither he nor anyone else suspected it in the least. One conclusion is that his mode of life in every respect was exactly the course most likely to aggravate it. It needs great quiet, vegetable food, and *no* bathing. I mention this, not in the least as regretting that it was so ; rather to show how utterly unavailing any care could have been. No one could tell the existence of the disorder till it appeared, and, except with reference to it, his course of living was exactly what suited him.

It is a noble and characteristic trait of Hull that he was present during the whole examination. He (Mr. Hull) is perfectly calm, exactly as usual, except that now and then you see his face wrung with agony. I went with him and Matthew to fix upon the place in the chapel for the burial. It is to be within the rails immediately before the Communion Table, that being the place usually allotted to the body of the founder, and as the real founder of the school is buried elsewhere, I think one may safely predict that there will never arise another who can dispute his claim to it. There was a painful struggle in Mrs. Arnold's mind whether he should be buried here or at Fox How, where she might hope to be buried with him. But she fixed at once that it should be here. ' Here was his work, and it will do more good here.' However, the masters, on being consulted, have allowed another niche to be made in the same vault, so that, when her time comes, she will be by his side. On going to the chapel Mr. Hull said, 'This is the only place which I never could stand. Twice I have come to chapel in your father's lifetime ; twice I have been forced to go out. I could not bear to see that congregation and know the intense interest your father took in them. He went there with the determinate purpose of doing them good and of nothing else. No man ever had a more definite object than he then had, and he has spoken of it to me till his eyes glistened and his finger-ends trembled.'

Letters, as usual, are the · greatest comfort to Mrs. Arnold—indeed, to all of us ; anything you hear about him or what people say of him will be most welcome. I forgot to say that the first thing Mrs. Arnold said to us yesterday when she could speak articulately was, 'What I chiefly think of is that he is free from the sight of sin. You know how that pained him above everything else, and now he will see it again no more.' It was a most just remark. I never knew any one to whom the sight of what he thought wicked gave such absolute suffering. I remember once Mrs. Arnold speaking of some little boy just come to school looking so innocent and good, and he checked her quite imploringly : 'Oh, my dear, do not speak of it. You know how it pains me to think of it, when I think how soon the devil will put his filthy paw upon him and mar it all.'

Mrs. Arnold will probably go on Monday. I shall stay here certainly till Tuesday, I hope, perhaps longer, because I see that I can be of use to the boys about the books &c. And I really cling to each day as it passes, remembering that it brings me to the last and fatal day which shall sever my connection, at least my dear and intimate connection, with the place for ever, and I know you will spare me.

They say that with this disorder he might have dropped down any day, in the water, abroad, or in the school. Think what a blessing that the manner of his death should have been so mercifully ordered, I may almost say, so majestically and above all characteristically arranged ! Price and Lake are both great comforts to me. No one else of the old pupils is here except Burbidge and three of the masters. Whether any will come I know not yet ; the sixth will all attend.

Another thing which Mrs. Arnold mentioned as re-markable during the last month was the complete calm-ness and carelessness about the reception of his volume of lectures. The last sermon to the boys expresses his doubt—his usual doubt, it is true, but, of course, *now* how solemn !—whether he should ever meet them again. The two little ones arrived from Fox How yesterday, their poor little faces quite swollen up with crying, but of course *they* will soon get over it. Willy, the sixth, has not been able to shed a tear ; he longs for it, but cannot. They all talk of him incessantly ; of course they are affected in different ways. Matthew spoke of one thing which seemed to me very natural and affecting : that the first thing which struck him when he saw the body was the thought that their sole source of *information* was gone, that all that they had ever known was contained in that lifeless head. They had consulted him so entirely on everything, and the strange feeling of their being cut off for ever one can well imagine as forcing itself upon them with almost disproportionate force.

I am better to-day than yesterday, slept more last night, and have found more relief in tears. But oh ! the future, the unceasing recollection of him at Rugby and at Oxford ! Do you hear anything about the professorship ? [1]

[1] Dr. Arnold was, at the time of his death, Regius Professor of Modern History in the University of Oxford [see XXII.]. His successor was Henry Halford Vaughan.

It may seem strange to think of myself again for it, and I do not know how I could stand it; but I feel that it would break the constant jarring to me if I were in his place instead of a total stranger. But I hardly like to think or speak of it, and most probably it is out of my reach. Of course I cannot help feeling what you suggest in your letter—that I loved him too much, and that it is both just as to the past, and good as to the future, that he should be taken away from me. The exclusiveness and vehemence of my veneration had naturally been abated by years, but I feel that I never saw, or shall see, his like again. Others, abler and better and wiser I may meet of course, but none who can stand in the same relation to me—none whose position and qualities so combine to attract respect and love.

Mrs. Bunsen, in her letter to Mrs. Arnold, spoke so admirably of looking round at the length and breadth of the calamity through the whole extent of the country, and yet always returning to the centre—the family—the widow. I have not seen any papers about him, but I hear there is something in the 'Morning Chronicle.' I cannot bear to think of him mixed up at this moment with party watchwords; the *man* stands forth in such tremendous prominence, the *opinions* recede into the extremest background.

Ever yours,
A. P. STANLEY.

I forgot this yesterday. I feel that up to to-day we have had only the luxury of sorrow—the mournful but inexpressible and inexhaustible delight of talking throughout the day to those who knew and loved him best, of his inexhaustible excellences. But after to-morrow will be the hard reality, and then I feel—I trust I feel—that God alone can support us. I feel as if the collected prayers of the nation were requisite to support the many hearts that, for weeks and months and years, will be groaning under the heavy trial.   And yet the dreadful news has to travel to the other side of the globe before it has wrought its work of sorrow fully—before the noblest and most beloved indeed of his pupils, Gell, will hear of it in Van Diemen's Land.

I saw the doctor yesterday, who gave me the whole account.   It is too long to repeat, and I cannot remember all the details ; but I was chiefly struck by the vast number of questions which Arnold put to him about the disease, with the utmost calmness, but with a fixity of look, which makes the doctor think he knew that his end was at hand. I must consider it again before I fully persuade myself that he did ; I have no doubt that he knew himself to be in great danger ; but one or two things make me doubt whether he knew that he was actually dying.   I was mistaken before in saying that Mrs. Arnold was out of the room at the last ; the spasm and the rattle in the throat came on when she was ; the doctor caught him in his arms, and screamed to them to come up ; the convulsion in the chest was violent. She herself rubbed his legs with hot flannel.   The children were all brought in ; one long-drawn sigh succeeded another ; and just as the second doctor who was called in entered, he breathed his last.

No words, the doctor says, can describe the agony of the scene that followed.   ' Oh ! is he really, really dead ? ' she exclaimed, and the children wept aloud and screamed. She had followed the doctor out of the room, after the first interview, and said, ' Is it *angina pectoris* ? ' then burst into tears.   And she clasped her hands in agony.   He said, ' You must command yourself,' and instantly she resumed her natural manner, and went into the room and read, as I told you before.   One thing I omitted then ; some verse she repeated to him, which he had been in the habit of reading to one of the old people in the almshouse, whom always, from time to time, but particularly during the last month, he had taken great pleasure in visiting. She said, ' This is old Mrs. Price's favourite verse,' and then there passed over his face one of those radiant smiles. The doctor thinks that one particular answer of his showed Arnold that the case was fatal, and he says that his countenance did not change a muscle. I have begged him to write out his account, and will then send it to you.

Moultrie [2] reads the service, which I mention that the Bishop need not think of his robes.

Ever yours,

A. P. STANLEY.

XXV.

A. P. S. to his Sisters.

THE LIFE OF DR. ARNOLD.

[The chief work of Stanley's life from 1842 to 1844 was the preparation of his ' Life and Correspondence of Thomas Arnold.' The book was published in May 1844, and before Christmas reached a fourth edition. While he was writing the ' Life,' he spent part of his vacations at Fox How, where Mrs. Arnold and her children were living. A letter describing the assistance which she gave him at this time and the reading of the last chapter of the Memoir to Archbishop Whately will be found in the ' Life of Stanley,' vol. i. pp. 320–21.

The visit to Rugby described in this letter was paid shortly after Dr. Tait, Arnold's successor as Head Master, married Catharine Spooner. The Rev. Hugh Pearson, afterwards Vicar of Sonning, was Stanley's closest and most intimate friend. In February 1841 they met at Naples, and spent Easter together at Rome. To the criticism of ' wise Hugh ' Stanley submitted all his projects and all his literary work. For many years scarcely a week passed in which the two friends did not interchange

---

[2] Rector of Rugby.

letters.   Of those from Stanley many hundreds have been
preserved ; of those from Pearson none are in existence.
On Stanley's desk, at the time of his death, lay an unfinished letter to ' H. P.'   Pearson had been at Harrow
under Dr. Longley, afterwards Archbishop of Canterbury.]

Fox How : September 1843.

My dear Children,—At last I have arrived at the place
of my destination.   The night journey passed off as
comfortably as that great evil can, and ten hours were
spent upon it—how I know not.   After three hours in Brook
Street, I had to start so abruptly to catch the Rugby train
as not to have time to go to Dover Street.   I got there in
the afternoon ; extracted, as is my custom, all the news in
the place from Cotton ;[3] then visited the school house,
and, finding Tait in school, sent up a message to Taitia
to announce my arrival.   Immediately there appeared a
little creature, pretty, gentle, with a fund of merriment,
and taking a great and brimming interest in the place.
We gradually advanced in intimacy, which was marked by
the gradual reiteration on both sides of ' Archie ' for ' Dr.
Tait.'   This was at last completed by the arrival of Archie,
and by a breakfast there the next morning, in which they
were exhibited together and discussed various subjects.
The little creature playfully rebuked her husband for his
attacks on Oxford, and perhaps she inclined too much to
the notions of her cousin Samuel Wilberforce altogether to
suit my notions of one who should occupy the house of
Rugby.   The great event of the neighbourhood had been
the sudden appearance of Julius[4] at Dunchurch to preach
a charity sermon for Mr. Sandford, rector of that place,
and he was made the lion of a large assembly, in which

---

[3] The Rev. G. E. L. Cotton, subsequently Head Master of Marlborough
College, and Bishop of Calcutta.   See LXVIII. and LXXXIX.
[4] Julius Hare.

the inhabitants of Rugby formed a large part. I with-hold the details for the present. The Prices completely approved of the closing part of the Memoir, which is all I had time to read to them.

In the afternoon of Thursday I proceeded to Lancaster, where I slept. Yesterday I arrived here at noon, and found the family as usual. Just as I was taking a solitary luncheon of bread and butter, my two expected friends, Hugh Pearson and Oliver Farrer, were announced, and carried me off for the afternoon to Lowood, where I dined and slept. They are, you know, the heroes of the happy meeting at Naples, and Pearson especially is so associated with some of the most pleasurable days of my life that the mere sight of him and recurrence of old travelling jokes always exhilarate me, and my afternoon with them quite set me up after my journey, which had rather jaded me. We met my luggage coming to Fox How, which nearly proved fatal to us, for the brilliant colours of the carpet bag so startled the horse of our car as to induce him to hurry us down a lofty bank with imminent danger of overturn. However, we recovered ourselves; the Memoir and a night-shirt we extracted from the bag, and the afternoon was spent in reading the MS. in a boat on Windermere, bathing, dining, and then walking by moon-light on the shore, imagining ourselves again by the Bay of Naples. The effect produced upon Pearson by the MS. was very satisfactory; the contrast with Longley was more forcibly brought out, and new points were dwelt upon. This morning I returned to Fox How.

Farewell, my children; I feel particularly well this morning.   Ever yours,

A. P. STANLEY.

XXVI

A. P. S. to Mary Stanley.

PRAGUE.

[In the first and last paragraphs Stanley refers to 'A Winter's Tale.' The third scene of the third act is laid in 'Bohemia. A desert Country near the Sea.' Antigonus asks the mariner:

> Thou art perfect then, our ship hath touch'd upon
> The deserts of Bohemia?

St. John Nepomuk was a native of Pomuk, near Pilsen. The legend is that, in 1383, King Wenceslaus commanded him to be tortured, and then thrown into the Moldau at night, with his hands and feet bound, because he refused to betray the confession of the Queen. Life was no sooner extinct than a heavenly light, appearing over his body, made known the secret of the King's crime. He was canonised in 1729. His memory is celebrated on May 16.

In 1419 John Ziska, the Hussite leader, threw the Burgomaster and thirteen of the councillors from the windows of the town hall. In 1618 a rising took place in Prague against the unconstitutional acts of the Emperor Mathias, and the Imperialist governors, Slawata and Martinitz, with their secretary Fabricius, were thrown from the windows of the Hradschin.

Albrecht von Waldstein, or Wallenstein, Duke of Friedland, the most remarkable of the Imperialist generals during the Thirty Years' War, commanded at Lützen, where Gustavus Adolphus was killed (November 1632). Suspected by the Emperor Ferdinand of plotting against the empire, he was murdered at Eger in Bohemia in February 1634.

Stanley's companion on the expedition was the late Master of Balliol, Benjamin Jowett.]

Dresden : Sept. 28, 1844.

My dear Child,—On Tuesday morning we started from Vienna by diligence and reached Prague on Wednesday night. The journey was awful; the roads so bad, and the sides of the diligence so hard, that after the night journey I thought I should have perished; and the country was so totally featureless that it seems like a blank in the tour, except that one felt that one was plunging deeper and deeper into the heart of Germany, and that the grotesqueness of Shakespeare's blunder about the seashore of Bohemia came upon me with the utmost possible force by seeing before my eyes how it is not only *an* inland country, but *par excellence the* inland country of Europe. And the only place of any historical interest was the field of Kolin, a name which rose like the ghost of long-forgotten reading—the scene of one of Frederick the Great's battles.[5]

But our fainting spirits were in some degree kept up by our fellow-travellers. Part of the way I went in front with the *conducteur*, an old Austrian soldier, who amused himself by alternately giving lessons in Bohemian and receiving lessons from me in English; and it was enough to enliven even the dreary plains of Bohemia to hear the roars of laughter and astonishment with which he heard that the English for 'pferd' was 'horse,' and for a 'hase' 'hare.' He had also a strong mixture of ignorance and knowledge, begged to be allowed to read a German life of Mahomet which I had, not as the life of the prophet, of whom he had obviously never heard, but of Mahomet Ali, and was thrown into convulsions of wonder at hearing that there were no Chinese in England after the war.

Of the passengers it was startling to find that, thus travelling in the centre of Germany, we two Englishmen were the only pure representatives of the German race. There was a Bohemian countess with her little boy and a friend, most gracious and pleasing, compassionating my

[5] June 18, 1757.

G

fatigue and anxious to give me tea, plums, &c. There was
an Italian travelling from the Lago Maggiore, with whom,
as not knowing a word of German, I alone of the passengers
was able to converse, and whom the young Bohemian
evidently regarded as a kind of monster. There was also
a rough Bohemian farmer-like man, who took me first for
a Turk because of a red handkerchief which I had put on
instead of a hat, and then for an Italian from my conversations with the Lombard. But the life of the party was
the young Count Otto. He was only eleven years old,
but he already looked very much older; and it was
curious to see in him the wild look, and untamed spirit,
and precocious growth, and restless activity and eagerness
of the young barbarian. Neither the night journey nor
the jolting road broke his energy. The joke of the Turk
was kept up with me for the whole two days, and at dinner
he amused himself with making passes with a carving-knife
at the body of the defenceless Italian.

Bad as this journey was, a much worse one would have
been well repaid by the two delightful days we had at
Prague. It fully equalled my expectations, whilst the influx
of new ideas was so great that I could hardly sleep from
them for the first of the two nights we passed there. I have
not yet disentangled them clearly enough to see distinctly
what Prague was, and is, and yet may be, what are the
various ways in which it strikes one as different from all
other cities I have yet seen, and by which it connects
itself with the history of Europe. It is not to my mind
strictly Oriental, nor even Sclavonic purely; it is, I think,
what one would expect from a city of a barbarian race
struggling in the arms of a civilised world. One or two
scenes out of it, however, I shall record.

Undoubtedly the great and characteristic feature, and
one not nearly enough dwelt upon, is the *bridge over the*

Moldau,[6] which divides the mass of the town from the
Hradschin (*i.e.* the citadel, palace, cathedral—in short,
the Kremlin of Prague). You suddenly emerge from the
streets of the town out of the huge buildings of the
university (the university of John Huss, and the oldest of
all the German universities, now so famous), and of the
seminary of the Jesuits, and you come in front of this magnificent bridge, incomparably the finest I ever saw, stretching over the Moldau, arch after arch, statue after statue,
till it ends at the foot of the Hradschin, which rises immediately above it one mass of palaces and churches, with
the cathedral towering out of them. The entrance of the
bridge is guarded by a watch tower, at the gate of which
took place one of the most striking and significant scenes
I ever heard of. It was here that, in the Thirty Years'
War, the Swedish army under Gustavus Adolphus was
on the point of taking the city by surprise, when a Jesuit
rushed out of the adjoining cottage, let down the portcullis,
and, like a second Cocles, defended the gate with three
students till assistance came, and thereby secured the cause
of the counter-reformation in Prague, in Germany, perhaps
in Europe. The whole scene bursts upon one with such
vividness that I can hardly help dreaming of it all night,
and in the mocking sculptures of Luther and his wife under
the gateway, and the long line of statues on the bridge
erected, since the war, to Roman Catholic saints, you see
the visible triumph of the Jesuits' cause.

You then walk along the bridge, most like of any that
I ever saw in its character and position to St. Angelo's at
Rome, inferior of course in interest, as it is superior in
magnificence, and at last, the eighth of the statues on the
right-hand side, a place worthy indeed of the patron saint
of bridges, stands the well-known figure of St. John

---

[6] The Karlsbrücke (1357–1503).

Nepomuk, with constellations of five gilded stars round on all sides—as marking the way by which his body was discovered—and his history sculptured round the bronze pedestal. The exact place of his being thrown over is also marked on the stone bridge a few feet off.

And here I must observe a new idea connected with his being thrown over. It is a remarkable coincidence, or rather it proves a singular trait in the Bohemian character, that a similar act, an 'herabsturz' as they call it, took place in every part of the town at various epochs of Bohemian history. Far down the river, from the rocks at the south end of the town, the fabulous Libussa, Amazonian foundress of Prague, threw down her lovers into the river; here on the bridge was the murder of St. John Nepomuk; from each of the two town halls, one in the old and one in the new town, the magistrates were thrown out of the windows into the street by the Hussites; and, lastly, from the third story of the palace, from a room which is still preserved exactly as it was, were thrown two councillors and their secretary at the beginning of the Thirty Years' War, as all the people will tell you with a vivacity as if it had happened yesterday.

It is useless to describe all the curious things and beautiful views which we saw. It was, however, exceedingly interesting to see the memorials of John Huss,[7] a huge liturgy with illuminations, and a festival in honour of his death, which gave me a new notion of the high position which his followers took up, and of the great spirit which must have been blended with their extraordinary ferocity and puritanism, two features which were also strongly brought out at Prague. Another, to me, delightful sight was the palace of Wallenstein, 'the Duke of Friedland' as they called him; his stuffed horse, his hall of reception, with

[7] Burned at Constance in July 1415.

himself in fresco in a triumphal car and guiding star, his rockwork in his garden, and his astrological tower. Two biographies evidently have to be written to set forth the Bohemian character, John Huss and Wallenstein.

And lastly there was the burial-place of the Jews, from 1100 to 1600, and since disused ; the old alders twined amongst the yet older gravestones, and the symbols of the bunch of grapes of the vineyard of the house of Israel. It was the eve too of the Feast of Tabernacles, and in the old synagogue they brought out the palm branches which were to be given to the people, and which came, they said, from near Genoa, evidently from the same grove which supplies Palm Sunday at Rome, and from which I carried off the branch which I have at Norwich. In the evening we went to the service there ; there was nothing, however, to me remarkable, over and above a wild kind of scream in the chant, except (1) the very much greater number of men than women ; (2) the way in which they talked to each other in the intervals of prayer and singing, evidently on ordinary matters—a practice which struck me as illustrating the manner in which conversations and disputes are described in the New Testament as going on in the midst of the synagogue worship in a way which one would never think of in a church.

It was with great reluctance that I left Prague. I should like to have known some one there to ask how far it is looked upon as the seat of Sclavonic feeling and literature in Europe. On that I should think must depend the question whether it is now dead, after having convulsed Europe by a few extraordinary movements, as those under Huss and Wallenstein, or whether it may yet again have a destiny to perform as the vanguard of that great race which, as one looked east from Prague, lay in one unbroken mass to the Volga. The bears on the seashore of Bohemia, which, as

I said, in approaching Prague struck me with a sense of almost intentional incongruity, struck me on leaving it with a sense of fanciful congruity. Bohemia was to an un-travelled Englishman in the sixteenth century the image of the *nearest* savage country on which a European could be thrown ; and the wild sea which rolled between it and the civilised world in Shakespeare's mind was a true symbol historically, though false geographically, of the great chasm which really divided races and nations in place so near to each other. One other thing I saw in the travellers' name-book at a convent in Prague, very striking—*Lord Nelson of the Nile*, and written with his left hand ; and immediately after *Sir W. and Lady Hamilton.* September 29, 1800.

Ever yours,
A. P. STANLEY.

XXVII.

A. P. S. to Mrs. Stanley.

SCHELLING, RANKE, AND NEANDER.

[Stanley was at this time staying in Berlin with Benjamin Jowett. The first of the distinguished men whom he mentions in the following letter is F. W. J. von Schelling, who in 1841 was summoned to the Chair of Philosophy at Berlin. Schelling, who had studied under Fichte at Jena, was born in 1775. Leopold von Ranke, the his-torian, had already published his History of the Popes and the greater part of his History of Germany during the Re-formation. Johann A. W. Neander was of Jewish parentage. Before his baptism his name was David Mendel ; but when he renounced Judaism (1806), in a very great measure the result of Schleiermacher's divinity lectures at Halle, he as-sumed the name of Neander ('new man'). He was Professor of Church History at Berlin from 1813 to 1850.

Ranke and Neander, in their conversation with Stanley, refer to the German Catholics who separated from the Roman Church in 1844. The immediate occasion of the schism was the exhibition of the Holy Coat at Trèves. In 1844 Bishop Arnoldi appointed a special pilgrimage to this relic. Against this proceeding Johannes Ronge, a suspended priest of Silesia, delivered a protest. A short time before, Czerski, a priest at Schneidemühl, in Posen, had seceded from the Roman Catholic Church and formed a congregation of 'Christian Apostolic Catholics.' Ronge and Czerski were thus drawn into a temporary union. Their confederacy was not, however, long-lived. While Czerski adhered closely to the doctrines and ritual of Rome, Ronge approximated nearer and nearer to the Rationalists, and his followers occupied themselves less with religion than with democratic politics. Lichtenberger ('History of German Theology in the Nineteenth Century') says : ' The support which Döllinger and Reinkens found in Bismarck and his policy has not been less compromising for the success of the reform which they professed to inaugurate, than the alliance of Ronge and Czerski with the demagogues of Frankfort and Baden was for their German Catholicism.']

Berlin : July 27, 1845.

My dear Mamma,—A week at Berlin has now passed, certainly very different from the week here last year. We began Hebrew on Monday, with a German student recommended to us by George Bunsen, and have been at work upon it ever since, with the exception of one half-day employed in a fruitless search after Humboldt at Potsdam, in the course of which I saw one or two of the palaces again. I think it has hitherto answered, and will answer— that is, I do not know where else I could have combined a teacher, a companion, and an equal freedom from outward excitement ; and I feel that the great difficulty has been surmounted ; the three first chapters of Genesis have been read, and I do not despair of getting, somehow or other, before the end of the vacation, through the greater part of the Pentateuch. It now begins to have some intrinsic interest, and one has the satisfaction of thinking that this is the last time one will ever have to go to school again, and repeat verbs, and learn to spell and parse and construe. And the relief of having got it over will be unspeakable.

All the sights I had seen before, and of the persons I will now only select the best. Humboldt unfortunately we missed, and he is now gone with the King to the Rhine. But Schelling I had not seen before, and he is well worth seeing. We had heard so much against him, partly as a courtier, partly as a false philosopher, from various quarters on our road, that the edge of our interest was rather taken off. But the one lecture which we heard, and in which we first saw him, was, as far as we could understand it, very striking, one of his course on the Philosophy of Religion, tracing the different forms of speculation on Theism from the old philosophy of the schoolmen to the modern philosophy of Kant &c. It was a fine sight to see so old a man still labouring in his vocation, and after so long a silence taking his place as the first philosopher of Europe in the same chair in which Hegel and Schleiermacher had lectured before him. There was a large audience, though not so large, they said, as when he first began—chiefly students, but also two or three old clergymen, and two or three young officers. After the lecture we called upon him with Bunsen's letter of introduction, and he received us with great kindness; not, as we had rather been led to expect, like Schlegel, with the air of a man who likes to be visited as a distinguished man, but with *real simple German friendliness*. There is something very pleasing in his countenance as it protrudes itself from under his snow-white hair. I had been told, I think by Julius,[8] that he was very like Socrates; this, at first, certainly did not strike me. It was more what Madame Restitz described it as being, like the face of a cat (a 'chat,' as she called it); but on seeing the bust of Socrates a day or two after in the Museum

[8] Julius Hare.

I see what is meant, and, taken under one point of view, there is a strong though partial resemblance. The strength and vigour and deeply marked character of the upper part of Socrates' face are wanting ; but the rest, especially the nose, is exceedingly like ; in fact, it has the same look of genius, but without the look of strength. He talked a little of the New Catholics, but disparagingly, like Erdmann. Of the exhibition of the Relic [9] at Trèves he spoke without the usual Protestant bitterness, but said that it was probably exhibited with a view of encouraging the politico-religious disaffection of the Rhenish Provinces, and that they would repent of it. He also spoke with a very kindly feeling of Coleridge ; said that he could not tell whether he had, or had not, seen him amongst the many English who had visited him in his youth at Jena ; that he had defended him in his lectures against the charge in Black-.wood of plagiarism from himself ; and expressed his gratitude to him for 'having in one striking expression on my theology (that it was tautegorical and not allegorical) collected all that I have thought out in many hours.'

Ranke also we have been to see, and I find him altogether more agreeable than. last year. He spoke more favourably and with greater interest of the New Catholics than any one else that we had seen, pointing·out to us their progress on a map which he had marked with green strokes wherever there was a New Catholic congregation. Swarming in Silesia, they became thinner and thinner as they approached the Rhine, and in Austria and Bavaria there was not one. He thought that the Protestants would not generally join them, from their Protestant dislike to the word 'Catholic' in any shape,—in this differing from most anticipations that we have heard. The strong interest in them lay, he said (comparing it, apparently with truth, to

* The Holy Coat.

the English feeling on Maynooth), in the middle classes, to the exclusion of the higher and lower. He was much amused at finding out our occupations in Berlin, and told us, what I thought was a pleasing trait—at least one would be surprised to have heard the same of Hallam or Macaulay—that he had himself taken up Hebrew again, after a long interval, and used to read the Psalms in Hebrew with his wife in the evenings.

Of things in general I hear most from the two Bunsens —chiefly from George, Charles being now much occupied with law. The account seems very uncomfortable ; a general disaffection to the Government ; the King almost universally unpopular, and knowing that he is so, but saying that he cannot concede anything to the popular demand ; that the national existence of Prussia depends on the preservation of the old military and monarchical system, and that by that system he must stand or fall. Ecclesiastical affairs too, George says, people are very anxious to free from the control of the Crown, and yet parties in theology are so fierce and so extreme, that one does not see how any system could hold them together without some such control. Charles describes amusingly the number of applications he has for settling divorces according to the German law, *pro tem.*, for all manner of causes. 'Do divorce me, pray do !'—in the most piteous strain.

We are now in lodgings at 66 Mittelstrasse—' convenient to remember,' says Schelling, ' as being an Apocalyptic number.'   Ever yours,

A. P. STANLEY.

Tuesday.—Neander has been visited again. He is very ill, and I fear from what they say cannot live long ; but he

talked with great spirit ; and in a more thoroughly Christian
spirit than any of the theologians I have seen this time. We
spoke to him of a foolish attack which has been recently
made on German Protestantism, and which he answered,
by an English clergyman at Hamburg ; and it was beautiful to hear the unfeigned respect with which he spoke of
his opponent, who really had been very provoking; then
of the complaint of the misunderstanding of the New
Catholic movement in England, where, as he said, people
spoke of it with delight as a desertion of the Pope,
as if it were not better to believe in Christ with the Pope
than not to believe in Christ without the Pope. At the
same time he acknowledged the excellence of Czerski.
He had not seen Blanco White's Life, but asked about it
with much interest, having once corresponded with him,
expressed great sorrow at hearing of his very great advances
in disbelief, but said that he had always been more of an
unconscious than of a conscious Christian. In the Maynooth Bill, too, he took much interest, and lamented that so
many good people should have so completely misunder-
stood so Christian an act. And he spoke much against
the indiscriminate attack on Popery as Antichrist, it having
been, as he said, much rather a school through which the
human race had had to pass. Altogether he was a striking contrast to Tholuck, when he talked of those things,
and gave one much more the impression of a man who
knew what he was saying. I longed to transplant him
into England and metamorphose him for a time into a
parochial Englishman. Yours ever,

A. P. S.

XXVIII.

A. P. S. to Mary Stanley.

NEWMAN'S ESSAY ON DEVELOPMENT.

[On October 9, 1845, John Henry Newman was received into the Church of Rome. His ' Essay on the Development of Christian Doctrine ' was written during the final struggle which ended in his leaving the Anglican Church. The work is an attempt to reconcile devotion to primitive Christianity with that capacity for growth which is a test of religious life. In its general argument it is a remarkable anticipation of the evolutionary principles which, in their biological aspects, have so powerfully influenced modern science.

The concluding passage, to which Stanley probably refers, was added as a postscript after Newman had finally determined no longer to delay his submission to Rome. ' Such were the thoughts concerning " The Blessed Vision of Peace " of one whose long-continued petition had been that the Most Merciful would not despise the work of His own Hands, nor leave him to himself ; while yet his eyes were dim, and his breast laden, and he could but employ Reason in the things of Faith. And now, dear reader, time is short, eternity is long. Put not from you what you have here found ; regard it not as mere matter of present controversy ; set not out resolved to refute it, and looking about for the best way of doing so ; seduce not yourself with the imagination that it comes of disappointment, or disgust, or restlessness, or wounded feeling, or undue sensibility, or other weakness. Wrap not yourself round in the associations of years past, nor determine that to be truth which you wish to be so, nor make an idol of cherished anticipations. Time is short, eternity is long. Nunc dimittis servum tuum, Domine, secundum verbum tuum in pace, quia viderunt oculi mei salutare tuum.'

Frederick William Faber, a former fellow of University College, Oxford, was Rector of Elton in Huntingdonshire. In November 1845 he was received into the Church of Rome. A complete collection of his hymns was published in 1862. He died in 1863 at the Brompton Oratory.]

University College, Oxford : December 7, 1845.

My dear Child,—I don't know which wrote last—but a long time has elapsed since either wrote.

Various important works have appeared in the interval ; one, a great work on Roman Chronology, for which you will care nothing ; another, Carlyle's Cromwell, which I reserve for the vacation, but which I expect to revolutionise people's notions on the seventeenth century ; the third, Newman's book, which I have read and which you will not : nor will people in general, it being too scientific and historical to make much popular impression, with the exception of the preface, and the last page, which will make on many a great impression, more, far more, than all the rest of the book together. The argument generally is addressed almost exclusively to his former followers, and, as an argument, touches very few besides, and appears to me so far to demolish Puseyism altogether. Very curious it is to see the running attack on his own books. There is one very brilliant historical chapter, though, in my humble opinion, capable of an historical answer ; and, though people here are disposed to pronounce it inferior to his former works, I do not think so. But, except so far as the force of his example goes, the whole fabric of Protestantism seems to me left untouched—and the attacks on Germany in particular are made, as it seems to me, in great ignorance of the real facts of the case.

Claughton has taken Elton (Faber's living), which will vacate the Head Tutorship at Easter, quite as soon as I shall be ready for it ; and he has been there once already to look after the place, and one of the churchwardens has been here. The accounts they give are very curious. It seems that Faber had devoted himself wholly to the parish, and, with the great energy of his character and fascination of his manners, had produced an effect on the people which I should think was really very extraordinary, whilst the faults which his friends knew did not strike them. He had lived on terms of great familiarity with them, having the young men &c. constantly to dine with him, and read with him in his own drawing-room, and having pulled down all the divisions in the Rectory grounds, so as to turn it into a kind of park, and throw it open to the whole parish to walk in, so that on Sunday evenings there used to be promenades of one hundred or three hundred people, the poorer classes, and he walking about from group to group and talking to them. And thus, whilst the old people liked him for his kindness, there had grown up a 'young Elton' which quite adored him, and most of whom (about sixteen) have gone over with him, and when Claughton came there he found these young farmer boys talking of 'the Church of St. Peter, out of which there is no salvation.'

The churchwarden described the last Sunday, and the departure on the Monday evening, as the most piteous sight he ever saw : all the people weeping and lamenting, and following him along the road as he went, and wandering about disconsolate all the next day. On the other hand, I think he must have gone to the verge of what was right, if not beyond it, in Romanising the people, while he was still himself doubting what he should do, nor has he behaved quite fairly since, it is said.

I hope to leave this on Saturday for two or three days at Rugby, and then to Norwich.

Ever yours,
A. P. STANLEY.

XXIX

A. P. S. to Mary Stanley.

THE NEW BISHOP OF OXFORD.

[Samuel Wilberforce, Archdeacon of Surrey, and Rector of Alverstoke, had been appointed Dean of Westminster in March 1845. In the following October he became Bishop of Oxford.]

University College, Oxford : October 31, 1845.

My dear Child,—You will be interested to hear that half an hour after I sent off my letter, in came the Alverstoke Curate, and we discussed at length the character of the late Rector. He spoke with enthusiastic appreciation of him, and insight was added to his testimony by two facts. One that he expressed himself unable to defend the retention of Alverstoke with the Deanery, on account of the public scandal which it was likely to cause ; though he thought it might be excused on the ground partly of the Bishop of Winchester's strong wish that he should keep it, but chiefly from the great loss which he would have been to the place, especially at that particular moment when he was busily engaged in carrying through Acts of Parliament and plans for the better arrangement of the parish which probably no one else could have managed. And he also thought it likely that he would not have kept it long. And, secondly, many things which he enlarged upon coincided exactly with our own limited experience ; as, for example, his great physical courage, his love of geology and the like, and his disregard for public opinion. The charge of insincerity he maintained to be unfounded, or founded only on his affectionate manner, which my informant believed to proceed from real warmth of heart, but which, from being shown towards so many, was usually thought to be unreal. His faults he stated to be looseness in statements of fact, and perhaps too great readiness to concede unessentials. The virtue on which he most dwelt was his remarkable unselfishness, his extreme consideration for the little comforts and the like of those with whom he had to do. He seemed to have talked freely with my friend about his prospects here, doubting what position he should take up towards the University, but his chief energies, it was supposed, would be directed to the unreclaimed wastes of Buckinghamshire, now for the first time attached to the diocese. He has been ill lately from an attack of influenza. At Westminster he had meditated great things for the school, which now I fear will be cut short. On the whole the impression left was very satisfactory. Send this report on to the Mother, as part of the ingredients necessary to an estimate of his character.

I forget what day you have to be in town, but send this there to catch you. Will you with the German books and cards send also any *shirts* of mine (if indeed there be any) which were left in town ?   Ever yours,

A. P. STANLEY.

XXX.

A. P. S. to Mary Stanley.

DR. BUCKLAND, DEAN OF WESTMINSTER.

[Dr. Buckland, Professor of Geology in the University of Oxford, and Canon of Christ Church, was born in 1784, appointed Dean of Westminster in succession to Samuel Wilberforce in 1845, and died in 1856. (See Life of William Buckland by his daughter, Mrs. Gordon. London, 1894.)]

Oxford : January 26, 1846.

My dear Child,—At 9.45 I embarked in the Great Western, and found myself sitting in the back of the carriage side by side with the new Dean of Westminster enveloped in a shaggy cloak, and bolstered up by a bag and basket which were displaced to make room for me. About five minutes after we had started, putting up a paper before his mouth that a gentleman and lady opposite might not hear what he was saying, he said, ' I will tell you a secret. After all the rain that has just fallen, the express train is very unsafe, and the engineer knows it to be so. I should not have come by it but for necessity. But never mind ; we are in the best place. We are in the middle carriage, and, going backwards, we shall only feel a violent shock. The gentleman opposite will probably be thrown forward, and break his skull against the projection on this side. But here we shall only be like a trunk, with all its contents dashed violently one against another.'

And with this pleasing information he commenced padding himself up behind with his cloak, I following his example, to break the shock whenever it should come, and, ever and anon, he pointed out the places where the soil had given way.

However, we came at a modified speed, and reached Oxford without any calamity. I am glad to say that he talked a great deal and very sensibly about the reform of Westminster School, the abuses of which he described at great length, particularly in the physical department— counterpanes in the dormitory not washed for eleven years, school not cleaned since Queen Elizabeth died, tyranny and cruelty amongst the boys, three of whom he had been instrumental in expelling. All this he meant thoroughly to look into, and thought of writing a pamphlet on the subject, and made me give him a detailed account of great parts of the system at Rugby.

Ever yours,

A. P. STANLEY.

H

A. P. S. to Mary Stanley.

VISIT TO THE BISHOP OF OXFORD.

[In October 1845 Stanley was appointed Select Preacher
at Oxford. His ' first sermon ' in the course, to which he
here alludes, was delivered in February 1846 ; the four
sermons which he preached during his tenure of the office
were published in 'Sermons and Essays on the Apostolical
Age.' The remainder of the letter describes a visit to the
new Bishop of Oxford, S. Wilberforce.]

Oxford : February 9, 1846.

My dear Child,—I had Price staying with me last week,
which hindered my writing. Meantime two events have
happened.

1. My first sermon.—The day before I was somewhat
alarmed by an access of sick headache, cold, and all the
usual accompaniments, which, growing worse and worse as
the evening drew on, at last ended in the old remedy of an
emetic, and with no further evil consequences than dreaming that I found myself at 7 A.M. on Sunday morning at
some village eight hours' distance from Oxford—with the
sermon impending at half-past ten. However, I was all
right in time, and duly drest up in cassock, bands, hood,
&c. It lasted not quite an hour, and is reported to have
been more audible than the last, though still admitting of
improvement.

I have not heard very many judgments, but on the
whole I should think it was successful. The undergraduates took it very well, and the practical part at the
end struck them more than I had expected, and our Master
declares his opinion that there was no reasonable ground
of offence to anyone. J. Boileau has begged to digest it at

leisure, which he is to do after it has gone through several other hands ; so that you may, perhaps, hear *his* judgment upon it. There is no chance, so far as I see, of another this term.

2. A visit to Cuddesdon.—I had been trying to arrange it for some days, but this was the last day, and the Bishop returns to London to-morrow. So I started with two companions at 2 P.M., and after encountering a snowstorm on the intervening hills, meeting two Oxford clergymen returning, who certified me that the Bishop was at home, and passing through beautiful views, far beyond the limit of my previous walking experiences, we reached Cuddesdon about 4 P.M. It is a very retired village on a rising ground with high trees, partly in an avenue, partly in a rookery, near the house. The Palace itself is larger than I expected —far larger than any ordinary rectory—in the midst of a pretty garden. I was shown into the dining-room first, where I waited for about a quarter of an hour with Mrs. Sargent, to whom I threw out various hints by way of informing her who I was—whether with success or not I do not know, for she committed herself to no statement of details on any subject whatever, perhaps because she was evidently wrapt up in the business of the approaching departures. It was a pleasant dining-room opening on the garden, somewhat larger than ours at Alderley.

I was then shown into the Bishop's study, where he was standing at a high desk writing, from whence he immediately descended, and after expressing his pleasure at seeing me, began with incredible activity at once to mend pens, and to leap from one subject to another without dwelling for two minutes on any. This, together with the evident signs of engagement which pervaded the whole household, made me unwilling to protract the interview ; and so at the risk of leaving on his mind a confused impression of my supposed Tractarianism by declining a controversy on Pusey's sermon, and at the cost of leaving unsaid various points which I really had wished to have said about Oxford, but which I had unfortunately not sufficiently prepared to throw in at the right gaps in the rapid conversation, I took my leave in about a quarter of an hour. During the dialogue he was perhaps a shade stiffer than when at Norwich; but in the interval between my rising and my disappearance through the front door, to which he conducted me, he was radiant with his best smiles, and very kind and agreeable, expressing hopes that he should see more of me on his return, and again discussing a variety of topics in our passage through the hall.

Again I was struck by the contrast between his want of power in handling theoretical, and his very great power in handling practical subjects; as for the mending of the pens, it was one of the most marvellous feats of manual agility that I ever witnessed. If every interview is similarly employed, hundreds upon hundreds must be the result; and one part of the dexterity of it was that it either was, or seemed, intended to relieve the interview from a too great appearance of tedium or stiffness. I rejoined my companions, whom I had left disporting themselves in the village, and reached Oxford by moonlight about 6 P.M. to partake with them of one of those quiet dinners on mutton chops, in one's own rooms, which are the greatest diversions of college life. The children were not visible.

Ever yours,

A. P. S.

XXXII.-XXXIII.

A. P. S. to Mary Stanley.

IMPRESSIONS OF SCOTLAND.

[The Free Church of Scotland was formed in 1843. Dr. Chalmers, to whose unrivalled influence the success of the movement had been largely due, was at this time Principal and Professor of Divinity at the Free Church College. Stanley, who only made his acquaintance shortly before his death in the following May (1847), warmly admired his character and intellectual power. He was fond of quoting the question which Chalmers had asked in the heat of the Disruption movement, 'Who cares about any Church, but as an instrument of Christian good?' Dr. Guthrie was at this time minister of Free St. John's, Edinburgh. He was not only prominent in the Free Church movement, but an ardent advocate for Ragged Schools, total abstinence, and compulsory national education. Dr. Candlish, who had been minister of St. George's, Edinburgh, was chosen to succeed Dr. Chalmers as Professor of Divinity at the Free Church College. From 1843 till his death in 1873 he was one of the recognised leaders in the Free Church. For a description of him by Erskine of Linlathen, see 'Life of Stanley,' vol. ii. p. 391.

The four battles in the 'Esdraelon of Scotland' to which Stanley alludes were : (1) Falkirk (1298), where Edward I. defeated Wallace ; (2) Bannockburn (1314), where Robert Bruce defeated Edward II. ; (3) Sauchieburn (1488), where the Scottish nobles defeated James III. ; (4) Falkirk (1746), where Prince Charles Edward defeated General Hawley.

The appearance to James IV. before the Battle of Flodden (1513) is probably a variation of the story told by Robert Lindsay of Pitscottie and by George Buchanan in his 'Historia.' Another story told by Pitscottie relates how, before the battle, a mysterious herald, standing at the Market Cross of Edinburgh, summoned by name a muster-roll of the Scottish gentry to meet his master in the other world. Rizzio was murdered at Holyrood in 1566. Mary Queen of Scots was imprisoned at Lochleven from July 1567 to May 1568, when she escaped from her island-prison.

The Regent, James Stuart, Earl of Murray, Mary's natural brother, was shot at Linlithgow by Hamilton of Bothwell-haugh in 1570.]

Edinburgh : July 25, 1846.

My dear Child,—At Newcastle I met my youthful companion, an amiable undergraduate of the name of James, who appeared there to meet me, having a few days at his disposal. We started at eight the next morning by a coach which took us as far as Melrose. It was certainly a very interesting journey ; first the wild moor of the border country, with the scene of Chevy Chase, Scotland and England, fable and history, blending together in indistinguishable confusion ; then the very marked frontier, where, on reaching the crest of the Cheviot Hills, you look over on the cultivated undulating prospect of the Scotch Lowlands. . . . . It was also curious to pass into a new country and hear the people instantly speaking broad Scotch, and yet no sea, no *douane*, no passport, no francs. I think these latter points almost compensate for the comparative want of novelty. . . . . .

From Melrose we walked to Abbotsford, a place to be seen once, but I hope never again. There is nothing of real interest, except just the study where the novels were written and perhaps a picture of the (beheaded) head of Mary Queen of Scots. Melrose Abbey is very beautiful both in itself and its situation, and here I observed the first instance of what seems a general practice in Scotland—the use of such ruins for burial-places down to the present time. Here also was the first Free church, all new, about a hundred yards from the old parish church on the hill—a most provoking sight.

The next day brought us by an easy journey to Edinburgh. The situation is quite equal to my expectations. Internally it is not unlike Prague ; the whole town extend-

ing all along one side of a deep ravine, above which stands
the Castle like the Hradschin ; the wooded banks sloping
down to the bottom, occupied indeed not by the Moldau,
but by the Glasgow Railway ; the new town rising on the
other side, and chiefly remarkable for its great magnificence of modern buildings, commanding, like the streets
of Valetta, glimpses of the sea at the different openings.
Externally (*i.e.* seen from a distance, or from the heights),
it certainly is extremely like Athens—a very Scotch Athens
it is true—Scotch both in the largeness and coarseness of
the features, compared with the great compactness and
delicacy of outline which characterises the view of Athens.
But still almost all the features are there more or less.
Arthur's Seat is Lycabettus ; Calton Hill, the Areopagus ;
the Castle, the Acropolis ; Leith, the Piræus ; the Firth
of Forth, the Saronic Gulf ; Inch Keith, Ægina ; the Fife-
shire Hills, the Argolic Mountains ; the Pentland Hills,
Hymettus. Parnes and Pentelicus are wanting, and this
takes off from the completeness of the view, and the entire
concentration of the whole round the Rock of the Acropolis,
which is the great glory of Athens.

All historical and architectural interest is confined to
the old town, which may be divided into two parts : (1) the
original city under the Castle, with the Grassmarket and
High Street—like the original City of London round the
Tower ; (2) the Canongate, of which the great interest is the
Palace and Chapel of Holyrood, which make this part the
Westminster of Edinburgh. The great height of the houses,
and the blackness and gloom of the whole street both
from within and without, are very striking ; and when one
remembers that, till within sixty years ago, all the Scotch
aristocracy lived there, it agrees with one's notions of the
half-civilised state in which Scotch society continued for
so long.

But there is nothing of individual interest except Holy-rood. The two great things there are the long hall with the imaginary pictures of the Scotch kings—scene of the Pretender's ball in 'Waverley'—and the suite of Mary's apartments through which you trace the scene of Rizzio's murder, beginning with the cabinet out of which he was dragged, and ending with the ante-room, where he was stabbed to death, and where I see no reason to doubt the stains of his blood.

Yours ever,

A. P. S.

Dunkeld : August 4, 1846.

My dear Child,—On Tuesday . . . . Tait and a contemporary of mine at Balliol, George Moncrieff, an English clergyman, but son of an old Scotch judge, Lord Moncrieff, came over to Edinburgh to be present at the examination and speeches of the chief school, 'The Edinburgh Academy,' at which they had both been educated, and accordingly I henceforth lived with them. I was much interested in the sight, the speeches, &c., and the boys. The contrast with similar scenes in England, whether at Oxford, Rugby, or Harrow, brought out the peculiarities of Scotland very strongly—speaking with an Englishman's feeling, I should say, for the most part very offensively. But it was very amusing. Partly then, partly by delivering my letters of introduction, I became acquainted with Lord Cockburn, Lord Moncrieff, Lord Jeffrey, Sir W. Hamilton, and others less known to fame. Sir W. Hamilton was certainly the most remarkable. . . . It was in some respects lamentable to see him, for, although a handsome vigorous man in the prime of life, he has had a paralytic stroke which has almost crippled him, and which sadly mars his articulation, so that at first I could hardly understand him. I did not venture to ask him whether he had read Julius's attack upon him ; but he was reading Melanchthon's letters, and entered at once on the subject of the Reformers as if he knew all about them —and certainly with considerable accuracy of detail, and more like a German than an Englishman ; still he evidently moved so entirely in a literary and philosophical sphere of thought, that I can imagine his being totally unable to appreciate their characters. . . . . .

Chalmers unfortunately had just left Edinburgh. And this introduces the mention of the Free Church, and such Scotch ecclesiastical affairs as have come across my notice. On Sunday I went in the morning to the Episcopal Chapel ; in the afternoon to the Free Church to hear a man whom I had been recommended to hear, Guthrie. What a contrast between the two services and sermons ! The extempore prayers I certainly dislike ; the mouthing and repetition are very unpleasant. On the other hand, the evident devotion of the whole congregation, the Psalms of the old barbarous Scotch version, sung by the Covenanters and by Cromwell's army, in which all the people joined, were very striking. Above all, I was pleased by a baptism which took place, in which the father stood up before the congregation, and received an extempore address from the minister on the nature of the ceremony and the duties of Christian parents. It was both very impressive in itself, and also extremely well done. The sermon was by way of being highly figurative and imaginative, and a certain coarse imagination there was, and a vehemence and variety of illustration which, even on a hot summer afternoon, kept even my eyes open, and it was interesting to hear him introduce so near the very spot, seemingly quite naturally, allusions to the sufferings of the Covenanters in the Grassmarket. However, the most remarkable reproduction of the scenes of the Covenanters was still to come.

On Thursday, after lionising Linlithgow and Stirling on the way (of which hereafter), I slept at Tait's, and from thence went on to Lord Moncrieff's, where I was beguiled to stay over the Sunday by the inducement of seeing Dr. Candlish, the Newman—or, as one should say, the Phillpotts —of the Free Church movement, who came there on a visit to preach in the neighbouring church. I was glad, too, of the opportunity of passing two days in a strict Presbyterian family, consisting of the old judge, his daughters, and his son, who, although, as I said, an English clergyman, is in Scotland a thoroughgoing Free Churchman. The place was Tullybole, an old castellated house, at which the kings of Scotland used to sleep on their road from Stirling to Edinburgh, and partly by its name, partly by its appearance, revived a pleasing recollection of Tullyveolan in ' Waverley.' My impression of Dr. Candlish, so far as one can judge of a man in two days, was of a very shrewd, acute, narrow-minded man, who managed to unite a considerable range of general information and worldly sagacity with a set, fixed formula of Scotch Calvinistic theology, and a dash of real enthusiasm against the principles of Establishment. He talked very freely, and I had two long discussions rather than arguments about Hook's pamphlet,[1] and about English Episcopacy, his historical knowledge, which was very considerable, furnishing a point of agreement for us amidst very great difference on almost all besides.

On the Sunday we went to the Free church of the parish ; but the crowds which had flocked to hear him, to the number of 700 or 800, could not be contained within the building, and so the day, though threatening, being fine, the whole

[1] The Rev. Walter Farquhar Hook, Vicar of Leeds (afterwards Dean of Chichester), preached a sermon before the Queen in 1838, which was subsequently published and went through twenty-eight editions. It is probably to this sermon, ' Hear the Church,' that allusion is made.

congregation sate down on the green grassy slope, which
descended from the chapel to the mountain stream at the
bottom of the valley, and there in the open air, quite as
one can imagine in former times, went up the sound of
their many voices in the psalms, and there for three hours
and a half they remained, without the slightest appearance
of weariness or discomfort or restlessness.   The only thing
which interfered with the picturesqueness of the scene was
what they call the 'Tent,' in which the preacher stood, a
wooden box exactly like Punch, the resemblance being
kept up in the most ridiculous manner by the alternate
appearance in the aperture of the precentor, or clerk, as
well as of the minister.   As in most country parishes in
Scotland, they had the extraordinary practice of having
two services, two sermons &c. in one.   Both sermons
grated on my ears ; they were powerful in expression, and
powerfully screamed ; but, with the exception of one really
beautiful and original passage, in which he very happily
brought in a thought which he had expressed in our walk
the day before, it was unpleasant to me as exhibiting so
very little resemblance to the natural man.   However, the
scene was very striking, and, as I told my Presbyterian
friends, awakened much the same kind of thoughts, though
in a different direction, as did the pilgrimage at Trèves—
the one a living reproduction, so far as was possible, of
the Middle Ages, the other of the age of the Covenanters.
The enthusiasm of the people about their Free Church is
indeed most extraordinary and indisputable ; but I cannot
reconcile myself to the waste of energy and the great
mismanagement which have caused such a useless division
throughout the whole country, and in every parish set up
two rival worships which do not even profess to differ,
which, in fact, glory in being exactly the same, the one as
the other ; and it struck a pang to my heart, though I have

no doubt it was the most grateful music to the ears of almost everyone else in that whole congregation, when just as the service was beginning, the bell of the regular parish church, which the great agitator had drained of its occupants, broke in from the hill on which it stood hard by, to call the scanty remnant which still adhered to the old established Communion. The Free Church feeling against the State, and the narrow, self-satisfied feeling at the Edinburgh Academy, seemed to me very much the concave and convex of the same half-sighted view of the world which displeases me in all I see of the Scotch; whilst, of course, there are in them a fervour and a religious earnestness which are really very instructive, and to which I know no parallel in England. So much for the Free Church, of which I could say much more, but as I knew hardly anything of it before I came, and you know still less, it would scarcely be intelligible, and so I return to the objects of interest on my tour.

At Linlithgow I stopped at the station, and was met by an excellent Scotch friend who lives near, and who lionised me completely over the church, where the apparition of St. John appeared to James IV. before Flodden, and the palace where Mary Queen of Scots was born, and the house from which the Regent Murray was assassinated. I find it extremely interesting to be lionised by Scotchmen: they seem to enter so much more into the local history than Englishmen. And so, in like manner, it was very satisfactory to be picked up by Tait at the station again, and with him I went over the great battlefield—the Esdraelon of Scotland—where were fought the battles of Falkirk, Bannockburn, and Sauchieburn. . . . Stirling, too, I saw with great pleasure. The situation is very interesting: the Castle rock rising island-like from the sea-like plain; the town climbing up its back, exactly a miniature of Edinburgh ; and the whole country round teeming with the stories of Wallace and Bruce.

The next day we saw Castle Campbell, a seat of the Argylls, rising out of a mass of wood not unlike the Wartburg, and, like the Wartburg also, the retreat of John Knox at one time, to whom the Duke of Argyll was what the Elector of Saxony was to Luther.

Tullybole is near Kinross, and there, after walking on the shores of Loch Leven, and seeing the whole scene of the escape, the boat darting out first to the east (as was proved by the direction of the cannon-balls found embedded when that part of the lake was drained), and then landing on the south . . . I was picked up by the Perth coach, and came on here. Perth disappointed me, though the resemblance, which is said to have struck the Roman army when they first saw it, is unquestionably correct. The bed of the river does exactly produce a spot like the Campus Martius. The country is flat till just as you approach Dunkeld, and here we evidently are on the threshold of the Highlands. I found my three pupils, who are reading here for the long vacation, very glad to see me, but whether they go on with me, or whether Jowett may arrive, remains to be determined.

Ever yours,

A. P. STANLEY.

XXXIV.

A. P. S. to Mary Stanley.

THE RUGBY DINNER.

University College, Oxford : February 10, 1847.

My dearest M.,—The chief event since I last wrote has been the Rugby dinner last night, the first really great meeting of Rugby men that has taken place not only since Arnold's death, but almost since his accession to Rugby. Various difficulties, such as the time, or place, or the still more insuperable objection of the intervention of the older generations who had no sympathy with us, had always before rendered them complete failures. This one therefore was undertaken with some misgivings, and it was to take place in Oxford as a new place, and consisted chiefly of Oxford men, and entirely those of the Arnold or Tait generations —myself in the chair, Lake and Clough as vice-presidents, Tait sitting on my right hand. Vaughan was to have been sitting on my left, but was, alas! prevented from coming at the last moment, and so his place was filled by a substitute who happened to be here accidentally on his bridal tour.

It was a party of seventy, from fellows of colleges down to the youngest undergraduates, with all the usual paraphernalia of toasts, speeches, &c., over which I, in this entirely new capacity, presided. A momentary gloom had been cast over it by Vaughan's absence; but this rapidly vanished before the complete and brilliant success, beyond all our anticipations. I hardly ever enjoyed anything of the kind so much. First the great cordiality and friendship of the meeting itself, and then the succession of speeches, of which hardly any were bad, and most so good, and with such variety, that my interest and spirits never flagged for a moment, nor my delight at the whole scene, except in the agonies of my own speeches, which consisted of the proposal of the two first toasts, of the prosperity of Rugby, and Tait's health;—the first describing what I meant by Rugby, and why also I wished for its prosperity; the second describing Tait, first as I knew him at Oxford, and then the results of his Mastership in the continuance of the ancient spirit. They were far more of set speeches than I ever before entered upon, and I got through them .

better than I expected, not without many falls, but still so as to give me some insight into what constitutes the materials of a real oration.

My health as chairman was proposed by Bradley,[2] whose speech I wish you could have heard, as well as the applause with which every sentence of it was followed, and the enthusiasm of the cheers with which it alone, besides the toast of the general prosperity of the school, was drunk at the end of his speech. You would have seen then what a cause I have for the affection and interest which I still feel to any Rugby boy who comes up here, and you can imagine how the floodgates of years seemed to be opened towards them. It was impossible to make any speech in reply. I could only say that truly their sympathy and support were the chief solace of my Oxford life, how truly, in the words of Pyrrhus to his soldiers, they were 'my wings.' It was a delightful scene which I shall not soon forget.   Ever yours,

                                        A. P. STANLEY.

XXXV.

A. P. S. to Mrs. Arnold.

VISIT OF JENNY LIND TO NORWICH.

[The Gospel to which Stanley alludes seems to be that for St. Matthew the Apostle (September 21).]

                    Palace, Norwich : September 28, 1847.

My dear Mrs. Arnold,—You must hear something about our illustrious guest of the last week. I must presuppose that you have heard of the Bishop's invitation to Jenny Lind, as a compliment to her excellent character, and that you

---

[2] Now Dean of Westminster.

have heard enough of her from him to appreciate the interest with which he awaited her arrival, delayed as it was by illness and uncertainty, and doubtful as it was how the visit could eventually compensate to the Bishop for the clamour raised against him for having invited an operatic singer to the Palace.

It is difficult to give you an impression of the increasing sensation which her presence occasioned. The mere excitement within and without doors was in itself very remarkable ; the crowds at the station, at the doors of the Concert Hall, the windows of the streets filled with faces and outstretched necks as she passed underneath, the dense throng which had to be forced asunder in the Cathedral on her way from there to the Palace—in short, in no respect inferior to the excitement produced by the Queen at Cambridge. And then you should have seen the flocking together of the whole household when the first notes of her warbling were heard in the Palace : the kitchenmaids lying prostrate on the stairs at one door ; the guests, all standing, at the other ; the flight of every single servant in the house to the second concert, so that I took the letters to the post myself.

However, all this, interesting as it was, was nothing compared with the interest of Jenny Lind herself. Her first appearance, except for its extreme simplicity and retiring bashfulness, is very plain and homely, much more so than you would suppose from the portraits of her. She was very much fatigued, and spoke but little at first, and was altogether so much occupied in preparing for the concert that the first day we saw but little of her. It was her appearance at the concert that first showed her extraordinary powers—I do not say of singing, for that produced no impression upon me—but of the fascination of her manner, of her attitude, of her curtseys, above all of her

wonderful smile ; and although this was all through most
conspicuous in the animation of singing, yet it was to be
seen more or less always, when she became more familiar
with us, and when we saw more of her. If I were to fix on
the one epithet which characterises her, I should say it was
gifted. Of course it is not often that one sees anyone possessed with what is obviously a gift, and with all the
circumstances of extreme delicacy and sensibility of organisation corresponding ; but it is still more rare to see anyone
possessed with such a perfect consciousness that it is a gift
—not her own, but given her by God. Hence the deep conviction of responsibility, of duty of using it for the good of
others ; hence the great humility. Conceive a young girl
having now for ten years lived in this whirlwind of enthusiasm and applause, and yet apparently not in the least
spoiled by it, always retiring to the lowest place, like a
servant or a child. At the same time there were a dignity
and resolution about her by which one could easily see
at what an immeasurable distance all the evil would be
kept which must be otherwise constantly in her way.
' C'est un don, pas un mérite,' and when my mother spoke
to her, on the last day, of her hope that, after having now
successfully overcome the difficulties of ten years, she was
for the future safe, ' Par la grâce de Dieu,' she said, ' oui.'

I have no time to go into further detail ; but I cannot
help reflecting with satisfaction that there have been three
guests in this house, each of whom it has been a glory to
entertain, not one of whom would at the time have been
entertained in any other Episcopal Palace in England—
Jenny Lind, Father Mathew, and yourselves. Whatever
doubt there might have been before about the propriety of
asking her here has been absolutely dispelled now. Even
the poor people speak of her as ' the good lady,' and I
think few who were in the house with her could have heard

the Gospel of last Tuesday without thinking that she was one of the most remarkable exemplifications of it that they had ever seen.

All the details I hope to give to you to-morrow, as I pass through town on my way to Cornwall, my first stage being *Palace, Salisbury,* my next, *Post Office, Wells,* (Monday), my third, *Liskeard.*

Ever yours,
A. P. STANLEY.

XXXVI.

A. P. S. to Mrs. Arnold.

IMPRESSIONS OF SPAIN AND PORTUGAL.

[Stanley, who was at this time Tutor and Dean of University College, Oxford, spent this Easter vacation in Spain and Portugal. He joined his two sisters abroad, where they had wintered owing to the illness of Miss Catherine Stanley. In speaking of Gibraltar, Stanley alludes to the supposed derivation of the name (Gebel-el-Tarik) from the Berber conqueror Tarik (711). The church of Belem was begun in 1500, to commemorate the voyage in which Vasco da Gama doubled the Cape of Good Hope and reached Calicut. The ships sailed on March 25 (the date is disputed), 1497, and returned September 18, 1499. King Manuel, 'the Fortunate,' reigned from 1495 to 1521.]

The Peninsular Steamer,
Between Vigo and Cape Finisterre :
April 23, 1847.

My dear Mrs. Arnold,—You may possibly have heard of the unexpected means by which the steamer from Cadiz started two days before the regular time, and so has left me here instead of beginning my lectures at Oxford. However, I will not trouble you with my private grievances, nor yet with the delight of the meeting of my

sisters at Seville, but will proceed at once to give you
some brief account of what I have seen and learned. You
will the more enter into it from the same tour having, at
least in some degree, been your intended tour also.

1. Spanish scenery.—I feel inclined to write, or to have
written, an essay on the scenery of the three Peninsulas,
so like in some respects, and in others so unlike. There
is much in vegetation which recalls Greece, much in the
intertwining of hill and valley which recalls Italy; but
still there is a peculiarity which renders it impossible for
you to mistake it for either. A tawny hue, analogous to
the purple shades of the Apennines and the hoary colour-
ing of the hills of Greece, a wildness and distracted
jumble of hill and valley, like the cross waves of the Bay
of Biscay, without the picturesqueness of Italy or the
simplicity of Greece. This is the outward complexion of
the whole country which you recognise at once. But there
is an inward texture which you can unravel easily, and
which also seemed to me very characteristic. Spain, if I
remember right, is described in the third volume of the
' History of Rome,' [3] as being like a huge tower, projecting,
beyond and above the rest of the continent of Europe,
with battlements rising from it. Yes, as far as I can
judge, it is exactly so. One illusion with which I came to
Spain, and which I suppose most people entertain, has
been quite dispelled, viz. the belief that the Sierras were
long serrated ranges extending parallel to each other. It
may be so in the north, and it is possible that, either from
these or from some supposed resemblance in particular
instances, the name may have been modified to suit the
image of a saw. But I never saw any such in Andalusia,

---

[3] Arnold's *History of Rome*, vol. iii. chap. xlvii. 'The Spanish peninsula
may be likened to one of the round bastion towers which stand out from the
walls of an old fortified town, lofty at once and massy.'

and the word, which I find is derived by some from an
Arabic word 'schrak,' meaning a high place, is used for
any hill, quite as much for an isolated peak as for a big
range, for a mud heap as for a sharp tooth.   And
accordingly I should say that the structure of the country generally is a mass of table-lands, partly cultivated,
but for the most part stony wastes, rising out of the flat
plain immediately on the coast, and themselves intersected
or encircled not so much by ranges as by clumps of
mountains, which, as seen from the plain below, have
precisely the appearance of castellated battlements rising
at intervals from each other.   These table-lands in themselves are wearisome and featureless in the highest degree.
From what I have heard they must give one some notion
of the central table-land on which stands Madrid, and of
which some one said to a friend of ours who travelled
thence to Lisbon, 'Do you remember *that tree* on the
road?'   Nor are the mountains which surround them
sufficiently varied or well formed to relieve the view.

Two redeeming characteristics, however, there are, which
I have never seen equalled anywhere.   First, there are the
valleys leading up from the last plain of the coast to the
'Puerta' or 'gate' in the mountain wall, which you scale
in order to enter upon those elevated wildernesses.   Of
course they are usually formed by the descent of rivers,
most of which have the Arabian prefix of 'Guad'—the
same word which you trace in the 'Wady,' or watercourse
of the Arabian desert.   Possibly the name [4] was applied to
all streams of whatever character; but all those which I
saw were exactly what the original word seems to imply,
not merely rivers, but rivers with wide straggling beds,
the habitations and vegetation of the valleys following their
irregular course.   And it is this vegetation which constitutes

[4] See *Sinai and Palestine*, ed. 1, pp. 15, 70; App. § 39.

their peculiar beauty, unrivalled as I have said in the valleys of Italy, or Greece, or Westmoreland : a wild and tangled luxuriance of oleanders, olives, myrtles ; orange groves like those of Sorrento, wild flowers of every colour ; at times, as in the backwoods near Gibraltar, forest glades, inferior, indeed, in majesty to those of England, but unequalled to my eyes anywhere else ; or long tracks of green sward reaching far up the hill against the brush-wood, the white flocks of goats browsing amongst them ; or the river, winding out from against the soft wooded hills into the plain below, disentangling itself from the mass of mountains which have confined it.

Secondly, there are the remarkable situations which occur, few and far between, on the table-lands themselves —towns rising not like those of Italy on the crests of isolated hills, but rather like those of Greece, on the side of some broken eminence in the folds of the plain, or on the skirts of the encircling mountains, where the river forces its way through a deep cleft. Such, I believe, is Toledo ; such are both Ronda and Granada. These two last are the great glories of Andalusian scenery. Ronda is in the midst of the plain, and is called the Spanish Tivoli, being, like Tivoli, remarkable from its position on a huge rock, over which the Spanish Anio bursts in cascades into the plain below ; but it is a very Spanish, *i.e.* a very coarse, edition of the real Tivoli, and I turn with far greater satisfaction to the recollection of Granada. There, too, the town is situated by the deep ravine of a river, and on the slope of the hills, overhanging a table-plain, and with monasteries rising immediately above it. But that ravine is the rich wooded glen of the Darro, which parts the city from the red fortress of the Alhambra ; that plain is the immortal Vega, which is, indeed, ' Beautiful as the garden of the Lord,' or at least,

if not so uniformly beautiful as I had expected, green with
a verdure beyond all earthly verdure that I ever saw for
so vast an extent, and contrasted with the snow, the very
purest mountain snow that I ever saw, of the Sierra
Nevada. It is, I suppose, the close juxtaposition of the
verdure and the snow that constitutes the singular beauty
of this view, certainly amongst the most beautiful I ever
beheld.

2. So much for the country ; now a few words for the
towns and the history—Cadiz, Seville, Ronda, Malaga,
Granada, and, although I only saw it through my sisters'
eyes, yet I have so thoroughly examined them, that I
think I may add, Cordova. The one pervading interest
is the struggle with the Moors ; and, with the exception of
the Cathedral at Seville, and the Royal Chapel at Granada,
the whole interest is exclusively Moorish and not Spanish.
I have, far more than anywhere else, far more even than in
Greece, seen the forms and breathed the spirit of the East.
Not being a great architecturalist I will not say much of
the Cathedral at Seville. So far as it is a Christian church
—*i.e.* in its magnificent interior, which has been well
described as Gothic architecture triumphant over the fall
of Mahomedanism—certainly the contrast of its height and
massiveness is as great as can be conceived to the low roof
and fragile tracery of the Moorish buildings. But its
exterior, in all essential features like that at Cordova, is a
Mosque. There you see the lofty tower, which was in fact
its minaret, the unmeaning outer wall, which appears to
be characteristic of all Eastern buildings as contrasting
with their internal splendour, the crescent horseshoe arch
opening into the court of orange trees and fountains, like
'trees planted in the courts of the house of the Lord' at
Jerusalem, the fountains for the endless ablutions, the huge
square form of the Cathedral, on the square site of the

original Mosque, giving no indications of the crosslike nave and transepts of the great church within. What it would have been within, had the Mosque remained, I can conceive from the accounts of Cordova—the absence of all light, except from lamps, again as in the Tabernacle and the temples of Egypt—the place of prayer for the Caliph—the sacred place, worn by the feet of the pilgrims as being the Holy of Holies which the Spanish Caliphs, like Jeroboam, set up in opposition to that of Mecca. Also in the houses of Seville and Cadiz you see the Oriental type everywhere prevailing—the court with its fountains and orange trees in the midst, the rooms of the inhabitants round it. But the one spot which transports you at once to Asia and the Arabian Nights, the Pompeii of the Moors, the image, not only of Oriental architecture, but (except in their worship, for the Mosque has unhappily perished) of Oriental life, is the Alhambra. I do not feel certain that he who would have so delighted in the view of the city of Granada would have equally enjoyed the sight of this its wonderful palace. Something I think he would have felt, as at Pompeii itself, of the sense of its presenting the image of the last elegances and refinements of a feeble and corrupted civilisation, not of the original vigour of a great and growing nation. To me, I confess, the mere consciousness of a new, an Eastern world; the sight of the Gate of Justice, of the court of lions, of the cloisters and of the recesses for putting off the slippers as a mark of reverence; the fairy delicacy; the sense of enjoyment, unbroken by any moral feeling whatever, which seems the characteristic of all Arabic poetry and fiction—all this was almost as affecting, although in a very different way, as my first view of the Capitol and the Forum.

3. One part of Spain, however, there is which he would

thoroughly have enjoyed from first to last, and that is in
fact hardly Spain at all, either now or formerly—Gibraltar.
There is something in the whole of that S.W. corner of
Andalusia which stands alone in historical interest. From
Cadiz to the Straits, I felt that I was looking on a scene
which has witnessed great events for a longer series of
years than any other part of the world : Tarshish, the
fleets of Solomon, the Temple of the Tyrian Hercules, the
vision of Hannibal, and Columbus ; the two great conti-
nents, Africa with its Atlantean pile of mountains, Europe
with its green undulations ; Cape Trafalgar ; and, lastly, the
great Rock itself of Gibraltar, with the Pillars of Hercules,
the mountain of the Moorish invader Tarik, and now the
most impregnable fortress of England. And independently
of all these great associations, how he would have delighted
in the majestic form, the magnificent precipices, the luxuriant groves and gardens and retired bays, and last, not
least, the thunder and flash of the morning and evening
gunfire, which reminds you in every part of the Rock
where, and in whose power, you are.

4. Portugal.—In other words, Lisbon and Cintra.
There is great beauty in both. The city on its three hills,
overlooking its sea-like river ; its broad deserted streets ; its
lovely gardens—so great a contrast to the neglected state
of those in Spain ; its variegated streets, red, green, yellow,
—also a striking contrast to the uniform whitewash of
Spanish cities ; its great square erected on the site of the
earthquake, whose rents are still visible in the convents
above. Cintra too, itself one continuous garden and pleasure ground, of which the peaks of its mountain range seem,
almost as if by artificial design, to be the natural rockeries.
But if I were to choose the one spot pre-eminently interesting within itself and historically, it would be—what very
likely you never heard of—the Convent Church of Belem,

built by Don Manuel to commemorate the great expedition to the East which set sail almost from its threshold. You know I am no great Cathedral worshipper, and therefore my judgment in architectural matters is worth but little; but I cannot call to mind the interior of any church which so much impressed me as the immense arch, the unearthly roseate shade, the union of Gothic space and awe with the fairy lightness of the Alhambra, which you see in Belem Church. In Spain and other countries you may see the two separate, or even side by side; but Portugal is, I fancy, the only nation which has blended them together. At Cintra there is a great deal of the same kind, but this is certainly the masterpiece. And then all the details of the architecture, so far beyond any other building that I ever saw, tell their own story of the epoch and object of their erection,—pillars formed of twisted cordage, capitals and mouldings of all the flowers and foliage of the East, the Refectory lined with pictures of the conversion of Indian tribes, candlesticks supported by rampant monsters, the souls of Don Manuel and his family riding on the backs of elephants. Such were the visions which naturally crossed my thoughts as, on my first visit to Lisbon, we steamed up that glorious river, the sun of a southern spring setting in a blaze of light in the Western ocean, and this wonderful church, which I did not see till my second visit, most completely realised them historically.

And now I think you have had enough. Something I meant to say of the impression produced by this glimpse, however short, of the Spanish nation, an impression certainly more favourable than one gets in the same length of time of the Italians—so thoroughly a nation of gentlemen, such courtesy, such self-respect, such generosity, and yet such a contradictory mixture of tenderness, of meanness, and avarice. Something, too, of Spanish travelling, and its three great drawbacks—the Roads, Rivers, and Robbers. Where else in the world do you find magnificent roads, broken up for miles and miles by mountain tracks worse than the worst Alpine passes? Where else, rivers flowing in the neighbourhood of great towns, which by a day's rain, for want of bridges, cut off all communication? Where else, at least in Europe, do you see the roadside studded with crosses till within a few years ago (now happily it is otherwise) to indicate the site of murders? Something, too, of Spanish Catholicism. How far inferior in feeling, in impressiveness, in simplicity to that of the Holy Week at Rome! I speak, of course, of the outward forms as I saw them at Seville, in the cathedral of whose Chapter one could not help remembering Blanco White had been a Canon. Whilst I write I cannot help telling you that we have within the last half-hour taken in from Vigo a bull which was sent out from England to improve the Galician breed, but which has been sent back, the people not being able to endure him as being a Protestant. And now, if you have read thus far, ' Farewell ;' you will know by receiving this that I am re-established back at Oxford, whither I must proceed instantly on landing to commence my suspended lectures.

' On what day is Mary Arnold to be married ?' said my sister Mary to me, on the memorable morning when we entered the mountain pass which led us to the table-lands of Granada, and which by its likeness to Dunmail Raise suggested the question. It was, was it not? on that very day—almost perhaps at that very hour—on the 8th of April. What a different scene—your bridal party at Rydal Chapel—we on our Spanish horses painfully toiling up that dreary ascent! (This, by the way, will of itself tell you of the almost complete cure of my sister Catherine.)

All happiness be with you.   Ever yours,

A. P. STANLEY.

XXXVII.

A. P. S. to Mary Stanley.

SALISBURY.

[The bishoprics of Sherborne and Ramsbury were re-united under Bishop Herman, and the episcopal seat, after the Council of London, 1075, transferred, about 1076, to Old Sarum. Osmund, his successor (canonised in 1456), was consecrated in 1078. Hoare, in his 'History of Wiltshire,' says : 'Peter of Blois, a contemporary writer, describes the place (Old Sarum) as barren, dry, and solitary, and the church as a captive on the hill where it was built, like the Ark of God in the profane House of Baal. He embodies, both in prose and verse, the general wish for a more eligible abode. " Let us," he says, " in God's name, descend into the plain ! There are rich champaign fields and fertile valleys abounding in the fruits of the earth, and watered by the living stream. There is a seat for the Virgin patroness of our Church, to which the world cannot produce a parallel." ' Old Sarum was deserted by its clergy and the mass of its lay inhabitants in 1220, when, on the feast of St. Vitalis (April 28), the foundations of the present Cathedral were laid by Bishop Poore. Forty years in building, the Cathedral was consecrated in 1258. The Chapter House and Cloisters were added about 1270, and the tower and spire between 1331 and 1375.

The boy-bishop was elected by the choir boys on St. Nicholas' Day (December 6), and held his office till Holy Innocents' Day (December 28). It is supposed that this boy-bishop must have died during his time of brief authority, though the genuineness of the monument has been disputed. The custom of electing boy-bishops was finally abolished by Queen Elizabeth.]

Bath : October 4, 1847.

My dear Child,—Now for New Sarum ! ' Three things,' say the old historians, induced the inhabitants of Old Sarum ' to make the change—the wind, which drowned the sound of the services, the absence of water, and the annoyance of being inclosed within the walls of a fortress.' And so, to obviate these, they descended to the present site, which tells its own story at once. It lies deep down in the valley, inclosed by the hills of Old Sarum on one side and Harnham Cliff on the other, with water rushing through every street, and all the corpses floating in water, and people who dined in the entrance hall of the Palace in former days finding their feet in water. It has no castle and no walls except those of the close. Certainly, the Cathedral is the image of repose, and Salisbury is truly a Cathedral city, growing up under the shade of the Cathedral and of the Cathedral only.

One very curious result of the removal is that not only the Cathedral but the town was built all at once, and therefore all the houses are arranged in ' chequers ' or squares, with streams inclosing and marking them off ; and thus the plan of Salisbury is exactly like an American town, everything at right angles. Did you discern this ? The whole thing admirably illustrates the history of Norwich. Old Sarum is exactly the Castle Hill, an old British encampment occupied by the Norman fortress, and the burgh or town inclosed within the Castle ditches, and a fine chapel attached to the Castle. Then comes the Papal decree and the general feeling enjoining that all cathedrals shall be removed from obscure places into distinguished towns ; and so Herbert comes from Thetford and Osmund from Sherborne, and the Cathedral in each case grew up under the shelter of the fortress. But the crest of the hill at Norwich being narrower than that of Old Sarum, the town had already burst the bounds, and as the Wensum was nearer than the Avon to the Castle, and as there was no room for the Cathedral on the hill, a compromise was effected, and Norwich Cathedral is thus in situation a mixture of Old and New Sarum ; it is on the river, like the new, yet it is not, like it, wholly disjoined from the Castle.

The Cathedral itself is in this way deeply historical ; the profound repose with which it sits upon the lawn, the unbroken harmony indicating the simultaneous growth of all its parts, no accidental excrescences like our side chapels, but multiplied transepts, essential members of the original plan ; the Lady Chapel not tacked on to the east end, as by an after-thought, but springing out of that beautiful colonnade, as the natural termination of the Cathedral. In these respects it stands alone in my recollection. In other respects, for these very reasons, it was to me very uninteresting ; no lengthened vista of ages in its growth, no trace of outward event or accident, and, as if to take away what historical interest it would have from its monuments, they certainly have much less from the fact that they have all been moved out of their places into two regular rows along the nave, so that you cannot speculate why this person was buried there or another here. Two, no doubt, are good— William, Earl of Salisbury, son of Fair Rosamund, with his long sword, and the boy-bishop.

·Ever yours,

A. P. STANLEY.

XXXVIII.

A. P. S. to Mrs. Arnold.

PARIS AFTER THE REVOLUTION OF FEBRUARY 1848.

[On April 9, 1848, Stanley, accompanied by Benjamin Jowett, F. Palgrave, and Robert Morier, arrived in Paris. On February 23 the tumults had taken place which led to the abdication of Louis Philippe and the formation of a Provisional Government, consisting of Lamartine, Dupont,

Arago, Marie, Garnier-Pagès, Crémieux, and Ledru Rollin. To these were afterwards added Marrast, Louis Blanc, Flocon, and Albert. Stanley was in Paris on April 16, when the energy of General Changarnier gave the first check to the extreme democrats, and on April 20, when, on pretence of a fraternisation with the National Guard and the Garde Mobile, the Regular troops were brought back to Paris. For his account of these events, see 'Life,' vol. i. pp. 396-402.]

Amiens : April 25, 1848.

My dear Mrs. Arnold,—A pause on my homeward journey allows me as usual to write you an account of my Easter vacation, which has been, although in a different way, almost as interesting as my last. It has been like *living*, not *reading* a romance. You will ask, I suppose, what were the outward signs of difference visible, and what my general impression of the inward state of things.

The first are perhaps less striking than you would expect ; tricolours flying out of every tenth window and over every public building, civil or ecclesiastical ; the trees of liberty in every open space, with the flag at the top, and the little garden round the foot ; the young trees in the Boulevards beginning to take the place of their predecessors, the victims of the Barricades ; the absence of carriages, of well-dressed people, and (till within the last few days) of soldiers, which made Paris look like a sun shorn of its beams ; the *Garde Mobile* shouldering the muskets, which most of them seemed too young to bear, still in their white blouses ; the windows of the Tuileries occupied by the 'invalids' of February, lolling in red nightcaps under the glitter of royal chandeliers ; little boys, of six or seven years old, running about with sham guns, swords and pistols ; and the word 'royal' superseded by 'national,' or leaving an ominous mark where it had once been ; the shattered ruins of the Château d'Eau still bearing on its blackened walls the white marks of the shot, and the stream of molten lead which ran down from its burning roof; the placards less numerous than I had expected, but still exceeding the natural limits of such publications, indicating by their different colours their official or non-official character. These are the chief external marks of the deluge which has engulfed the monarchy of France.

Of the real effects, or, rather, of the present internal state of the popular feeling, two or three things remain fixed after the varying impressions which one receives. There is, first, a general absence of enthusiasm. 'The King is gone;' 'he was a rogue who cheated everybody and was cheated by anybody;' that is no doubt felt or expressed almost universally. But the Republic—for its own sake—appeared to me to be welcomed only by the very few theoretical republicans who had assisted in bringing it about. 'We must endure it; we must go through with it; but the sooner we are done with it the better,' is certainly the feeling of all the *middle* classes, and the entire feeling of the lower orders is not sufficiently strong to produce any great effect in an opposite direction, unless worked up by demagogues.

Secondly, perhaps as the natural result of this, there is a great regard for order and peace amongst all classes. Nothing could be more good-humoured or courteous or pacific than the appearance and behaviour of everyone, even on the two great days of April 16 and 20, on the first of which 150,000 armed men, and on the second 400,000, defiled through the streets of Paris amidst the wonder of a crowd equal to themselves in number.

Thirdly, there is a very strong distrust of the Provisional Government. Lamartine stands far the highest, as in popular favour, so in popular esteem; but even he, I fear, cannot be regarded as truly great, and of almost all the others of any eminence, there is something which gives an uncomfortable impression of their honesty. Perhaps I should except Arago. It is impossible that they can hold together after the meeting of the Assembly; and what will be the result of the disruption I do not venture to predict. Possibly Ledru Rollin will fall at once; possibly he may rally round him the baser elements of the Parisian mob, and establish a temporary—it can be but a temporary— Reign of Terror, which will end in a civil war, which will end in the restoration of Henry the 5th or the Comte de Paris.

This is a representation rather from a conservative point of view, which Clough doubtless will modify next week. My own result, however, certainly is to like the French people much more, and the Revolution much less, than when I went. As a judgment on Louis Philippe and his corrupt government, I hope we may all still regard it with satisfaction; but a deliberate expression of the national mind it certainly was not, if anyone can be trusted about anything. No doubt some great change must have come on sooner or later, and the rapidity with which the fall of the dynasty has been effected shows that the old state of things had no hold on the feelings of the people. But the revolution was brought about by the fatal discharge on the night of the 23rd and by nothing else, and the republic by a few determined men suggesting and urging it upon a mob, which one night before had gladly acquiesced in the change of ministry.

I hope to be in England to-morrow, and at Norwich on Friday, having snatched away these few days for home, in order that I may, if the Assembly holds to its intentions of meeting on the 4th, run over once again to see it before the beginning of term.   Ever yours,

A. P. STANLEY.

XXXIX

A. P. S. to Mrs. Arnold.

LAMARTINE.

[Stanley was a very warm admirer of Lamartine, as a man of letters and an orator, and he followed his career during the Revolution with the keenest interest. Lamartine married an English wife, Marianne Birch. He was returned to the Assembly, which met in May 1848, by Paris and by nine other principal departments, and was appointed one of the five members of the Executive Committee which succeeded the Provisional Government. From that time his influence dwindled. He had not the vigour and force of character which were necessary to cope with the extreme democratic party under Ledru Rollin and Louis Blanc, and his weak but well-intentioned efforts to restrain them were regarded as indications of sympathy with their objects. The final struggle, which was averted on April 16 and May 15, was fought out on June 23. The Executive Committee resigned their functions into the hands of General Cavaignac, who put down the insurrection by aid of the troops after three days' fighting.

The Ministry, to which M. Guizot (Foreign Affairs) gave his name, was in office from October 1840 to February 23, 1848. Its pacific policy and its opposition to the cry for electoral changes contributed to the disaffection that resulted in the fall of the Monarchy.]

38 Lower Brook Street : July 21, 1848.

My dear Mrs. Arnold,—I should have answered your letter long ago, but that I thought you would prefer that I should wait till after having heard of Madame Lamartine's vindication of her husband, from some cousins with whom they had lived on the most intimate terms during the eventful days preceding and following the Revolution. Of course they are much grieved by the eclipse ; but they console themselves by ascribing it to the compact with

K

Ledru Rollin, which they represent as originating not the
least in any real sympathy between the two men, but solely
in Lamartine's conviction, whether right or wrong, that
Ledru Rollin's power could only be clipped by retaining
him in the Government, and that to this precaution France
is probably indebted for the bloodless suppression of the
conspiracy of April 16 and May 15, and the formation of
the party of order in strength sufficient to put down the
final insurrection of June 23. I think this is a possible
explanation, though it still leaves some points in the dark—
e.g. the twelve or six hours of inaction on June 23, during
which the new barricades were erected. This, however, is
less important as far as regards Lamartine personally,
because it equally involves the whole of the Executive
Committee, including Marie, whom no one seems to suspect.
If you add to this the total difference of the two spheres in
which he has had to act before and after May 4, and his
acknowledged capacity for the first, and incapacity or at
least uncongeniality for the second, I think there is enough
to account for his submersion without calling in any of the
darker motives, to which I am the less disposed to attach
credit, from having seen even within my own narrow experience of revolutionised Paris how fertile it is in all con-
ceivable stories which envy or party or mere imagination
can invent. Now nothing, *e.g.*, was more firmly believed
in England, I suppose because of its propagation in Paris,
than the story that Lamartine had in March and April
advised every Englishman to leave Paris, and had even
taken farewell of his own family, than which I know nothing
could be more entirely false. On the whole, then, I hope
we may still be allowed to look upon Lamartine, not indeed
as a hero, but as having, in the 120 days of his power, performed services to the cause of moderation which no one
else, not even Cavaignac, could then have performed, and

as not having forfeited our admiration by any subsequent acts of treachery or inordinate weakness.

I had wished very much to see Paris once again ; but so many representations of its present insecurity were made that I gave it up. The most extraordinary facts which I have heard from eyewitnesses of its present state relate to the levity with which both parties speak of the late catastrophe ; each admiring the courage of the other, but neither with any sense of the horror of the event, nor (which in one sense is satisfactory) with any feeling of exasperation against each other (except in the case of the Garde Mobile) ; both alike prostrate before Cavaignac as they were a few days ago before Louis Napoleon, and two months ago before Lamartine. The strategic operations of the insurgents are said to have been masterpieces, and the activity of the Gardes Mobiles also most astonishing.

But I still recur to the three days of February with unabated interest, as throwing all else into the shade. With every deduction of accident, plot, juggling, it still remains the first and greatest of these convulsions, although the subsequent horrors incline one to look upon it with much less hope, and upon the King and Guizot with less severity. Guizot I have seen twice ; and deeply interesting it was to hear from his own lips his judgment of the events in which he had borne so great a part. His daughter spoke to me of the great pleasure with which she was reading the 'Life,' and how much she and her father regretted that there was now no longer the same inducement to send his boy to any public school. One is very much struck in seeing Guizot with the great contrast between him and his countrymen generally. One can imagine how difficult it must have been for a man to have had any hold on their affections who has so little sympathy with their follies. 'If it were not for the magnitude of the interests at stake,' he said the other night, ' I could sit down and laugh over the absurdities of which the French nation have been guilty.'

And now, shall you be at Fox How during any part of August? I have to take my sister to Scotland and leave her there for a fortnight, and should enjoy beyond anything coming to you then, or on my return, if you will give me your dates of going and coming.   Ever yours,

A. P. STANLEY.

XL.

A. P. S. to Mrs. Arnold.

DEATH OF THE BISHOP OF NORWICH.

[Edward Stanley was born in 1779. He was not allowed to gratify his boyish passion for the sea, but, with little previous education, was sent to Cambridge, where he took his degree as 16th wrangler in 1802. Ordained shortly afterwards, he was in 1805 presented by his father to the Rectory of Alderley. In 1810 he married Catherine Leycester, who survived her husband many years, and died in 1863. At Alderley he remained till November 1838, when he was appointed Bishop of Norwich. He died, as the following letter describes, on September 6, 1849. His tastes, unlike those of his son, were scientific. His 'Familiar History of Birds, their Nature, Habits, and Instincts,' was published in 1835, and has since passed through many editions. At the time of his father's death, Stanley had made all preparations for a visit to the Holy Land. His plans were completely altered by the event, and the tour was postponed till 1852-3. In his ' Addresses and Charges of E. Stanley, Bishop of Norwich' (1851), and in his 'Memorials of Edward and Catherine Stanley' (1879), he has told the story of his father's life as Rector of Alderley and Bishop of Norwich. For an account of the funeral at Norwich see 'Life,' vol. i. ch. xii.]

Brahan Castle, Dingwall : Sept. 8, 1849.

My dear Mrs. Arnold,—It is hardly necessary to write again to tell you that all is over. All Thursday he lay

in the same unconscious state, heavy breathings the only
indications that life yet remained.   These gradually grew
fainter and feebler, and at half-past eleven at night they
grew less and less frequent; the last sigh escaped, and all
was silent.   That sight you know I never saw before, nor
yet the sight of the next morning, the stone-like repose of
the beloved countenance, with none of its energy or fire,
but with nothing of the suffering of that long-protracted
struggle of expiring nature, nor yet of the restlessness of
his often overworked and over-excited life.   Thank God
with us that he was spared the trial of surviving any of us;
above all that he was spared the misery, as it would have
been to him, of what could have been only a partial
recovery.

We move, I hope, from hence on Tuesday, intending, if
possible, to arrive at Norwich on Friday night.   There it
had long been his express wish to be buried, and there he
will lie in his own Cathedral in the midst of the scene of
his labours, in the midst also, I truly believe—now that he
is taken from them and that they will feel his loss—of the
blessings and lamentations of a grateful population and of
a grateful diocese.   How thankfully I recur at this moment
to the recollection of how truly he honoured and was
honoured by him whose death is the only event within my
personal experience that I can compare to this!   They
were very different in many ways; the differences of
tastes and of education were so great that one almost
wondered how they could understand each other; yet, in
spite of this, there was the same manly, generous love of
truth and justice united with purity and devotion in that
rare union which outweighs hundreds of books of evidences,
and each felt it in the other, and it was reserved for him to
be the one Bishop in England who delighted to receive
and honour him whom all England has since delighted to

honour ; and he, I trust, will in like manner receive *his* praise when he has been removed from the scene where he earned it.   Ever yours,

                              A. P. STANLEY.

XLI.

Rev. B. Jowett to A. P. S.

DEATH OF THE BISHOP OF NORWICH.

Sept. 1849.

My dear Arthur,—It was only this evening that I learnt from the newspapers the death of your father. I know how idle all words of comfort are except such as can be supplied by ourselves. I hope you will write and tell me about yourself and your mother. It would be a great happiness to me to be with you if I could be of the least use in alleviating this overwhelming affliction.

I am afraid this must be a great blow indeed to your mother—the greatest that any one can suffer in the course of life, however many moments and happy recollections of the past they may have. I cannot sympathise in all the grounds of consolation that are sometimes offered on these melancholy occasions ; but there are two things that have always seemed to me unchangeable—first, that the dead are in the hands of God, who can do for them more than we can ask or think, and, secondly, with respect to ourselves, that such losses deepen our views of life, and make us feel that we would not always be here.

It is indeed a melancholy thought that so happy a family as you have been should lose its main prop and centre ; but I trust that you may be all strengthened to bear this great blow, and, although it is impossible you should all be exactly as you have been, that you may find a peace and happiness not less real in thinking of your father's memory than his presence among you was formerly able to bestow.

It gives me great pleasure to think that I knew him, and, as I have received so many kindnesses from him, am better able to understand your sorrow for him.   I wish I knew your address : I think I should have ventured to come to you at once.   If you receive this to-morrow (Thursday), will you send me a line addressed to P. O., White Haven ; if later, address Douglas, I. of Man ? Would you like me to come to you ?   If so, I should like to stay in lodgings near you rather than in the same house.

May God bless you and your family !

Believe me, my dear Arthur,

Your affectionate friend,

B. JOWETT.

XLII.

A. P. S. to Rev. B. Jowett.

DEATH OF THE BISHOP OF NORWICH.

[All the letters from Stanley to Jowett printed in this volume are taken from a selection made by the late Master of Balliol, some years before his death, for the purpose of being used in his friend's biography.]

Palace, Norwich : Sept. 15, 1849.

My dear Jowett,—I had been in hopes that a note from Edinburgh to Myers would have caught you before you left Keswick, and prepared you for the alarm.   And I wrote again two letters—one in the first distraction of distress on arriving at Brahan, another to tell you that all was over, which I sent to St. Michael's, Isle of Man.

Very many thanks for your kind thoughtfulness in proposing to come.   No, my dear friend, it was not needed then, and is not now. We are enough in ourselves for ourselves, and hereafter I will not fail to let you know whether you can be of the slightest service to us.

I will not go over again the sad story which I wrote to you from Brahan, though in fact I hardly remember what I did say. You will have more pleasure in hearing that my dearest mother and sisters bore the long journey of four days from Ross-shire to this place well, and that they are able to look on the brighter, as well as on the darker side of the great change which has fallen upon us. That my dear father should have been taken away, not after the decay of his faculties, which was what she always dreaded for him, but from the midst of his labours and his usefulness, is a matter of thankfulness beyond words; and when I think of what he was, and what he did in spite of what obstacles, I confess I feel a proud satisfaction, or, if that be not the word to use now, a grateful satisfaction, at having known him and increasingly honoured him, with the feelings which only a son can have to a father, and now of seeing him, as I trust, at last appreciated and valued as he deserved.

We remain here, I suppose, for some weeks to come; and then in all probability our abode will be in London. Till the entire uprooting and transplanting have taken place, of course I do not leave them for a minute, and therefore shall not be in Oxford, at least at the beginning of next term. I have written to Ffolliott to tell him of the abandonment of the Eastern tour.

Thank God, I was still within reach.

Ever yours affectionately,

A. P. STANLEY.

XLIII

A. P. S. to Rev. B. Jowett.

REFUSAL OF THE DEANERY OF CARLISLE.

[The Deanery of Carlisle, vacant by the appointment of Dr. Hinds to the See of Norwich, was offered to Stanley by Lord John Russell, partly, as the Prime Minister's letter stated, 'as a tribute of respect to the memory of the late Bishop of Norwich.' Stanley declined the offer on Sept. 26, 1849, preferring to remain at Oxford.]

Palace, Norwich : Oct. 1, 1849.

My dear Jowett,—I ought to have written some days since to tell you that on Wednesday last I received from Lord John Russell the offer of the Deanery of Carlisle (vacant by Dr. Hinds' translation here), which I declined at once. In many ways it had attractions, and chiefly the opportunity of at once offering a new home and new centre of interest to my mother and sisters, and as calling the attention of the world to the tribute of respect which the Government or the Queen (whichever it might be) expressly intended to be thereby paid to my dear father's memory. Perhaps these two considerations, combined with the possibility which sometimes crosses my mind that I shall really be able to pursue a more independent, and therefore happier and more useful, career away from Oxford, ought to have outweighed all besides. But *they* had no wish to go to Carlisle, and therefore I did not feel that the momentary feeling of gratitude and emotion would justify the abandonment of Oxford; which the eight months' residence in so remote a place would have almost necessitated.

Something seemed to me to be due to the professions which I have made, I hope sincerely, of the importance of adherence to Oxford, and if the refusal of the Deanery be a mistake, it is not so irreparable a one as the acceptance of it would have been, supposing it to be a mistake. I shall be very glad if you can say that you approve of the step. I am sorry to find that all my friends, from whom I have heard, think that it was wrong.

Many thanks for your last kind letter. Many thoughts indeed rush in at such a moment, in the light of which the speculations of books seem to fade away, or else to stand out in a new aspect. The words of the Bible are truly justified by their astonishing force at a time like this.

There is one thing which I have often thought of saying to you, and which the closing sentences of your letter partly invite me to say now—now especially when I have burnt my ships behind me, and must look forward to Oxford and to theology as my final home and resources. You know that I believe myself to have learned more from you than from any one else since Arnold's removal; and therefore I hope you will not misunderstand me when I say that I sometimes feel so much oppressed and depressed in talking to you about these things that I seem to have lost all will of my own. Some means must be taken for avoiding this. Perhaps the long interval and separation from all such topics will of themselves produce all the independence which is requisite. Nor do I wish for the slightest change in our relations on the subject. I only mention it that you may understand why it has been that of late years I have not been able to sustain in your presence the same buoyancy of interest that I used to feel in discussing these matters, and also that I may not be for ever having to explain and apologise for following my own devices, not as the best in themselves, but as the best for me.

You will wish to have a few words about ourselves.

We are all well. I dread for them only the void into which we shall pass when we leave this. It is the breaking of the string of the bow of our life that seems to relax everything. I trust this may be repaired as soon as possible, and from this cause I think I shall stay with them as long as I can, with the exception of a few days' visit in November. Dr. Hinds comes here next week for two days; all the accounts of him are satisfactory. This will be a week well over.

Kind remembrances to Ffolliott and Morier.

Ever yours affectionately,

A. P. STANLEY.

I have been reading your letter again—this is a sad worldly answer to send in reply to it—but I do hope indeed that it may not be in a worldly spirit that I have written.

XLIV.

Rev. B. Jowett to A. P. S.

Balliol : Oct. 23, 1849.

My dear Stanley,—A day or two since I received a kind letter from you dated October 1st, *viâ* Ffolliott, who had kept it in hopes of my coming there.

Almost every one here thinks you were right in giving up the Deanery—Lonsdale and Temple most strongly, whose opinions, from my long experience, I am inclined to put more faith in than almost any one's. I ought to except the Dean of Wells from this general ' consensus,' who feels the same kind of difficulties that he did on the occasion of Oakley's resignation of his fellowship.

I could not help feeling pained at the latter part of your very kind letter. I know well how much better and

wiser I ought to be at all to be worthy of the high opinion
you express.   It will always be a motive with me to try
and make myself very different from what I am.   I think
it is true (and I am glad you mentioned it) that we have
not had the same mental interest in talking over subjects
of theology that we had formerly.   They have lost their
novelty, I suppose ; we know better where we are, having
rolled to the bottom together, and being now only able to
make a few uphill steps.   I acknowledge fully my own
want of freshness ; my mind seems at times quite dried up—
partly, I think, from being strained out of proportion to the
physical powers.   And at times I have felt an unsatisfied
desire after a better and higher sort of life, which makes
me impatient of the details of theology.   It is from this
source only that I can ever look for any 'times of refreshment.'   Had I always done rightly, my life would doubtless have been happier and my mind clearer.

I think sometimes we have been a little too intellectual
and over-curious in our conversations about theology.
We have not found rest and peace in them so much as we
might have done.   As to the other point you mention, I
am quite sure you cannot be too independent.   Your supposed want of judgment is a mere delusion, and if it were
not, and I were really able to guide you, it is the greatest
absurdity for one man to submit his will to another, merely
because he has the power of sympathising with him and
has greater energy at a particular moment.   I think I see,
more clearly than formerly, that you and I and all men
must take our own line and act accordingly to our own
character, with many errors and imperfections and half-
views, yet upon the whole, we trust, for good.   We must
act boldly and feel the world around us, as a swimmer
feels the resisting stream.   There is no use in desultory
excitement, of which perhaps we have had too much.

Steady perseverance and judgment are the requisites.
And Oxford is as happy and promising a field as any,
such as we are, could desire.

I earnestly hope that the friendship which commenced
between us many years ago may be a blessing to last us
through life. I feel that, if it is to be so, we must both
go onward : otherwise the wear and tear of life and the
' having travelled over each other's minds ' and a thousand
accidents will be sufficient to break it off. I have often felt
the inability to converse with you, but never for an instant
the least alienation. There is no one who would not think
me happy in having such a friend. We will have no more
of this semi-egotistical talk : only I want you to know
that I will do all I can to remedy the evil, which is chiefly
my fault.   Your affectionate friend,

                                B. JOWETT.

XLV.

A. P. S. to Rev. B. Jowett.

[The Deanery of Carlisle was offered to, and accepted
    by, Dr. Tait, then Head Master of Rugby.]

Palace, Norwich : October 24, 1849.

My dear Jowett,—Many thanks for your kind good
letter. I am relieved for once to have spoken out my
mind, and now let us dismiss the subject. I am sure I
shall be happier for having done so ; therefore you must
forgive me if it at all grieved you. And for the other
subject, the Carlisle Deanery, I am sorry that I troubled
you or any one else about it after I had once made up my
mind. What misgivings I had were, I believe, the result
only of a gloom which overspread our horizon at that time
from a stronger sense of the blank and trackless world

which seemed opening before us.   But they are now quite passed away, and I feel myself more than repaid for the many other anxieties I may have had about the refusal by its having issued in this delightful appointment of Tait. I am sorry that Rugby is to be again at sea ; but, for his sake and with the great risk of his continuance there, I cannot imagine a place which would suit him better. I reflect upon it with curious joy every hour of the day.

I forget whether I told you that we shall now be here, in all probability, till the end of November ; then to London, and I straight to Oxford, where I shall hope to be for a week or so.   We much enjoy these halcyon days, of which the repose will, I trust, not unfit but prepare us for their end.

I long to see you, for there is much to say.

Ever yours most truly,

A. P. STANLEY.

XLVI.

A. P. S. to Mrs. Stanley.

THE BISHOP OF NORWICH AS RECTOR OF ALDERLEY.

[Ellen Baskerville was kitchen-maid at Alderley Rectory in 1811.   The 'second news' to which she refers in the following letter was, no doubt, the news, which arrived in December 1849, of the death of Captain Charles Stanley, R.E., the Bishop's youngest son, at Hobart Town, Van Diemen's Land.   Alderley Rectory had been offered to, and declined by, Stanley.   Owen Stanley, the eldest son of the Bishop, died suddenly, in February 1850, on board his ship H.M.S. 'Rattlesnake' in Sydney Harbour.]

Alderley : January 9, 1850.

My dearest Mother,—You must hear the account of my first round of visits to Mrs. Twiss (of which Mary will have told you in part), Jane Dunville, Ellen Baskerville, and Hannah Burgess.

Ellen was of course by far the best. It is really wonderful to see how a remarkable character emerges from the mass in humbler as well as in higher life. She said she had been much more 'hurt' by the second news than by the first. 'I don't know how it was; but when I heard of the Bishop's death I did not fret over it at all. I did not take it nearly so much to heart as when he left Alderley. I thought to myself over everything, and I believed that he was happy, and that was enough. And besides, when last I saw him, I somehow felt sure that I should never see him again. It was not that he was aged. He was very cheerful, and when I stroked his hair (for it was so beautiful and white that I could not keep my hands off from his head), and said, "You are growing old," he said, "Oh, yes, Ellen! we all grow older; but never mind that." But he went on to speak of the angels in heaven beckoning away those that remain on earth, and he said, "Whichever of us is taken away first must beckon to the others to come too." And so when I heard that he was gone, I thought of these words, and comforted myself.'

She had heard of his illness before, and of his death on the Sunday after church; and when she came home a gentleman—she thought he must have been from Norwich—who was staying at one of the new houses on the other side of the road, came and knocked at the door to ask whether it was true that the Bishop was gone. 'And I said, "Yes, I believe that the Bishop has gone." And then he seemed almost as much hurt as I was, and walked up and down before the house and sat down and seemed quite sorry. And he came every day for the next week to ask whether I had heard anything more, and brought me the Norwich papers to read. . . . I often and often look backwards, and

think that I see him. I recollect him as he used to come
on his horse up the hill, and call out, " Ellen, Ellen," as he
came nearer the house that I might come out to him. How
I did miss that voice when he went away ! He was my
father and leader in the right way. It gave me a shock to
see him when he came back.' Once, especially she mentioned, ' I was sitting in our pew between the pulpit
and the Park pew, where we could just see any one if
they looked over, and I did not know that he was there,
when suddenly he looked over, and when I saw him I felt
such a shock that I almost fell down in the pew. And
another time I was going across the road to meet the
butcher's cart, and saw an open carriage coming across the
road, and he got up in it, and when I saw him I could not
help screaming aloud. It was a shock, you understand,
like grief; but it always ended in gladness.' She asked
many questions about his illness, and about Charley,
mentioning how I had told her, as she had walked with me
along the road in the summer, how he lived under our feet,
and she had often thought about my tour to Jerusalem, and
how she should hear all the particulars. And then she
began to regret about my not having taken the Rectory ;
but put it from her at once, saying, ' But it was not to be.'

She then went on to speak of her delight in former
times at going to the Rectory in any half-hour that she
could spare. ' Owen,' she said, 'was my favourite, perhaps
because I was in the house when he was born. I recollect
how I stayed up by the kitchen fire waiting for it, and at
last master came running down in the night to say that
" there was a baby born," but he did not know what ; and
then again to say that " it was a boy," and that by the time
he was ten years old he should be " *on the sea.*" I marked
it at the time, and know it is correct, because I thought it
hard and cruel that he should think so about the baby

when it was but just born ; and when the tenth year came I
marked it, and he was not then gone to sea ; but he was at
eleven or twelve. But Owen was always so partial to the
water ; when he was in the tub he did not care how much
water he had poured over him everywhere. He was such
a beautiful child.' The Bishop, she said, was such 'a dear
lover of children.' When he came to her, he used to sit and
talk, not read the Bible, but ' lay down ' any questions that
she asked him out of it. One night she had dreamt that
she had seen him sitting in her chair, and 'a few days
afterwards he came to Alderley unexpectedly, and I never
wished to see him more than once. I knew that he had so
many to see ; once always satisfied me.

'I was quite struck when first I heard of his death ;
but then, when I thought of all this, it seemed to me so
glorious that he should be an angel in heaven. Margaret
will be there too, and many, many faces that he has
known here. And wide and broad as is the distance of
the place where Mr. Charles died, that is all over now.
Never, never did I hear any speak ill of him, much
rather the reverse ; and many strange faces, from wide
and broad, came to church when they heard that he was
to preach.'

Jane Dunville : ' The children were not afraid of him ;
when he came in, it was so different to any one else ; he did
not look just once round at all, but he had something to
say to each. They used to say, " Mother, mother, wash my
face, the Rector's coming."'

Peggie Burgess sate in her chair and hardly said a word,
tears rolling down her face, but nothing more. Hannah
(her daughter) spoke much of his last sermon, as did also
Margaret afterwards ; how at the end of it he had leaned
over the pulpit, and turned first to the children in the
chancel, then to the old, and shed tears as he ended, as

L

some one else expressed it, 'God blessed them all'—quite a *Father*, they said, to the parish.

Will Powell was out when I came in. It was very affecting to see his rough face struggling with emotion. He tried in vain to give me an account of his last sermon at Birtles. 'It was explaining,' he said, 'how one party is prosperous, but not good.' And then at the thought of the preaching he burst into tears, and then went on again: 'another party suffering, but good.' 'He was,' he said, such a gentleman: he treated me so like a gentleman about my place.' Margaret said, 'It was so hurtful; I never felt so sorry in my life.' Old Betsy Brocklehurst came out of the house when she saw us coming, and for a time could say nothing but 'the Lord Bishop,' 'the Lord Bishop.' She said, when she got into the house, 'I am all of a tremble; I canna stand; I maun sit down. I knew who it was from his likeness to his father; there was some-thing of a look—I canna say what it was—something like.' 'I have read over the paper to the parishioners,' she said, 'many many times, as often as I could for tears.' 'He used to come in,' she said, 'no matter whether we were clean or rough, always as if we were his *equals*.' She sate there on the chair with one of our hands in each of hers, and looking round at her family, and there was something almost majestic in the manner in which she said, 'Bring me the Bible' (in order to try the spectacles). She described exactly the moment when she first saw him, her father doing something with the wool, all which was described in such detail as to be quite unintelligible; but evidently the whole scene was before her, as if it had happened to-day. It 'made sport for him.'

Phœbe Earlham sate motionless in her chair, the tears streaming down her cheeks, and dimming her aged eyes, so that she took Mary for you—for 'the Lady-Bishop.' She

could say very little coherently. One image seemed to be
constantly before her—' Whenever Lady Stanley, or Miss
Stanley, or Miss Louisa comes in, it sets me off directly.
I should have been more comfortable if he had been laid
here.' Her countenance lighted up through her tears when
the spectacles were brought out for her to choose from, and,
when she had fixed upon her pair, she held them in her
hands, and said solemnly : ' I would not take five shillings
for these, even if there were not a bit of bread in the house
to eat so long as I live.' ' And after that,' broke in her
daughter, ' I will have them, and they shall never go out of
the family.' She said to me (when first taking Mary for
you), ' Be a comfort and support to her.' And when we
went away, ' Tell Lord Stanley that I am much obliged to
him for having lent you his carriage to come and see me ;
mind you tell him.'

The daughter spoke much of his affection for children,
of the many pair of shoes he had given to some poor
motherless child in the school because it was motherless.
' The last time he was here was just at the edge of dark,
and mother was afraid he would be bewildered as he went
home. But he said, " Oh, I know the lanes well enough,"
and down the lanes he skipped like lightning out of sight.'

Martha Whitney came out to meet us, also with streaming eyes. ' The last time he came to see me, he said, " Well,
Martha, if I do not see you again, I hope we shall meet
in heaven." It was not every rich man or gentleman who
would have thought of that, to meet a poor body like me
then, when he would have thought he had done with me.'
' I think now I hear him coming up galloping, galloping,
galloping, and call out " Anne ! "—and then he come in and
say, " Well, Anne ; " and once I recollect Miss Catherine
riding with him ; and when he had sat a time he would turn
round and say to her, " Come, Catherine," and off they would

L 2

both go spanking together. There he would have sate praying, and reading and talking.'

Mrs. Adams (Becky Bratt) said that she had so often grieved to see him go by without calling upon her (after he had left Alderley) that she at last begged him to come; and he said, ' Why, you know, the reason is that I could not manage to go to any one out of the parish.' ' He took so much trouble in whatever he did; whatever he took in hand, he never spared any trouble about it. I don't think, nowadays, gentlemen take as much trouble as he did. Do you think they do, sir? My mother never cared much about waiting on great people at Monkesheath; but she would do anything for the Rector.'

Ellen Baskerville again: ' Do you recollect the time of the fighting by your house?' ' Hundreds and hundreds of times have I told that,' she said; ' the fight had been put off in the morning by the constables from Wilmslow, and we thought it was all at an end. Then in the afternoon I saw a great quantity of men coming up the road abreast, so thick that they made the road one head. I said, "What's to do?" and they said, "We have not been able to have the fight in Wilmslow, so we'll have it in Alderley!" And I was quite struck, and said, " Oh, for God's sake, not in our fields!" Well, they passed by our fields, just below, and the whole field was filled, and all the trees round about, and I could hear the sound of the blows; and in about a quarter of an hour I saw the Bishop coming up the road on his pony, as quick as lightning; and I trembled for fear they should harm him, for I saw what he was come for. And he rode into the field, and just looked quick round, as if he thought the same, to see who there was that would be on his side   But it was not needed; for in one moment it was all over. It was as if they would all have wished to cover themselves up in the earth. From the trees they all dropped down directly, and no one said anything. There was one vagabond man in the field, drunken and bad, who after that day was quite changed and became a good man. I never knew quite what became of the men who were fighting ; but one of them afterwards became quite steady. He sent for them, not to scold them, but to talk to them. I never knew any disturbance so great as this ; but whenever there was a drunken fight down at the village, and he knew of it, he would always come out to stop it. There was such a spirit in him.'

'Do you recollect when you first heard of his leaving Alderley?' 'I could show you the very foot-breadth. It was as I was walking back from church on Sunday, at the corner of the smithy lane-end, and Mrs. Dunville said to me, "Do you hear the Rector is going to leave us?" And I did not believe it, because I recollected that he had not taken Manchester ; and she said, "Yes ! but this is true," and then we both shed tears together. I came down to the Rectory to see him at the last, and went all through the rooms, and took my leave, and have never been there since, but to the door. Oh ! it was a sad time. When he went away, I had said that sooner than lose him I would have given up my only child. She was then quite well ; but in six months she fell sick, and then this very trial of which I had spoken came upon me.' He used then to write to her. 'I have lost my father, mother, husband, but that was nothing to what it was when I lost my child. I never wished her back, but I wished to go to her. And then he used to comfort me and tell me about the angels in heaven.'

I shall continue Jane Dunville's conversation from this morning. She said that the change had been very great in the parish from the time he came. In Carr's time the clerk used to go out to the walk leading to Harwood to see whether there were any more coming to church, to make it worth while to have a service, there being seldom enough for a congregation. No one had ever spoken ill of him that she remembered ; those few drunken reprobates that he was always attacking had only said, when he went away to Norwich, that they wished they could have the satisfaction of shaking hands with him. She said that she did not think she had ever recovered the sight of the packing-cases at the kitchen door.

Anne Barker was having a tea-party with two married daughters of John Swindells from Wilmslow, who had lived with their aunt Elizabeth. They had several letters, they said, to their aunt, from Mr. Charles and Miss Catherine, beginning 'Dear Nanna,' and they remembered the two children coming into her house, and leaping upon her knee, and saying, 'Bless you, dear Nanna ; let me kiss you,' with their arms round her neck at once, and they had a horn box which Catherine had given her for a keepsake when she left Alderley. William Barker spoke much of the benefit of the *schools*, contrasted with the profound ignorance under the reign of Carr. Anne said that the last time he had called upon her (the last time she had seen him he had shaken hands with her in her pew in church) he had said, 'Do you know my *stone* in the churchyard ?' and had told her which it was. 'There I should have laid if I had stayed ; but now I must rest where I have been last.' So *she* was quite satisfied.   Ever yours,

A. P. STANLEY.

XLVII.–XLVIII.

George Grote to A. P. S.

THE 'HISTORY OF GREECE' AND CHARACTER OF SOCRATES.

[The two following letters refer to two articles which Stanley contributed to the 'Quarterly Review' on Grote's

'History of Greece,' vols. iii.-viii. The first article appeared in March 1850, the second in December 1850.]

12 Savile Row : April 1, 1850.

My dear Mr. Stanley,—I have just had the pleasure
of reading your kind and flattering notice of my 'History'
in the 'Quarterly.' It is highly gratifying to me to see
that the spirit, in which I have *sought* to compose it, is so
worthily appreciated by a reader like yourself. The points
of success for which you give me credit are exactly those
upon which I myself set the greatest value : earnestness
of moral interest, combined with laborious study of the
evidence, so as neither to overlook anything which it does
contain, nor to make it serve as a vehicle for inferences
which it does not fairly warrant. In respect to earnest
moral interest, I am happy to find that there is so warm a
sympathy between us, in spite of the difference in some
points between our views : which difference, with a
generous and catholic mind like yours, does not prevent
you from doing justice to all that you find, even while you
remark the absence of that which you think ought to have
been added. The liberal and scholarlike composition of
your article, combined with the warmth of the praise
which you are indulgent enough to bestow, cannot fail to
impart to the work an additional circulation, for which I
shall have to thank you.

You have brought out (pages 386-387) one circumstance which has always been strongly impressed upon my
mind during the composition of the work—the necessity
of looking upon Grecian history as a moving and progres-
sive scene, in which the characters of one generation are
different (for better or worse, as it may be) from those
of another. This has been (in my judgment) never
sufficiently attended to by those who have written Grecian

history before. Most of them treat all the characters in Grecian narrative as being at the same distance from the point of vision—to use your simile of the *fixed stars*, which is very happy, and which I should certainly have put into my history if it had occurred to me.

I shall endeavour to profit by your less favourable criticisms, in my future volumes. Of many among those criticisms I feel the force, even when I do not see how I can carry them out without sacrifices more than commensurate on other points. Your picture of the battle of Marathon is at once exact and animated ; but I incline to fancy that it would hardly do for one or two pages of a long and continuous history, though highly striking in a short composition, or as the speech of a reciting Messenger in a Greek tragedy. I remember a remark of Bishop Butler that a certain *oneness of style* is always the mark of one who writes with simplicity and in earnest : were I to paint so highly, on particular occasions, I should perhaps lose more by seeming to dress up for a purpose, than I should gain by the stronger impression made upon the reader. I will also confess that the tendency of the present age seems to me to run rather too strongly towards the *pictorial* in history, of which Macaulay is so remarkable a specimen. Of course it is absolutely essential to bring out the significant points and to make the reader clearly conceive the scene that is passing, together with the motives and sentiments animating the actors : in so far as I fail in this, it is from want of ability, and not from want of will ; but I have a certain fear of running into poetical exuberance, and of overstepping what is permitted to a faithful deposing witness and a sound expository philosopher.

Moreover there is another point to which I would beg your attention, in reference to my manner of handling, and to the way in which (as you observe) I blend narrative with evidence and dissertation, making my authorities speak for themselves. The facts of Grecian history (different in this respect from English or any other history) come before young men when they are receiving their education and when they are reading the best of the Greek authors. One of my particular objects in writing it has been, that my book should be the best and most useful accompaniment which a young man can take who is studying Herodotus or Thucydides. To give results simply, without references, examinations of evidence, clearing up of obscurities and difficulties &c., would not have answered this object. There is hardly any compliment in your article which I feel more strongly, than that in which you say that it almost amounts to a *new edition of Thucydides* (p. 388). You observe indeed, very truly, that this is tedious and uninstructive to all readers who are not *patient students*; but to those who *are* patient students it will be all the more instructive ; and in English education all the young minds pass more or less through this phase. Macaulay has *no* readers who are *patient students*, and therefore would have no occasion to write for them.

Lastly, I know that my views on Grecian history are contrary to those which are received and popular ; and that my opinions on many other subjects, formed by my own reflection, dissent materially from all the great currents of English sentiment. I have no chance of being listened to except such as may arise from the reasons which I can produce ; and this is one among many causes making me habitually careful of advancing anything without grounds assigned—perhaps sometimes even to excess. It might be otherwise if my task were (like that of so many other authors) merely to amplify and vivify in the minds of readers conclusions of which the basis was already laid.

Your remarks about defective arrangement I shall

certainly lay to heart. I do not doubt that I am more or less chargeable with it : for there is great difficulty in determining at what point of the history the natural place of various important matters is to be found.

Believe me, my dear Mr. Stanley,

Yours very sincerely,

GEO. GROTE.

Rev. A. Stanley.

George Grote to A. P. S.

London, 12 Savile Row : Jan. 24, [1851].

My dear Sir,—Pardon me if I have been tardy in adverting to your article in the 'Quarterly Review.' I had other matters in my mind which I wished to throw off upon paper before I took it up.

I beg you to believe that I have read it with sincere pleasure and strong sympathy. The warmth of feeling which it displays, combined with a conception at once so animated and so just of the character of Sokrates, was most gratifying to me, and cannot fail, I think, to inspire a similar interest to readers generally, even if they approach the subject with ever so little favourable predisposition. For the manner in which you speak of myself and my work, I have to thank you much : it is indeed a compliment of high value, if I can flatter myself with having presented so familiar a character as Sokrates under points of view in which he has been little remarked before. It is an additional motive to persist in the plan which I have laid down to myself—of trusting nothing but impressions derived from fresh study and intense meditation of the original evidence. That you should dwell upon and expand the analogies connected with the religious character of Sokrates is a circumstance perfectly natural. As in your former article, I have reason to be grateful for the liberal candour

with which, while expressing yourself with that earnest
positive conviction inherent in your character, on the religious part of the subject, you abstain from any unfriendly
expressions towards persons dissenting from you. And,
what is of still greater moment than any feeling personal
to myself, you bring out into full relief the intellectual
Sokrates, especially in the last pages of your article : you
praise, with an emphasis rare to find yet still amply
deserved, even his most unpopular intellectual qualities—
his fearless cross-examination of existing opinions, and his
application of the negative test as an essential condition
for getting at truth and knowing when a man has got it.

I shall not touch upon particular points of difference
where the general impression left upon me by your whole
article is so satisfactory, and where I am persuaded that its
effect upon readers is likely to be suggestive as well as
instructive. I cannot, however, pass over without notice
your note on page 53, in which you sum up, in a few
sentences, the general contrast between my views and those
of other historians respecting the Sophists. Nothing can
be more perspicuous and accurate than the sentences in
which this contrast is set forth. Though you do not
ostensibly handle this chapter of my work, you have put
people exactly on the look-out for what they will really
find in it. I was talking over your article yesterday afternoon with Mr. Mill (author of 'The Elements of Logic'),
who, while coinciding fully in my general estimate of its
merit, singled out particularly this note upon the Sophists,
as I had done when reading it. I presume that on p. 67,
where you allude to the position of 'philosophers who do
not aim at founding a school,' you had in view Dr. Arnold ?

Believe me to be, my dear Sir,

Yours very sincerely,

Rev. A. Stanley.   GEORGE GROTE.

XLIX.

A. P. S. to Rev. Hugh Pearson.

THE CLOSE OF THE GREAT EXHIBITION.

[When this letter was written, Stanley had been appointed secretary to the Commission of Inquiry into the state of the University of Oxford. The Commission issued on August 31, 1850. Its elaborate Report, the preparation of which was mainly Stanley's work, was published in May 1852.

Three months before the date of this letter (July 1851) he had accepted a Canonry at Canterbury. But he did not resign his work at University College, Oxford, till the end of the October term which was just about to commence. For an account of the opening of the Exhibition, May 1, 1851, see 'Life,' vol. i. pp. 423–26.]

6 Grosvenor Crescent : Oct. 11, 1851.

My dear H. P.,—A few words of the close of the Exhibition. At 4.30 we, the sister and I, mounted the east corner of the south-west gallery. Multitudes, multitudes, far more than we saw the other night, far down each nave, but thickening towards the transepts ; a deep sea of black heads ; the most were men, out of which rose the white statues ; here Diana, bow in hand, conversing with the people at her feet ; there Victoria presiding over them.

At 10 minutes before 5 there was a sudden pause in the roar of many voices. It was the sensation caused by the cessation of the crystal fountain, the first sign of the approaching dissolution. An aged minister close by, whom I imagined to be a Wesleyan, observed, 'There is but one fountain which never stops.' Was it sublime or ridiculous ?

At 5 P.M. the clocks struck in order one after another.

As the last and shrillest clock ceased, a band of trumpets struck up from the south-west corner; organs dimly streamed from the naves; singers, stationed seemingly in different parts, sang audibly ' God save the Queen ; ' the multitudes below turned up their faces, not seeing whence the sounds came. The sounds, however, were fully audible, and still more so when, on the close of the singing, the whole assembled crowd burst forth into a loud hurrah, many times repeated, and lasting till the breaking in of the great bell, which rang from end to end.

From that moment the crowd gradually dissolved ; the fountains all ceased. In any interval of the bells, the crowd, still lingering in galleries and naves, shouted and cheered, much as in the Oxford theatre, calling out names, 'the Queen,' 'the Duke,' &c., and ever and anon a speech from some individual on the borders of the crystal fountain, which was immediately drowned in the renewed crash of bells and gongs, evidently set on with redoubled vehemence at the instigation of the police.

By this time we had descended into the area ; the gas lights illuminated the roofs and fountains ; and we watched the emptying of the galleries and naves. By a quarter past six all was clear except the transepts. The police and the company of sappers and miners then formed a cordon round the centre, gradually sweeping every one within it, and pressing the crowd round the crystal fountain, who were then made to file out by the south transept. They passed by its dark waters, and most drank of it. The police then formed close round it, and drove us on from behind, the soldiers flanking us. We passed close under the bell, ringing as if its heart would break, and out into the space where the tree stands in the south entrance. There we saw the last file emerge, the blinds drawn up, and heard the last peal of the bell, drowned, however, in a loud cheer from the crowd outside. The whole scene was certainly very fine, a little wanting in point, you would say, like Carnac, but still impressive ; there was nothing melancholy. The Exhibition ended amidst universal applause.

If you do not hear to the contrary, I shall·come by a late train on Thursday. Ever yours,

       A. P. STANLEY.

L.

A. P. S. to Rev. Hugh Pearson.

RAVENNA.

[In May 1852, Stanley, who had resigned his Fellow-ship at University College, and kept his first residence at Canterbury as Canon, was released from his work as secretary of the Oxford University Commission by the publication of the Report. In August 1852 he left Eng-land for a tour abroad with his mother, his sister Mary, and his cousin, Miss Penrhyn. The three following letters, describing Ravenna, Loretto, and All Souls Day at Rome, were written on this tour.

The Duke of Wellington died September 14, 1852. His public funeral, at which Stanley was present, took place on November 18, 1852. He was succeeded as Chan-cellor of Oxford University by the Earl of Derby.

The history of Ravenna, which is, as Gregorovius after-wards said, 'the Pompeii of the Gothic and Byzantine times,' interested Stanley for five reasons :

1. *As the refuge of the Western Empire*, A.D. 402–476. Galla Placidia, daughter of Theodosius, and sister of Honorius and Arcadius, spent much of her life here. Made prisoner at Rome in 410 by Alaric, she married her captor's brother-in-law Adolphus, king of the Visigoths. When her husband was murdered in 414, she returned to her brother Honorius at Ravenna. There she married the successful general, Con-stantius, by whom she had a son, afterwards Valentinian III. In the name of her feeble son she ruled the Western Empire for twenty-five years till her death in 450. Boniface and

Aëtius, whom Gibbon styles 'the last of the Romans,' were her generals.

2. *As the seat of the Gothic kingdom of Italy.* The capitulation and murder of Odoacer in 493, after Ravenna had stood a siege of three years, left Theodoric undisputed master of Italy (493–526). Himself an Arian, he was induced at the close of his reign to persecute the orthodox Christians. He caused Boethius, the author of the 'Consolations of Philosophy,' to be executed, as well as the philosopher's father-in-law, the patrician Symmachus (525). In the head of a large fish served at the royal table, Theodoric thought that he beheld the angry countenance of Symmachus. He retired to his chamber, and died a few days afterwards.

3. *As the seat of Byzantine dominion in Italy.* Belisarius, in 540, gained possession of Ravenna for his master Justinian, and for 200 years it was governed by Exarchs in the name of the Emperors of the East.

4. *As the See of an almost independent Archbishop.* Apollinaris, first Bishop of Ravenna, was, according to Bede, martyred in the reign of Vespasian. Gregory the Great, in his letter to Castorius Notarius, confirmed the custom of swearing parties at law before his tomb. Romuald was born about 956, a son of a noble of Ravenna. He founded his order at Camaldoli, near Arezzo. The Camaldoli habit was white, because, in the vision to which Stanley alludes, all those who had appeared ascending the ladder to heaven were so clothed. In 998 the Saxon emperor, Otho III., put down an insurrection at Rome, and, contrary to his promise, executed its leader, the Senator Crescentius, whom Gibbon calls 'the Brutus of the Republic.' For this crime he did penance at the bidding of Romuald.

5. *For its associations with the life and death of Dante.* Dante died at Ravenna in 1321. The inscription on his tomb is as follows :

Jura Monarchiæ, Superos, Phlegethonta lacusque
Lustrando cecini, voluerunt fata quousque,
Sed quia pars cessit melioribus hospita castris,
Auctoremque suum petiit felicior astris,
Hic claudor Dantes, patriis extorris ab oris,
Quem genuit parvi Florencia mater amoris.]

Ravenna : Sept. 26, 1852.

My dear H. P.,—This letter must be begun here for
the sake of the date.   Since last I wrote, we have entered
the Papal States.

Ferrara is a deeply uninteresting place.   We saw
everything, and condemned everything, except the vast
castle (seat of the Estes and cradle of the Brunswicks), and
the curious front of the cathedral (in which was held that
grotesque council, so ludicrously described by Gibbon,
when the Greek emperor and patriarch came over to
Ferrara, as the town nearest to Greece, to confer with the
Latin Church, and, on the plea of pestilence, were then
hurried off to Florence and there reconciled for a month
or two).   The relics of Tasso and Ariosto are mere fetish
relics, of no illustrative force.

From thence we flew to Bologna, which charmed us.
You know I had but just caught a glimpse of it in 1840.
There for the first time, and I think even more than in
1840, I realised the ‘ States of the Church.’   What a fairy-
land it must appear to ecclesiologists—a great city ruled
by a cardinal, Pontiffs in bronze or marble towering over
every square, and the keys blazing on every gate, custom-
house, and shield !   The arcades, the vast church of St.
Petronius—scene of Charles V.'s coronation, and of the
adjourned Tridentines—the tomb of St. Dominic, the lean-
ing tower or towers, the view from S. Michele, and, above
all, the truly magnificent view from the Monte della
Guardia, ascended by its unparalleled cloister, three miles
in length, and commanding the city, the plain, and the
Apennines.   To these I must add a visit, concerted for my
private gratification, to a wretched island in the wide,
unsightly Reno, where Antony, Augustus, and Lepidus
met to proscribe their friends and enemies.

It was at Bologna, on the 22nd, that 'Galignani' revealed
'the *late* Duke of Wellington.' It was a great shock,
though, on coming to meditate upon it, no public death
has contained so many grounds of consolation. After the
first considerations of the void occasioned by the absence
of the greatest man in England, Europe, the world, my
thoughts turn with some anxiety to his successor at
Oxford. Pray let me hear all comments and details of
and on the death, and, if so be, the funeral.

The first shadow cast across the Papal States was the
unpleasant sight of a Roman princess travelling with an
armed escort from Imola.

And now for *Ravenna.* First let me relieve you by the
assurance that you would certainly be disappointed. There
is nothing whatever of impressiveness, solemnity, or beauty
in the situation or outward appearance of the city, or in
any one of its buildings (with two exceptions perhaps).
It is a town of mean, scrambling, second-rate, modern
streets : its best churches not aspiring beyond the humblest
of those at Poitiers, its immediate neighbourhood—fields,
hedges, and occasional ditches. The two exceptions as to
situation are the two deserted churches of St. Maria in
Porto Fuori, and St. Apollinare in Classe. These two
stand about a mile asunder, and two or three miles from
the town, absolutely alone in the wide flat plain, once the
harbour of the Roman fleets. St. Paul's at Rome (fuori le
Mura) is the nearest approach to them that I remember.
The clergy, the monks, the inhabitants, have all retired, and
green damp steals over the walls, devouring in the one the
frescoes of Giotto, in the other the mosaics of the empire.

The main, if not the whole, interest, therefore, of
Ravenna centres in its history, as displayed in its tombs
and mosaics within the churches. I will go briefly through
its several points.

M

First the last refuge of the Western Empire. This is centred in the extraordinary tomb of Galla Placidia. A low brick wall, a low brick octagon tower—this is the exterior. The interior is a dark chapel, with three recesses, every vault and arch of which glitters or darkens, as the case may be, with mosaics—those well-known old mosaics of the stags at the water brooks, and the youthful shepherd sitting with his flocks, and the Evangelistic beasts; and in each of the three recesses a huge marble sarcophagus—Galla Placidia in the centre, Honorius on the right, Constantius on the left. As late as 1577, Placidia herself was to be seen sitting, like Charlemagne in later times, wrapped in her imperial robes, seated on a throne of cypress. Through the aperture which revealed this wonderful sight three children put in a light; the robes caught fire; and in a few moments all that remained of the daughter of Theodosius, the sister of Arcadius and Honorius, the wife of Adolphus and Constantius, the Empress of Aëtius, and Boniface, the mother of Valentinian III., was reduced to ashes. 'Adesso,' said the guide with a grim smile, 'non c'è Galla Placidia.' But, though this be so, it is still a spot of unique interest, so little changed since those awful times of a dissolving world, so humble without and so proud within, the close of the most romantic life in the Imperial family!

Secondly, the Gothic kingdom. Three monuments remain : the palace of Theodoric, where he died of seeing the ghost of Symmachus in the large fish on his table, a mere fragment ; the Basilica close by (of which more anon) as St. Mark's at Venice for the Doge ; and outside the walls, in the green fields and hedges, a huge well-built mausoleum like Cecilia Metella's, or Hadrian's, on the top of which once rested his ashes till they were scattered, as Arian, by the Athanasian Greeks. On the whole this Gothic period is the least impressive.

Thirdly, the Exarchate. All the most interesting mosaics, and two of the chief churches, St. Vitalis and St. Apollinaris, both built by a Ravenna banker (Julianus and Co.) at the same time, one within, one without the walls are of this period. The most remarkable are the great representations, in St. Vitalis, of Justinian and Theodora, 'that great man and that wicked woman' (as Sir F. Palgrave said, who, by a singular coincidence, has been here the whole time), and in St. Apollinaris, of Constantine Pogonatus with his two brothers. They seem to be the only existing pictures of the Byzantine court, and, though stiff like all mosaics, it is something to look on the very figures of those departed potentates. Justinian, as also Constantine, is headless, clothed in purple, with a diadem and a glory as of a saint round his head. Theodora, the infamous Theodora, has the same; her eyes are very large, her face thin, her mouth small. Her benefactions to this church were amongst the last acts of her life. She died in the year it was finished; so we here see the last of her. Beside Justinian stand the Varangian guards, Anglo-Saxons, now first appearing in historical monuments, with brown hair and light trousers.

I omit the tomb of Exarch Isaac as of little importance, and pass, fourthly, to the *Church of Ravenna*, which seems to have maintained a great, and claimed a higher, independence all through these struggles, hoping at one time to be Papal, though sadly baffled in the event. Its Peter was Apollinaris, a dim shadow on the Apostolic age, ordained ('si diu') by Peter on the Janiculum, and first Bishop of Ravenna. He lies entombed (so we are enjoined, under pain of anathema, to believe by declarations posted up in every part of the church with a vehemence which, if it were worth while, would make one doubt the fact) in the great church which bears his name, and of which I have already spoken, in the deserted 'Classis' outside the walls. His grave was so sacred that oaths were sworn upon it. The Camaldolese Order sprang from a vision of Apollinaris to St. Romuald as he prayed at its altar. Otho III. performed a more than Henrican penitence there for the murder of Crescentius. His eleven immediate successors were created (so assert witnesses) in the little church, thence named S. Spirito, by the descent of a dove, which on every vacancy of the see whispered in the ear of the Archbishop (so) elect ; the window through which the dove came, the stone on which it rested, the little house where Severus, the last Prelate so named, lived, are all preserved. From that time the succession has continued regularly through 126 Archbishops to the present day, and they go round the walls of St. Apollinaris, like the Popes in St. Paul F. M. I conclude the Ravennese churches with the most striking mosaic in the place, the most striking I have ever seen, placed by an orthodox Archbishop in the Basilica of Theodoric—two long processions advancing along the frieze of each side of the church, one of male, the other of female saints ; one advancing from the city of Ravenna, rudely represented by the actual portraiture of Theodoric's palace ; the other from 'Classis,' with the port and ships ; one approaching our Saviour, the other the Virgin. And this last (about A.D. 550) is said to be the first undoubted representation of the reverence of the Virgin. There is something very august in this slowly moving procession, though uncouth and quaint. Altogether the mosaics, whether sacred or profane, give a notion of an extinct race of men and ideas. The interest they excite is quite different from that of classical or mediæval art. They belong to a mysterious age, which we shall see no more again for ever.

And now, fifthly, one more scene remains. Alas ! 'quanto præstantius esset,' if they had left the world-worn poet in the chapel, 'squalid with filth,' as the Latin inscriptions testify, where he was deposited first, than to have decked out his tomb with an absurd cupola in the street, locked up with grate, custodian, and all else to make it distasteful. However, there Dante lies in a marble sarcophagus with his own epitaph (undoubtedly his own from internal evidence) inscribed upon it. He lived, they say, hard by the church, the Franciscan church (observe its congeniality to his old fancy) where he was buried, and where is still to be seen a tomb of one of the Polenta family who were his hosts. But in the town, for all the reasons before stated, you cannot realise his presence. The canto on Justinian may have been inspired by that strange mosaic ; and the separation of Ravenna from all the rest of Italy may have enhanced the exile.

But, after all, the only truly poetical locality in or about the place is the Pineta, whence I doubt not he took his notion of the 'antica silva' in the Purgatorio, and of which you shall now hear. (Thus far I had written before leaving Ravenna, and I must somewhat modify what I have said about its situation. The true approach to it is from Rimini, and through this, supposing you to advance as we departed, I shall now conduct you.) You enter the skirts of the forest about two miles south of Ravenna, scattered pines standing here and there on the roadside, but large masses gathering in long lines hard by, with endless lanes beneath. These masses become wider and deeper, and the glades more tangled, as you proceed. At length you leave them and emerge on a wide unending plain, which breaks the line of the forest, being in fact the ancient port of Ravenna. Two solitary towers alone interrupt the vast desolation, the towers of the churches before noticed of St. Apollinaris in Classe, and St. Maria in Porto. On the southern horizon behind rises the jagged sweep of the blue Apennines ; on

the north, the long line of the towers and domes of Ravenna.
The forest may be entered either in this part, or (as we did,
perhaps erroneously, through the obstinacy of a driver) in
the continuation of it, north of the city. The taller pines rise
above the others, so that there are, as it were, two stories
of trees. The outskirts consist of isolated pines. Once
within, however, the labyrinth seems endless; not a gloomy
shade like northern firs, but, above, a bright perennial green
of the spreading pine-tops, and, beneath, lawns and glades,
opening each into each, widening and narrowing in endless
variety, bowers of underwood festooning, climbing, and falling around, and in spring, we are told, flowers of every
kind. A truly enchanted scene! those old pines of the
Roman fleets—to Rome, what the oaks were to England—
and here, doubtless, the great Dante wandered, and imagined
Beatrice approaching through the vista. When I think of
the prosaic materials of modern Ravenna, I recur to this
wild evergreen belt which girds it in, and kings, emperors,
exarchs, and poet, all seem fitly inclosed within the magic
circle.

Farewell Ravenna! We crossed the Rubicon, and,
again joining my old route with E. M. Goulburn in 1840,
passed into the old familiar scenes of Rimini, whence I now
write. One new object of course we saw—the picture of
Rimini. What shall I say? Very briefly this: that the
picture is singularly beautiful and impressive, which in
itself explains, or renders rational, the great enthusiasm
when once excited; and, secondly, that the belief of the
motion of the eyes is occasioned by a peculiar softness and
sensitiveness with which the eyes are painted, and which
make it extremely difficult, when you look long at them,
to say whether they move or not, just as in the case of the
tower of Pisa. There is evidently no fraud, unless you so
call the advantage taken of the natural effect of such a

picture on the contagious enthusiasm of an excitable
population.   Farewell!   On the fifth think of us, and write
to us at Rome.   Ever yours,

A. P. STANLEY.

LI.

A. P. S. to Rev. B. Jowett.

LORETO.

[For a detailed account of the Grotto at Nazareth
see LVIII.]

Loreto [5] : Sept. 29, 1852.

My dear Jowett,—I begin my letter from hence, according to promise, and that I may date it from this extraordinary place, though doubtless finishing it elsewhere.

Loreto is one of 'tot congesta manu præruptis oppida
saxis' so characteristic of Central Italy, seated on a spur of
the Eastern Apennines, and overlooking a rich plain and
wide bay of the Adriatic Sea.   The whole town hangs,
begs, lives, on the Sanctuary.

The Sanctuary is a vast modern church, its exterior
striking, and indeed, as a church, unique in my experience,
from its eastern front presenting the appearance of a gigantic
fortress, its apses rising, like huge bastions, to guard the
treasure within from the assaults of Turkish pirates.

The interior has nothing but size to recommend it, and
in fact its whole arrangement partakes of one of those fatal
mistakes of policy and taste by which the highest Pontiffs,
as well as the lowest churchwardens, destroy the effect of
their own works.   If the House stood, unveiled, under the
dim light of a Gothic cathedral, or even visible at all, I can
conceive the impression being very great.   As it is, it is so

---

[5] Such is the approved mode of spelling this famous name.—[A. P. S.]

entirely encased with marble, and sculptured with fine, though second-rate, statues, that its outer walls are invisible, and probably will be so till the fatal day shall come, and the dark made light, and the wrong made right, at Loreto as elsewhere.

But the inside is sufficiently disclosed to admit of a very fair investigation. It is a chamber thirty-six feet by seventeen, built of red stones compacted together like bricks. It confesses to have received some alterations, and bears traces of having received more, from later hands—three new doors added to the original one, a window blocked up, an enlargement in that one 'through which' (*horresco referens*) 'the Angel Gabriel flew to make the salutation.' But it has indisputable marks of age ; and I doubt not bears the same relation to other houses as the 'heiliger Rock' at Trèves bears to other coats.

But it is a mournful spot to see, and to have seen. At 4.15 every morning, as I saw it that morning by the moonlight before sunrise, the doors of the church are opened : a few peasants—on Sundays, they say, increased to hundreds, and on the great festivals to thousands—already there to enter ; Capuchins are seen kneeling, as they have knelt there all night long. Immediately begin the masses, of which 120 are said daily ; a hundred priests are in attendance, more or less constant, on the services ; confessionals are open for all languages ; accounts of the House are hung round the walls, not only in Latin and Italian, but in English, in Welsh, and—what is very curious in an historical and philological point of view, as showing that, at that time (1630), the two dialects were regarded as distinct languages—in *Lowland Scotch*.

A deep swerving line is marked in the marble pavement round the shrine by the knees of the pilgrims : the poor people retire backwards through the nave when they leave

it. The 'Santa Casa' is spoken of as if it were a person.
It possesses all the property of the rich plain which it overlooks, and its treasures, though doubtless much diminished
since Sixtus V. built the vast walls to defend it from the
corsairs, still require two soldiers to stand by and guard it
with drawn swords from sunrise to sunset. No other
church exists, or is allowed to exist, in the town or neighbourhood to interfere with its sole and sovereign sanctity.

It struck me as especially mournful from the irre-
concilably opposite aspects which it presents to us and to
them. The Protestant's associations of Loreto are merely
of a gross and monstrous fiction. In the mind of the
Catholics, it is not merely that they do not reject the fiction,
but that it seems hardly to enter into their consideration of
the place. It seemed to me that the miraculous transporta-
tion occupied a very subordinate place in the minds of the
common people. They contented themselves with the
disjunctive syllogism : ' The House is not at Nazareth, nor
in Dalmatia : therefore it must be here.' They look upon
it simply as a part of Palestine become their own—the
most holy spot on earth, the scene of the Incarnation.

Is there any middle term, or any explanation of the
fable, capable of an innocent or rational meaning? You
know the story. In 1292 it lighted in Dalmatia, in 1294
at Loreto, and, after two changes, fixed on its present site.
The most probable origin seems to me that, when the final
occupation of Palestine by the Mahometans precluded
further pilgrimages, the European Christians determined
that, as they could not come to the mountain, the mountain
should come to them. Varallo and other places in Italy
exhibit representations of Jerusalem, Bethlehem, &c. This
may have been an attempt at a reproduction of Nazareth.
I gather from the accounts, and shall perhaps be able to see
for myself, that there is a likeness of situation. The holy

house of St. Francis, just before that time inclosed at Assisi, would suggest the notion.   In the wild forest, as it then was, a house might be built, its origin forgotten or mistaken, and, when fresh discovered to the world, welcomed as the very house of which it was the representation. Pope Clement VIII.'s commissioners reported the stones to be wholly unlike those of Italy and like those of Nazareth. To me the older houses of neighbouring towns did, I confess, appear marvellously like in material and construction. So I console myself by looking at the whole as the last and deepest sigh of the expiring Crusades.   I cannot but think that the best work for Angels now would be to lift up the House once again, and drown it in the depths of Adria.

I have left no space for aught else.   At Terni we had a fall of our own.   We were actually overturned, happily with no worse results than cuts and bruises now subsiding. At Rimini and Ancona we saw the so-called winking pictures.   The pictures (at least the former) are very beautiful, and it is clear that the movement is not a fraud, but the effect of imagination gazing on eyes peculiarly sensitive and soft in the expression of the painting.   With a very slight deviation, if any, from the truth of what I saw, I could have put the whole population of Ancona into a fervour of enthusiasm.   Ever yours,

A. P. Stanley.

LII.

A. P. S. to Rev Hugh Pearson.

ALL SOULS DAY IN THE SISTINE CHAPEL.

All Souls Day, Rome : November 2, 1852.

My dear H. P.,—This day suggests a letter, the more as it was all new to me.   At 9.30 A.M. behold us rolling down

to the Vatican, I all in black and white. Up that well-
known staircase; no crowd or rush, however, as on the
Wednesday in the Holy Week (for the English nation has
not yet gathered its forces into Rome), but gradually
mounting till we arrived at the Sala Regia, where an ex-
pectant party, male and female, waits at the closed doors of
the Sistine Chapel.

There, during the interval, I pointed out to an Irish
clergyman, what I do not think you and I saw, at least I
never before thoroughly mastered it, the representation of
the massacre of St. Bartholomew in the midst of the frescoes which displayed the triumphs of the papacy. It is at
the end opposite the Pauline Chapel in three compartments,
one of which exhibits the murder of Coligny ; the second,
the slaughter generally ; the third, the justification of it to
the Parliament by Charles IX. The Irish clergyman was
so horror-stricken and excited at this unexpected display
of papal atrocity that I hastened to calm him by pointing
out what is indeed only less remarkable than the pictures
themselves, namely, the erasure of the inscription indicating
a subject. You can still trace a few words here and there
dimly looming through the shade, enough to indicate the
fallibility, and at the same time the improved humanity or
enlightenment, of the chair of Peter.

By this time the doors were open, and I advanced to
the front row of the strangers' seats. I never had before
realised fully that the Sistine Chapel is simply a chapel of
the Papal Court. No one else is supposed to be present,
and so rigidly is this enforced that Swiss guards are stationed to prevent you even from putting your fingers on
the inside of the barriers. Nothing but your head is allowed
to appear above.

Meanwhile the chapel itself remains vast and empty.
At last the Cardinals dropped in one by one in crimson and

purple, this being a substitute for scarlet in honour of the funereal character of the day. . . . Each kneels for the moment ; an attendant priest clothed in purple unwinds his train ; he rises, bows to the altar, and seats himself on the long seats that run round the chapel. Another, and another, and another, each kneeling, and rising, and bowing, first to the altar and then to the Cardinals already seated, who in return rise, and bow, and sit again, the purple priests sitting at their feet and readjusting their robes.

The name of each was whispered by some one among the spectators. There was the little Barberini, a lively little old man ; Antonelli, chief secretary of state, in full vigour of age, very striking, strong, clear, yet not malevolent features, seated himself in a moment, and talked incessantly till the service began ; then came old Prince Altieri, oldest of the Cardinals ; and, though not the oldest, yet the most infirm, tottering in, the companion of Gregory,[6] our own Gregory, old grey-headed Lambreschini. The rest were ordinary enough ; some read their books, others took snuff, others talked. Any one who has seen the heads of Houses drop into Adam de Brom's chapel before the University sermon has a very fair notion of the aspect of the conclave. There is just the same mixture of a few very able with many very weak faces ; the same look of ecclesiastics, yet not ecclesiastics ; the same appearance of an ancient institution outliving itself, yet determined not to die. All this, carried to the highest pitch, is the meeting of the Cardinals in the Sistine Chapel.

You will perceive from this description that, with each successive entrance, the show, or game as it almost seemed, became more and more complicated, all rising as the others entered. At last the great catastrophe arrived. The door

---

[6] Pope Gregory XVI., whom Pearson and Stanley had seen at Rome in 1841. (See *Life*, vol. i. ch. viii.)

on the left of the altar, after having poured in a host of magnificently arrayed canons round the Cardinal Archbishop who was to perform the service, and of scarlet prelates, opened finally. ' Il Pontefice,' whispered the spectators ; the cardinals rose *en masse.*

In walked Pius IX., with a high white mitre, white, but with a richly embroidered coat, a long train borne by two scarlet Monsignori, one of whom was our old acquaintance Talbot of Balliol. What with the turning inwards of the whole body towards him, the robes, the train, and mitre, and also a portly person and large-featured face, there was something almost colossal about him—something very different from the dead corpse-like figure of Gregory XVI.

Behold him, then, at last deposited on his throne, right of the altar, the service being commenced the very instant he entered the chapel ! There was the usual ceremonial, which after being seen many times still seems as strange as ever. Thrice at least he descended from the throne to be clothed and unclothed, mitred and unmitred, spread and unspread, and the whole service seemed to move in equal relations round him and round the altar. Never for a moment were you allowed to forget that the highest potentate of this earth was present in the chapel ; never could you forget that you looked on an aged human being, living in this passing generation of the nineteenth century, but laden with the traditions and courtesies, and, must I add ? superstitions and falsehoods of 1,500 years. The last words of the service he read himself, or rather chanted. Once too he tossed the incense, and thrice he shook I know not what.

Two parts of the service were, however, truly impressive, irrespective of the pontifical presence. Almost at its very beginning the choir burst forth with the long sustained chant of ' Dies iræ, dies illa.' A thrill passed through me as I caught dimly the words 'Teste David cum sibylla' under that immortal roof, alive with the prophets and sibyls who vainly tried to sound the depths of their own prophetic thoughts, and when the whole judgment was un-rolled in the presence of that great malediction, miscalled a judgment, on whose deep blue sky and central figures the November sun was shining full and bright over the altar.

This was the first point. The second, as of course it always must be, was the moment of the elevation. I saw the attendant snatch off the white skull-cap from Pio's head and disclose the bare tonsured hair, and then saw no more; for down went every head, cardinals and guards, and all but one or two sturdy Protestants in the background, and all was for a few moments both silent and invisible.

The day was marked by a large velvet coffin being placed before the altar. The assembly broke up in a moment. The Pontiff vanished; the cardinals and atten-dants instantly twisted up their long trains, and so the pageant dissolved.

In the afternoon we drove out on the Appian Way, but far beyond what you and I ever saw. For they have now excavated and made a road for about three miles beyond the tomb of Cecilia Metella, through which, in the course of a year or two, will run the great road from Naples. And in this newly accessible part you pass through three miles of tombs, as closely succeeding each other as the street of tombs at Pompeii, broken of course, often nothing but the basement, but still perfectly distinct, the pavement often appearing; inscriptions, statues, bas-reliefs of brothers and husbands and wives joined hand in hand, fragments of capitals, squares with the cavities for ashes, and then, from time to time, huge masses only less than the tomb of Hadrian, one supporting a tower, another a house, and olive groves on the top. This long avenue extends straight as an arrow into the blue bosom of the Alban hills on one side and the line of Rome's white clusters on the other. Truly an august cemetery, and a fitting place wherein to contemplate ' All Souls !'

> Tuba mirum spargens sonum
> Per sepulchra regionum
> Cogit omnes ante thronum.

Where are they all now, these old heathen heroes, and where will they be ? And what another thought shoots along this oldest of Roman roads, this greatest of European burial-places, when you remember with absolute certainty that over this pavement, and through this long-continued street of seven miles of tombs, came the great Apostle ! We turned aside from the Appian Way on our return and entered the city by the gate of St. John Lateran. After all, this is to me the most solemn place within the walls of Rome, the first beginnings of the papacy, and so completely commanding the ruins of the old Babylon.

One other incident occurred to amuse you. Hohl [7] went with us to the Sistine Chapel, was excluded for his frock coat, flew into the Sala Regia, pinned back the skirts of the same, and claimed and received admission as being now in a dress coat. Also the Piazza di Spagna has been thrown into a state of dismal commotion by the sudden death of the Spanish ambassador, who killed himself, they say, by eating mushrooms.   Ever yours,

A. P. STANLEY

---

[7] The courier.

LIII

A. P. S. to Mary Stanley.

CELEBRATION OF THE BIRTHDAY OF MAHOMET (DE-
CEMBER 23) AT CAIRO—THE 'DOSEH' OR TREADING
OF THE DERVISHES.

[The ten following letters were written by Stanley on
his Eastern tour, which lasted from December 1852 to
June 1853. His companions were Mr. Theodore Walrond,
Mr. Fremantle, and Mr. Findlay. The substance of most of
the letters was published in 'Sinai and Palestine' or in the
'Lectures on the Eastern Church;' but the freshness and
vividness of the first impressions seem to give the originals
an interest of their own.]

Cairo : December 22, 1852.

Now that our arrangements are made, you will wish, I
suppose, to hear something of them.

We have been galloping about Cairo under the auspices
of a guide, who has to describe the glories of the East to
us in scraps of English picked up from the slang of the
inn, without conjugations, genders, or prepositions, and,
like all his countrymen, falling into the traps of leading
questions. Abbas Pasha's mother, the River Nile, the
Prophets, the whole population of asses, are equally 'he'
and 'him.' The groans of the dervishes are described as
'the fellows, you know, talking about the God, you know.'
The Patriarch Joseph and his namesake, the Sultan, are
indistinguishably blended in 'Joseph, you know, who is in
the book, you know.' All this is highly entertaining for a
time ; but it made us somewhat long for a more copious
channel of intercourse.

Meanwhile the grand question of the Nile was pending.
An excellent dragoman, known to T. Walrond through a
friend with whom he had travelled, has presented himself,

and we are now in his hands.   Cook, boat, and boy are all
fixed upon.   We are to start on the 24th, and get to the
First Cataract, if we can, returning here probably by February 20, which every one says will be time enough.   Of course
we are late in starting, but Thebes must be seen, and I
consider ourselves amply repaid by being at Cairo this
great week of the Prophet's Festival.   The ceremony of
to-morrow is what I have looked forward to for years.

   To-night we have been again to see the dervishes, and
also last night.   There was one circle which, with all its
strangeness, did rise into something like adoration or
praise—lifting up their hands, and then clapping them
violently together, with the shout of ' Al-lah ! '   Otherwise
the first impression was confirmed.   I find that it *is* a
question amongst Arabic theologians how far this is truly
in accordance with the Koran, and some declare such
vehement motion cannot be in agreement with the practice
of the Prophet and his followers, 'who prayed in such
tranquillity that a bird might have settled on their heads
without being disturbed.'

   A possible explanation of its origin occurred to me to-
night, when, in his barbarous English, our guide introduced
us to a friend of his in the streets : ' Very good man ; he
has been five times to Mecca ; he is called Sheikh Gemel
(Sheikh of the Camels) ; he has shaken his head to the
camel all the way.'   And the Sheikh acknowledged and
verified the compliment by immediately beginning the
everlasting wag to and fro, as if it were his natural motion.
This ' shaking of the head to the camel' is, in fact, only a
little beyond what the movement of the camel itself suggests ; the tremendous swing of the creature's body may
really have contributed to the notion of merit in a corresponding movement of the pilgrims who ride upon it, and
thus these tossings of the Cairo dervishes may be a sort of

stay-at-home pilgrimage. Strange, if so, the influence of the beast over the man, and the new chapter added to the wonderful history of the ship of the desert.

This is the eve of the birthday of Mahomet. How striking a contrast to the eve of that other birthday which will immediately succeed it! To-morrow is the Nativity of Mahomet; Saturday is the Nativity of Christ. I shall say no more than to describe the great ceremony of the day, to which I look anxiously forward—certainly with no fear as to the comparison.

December 23.—At 11 A.M. we were stationed in the court of the house of the Sheikh-al-Bekr. You must understand who this great man is. He is the living representative of Abu-Bekr, first Caliph, and immediate successor of the Prophet, and is the highest ecclesiastical personage in Cairo. The present Sheikh, moreover, is so eminent for his sanctity that he alone of men is permitted to enter the Pasha's harem to pray over the sick wives, though even he with his eyes bandaged and his hands pinioned. He is the Archbishop of Canterbury, and you must imagine us seated in the entrance court of Lambeth Palace to witness the Cairo celebration of what to them is, as I have said, Christmas Day.

It was a small court, like those in the Moorish houses in Spain, open to the sky, with high raised stone divans round two sides; doors at each corner; the whole about the size of the library at Norwich. We were graciously received by a lean scraggy person, known by the name, apparently official, of Mohamed Effendi, who, in the absence of the Sheikh, who was ill, performed the honours. Most of the Europeans in Cairo were there, seated on benches or on the divans. Coffee mixed with rosewater was handed round. The rest of the seats were occupied by the canons, *i.e.* the Sheikhs of the various mosques, and by the Lord Mayor—the chief Cadi of Cairo. A crowd of servants and populace filled up the vacant places by the doors. The central space was free, though broken from time to time by the entrance of a veiled lady on an ass, who was forthwith conveyed to the upper story to look through the lattices. An open chamber above contained a crowd of young pashas, like the Westminster boys at the Coronation.

The proceedings opened by the entrance of about twenty dervishes, who groaned and nodded for about ten minutes, and then left the space clear for the following scenes, which, it must be remembered, were not simple amusements, but religious ceremonies.

First, a boy and man, fantastically dressed, who fought a sham fight with spear and shield. Secondly, two wild figures, one bald, the other with long shaggy hair, their naked bodies only covered with a rough pair of drawers, who tumbled each other about in a sham wrestle. Nothing but the grave dullness of their countenances distinguished these two acts from mere child's play. The third was more serious: a savage set, dressed, or undressed, like their predecessors, danced in, some with iron pikes, frizzled at the top with chains and spikes, like the brands of Furies or the horrid Turkish clubs which I have seen, I think, in the armouries at Vienna. These they brandished about, and planted, or seemed to plant, one in his cheek, another in his eye, and then pull them out with a tremendous screech, yet leaving neither hole nor blood behind. Others tumbled over swords, or stuck the swords into their naked stomachs, or drew them across each other's necks—also with as little result. Whether their skins were hard, or the swords blunt, or there was some other trick, I know and care not. The object was to show that they were invulnerable, as long as they had faith to cry '*Allah!*

Allah!'—which accordingly came rolling out through the whole of these hideous gambols.

This group had hardly been cleared out when two men burst in, holding in their arms a third, apparently in a state of possession or idiocy, foaming at the mouth, and holding in his hands a large live snake, which in each successive paroxysm he tore with his teeth, and devoured piece by piece, leaving the large red gash visible in the body of the writhing serpent. As he was carried round and round, one of the naked faquirs darted upon him from the crowd, and clutched with hands and teeth at the snake, also tearing away portions, and struggling for more. Another man, with rolling eyes and diabolical features, but taking no part in the act, stood by, and (so his cries were interpreted by an Englishman who knew Arabic and was sitting by me) called out, 'Eat! eat! for the sake of God.' Anything so dreadful I never saw. The Easterns seemed to be unmoved; but every European face, after the first thrill of astonishment, was distended with horror. At last the son of the Sheikh stepped in, and put an end to the horrible exhibition. At the end of each of these performances the actors, or devotees, whichever they are to be called, came round for 'backsheesh' (*buona mano*). It was a satisfaction after this frightful sight was over to hear Walrond's voice, trembling with honest indignation, say, 'No! no! no backsheesh for *this*.'

I think that the next appearance was of a negro, dressed up like a fool, in a patchwork made up, seemingly, of scraps from some European warehouse, and with the large letters still printed upon them—'Nata Frères,' 'Saxon,' &c. This creature walked to and fro, blowing a ram's horn, for some minutes. Then the swordsmen tumbled in again, and then there was a pause of an hour or more with no incident worth recording.

During this time I inquired from an aged sheikh through an interpreter the origin of the ceremony which was to crown the day. 'Eight hundred years ago, the Sheikh of the Saadyeh dervishes' (*i.e.* the head or founder of this particular order, as St. Francis of the Franciscans or St. Dominic of the Dominicans) 'entered Cairo and was refused admission. He said that he would prove, by two certain signs, that Cairo belonged to the people of God. The first sign was that he should ride over bottles of glass without breaking them ; the second, that he should stand in an oven and throw out the loaves as they were baked, himself unhurt. He succeeded in both, and the memory of the first is preserved in the " Doseh," or *treading* on the dervishes, who now supply the place of the bottles to show their faith that he who rode over glass without breaking it can do the like over men.'

Year after year, accordingly, on the Prophet's birthday, the Sheikh so rides. The custom is peculiar to Egypt, and the more enlightened Mussulmans reject it as no part of their creed. Still, in spite of himself, the Sheikh is obliged to perform the ceremony, and even sometimes, they say, the Sheikh-al-Bekr himself has undertaken it. On this occasion it was his eldest son, who is the Sheikh of the Order. He was to begin in the great square, and, after riding over thousands of prostrate dervishes there, was to close by a similar 'tread' in the court of his father's house.

After the long pause above described, a visible agitation and a sound of kettledrums without announced the approach of the sacred moment. The space was cleared, whilst, at the same time, a crowd of frantic people burst in and piled themselves up in the corners opposite us. Between them and the benches on which we stood—for from this instant every one was on his feet, his chair, or his bench—

a long lane was formed, from door to door, through the
whole length of which, to the number of at least one hundred, the dervishes (I call them so, but there was nothing
in dress or appearance to distinguish them from the surrounding crowd, and there were men and boys of all sizes)
flung themselves down on their faces. Attendants or bystanders packed them as they lay, partly, it would seem,
for the sake of the more easy transit, partly for the sake of
making greater room, for, as the avenue became filled, there
were men fighting for places, thrusting aside those who were
already prostrate, or pushing themselves into the thinnest
intervals.

At last the whole line was packed, and smoothed, from
end to end. I looked down immediately upon it. The
bodies lay motionless, except a slight heave occasioned by
the murmur of the everlasting word '*Allah*,' and, in many
instances, by the shaking of the head even in that prostrate
position. Above them, all groaning or muttering '*Allah*,'
a dense mass of turbaned heads, filling all the rest of the
platform, was tossing to and fro in wild excitement. Every
face was turned to the arch of the gateway. The very
air of the court seemed to quiver and reverberate with the
sound and the agitation.

Finally an enormous pole, ending in a spiked ball and
green flag, appeared horizontally through the gateway. It
was raised, and came in, borne by two or three men—
dervishes, I suppose—who, followed by five or six more,
walked steadily, though quickly, over the bodies. Then,
led by two of them, appeared the Sheikh himself, dressed
chiefly in dark brown, and on a brown horse. The murmur
burst into a deafening shout of '*Allah-ya* ;' the whole mass
of Mussulman spectators swayed to and fro as one man ;
the horse advanced at a quiet foot's pace, and stepped over
the bodies as over a cushioned floor, the horseshoes—for he

was certainly shod—leaving no visible mark as he passed on. The Sheikh himself, a large heavy figure in the prime of life, sate with his eyes shut, and his countenance compressed into a state of insensibility—as if, I must do him the justice to say, he could not, or would not, look on the scene of which he was the chief figure. It was over in three minutes or less; the moment the horse reached the opposite door, the Sheikh was hurried into the house, and the horse was led out at another corner.

At that same moment the line of bodies sprang to their feet: the crowd rushed in upon them, and the whole area was a whirl of wild embraces and contortions, some fainting in apparent stupor, others clutching each other seemingly in congratulation at the miraculous escape, others howling and groaning, one, or perhaps two, wreathing live snakes, like Michael Angelo's 'Last Judgment,' round their necks and waists. In a few minutes the confusion subsided, the space was cleared, and we all retired. Whether the men were hurt, or were likely to have been hurt, was a matter of very various opinion. Our guide said that many had been much injured about the legs, but that seven strokes of the Sheikh-al-Bekr's hand restored them to health. You will see a full account (with a picture) in Lane's ' Modern Egyptians,' ch. xxiv. Nothing that I have ever seen can be at all compared to the moment of the entrance in strangeness.

Ever yours,
A. P. STANLEY.

LIV.

A. P. S. to Mary Stanley.

THEBES (FIRST VISIT).

[Thebes was at the height of its glory in the period of the 'New Empire,' after the expulsion of the Shepherd

Kings, under the rule of the 18th and 19th dynasties (1530–1050 B C., or, according to other chronologists, 1700–1200 B.C.). Egypt now aspired to foreign conquests, pushed its victories to the Euphrates, and established a vast empire.

Thothmes III., who belonged to the 18th dynasty, may be justly called the greatest and most powerful of Egyptian kings. His successor was Amenhotep (Amenophis) III. Rameses II. was the son of Seti I. (Sethos), the virtual founder of the 19th dynasty. He has been sometimes identified with the Pharaoh of the oppression. It has been supposed that the legendary exploits of Sesostris were the combined achievements of these conquerors. The statue of Rameses II. is celebrated in Shelley's sonnet on Ozymandias.

Stanley, as was to be expected, was no admirer of Shelley. Few allusions appear in his numerous letters to his poetry. But Southey was one of his chief favourites, and he finds a parallel to the pride of Rameses, the conqueror, in Kehama, the Almighty Rajah of the Earth, the omnipotent Lord of Heaven, who aspired to rule also over Yamen, the Lord of Padalon or Hell. The struggle between the rivals was short. As the gloom opened, fallen Yamen lay on the ground, his neck beneath the feet of Kehama.

> Silent the Man-Almighty sate ; a smile
> Gleam'd on his dreadful lips, the while
> Dallying with power, he paused from following up
> His conquest, as a man in social hour
> Sips of the grateful cup,
> Again and yet again with curious taste
> Searching its subtle flavour ere he drink ;
> Even so Kehama now forbore his haste,
> Having within his reach whate'er he sought ;
> On his own haughty power he seem'd to muse,
> Pampering his arrogant heart with silent thought.]

The Nile : Jan. 10, 1853.

At last we have reached and caught a glimpse of *Thebes*. Finding that the boat would be a long time in effecting the circuit of the river, we disembarked at Negaldeh, and walked and rode by land for three hours, reaching Thebes at 3.30 P.M., and rejoining the boat at 7 P.M. I shall not now attempt an account of my impression of Thebes. I feel as if I had but seen one foot or hand of the great colossus—to use a figure which this day's sight has suggested—never to be forgotten. I shall therefore wait till I have seen the whole, as I hope, on our return.

Jan. 11.—So far last night. But I cannot forbear to give my first impression of even the smallest part of this wonderful place.

What I wish to dwell on is this. Nothing that I have ever been told has given me any adequate impression of the effect, past and present, of the colossal figures of the kings. What spires are to a modern city—what the towers of a cathedral are to its nave and choir—that the statues of the Pharaohs were to the streets and temples of Thebes. The ground is strewn with their fragments. There were avenues of them, towering high above plain or houses. Three of gigantic size still remain. One was the granite statue of Rameses II. himself, who sate, with his hands on his knees, on the right side of the entrance to his palace. By some extraordinary catastrophe, the statue has been thrown down, and the Arabs have scooped their millstones out of his face. But you can still see what he was—the largest statue in the world. He must have been, even sitting, a hundred feet high.

Far and wide that enormous head must have been seen —eyes, and nose, and ears. Far and wide you must have seen his vast hands resting on his elephantine knees ; the toes, even without the nails, are two feet seven inches long. You sit on his breast and look on the Osiride statues which support the temple, and which, anywhere else, would put to shame even the cherubs and statues of St. Peter's. But they seem pigmies before him. His arm is thicker than their whole bodies.   The only part of the temple or palace at all in proportion to him must have been the gateway, which rose in pyramidal towers, now broken down.

Nothing which now exists can give any notion of what the effect must have been when he stood erect.   Nero towering above the Colosseum may have been something like it ; but he was of bronze, and Rameses II. was of solid granite.   Nero was standing without any meaning ; Rameses was resting in awful majesty after the conquest of the then known world.   No one who entered that building, whether palace or temple, would have thought of anything else but that stupendous being, who thus had raised himself up above the whole world of gods and men. Kehama, as he entered Padalon, is the sort of notion he suggests, if you can substitute the Egyptian repose for the Indian fanaticism.

And when from the statue you descend into the palace the same impression is kept up.   It is the earliest instance of the great historical glories of a nation, such as Versailles and the Vatican.   You see the king everywhere, conquering, worshipping, ruling.   But everywhere the same colossal proportions are preserved.   He and his horses are ten times the size of the rest of the army, as he appears in battle.   In worship he is of the same stature as the gods themselves.   You see the familiar gentleness with which, one on each side, they take him by each hand, as one of their own order, and in the next compartment introduce him to Ammon and the lion-headed goddess.   All distinction, except of degree, between divinity and royalty is entirely levelled, and the royal majesty is always represented by making the king—not, like Saul or Agamemnon, from the head and shoulders, but from the foot and ankle upwards—higher than the rest of the people.

It carries one back to the days ' when there were giants

in the earth.' It shows how the king was, in that first monarchy, the visible god upon earth. The only thing like it can have been the deification of the Roman emperors, and it appears to me to shatter to pieces Miss Martineau's representation of the old Egyptian religion. No pure monotheism could for a moment have been compatible with such an intense exaltation of the reigning king. 'I am Pharaoh,' ' By the life of Pharaoh,' ' Say unto Pharaoh, Whom art thou like in thy greatness ?'—all these expressions seem to me to acquire new life from the sight of this monster statue.

And now let us pass to the two others. They are the only statues remaining of an avenue of eighteen similar, or nearly similar, statues, some of whose remnants lie in the fields which lead to the palace of Amenophis III. Every one of the statues is Amenophis himself, thus gaining in multiplication what Rameses gained in solitary elevation. He lived some reigns earlier than Rameses, and the statues are of ruder workmanship and coarser stone. To me they were much more striking close at hand, when their human form was distinctly visible, than at a distance, where they looked like two towers or landmarks. The sun was setting ; the African range glowed red behind them ; the green plain was dyed a deeper green beneath them ; and the shades of evening veiled the vast rents and fissures in their aged frames. They too sit, hands on knees, and they are sixty feet high. Imagine Alderley Church steeple suddenly transformed into a sitting figure !

As I looked back at them in the sunset, and they rose up in front of the background of the mountain, they seemed indeed as if they belonged to some natural creation rather than to any work of art. And yet, as I have said, when anywhere in their neighbourhood, the human character is never lost. Their faces are dreadfully mutilated. Indeed the largest has no face at all, but is from the waist upwards (as I will explain presently) a mass of stones or rocks piled together in the form of a man's head and body. Still, especially in that dim light, and from the distance which, even when at their feet, intervenes between you and them, they seem to have faces only of hideous and grinning ugliness.

And now a few words about their history, not as Pharaohs, but as statues. Who was it that strewed the plain with these countless fragments? Who had power to throw down the colossus of Rameses II.? Who broke the statue of Amenophis III. from the middle upwards?

From the time of the Roman travellers, who have carved their names in numbers innumerable on the foot of Amenophis, there has been but one answer: Cambyses. He is the Cromwell of Egypt. Of the great Rameses it really seems to be true, and so of many of the others. If so, what an effort of fanatical or religious zeal! what an impression it gives of that Persian hatred of idols, which is described in the Bible, only here carried to excess against these majestic kings! ‘Bel boweth down, and Nebo stoopeth.' Well might the idols of Babylon tremble before Cyrus, if such was the fate of the Egyptian Pharaohs before Cambyses. Of Amenophis III., however, it seems probable that an earthquake, twenty-seven years before the Christian era, was the destroyer. There was such an earthquake, and so Strabo was told a few years later, when he saw the statue, not as we now see it, but literally headless and bodiless.

And then first began the story of its musical sounds, and gradually it came to be called by the name of the Greek hero, Memnon, and, looking eastward as it does, was thought to be greeting his mother Aurora; and then, strange to say, people from all parts of the Roman Empire came to witness the miracle, making offerings, writing verses, thinking (as I shall think of you all, dearest, when I see it again), thinking of those whom they loved best, pleased if they heard the music, frightened if they did not, speculating whether they did—like the pilgrims of Loreto and Rimini. So it went on till Septimius Severus put together the upper part—by way of doing it honour—as we now see it, and then the sound and the pilgrimages ceased. An Arab climbed up into the lap, and, by striking, produced a sort of metallic ringing : but I hardly think it could have been that. More likely it was something connected with its former fragmentary state.

I do trust that you are all happy and able to read these letters with anything like the pleasure with which I write them. Ever yours,

A. P. STANLEY.

LV.

A. P. S. to Mary Stanley.

THEBES (SECOND VISIT).

February 5 : Between Thebes and Dendyra.

A most delightful hour I have before me, the description of the most interesting place in the world—after Rome and Athens—that I have yet seen. Everything that has gone wrong seems compensated by the three glorious days at Thebes.

Let me give you, first, a general view of the whole city, such a view as I have been unable myself to draw from any description. Will this be any better ?

Alone of all the great scenes of Egypt, the situation of Thebes is really beautiful. Then it is that, for the first time, as you ascend the river, the monotonous ranges on either side assume a new character. That on the western side is chiefly varied by a loftier, bolder, and more massive formation. It is this which makes the backbone, as it were, of the great plain, and, by a long strong arm which it throws out to the river channel, entirely shuts it in on the northern side by a natural bulwark.

On this side of the river, probably, the larger part of the city was always to be found, and in later times, when Thebes had fallen into ruins, a town grew up round the Christian monasteries sufficiently large to deserve the name of a city once more—'Medinet-Habou.' After the Mahometan conquest this town declined and is now shrunk to a wretched condition of mud hovels, which, however, I mention here as giving its name to the chief ruin on the western bank.

But the original sanctuary of Ammon, from which, as far as I can understand, the ancient city of No-Amon, which the Greeks by a foolish mistake called Thebes, first sprang, was on the eastern bank, and thus the great 'capital'—for that is the meaning of 'Thebes'—had the singular peculiarity of stretching over both shores of the Nile. Unlike Memphis or Cairo, but like Babylon on the Euphrates, or like London and Paris, it presented the magnificent sight of a city with a river for its thoroughfare, and that river the most venerable and extraordinary of all the rivers of the earth. 'Art thou better than No-Amon, that was situate by the rivers of the Nile, that had the waters round about it, whose rampart was the sealike stream, and whose wall was the sealike stream?'[8]

But the peculiar beauty of the situation of Thebes is that the green plain—green with the verdure of Egypt, green

---

[8] Nahum iii. 8, A.V.: 'Art thou better than populous No, that was situate among the rivers, *that had* the waters round about it, whose rampart *was* the sea, *and* her wall *was* from the sea?'

as the Vega of Granada—which spreads, east and west, for
an unwonted circuit on each side the river, is here inclosed,
not as usual within the two ranges which belong to the
whole country, but within a circle peculiarly its own.   The
western barrier I have already described, and it has often
been described, for reasons which will appear hereafter.
But the eastern barrier was what I was not prepared to see.
It stands far off, but still sufficiently near to form the
frame of the whole picture, to act the same part to the
view of Thebes as the Argolic mountains to the plain of
Athens.   It consists of a various and broken chain, rising
and falling in almost Grecian outline, though cast into that
conical form which marks the Nubian hills farther south,
and which perhaps suggested the shape of the Pyramids.
Here, alone in Egypt, as you sit on the great gateways at
sunset, and look out on those lovely hills rising over the
green plain at their feet, you feel that Nature is more
beautiful than Art.   You feel that, whether or not these
pyramidal shapes suggested those in Lower Egypt, they
made it impossible to have built pyramids at Thebes.

This, then, is the natural situation of the city.   Now
for the city itself.

Two great features it presents which you can see
nowhere else.   The colossal statues which I described
before, and which must have been to it, as I then said, like
the spires of a modern town, may be seen at Ipsambul.
The temples, merely as temples, are less perfect than those
of Nubia, where the fact of their being hewn in the rock
has preserved all their arrangements far better than in
these broken edifices.   But Thebes is pre-eminently the
city of *palaces* and of *gateways.*

It is very difficult, doubtless, to distinguish between
Egyptian palaces and Egyptian temples.   They were both
in one, as their kings were priests and gods as well as

kings.   Still there is a grandeur and multiplication of
parts in the Theban ruins which has no parallel in the
temples.   In the great outworks of Medinet-Habou, the
palace of Rameses III., there are clearly chambers for
dwelling—like those in feudal castles, in their massive
towers and walls—though, as you will hear afterwards, like
our drawing-rooms in decoration and furniture.   In the
Rameseum too—the palace of Rameses II.—there is a room
which you can hardly doubt to be what Diodorus describes
as the library.   Astronomical devices cover the roof, and
in the sculptures is the writing of the king's name on the
fruit of the sacred pearl tree by Thoth, the ibis-headed
god, who was in Egyptian mythology the personification
of all authorship, a sort of deified Murray, to whom all
books, by whomsoever written, were ascribed.   In the little
temple of Osiris there are chambers also quite unlike those
of the southern sanctuaries ; and, lastly, in the great palace
of Karnac there is the hall, which certainly is absolutely
singular in all the arrangements of these sacred buildings.

And now that I have mentioned the name of Karnac,
to Karnac we must go.   For Karnac is, after all, the real
glory of Thebes, the sight which, the more you see and
think of it, the more fully does it realise all you have ever
heard of Egyptian grandeur.   It is useless to go through
the details of Karnac to any one at a distance.   On the spot
you must do so to form an idea of the whole.   But for those
who have not seen it, a general notion of the whole is, I
think, the best and only one that they can form.

Imagine, therefore, a long vista of courts and gateways
and halls—and gateways and courts, and colonnades and
halls—here and there an obelisk, shooting up out of the
ruins, and interrupting the opening view of the forest of
columns.   Imagine yourself seated on the top of one of
these halls or gateways, and looking over the plain around.

You find that this mass of ruins—some rolled down in avalanches of stone, others perfect and painted as when they were first built—is approached on every side by avenues of gateways as grand as that on which you are presumably standing. East and west, and north and south, these vast approaches are found. Some are shattered. But in every approach some remain, and in some you can trace, besides, the further avenues, once extending for a mile and a half, and still in part remaining, as thickly packed as troops of soldiers—by hundreds together—avenues of ram-headed sphinxes.

A word on the gateways themselves. I have said that they are one of the most distinguishing features of Thebes. It is true that every Egyptian temple has, or ought to have, one of these great gateways, formed of two sloping towers with the high perpendicular portal between. But what makes them remarkable at Thebes is their number and their multiplication and concentration on the one point of Karnac. For any distant view they are, strange to say, the chief drawback to the beauty and grandeur of the view. Their form is not striking, and their size shuts out from sight all the colonnades and buildings within. But when within or upon them, they are most imposing. Well might Thebes be called by Homer ' the city of the hundred gates,' and, in ancient times, even from a distance, they must have been beautiful. For instead of the brown mass of sand-stone which they now present, the great sculptures of the gods and conquering kings, which they uniformly display, were gorgeously painted, within and without ; and in the deep grooves, which you still see, twofold or fourfold, on each side of the portal, with enormous holes for the trans-verse beams to support them, were, as you shall hear, immense red flagstaffs, like those in the Piazza of St. Mark, with Isis-headed standards—red and blue streamers floating

O

from them. Before almost every gateway in this vast army, besides the long line of sphinxes, were the granite colossal figures—usually of the great Rameses, sometimes in white or red marble of Amenophis or Thothmes—whose fragments still remain, and pairs of towering obelisks, which you can generally trace by pedestals, on either side, or by the solitary twin, mourning for its brother, either lying broken beside it or far away in some northern region, at Rome, at Petersburg, or at Paris. I shall now never again see the obelisk of the Place de la Concorde without the vision of the great gateway of Luxor, with its shattered statues and deserted obelisk, from the side of which the other was taken to witness a new series of history in France.

I have spoken of the general view from the top of the great gateway which overlooks the whole array of avenues. I must speak also of the next most striking, which is, I think, as you stand at the other end and look through the whole series of ruins, each succeeding the other in unbroken succession. It is a view something of the kind of that up the Forum from the Colosseum to the Capitol—like it, I mean, in the luxury of ruin, though unlike it in almost everything else. You stand in front of a stately gateway, built by the Ptolemies. Immediately in the foreground are two Osiride pillars, their placid faces fixed upon you—a strange and striking contrast to the crash of temple and tower behind. That crash, however, great as it is, has not, like that of the fall of Rome, left mere empty spaces where only imagination can supply what once was there. No! there is not an inch of this Egyptian Forum, so to call it, which is not crowded with fragments, if not buildings, of the past. To figure the scene, as it once was, you have only to set up again the fallen obelisks which lie at your feet ; to conceive the columns, as they are still seen in part, overspreading the whole ; to reproduce all the statues, like those which still remain in their august niches—and you have ancient Thebes before you. And what a series of history it is! In that long defile of ruins every age has borne its part—from Osirtasen I. to the latest Ptolemy— from the time of Joseph to the Christian era. Through the whole period of Jewish history, and of the ancient world, the splendour of the earth kept pouring into that space, for two thousand years, as in the next five hundred years it poured into the Roman Forum.

And now you will ask what else remains to be described. Something far more wonderful even than Karnac.

You remember the western barrier of the Theban plain. It is a mass of high limestone cliffs, with two deep gorges —one running up behind the plain and into the very heart of the hills ; the other running up from the plain, so as to be enclosed within the hills, but having its face open to the city. The former is the Valley of the Tombs of the Kings, the Westminster Abbey of Thebes ; the latter the Valley of the Tombs of the Priests and Princes, its Canterbury Cathedral. The whole range is, in short, the cemetery of Thebes.

Ascend, therefore, with me the first of these two gorges. It is the very ideal of desolation. Bare rocks, without a particle of vegetation, overhanging and enclosing, in a still narrower and narrower embrace, a valley as rocky and bare as themselves, with no human habitation possible, and the whole stir of the city entirely excluded. Such is, such always has been, the awful resting-place of the Theban kings.

Pyramids, as I have said, were to them impossible. But they knew how to make tombs, certainly, except the Pyramids, the most magnificent that the world has ever seen. Nothing that has been said about them had prepared me for their extraordinary grandeur. You enter a sculptured portal in the face of these wild cliffs, and find yourself in a long and lofty gallery, opening or narrowing, as the case may be, into successive halls and chambers, all of which are covered with white casing, and this white casing brilliant with colours fresh as they were thousands of years ago, but on a scale and with a splendour that I can only compare to the Vatican Library. Some, of course, are more magnificent than others ; but of the seven which we saw, all were of this character. They are, in fact, gorgeous palaces hewn out of the rock, and painted with all the decorations that could have been seen in the palaces. No modern galleries or halls could be more completely ornamented.

But, splendid as they would be even as palaces, their interest is enhanced tenfold by being what they are— tombs. There lie ' all the kings in glory, each one in his own house.' Every Egyptian potentate, but especially every Egyptian king, seems to have begun his reign by preparing his sepulchre. It was so in the case of the Pyramids, where each successive layer marked the successive years of the reign. It was so equally in these Theban tombs, where you can trace the longer or shorter reign by the length of the chambers or the completeness of their finish. In one or two instances you pass at once from the most brilliant decorations to rough unhewn rock. The king had died, and the grave closed over his imperfect work. At the entrance of each tomb you see him making offerings to the sun, who, with his hawk's head, wishes him a long life to complete his labour. Thus the most magnificent of the tombs is that of the builder of the most magnificent of the works of Thebes—the Hall of Karnac—Osiris I., the father of the great Rameses. We know hardly anything more of him. But the two facts speak for each other.

Two ideas seem to reign throughout the sculptures. First, the endeavour to reproduce, as far as possible, the life of man, so that the mummy of the dead king, whether in his long sleep or on his awakening, might be encompassed by the old familiar objects. Egypt, with all its peculiarities, was to be perpetuated in the depths of the grave ; and truly they have succeeded. This is what makes this valley of tombs like the galleries of a vast museum. Not the collections of Pompeii at Naples give half the same knowledge of Greek or Roman life as these do of Egypt. The kitchen, the dinners, the boating, the dancing, the trades—all are there. I need not describe them. They are given in detail in Wilkinson's 'Egypt.' The wonder is to see them there in long successions of pictures, all fresh from the hands of the Raphaels of the primeval world.

The other idea is that of conducting the king to the world of death. Here, I am sorry to say, ignorance prevented the same instruction or pleasure as in the other parts. It was tantalising to see yards of sculpture lost to you from not having the key to explain them. Nor was the notion of the final judgment before Osiris brought out with that clearness which the case seemed to demand. But the farther you advance into the tomb, the deeper you become involved in endless processions of jackal-headed gods, and monstrous forms of genii, good and evil, and the goddess of justice, with her single ostrich feather, and barges carrying mummies, raised aloft over the sacred lake, and figures of mummies themselves, and, above all, endless convolutions of serpents in every possible form and attitude, human-legged, human-headed, crowned, entwining mummies, enwreathing or embraced by processions extending down whole galleries, so that, meeting the head of the serpent at the top of a staircase, you had to descend to its very end before you met with his tail. At last you reach the close of all—the Vaulted Hall, in the centre of which lies the immense granite sarcophagus, which ought to contain the body of the king.   Here the processions, above, below, and around, reach their highest pitch.   You see them marching round and round, white, and black, and red, and blue—legs, and arms, and wings spreading in enormous fans over the ceiling—and below lies, as I have said, the coffin itself.

And this brings me to the most curious and striking fact of all.   It seems certain that all this gorgeous decoration was, on the burial of the king, immediately closed, and meant to be closed for ever, so that what we now see was intended never to be seen by any mortal eye, except that of the king himself when he awoke from his slumbers. Not only was the entrance closed, but in some cases, chiefly in that of the great sepulchre of Osiris, the passages were cut in the most devious directions, and the approaches to them so walled up as to give the appearance of a termination long before you arrived at the actual chamber, lest by any chance the body of the king should be disturbed.   And yet, in spite of all these precautions, what was most extraordinary of all, in no instance, I believe, has the mummy been discovered.   When Belzoni broke through gallery after gallery of this gigantic fortress, and arrived at last at the sarcophagus, it was empty.   Two explanations are given.   One that the king after all, to render security doubly sure, was buried deeper still, the other that plunderers had broken in through passages which do exist through other parts of the rock.

You may suppose that these tombs would require weeks and months to study.   But, not having these, I do not know whether one single day was not sufficient.   I carry away, it is true, but few distinct impressions.   But I feel that I have had a glorious vision of the past, and that all I shall now read or hear about them will have an interest which else would never have existed.

Amongst the inscriptions of early travellers is one of peculiar interest. It was the 'torch-bearer of the Eleusinian mysteries' who records that he visited these tombs 'many years after the divine Plato'—thanks 'to the gods and to the most pious Emperor Constantine who afforded him this favour.' It is written in the vacant space under the figure of a wicked soul returning from the presence of Osiris in the form of a pig, which probably arrested the attention of the Athenian by reminding him of his own mysteries. Such a confluence of religions—of various religious associations—could hardly be elsewhere found ; a Greek priest-philosopher recording his admiration of the Egyptian worship in the time of Constantine, on the eve of the abolition of both Greek and Egyptian religions by Christianity.

It was on the eve of our last day that we climbed the steep side of that grand and mysterious valley, and from the top of the ridge had the last view of the valley itself as we looked back upon it, and of the glorious plain of Thebes as we looked forward over it. No distant prospect of the ruins can ever do them justice ; but it was a noble point from which to see once more the dim masses of stone rising here and there out of the rich green, and to know that this was Karnac with its gateways, and that Luxor with its long colonnade, and those nearer fragments the Rameseum and Medinet-Habou ; and further, the wide depression in the soil, once the funereal lake.

Immediately below lay the valley of Assasif, where, in a deep recess under towering crags like those of Delphi, lay the tombs of the priests and princes. The largest of these, in extent the largest of any, is that of Petumenap, chief priest in the reign of Pharaoh Necho. Its winding galleries are covered with hieroglyphics, as if hung with tapestry. The only figures which it contains are those which appear again and again in these priestly tombs, the touching effigies of himself and his wife—the best image that can be carried away of Joseph and Asenath—sitting side by side, their arms affectionately and solemnly entwined round each other's necks.

To have seen the tombs of Thebes is to have seen the Egyptians as they lived and moved before the eyes of Moses, is to have seen the utmost display of funereal grandeur which has ever possessed the human mind.

Ever yours,

A. P. S.

LVI.

A. P. S. to Mary Stanley.

BETHLEHEM AND THE APPROACH TO JERUSALEM
FROM HEBRON.

Easter Eve [1853] : Jerusalem.

I cannot rest to-night, dearest, without saying something of this wonderful day.

We started by walking round the gigantic walls of the mosque of Hebron ; all that we were permitted to see of that most venerable of graves—walls built round it, there seems but little doubt, by the kings of Judah, and of a style quite peculiar. Above it rises the ordinary Mahometan structure, which since the Crusades only two Europeans are known to have seen. It is at any rate a satisfaction to think that it is in the possession of one branch at least of the descendants of Abraham, and my heart quite went with our old cook when he announced that he was going to pay his devotions to ' El Khalil,' ' The Friend ' of God.

In a long train of horses and mules—to me, a sad exchange for the dromedary—we left Hebron. Two more relics of Abraham we saw. One was a beautiful and massive ilex, called by his name, which, with two or three near it, at least enables one to figure the scene in Genesis xviii., and to understand why it is that the spot was called ' the oaks ' (mistranslated ' the plains ') of Mamre. Whether this be the exact spot, or the exact kind of tree, seems doubtful, for the next spot we saw was one of those solid and vast enclosures which seem to coincide with the account of the place that Josephus mentions as the site of what he calls the ' terebinth of Abraham.' However, there was the wide scenery, the vineyards too, with their towers, reaching down on every side of the valley of Eshcol, whence came the famous clusters, and the red anemones, and white roses on their briar bushes.

Next came, in one of those gray and green valleys, one below the other, the pools of Solomon. I must again say ' venerable,' for I know no other word to describe that simple, massive architecture in ruin, yet not in ruin. And, behold ! there are the very gardens, not now indeed beautiful as when he came in state, so Josephus describes, with his gold-powdered servants, to see them, but marked by the long winding defile, green and fresh and winding as a river, which leads towards Jerusalem. Along the mountain-side runs the water through the channel begun by him, but —strange and unexpected conjunction—restored by Pontius Pilate.

Far away to the east rises the conical hill where Herod died, and now you mount the ridge of which that hill is the end, and covering the crest of the opposite ridge is the long line of lofty houses and of the still more massive and lofty convent. A shout ran down the long file of horsemen, followed by deep silence—BETHLEHEM !

I have not time, here or elsewhere, to describe all in detail. There is, I think I may say, no beauty. It is a wild, bleak hill, amidst hills that are equally bleak, if 'bleak' may be applied to hills which are covered with vineyards, in autumn rich and green, and which now, in fact, wave with corn. One only green plain—I believe, of grass—hangs behind the town. It is the traditional scene of the shepherds' watch by night. But the elevation of the whole place, and, above all, that most striking feature, which was to me quite unexpected, the immense wall of the mountains of Moab, seeming to overhang the lower hills of Judah, from which they are only separated by that deep mysterious gulf of the Dead Sea, are most impressive. Well might Moses from their summits overlook the Promised Land ! Well might Orpah return as to a near country ! Well might Naomi be reminded of her sorrows !

Of the one great event of Bethlehem you are, of course, reminded by the enormous convent, or convents, Latin, Greek, and Armenian, clustering round the church, the original work of Helena, which is the prototype of the Roman St. Paul's and the Apollinaris of Ravenna. The manger is in a *cave*. I do not think this is probable. Yet there is the deep interest of knowing that this is the oldest special locality fixed upon by the Christian Church. Before the sepulchre, before the Ascension, before any of the other countless scenes of our Saviour's life had been consecrated, the famous passage in Justin Martyr proves that the cave of Bethlehem was already known as the scene of the Nativity. And one of the earliest and most striking instances of this reverence exists in a cave, or rather in one of the many winding caves which form the vaults of the church, the cell where Jerome lived and died that he might be near the sacred spot, where he wrote that renowned version of the Scripture, the Vulgate, where is the very

scene of that wonderful picture in the Vatican, his last
communion.

I have said that you are reminded of the Nativity by
the convent. But, in truth, I almost think that it detracts
from it. From the first moment that those towers and
hills and valleys burst upon you, you have before you the
thought that now at last you are in the Holy Land : it
pervades the atmosphere ; even Ruth and David wax faint
in its presence. No feeling that I have experienced in
seeing famous places has been at all like it. If I were to
describe it at all, I should say that it seemed to turn one's
heart into stone.

One recollection of David I ought not to omit. I see
no reason whatever to doubt the authenticity of the well
or wells, on the ridge of Bethlehem, for which the three
friends broke through the Philistine camp.[9] Next came
Rachel's tomb, a modern mosque, but the site must be the
true one.

And then, far on the top of the hill opposite Bethlehem,
was the convent of St. Elias, seen from Bethlehem, and
from which I knew we should see Jerusalem. It is the one
place which commands the view of both. From that hill
I saw a wide descent and ascent, and a white line rising, of
I knew not what buildings, but I knew that it was Jerusalem. I have no thoughts nor impressions to record, save
the only feeling that I now saw the sight that for years I
had most longed to see. Yet, unlike Athens and Sinai,
there were many new features in it. First, there was still
that mighty wall of Moab. Secondly, there was the broad
green approach of the valley of Rephaim, so long, so broad,
so green, that it almost seemed a natural advance to the
city, which still remained suspended, as it were, above it,
for you saw that white line increasing in height and length

* 2 Sam. xxiii. 14-17.

as you neared it, yet saw not the deep ravines that parted you from it.

Shall I say that I was glad or sorry that the first conspicuous building which catches your eye is the English church?   Then the castle, then the minaret over the so-called mosque of David.   The mosque of Omar, and even the Mount of Olives, were for a long time shut out by the hill which, with its solitary tree, intercepted all the view to the east.   High, beyond, to the north, towered Ramah of Benjamin.   At last the deep descent of the Valley of Hinnom appeared.   The chief thing that struck me as new was the rush, so to speak, of both the valleys to the south-west corner.   We entered the Jaffa gate about 4.30 P.M.

Easter Sunday.—I rose at 5.30 A.M., partly to have the pleasure, for once, of seeing the sun of Easter Day rise, 'very early in the morning,' over the shoulder of the Mount of Olives, partly to see if any ceremonies welcomed it in the great church.   But there was nought.   Strangely enough, here, as at Seville, Easter Day is nothing.   There were groups scattered here and there as at the like hour in Loreto, but no burst of joy or emotion.   Our own service was at ten.   I called on the bishop to offer my help, and had the great delight of reading the whole service.   In the afternoon we walked down the Via Dolorosa by Gethsemane, up the Mount of Olives, round the valley of Jehoshaphat and Hinnom.

There is no doubt that to see Jerusalem, and to think of yourself as being there, require an effort of abstraction from all the surrounding circumstances.   There is a matter-of-fact appearance about the hills and scenery that does not of itself, as at Sinai, raise you above the earth.   'He is not here; He is risen,' seems to me the prevailing truth that you have before you.   But yet in this matter-of-fact homely appearance perhaps lies the chief instruction ; the hills are featureless, the olives scanty, the fields bare, and I do not know whether more romantic surroundings would be better for one's thoughts.

This, I think, is what must first strike any one. I can only say generally that the city is in ruins—ruins of Crusaders, Saracens, Turks ; that the old city lies buried thirty or forty feet below the surface ; that the only Jewish remains are the gigantic substructures of the Temple, which are indeed venerable beyond expression ; that the view from the Mount of Olives, in spite of all that I have said, is one of the most striking that the eye can rest upon—the wall of Moab, the long waters of the Dead Sea, the black line of the Jordan, the masses of the city below, with that most beautiful scene, the enclosure of the mosque of Omar.

Gethsemane ! dearest Kit ; [1] I have seen it with the bodily eye, but I have not yet been able to enter. The garden gate was locked. But I do not feel entire confidence in the site. It is too exposed to public view, too close to the road, to meet either one's views of the place, or the account in the Gospel. Other secluded spots there are just round the corner of the hill, where no doubt could have arisen.

But of all the scenes there is to me none like Bethany. This afternoon we walked round the north skirts of Olivet, so as to come upon the village from behind. It is a wild mountain hamlet, perched high up on the hillside. It was a stormy day, and the clouds drifted past, almost touching the secluded hill above the town—the real site, in all probability, of the Ascension, now misplaced to the top of the mountain.

There was a rough but well-defined road sweeping round the lower shoulder of Mount Olivet on the south. I

[1] His sister Catherine, now Mrs. Vaughan.

have hardly a doubt that this was the course of that great procession. I walked along it with St. Luke's account in my hand, waiting with intense expectation for the two views of the city, which are implied in the narrative—the first which called forth the shout of the multitude, the second which called forth the burst of sorrow. Each came. The first was the view of Mount Zion only, the temple being hid by the slope of Olivet—Mount Zion with the palace of David—' Hosanna to the *Son of David !* ' Then the city withdraws as you descend a declivity, and then you rise once again, and stand on a long ledge of rock. In one moment the whole city bursts upon you. No view that I have seen is comparable to it ; this is the only spot from which you can see it, and it comes precisely at the point where you would expect it. And here the ledge remains, undefiled by mosque or marble, unmarked, I believe, by any tradition. As now the great dome of the mosque of Omar rises like a ghost from the ground, so then the tower of the Temple ; as now the vast inclosures, so then the courts of the Temple.

I have now been inside the garden of Gethsemane, and cease to wonder at the emotion it inspires. It is not the situation. It is those aged olives, the more striking from their total unlikeness to all the others. They could not have seen the Agony. No ! But they have seen the tears of generations of pilgrims, and more than anything else in Jerusalem, except the everlasting hills themselves, they carry you back to that day. Of all trees that I ever saw or shall see, they are the most venerable. Farewell.

Ever yours,

A. P. STANLEY.

LVII.

A. P. S. to Mary Stanley.

BETHEL ; SHILOH ; SHECHEM ; JACOB'S WELL ;
THE SAMARITAN SYNAGOGUE.

Nazareth : April 3, 1853.

We left Jerusalem on the 31st, and came by Anathoth, Michmash, Bethel, Shiloh, Shechem, Samaria, Jezreel, hither.

The first day was amongst the northern mountains of Judæa. Of the scenery, with such exceptions as I shall mention, I have the one thing to say—that it is like the Lowlands of Wales or Scotland—grey rock, intermixed with green waving cornfields. Its defect is that it is almost entirely featureless—one hill like another—no imposing situation or view. Even Bethel and Shiloh, those two renowned sanctuaries, would not, I think, arrest the traveller by any natural peculiarity. Still there is the indescribable charm of the knowledge that you are in these places, which succeed each other as rapidly as the famous places of Greece. One feature, too, there is, which always relieves the insipidity of the view, whenever you catch glimpses of it, as you do again and again in that first day's ride to Bethel, the deep cut of the Jordan valley, marked by its precipitous wall of eastern mountains. It is, I believe, the deepest fissure on the face of the earth, and that is quite the impression it leaves upon you. The mountains, which I have so often mentioned, of Moab, and now of Ammon, are not really so high as the Mount of Olives ; but from this tremendous descent you see them, not as you see most mountains, raised far above the level of the sea, at their bases, but, on the contrary, far below the level, so that the deep precipice is thus deepened to your view beyond what you could think possible.

Amongst these ordinary hills, then, set off by this marvellous background, you are now to wander up and down for a day and a half. Three lofty points tower above the rest from almost any point of view. They are Gibeah of Saul, Mizpeh, and Ramah, whether of Samuel or not is difficult to say. In the centre of these is Mukhmas —the old Michmash, possibly the old Ai—scene of the exploits of Jonathan. These we ascended, and then for one piastre the Arabs presented us with an English letter they had found. I hope we were not wrong in reading it. It introduced us at once into the bosom of an urban family circle, which quite enlivened our day's journey. The Arabs told Abdullah that it was worth one hundred piastres to see that it made us laugh so much, and we then tore it to shreds lest others might not make so good a use of it.

From Mukhmas we came to Bethel. It is one of the many places which Robinson has the great credit of discovering. There are four points in it of great interest. The first is the hill 'eastward of Bethel,' which commands a view on the east over the vale of the Jordan, winding dark through his thicket maze to the waters of the Dead Sea, on the south over the wide wild hills to Hebron. You cannot doubt that this is the very point of view described in the separation of Abraham and Lot, that parting of fortunes which has been repeated again and again in the moral world, the real 'choice of Hercules,' which here you see before your very eyes. Secondly, there is on the west, on the direct road for Jericho, another lower hill, covered with large flat rocks, almost like gravestones. Here again, in like manner, is the very scene of Jacob's rest. 'This is none other than the house of God, this is the gate of heaven.' There is, as I have said, nothing to distinguish it; it is one

of the common hills of the country.   So much the more
striking is the moral.   Thirdly, there is a hill between the
two, occupied by some ancient building.   There, I think,
probably stood the sanctuary of the Calf, at the southern
extremity of Ephraim, for here you have just left the hills
of Judah ; they end at Bireh or the old Beeroth, which you
see high on the hill opposite, the traditional scene, and one
highly probable, of the first halt of the Nazareth caravan
described in Luke ii.   Fourthly, there are, in the long valley
leading up to Bethel from the east, many sepulchres hewn
in the rock, all old, one of them in all probability containing the bones of the old prophet and the prophet of Judah.

This was enough for the day's journey.   I have said nothing about seeing Ophrah of Gideon, probably the Ephraim
to which Christ retired after the raising of Lazarus (perched
high on its mountain-top like the towns of the Apennines),
and Anathoth, birthplace of Jeremiah, and ancient structures
ascribed to the remnant of the Amalekites.

The next day brought us through the hills to Shiloh.
This, like Bethel, had nothing marked except its seclusion
and central situation, a hill rising amongst other hills
amidst bowers of green cornfields.   But there was an old
well hard by, where the daughters of Shiloh had no doubt
danced, and there again were sepulchres which, no doubt,
had contained the bones of Eli, of Hophni, and of Phinehas.
From Shiloh you descend from these hills and enter a wide
plain, one mass of corn, unbroken by boundary or hedge,
a sea of corn with olive trees shooting up from the midst
of it.   At the north end of this, far away, rose the snowy
ridge of Hermon.   At last you come to an opening in the
hills on its west side.   Those hills are Gerizim and Ebal.
Up that opening, though not as yet seen, lies the city of
Shechem or Sychar.

At the mouth of this valley, and in the midst of the

corn plain that I have described, you see two slight mounds, one a white Mahometan tomb, the other a few fragments of stone. The first of these is Joseph's grave, where, in all probability, his embalmed body still lies ; the other · marks the site of the neglected and choked well, which is the very Jacob's Well memorable to all time as the first property, distinct from mere sepulchres, which Israel acquired in the Holy Land. This plain of waving corn suggests that the pastoral life of the early patriarchs was now to be exchanged for the settled life of the founder of a mighty nation, the well dug in this 'parcel of ground' indicating (as Robinson observes) that Jacob would not trust to the springs higher up the valley, which belonged to the Shechemites ; its situation thus remains as an actually existing monument of the prudential character of the old patriarch, as clearly as if you saw him administering the mess of pottage, or compassing his ends with Laban ; and there, hard by, lies, as I have said, the tomb of his favourite son. But, if interesting for its connection with Jacob, how much more for its connection with a greater than Jacob!

Of all the special localities connected with our Lord's life in Palestine, this alone, I believe, is absolutely undoubted. Here, by the very edge of this well, 'Quærens me, sedisti lassus.' With one exception everything corresponds. There is the well ; there is the passage through the mouth of the valley to the city which He did not enter ; there are the cornfields with four months already to the harvest ; there is 'this mountain' of Gerizim, with its temple on the top, immediately overhanging the spot ; there is the woman coming to draw water, as on this very day at Shiloh, and at another well, halfway between the two, we found the 'women of Samaria' gathered round the well and eager to talk to us or any one else who came. One only circum-

stance fails, and that is the quantity of living—that is, fresh
spring—water as soon as you enter the valley of Shechem;
and, if so, why the woman's speech? Explanations are
given; none appear to me quite satisfactory. But the
difficulty is not so great as to shake the general conviction
that it is the very spot.

From this point—which, I hope, remains fixed in my
memory, never to depart—we passed at once into the narrow
vale of Shechem, or, as it is now called, Nablus. I need
not go over the historical recollections of this first primeval
capital of Palestine, then the seat of the northern kingdom,
and then of the Samaritan sect. But, bearing this in mind,
you must figure to yourself a valley green with grass, gray
with olives, gardens sloping down on each side, fresh springs
rushing down in all directions, at the end a white town embowered in all this verdure, almost like Chiavenna, lodged
between the two long mountains extending on each side
of the valley—that on the south, Gerizim; that on the
north, Ebal. It is to Palestine, to the dry rocky hills of
Palestine, what the Wady Feiran is to the desert. And
now ascend Gerizim just before sunset. Glorious indeed
was the view! On the west the Mediterranean Sea, and
on the south the everlasting wall of the trans-Jordanic
mountains; Ramoth Gilead almost in sight, and, what to
me was more striking than all besides, a deep opening in
this wall immediately facing us—the mouth of the valley
of the Jabbok—down which Jacob came from Mesopotamia,
and from which he marched at once, and, as has been
said with obvious purpose, direct to his first settlement
underneath Gerizim. And when from the view you turned
to the mountain itself, there, in the very face of the
declaration that all local worship was to cease, remains the
strongest example of local worship now existing in the
world. There is the road worn in the hillside by which,

P 2

four times a year, the Samaritans ascend to celebrate the
Jewish festivals ; there is the hole deep in the ground where
every Passover they roast their seven lambs ; there are the
twelve rough rocks which they believe to be, or to cover,
the twelve stones of Joshua ; there is the spot where,
according to them, Abraham offered Isaac ; there is the
bare ledge of rock which they believe to be the holiest of
places, and to which they turn as faithfully as Mahometans
to Mecca.

The Samaritans combine the two extraordinary claims
of being at once the oldest and the smallest sect in the
world : the oldest, because by them the Jewish worship has
been continued unbroken, whilst in the main branch of the
nation it has perished ; the smallest, because they consist of
thirty families living in Nablus. They are amongst churches
what St. Marino is amongst states. I had long set my
heart on seeing their great sacrifice. This, however, was
impossible. But it struck me as we neared Nablus that
it was Friday evening, and that possibly on Saturday
morning I might see their early service. I found that it
was at 6 A.M., and accordingly went. It lasted about an
hour, and was to me one of the most interesting and
affecting sights I have ever seen. In a humble synagogue,
which I entered without my shoes, was assembled the whole
· Samaritan sect—that is, the whole male part—about thirty
men and ten boys. They wore white turbans, and each as
he came in dropped down a white tippet, like a train, so as
to enter in complete white. These white figures, men and
boys, after stroking their faces and (those who had them)
beards, sate or stood—kneeling, I believe, is a posture unknown to Oriental devotion—joining in a wild and eager
chant led by a priest, who stood in a recess. The essential
part of the service, however, was the ' elevation,' not of the
Host, but of the Pentateuch. The Samaritans receive only

the Pentateuch, and they believe that their copy of it was written by the great-grandson of Aaron. It was this parchment, stretched between two brazen rollers, that the priest raised above his head, turned round in every direction, and brought to the centre of the congregation, exactly like the Host ; and to it, with one exception, the whole devotion converged. That one exception was the Holy Place on Gerizim. Thrice at least in the service, whether on the successive elevations of the Law I cannot certainly say, the whole assembly threw themselves flat on their faces, not in the direction of the priest, or Law, or any-thing within the building, but obliquely across the floor, to what I knew, from what I had seen on the previous night, was the point of worship on the mountain.

They are a noble-looking race, but there was that strange indifference to the service—talking and smiling—which I have seen amongst Jews generally. No others, they said, existed anywhere else.

It was on coming out of this synagogue, and just as we were making for Samaria, that I received the letter which mingled with all the other sights of that day. Unfortunately, a thick mist set in, which shut out the view from the top of the beautiful hill of Samaria. This we reached in about three hours from Nablus. The fertility and freshness still continue, and it is evident that, whilst Jerusalem must always have been the most venerable, Shechem and Samaria must always have been the most beautiful and luxurious of the Jewish capital cities. That evening we left Samaria and Ephraim, and entered Galilee, Issachar, Zebulun, and Naphthali. These I must reserve for my next letter. A traveller hence carries this to Beyrout.

All well.   Ever yours,

A. P. STANLEY.

LVIII.

A. P. S. to Mary Stanley.

[Stanley quotes from Keble's ' Christian Year ' a passage in the poem for the Third Sunday in Advent. The epithet ' mossy,' to which he objects as inexact, occurs in the third stanza.

> The Paschal moon above
> Seems like a saint to rove,
> Left shining in the world with Christ alone ;
> Below, the lake's still face
> Sleeps sweetly in th' embrace
> Of mountains terrass'd high with mossy stone.]

April 8 : on the road to Damascus.

It was after descending from the hills of Samaria that we entered the Roman province of Galilee, the territories of Issachar, Zebulun, and Naphthali. Two objects of wonderful though most different interest presented themselves : the great battlefield of the whole Jewish history in the plain of Esdraelon, and the chief ministrations of our Lord.

After the endless undulations of hills and valleys, almost indistinguishable, which had been our lot from Hebron, one may say, to Samaria, it was a striking contrast to enter on a geographical feature so strongly marked as this famous plain. Its peculiarities are soon told. It is a wide rut between the hills of Southern Palestine, which I have already described, and the bolder mountains of Northern Palestine, which are in fact the roots of Lebanon. It consists of a plain at the west end with three legs running eastward, of which the southernmost is a *cul de sac* ; but the central one and the northernmost run down to the valley of the Jordan. These branches, or legs as I call them, which you see stand in the same relation to the east plain as the legs of Como to the lake at Colico, are divided from each other by nearly isolated ranges, Gilboa, Little Hermon, and Mount Tabor. The only stream which flows through this wide plain is the Kishon, which, however, has perennial water only at its west end. The mere enumeration of the names will tell you what a map, not only of geography but of history, thus lay open before me.

On Mount Tabor were assembled the forces of Barak, and in the plain was fought the battle with Sisera. There too fell Josiah. In the central branch was the defeat of the Midianites by Gideon, and of Saul by the Philistines, and of the Syrians by Ahab. And the whole plain is the scene chosen in the Revelation to express the last great battle of Ar (that is, the mountains of) Megiddo.

But you will ask, not only for a map, but for a picture of this world-renowned field. You know, dearest mother, how long I had known it and all its parts by name. You can imagine how I feasted my eyes upon it, in the three great views I had of it, from the hill above Jenin, from Jezreel, and from Tabor. It is for the most part a vast waving cornfield, olive trees here and there springing from it. It is very rare to see so wide and long a plain, especially such as this which forms the watershed, though, as most of the watersheds of Palestine, almost imperceptible between two seas, with so slight a trace of water. The Kishon, as I have said, has ordinarily none till near its mouth, which I have not yet seen. There no doubt, when swollen by the storm, it 'swept away' the forces of Sisera. The two ranges of Little Hermon and Gilboa which rise out of it are almost entirely bare ; so also is the long range which bounds it on the north. But so is not that strange and beautiful mountain which rises in the eastern end of the northern branch—Tabor. It was from Nazareth that I first saw it. It towered like a dome over the monotonous undulations of the other hills ; from other directions it is more like a long wooded mound. It is not what we should call a wooded hill, because its trees stand apart from each other ; but it is so thickly studded with them as to stand quite alone in its verdure amongst the neighbouring mountains. Its sides are extremely like the scattered glades on the outskirts of the New Forest ; its top is an alternation of shade and greensward, that was made for a national festivity, broad and varied, and with the wide views up and down the plain. This of itself will tell you that it is not that peaked height which we imagine for the Transfiguration, and there are besides the ruins everywhere of that town or fortress which, existing there as it seems to have done at the very time of the Christian era, renders the tradition impossible. But if it must lose that last crowning glory, it has all the old associations undisturbed ; one sees Barak with his ten thousand men encamped on the top, and one understands how the Psalmist joins its name with the great Hermon which can be seen, though at a distance, from its summit, as well as from the surrounding valleys.

But I must descend once more to the plain which you see from it, and of which the last characteristic that I shall notice is its villages, most of them keeping the ancient names unchanged. Unlike the towns of Judæa, which are mostly on the hill-tops, or of Samaria, which lie deep in the valleys, these are on the slopes of the ranges which intersect or bound the plain, or else on slight eminences rising from it. It is delightful to see how well they suit the history. Far down on the slope of the plain of Megiddo is Taanach ; on the northern slope of Little

Hermon is Endor, on its southern Shunem, both so deeply linked with the fatal fight of Gilboa. Most striking of all, however, is Jezreel, now the wretched village of Zerin ; but its situation on a beautiful green swell at the entrance of the central branch of the plain marks it out at once as the capital of the whole. Westward you look over the plain to Carmel, whence Elijah ' ran to meet Ahab ' at the gate. Eastward you look down the descent of 'the valley of Jezreel,' closed by the black mountains of Ramoth Gilead on the other side the Jordan, whence Jehu came, 'driving furiously' up this very valley, and seen from its watch-towers as he approached. You imagine too the shout with which we welcomed the dogs of the village as they rushed out at us. ' The dogs shall eat Jezebel in the portion of Jezreel.' Bethshan too you see on the farther slopes of Gilboa, near enough to the deep chasm of the Jordan to make you understand the exploit of the men of Jabesh Gilead in rescuing the bodies of their benefactors. Deep down in the valley too is the famous ' fountain ' or spring of Jezreel, the camping-place of Gideon and of Saul.

It was on Sunday morning that we crossed the plain, Walrond reading aloud the song of Deborah and the lamentation of David in the intervals of the heavy storms, which from this time forward have troubled our journey. To one village we turned aside, not connected with the warlike reminiscences of Esdraelon, though close to Endor —Nain—still bearing the same name, and on the rough slope of Little Hermon. One entrance alone it could have had, up the hill-side ; and it was in that steep descent, doubtless, that the bier was stopped. And now we are on that track, we shall not leave it again.

We arrived at Nazareth in the early afternoon—wet through, and glad of the hospitable walls of the Convent— before our baggage arrived. Nazareth lies high up in the mountains, which, as I have said, being the offshoots of Lebanon, itself invisible and far away, form the northern boundary of the plain of Esdraelon. It seems the peculiarity of these hills, as distinct from all that I have hitherto mentioned, that they contain or sustain green basins of table-land just below their ridges. Some such we saw from Tabor, others from the heights of Banias. One of these is Nazareth, which lies on the steep slope of such a circle of green hills which run round it and above it, just screening it from the view which the tops of those hills afford. One such view from a hill, half an hour's walk above the town, would, if it had been clear, have been one of the most beautiful in Palestine and in the world—finer, I think, even than that from Tabor. It commands, what Tabor does not command, Carmel and the Mediterranean, Tabor itself, Hermon also—a conjunction I should imagine quite unique—and, besides, the tangled uplands of the range of which it forms a part, and, close below, the peaceful basin of Nazareth itself, the green hills just touching its precipitous rock 'on the brow of the hill whereon' (that must be, on the side of which) 'the city stood.'

These are the natural features, unaltered, which for nearly thirty years were within the daily view of Him who 'increased in wisdom and stature' within this beautiful seclusion. Now to descend to the modern town and its traditional sights. The most prominent object is the Franciscan Convent in which we lodged. The church is built over the site of the 'house.' Accordingly, as at Canterbury, the altar is raised very high, and this of itself gives an impressive effect to the building; the vespers were going on, and it was very striking to hear the congregation join in the responses, with more fervour, I think, than I ever heard in a Roman Catholic Church. It was the more striking from the fact that most of the congregation were Arabs, some dressed in the wild Bedouin costume with robe and kefyeh, apparently dependent upon the Convent. One of the little boys who acted as our guide was an excellent specimen of the rest. Altogether it seemed an establishment worthy of the place. When the vespers were ended, we descended to the vault under the altar. On the supposed site of the house is an oblong vestibule, about twenty-six paces long and, I think, nine broad, which opens by a wide door on the east side into a large grotto, of which the natural rock in part remains. This is to them the great sight. The 'house' was treated by the Sacristan with indifference. Whether it had been destroyed by the Turks, or removed to Loretto, he did not seem to know or care. All that he maintained was, that it had stood on the site of the vestibule and opened into the grotto, and that there, on a place marked by a stone and by the same inscription as at Loretto, ' Here the Word was made flesh,' stood the Virgin. This was kissed devoutly as usual by every one. On the left hand as you enter from the vestibule is a window in the grotto walls, 'through which the angel flew,' and a pillar inscribed where he stood. In short, as you see, all that is made much of in the house at Loretto, is here transferred to the grotto : characteristic enough of the two countries. Nor did I see how the arrangements could be reconciled ; for the entrance to the grotto implied a large door in the house where no door could have existed in that of Loretto, and the aperture to the grotto another window. On the measurements I lay no stress (nor indeed do I remember whether they agree), as they clearly had no knowledge or tradition as to how far the vestibule, as it now stands, exactly coincides with the house as it stood. It should be mentioned that the Greek Church has another spot at the other end of the town in the chief church which is shown as its traditional site of the same event. The grotto in the Franciscan Convent opens into a larger grotto behind, said to be the house of the neighbour who kept the Virgin's house when she went to see Elizabeth—a curious and innocent tradition as it seemed to me. In and about the grotto itself there is no building, nor any traces of foundations of the house, only some stonework said to be by Helena. But at a short distance is what is said to be the workshop of Joseph with a few fragments of what they say is the original wall. There is not the slightest resemblance between them and the stones at Loretto. They are a rough gray limestone like the actual buildings of the village, made, as they naturally would be, of the stone of the country. One other remark on the connection of Nazareth and Loretto. I had thought before I came that possibly a likeness of situation might have suggested the story. There is, as you will have seen, none such.

We left the Convent on Monday, and rode first to Tabor, which I have described, and then to Tiberias. North-east of Tabor a wild upland plain runs between the hill of Nazareth and Safed, which I called for convenience sake the roots of Lebanon, and in the midst of this rises a long low ridge ending in a curiously shaped hill, called from its two points the Horns of Hattin. It is said by tradition to be the Mount of the Beatitudes—that is, of the Sermon. We passed close under it, but without ascending it, which I regretted the more especially because every time that I saw it from the Sea of Galilee made me think it more and more probable that it may have been the place. It is the only conspicuous mountain seen from there; it is easily accessible; the level top suits the accounts; and though the situation no doubt suggested the tradition to the Crusaders who gave it the name, yet the situation also agrees with the Gospel narrative. The

Crusaders gave it the name, and it has another fatal association with their history.   On that long ridge the battle was fought by which Saladin became master of Palestine—fought in the presence of the holiest places of Christianity, and miserably lost.   From the top of Tabor we had the first glimpse of the waters of the Sea of Galilee. But it was only a glimpse.   The first full view flashes upon you as you descend from the upland plain which I have described, through the mountains which form the west side of the lake.

I must confess that this was a moment when the recollections of the past disarmed all criticism of the scenery. Whether the lake be as tame and poor as many accounts describe, I cannot say.   Yet I think that there is a character about it which at any rate distinguishes it from other lakes, and by this I will try to describe it.   According to Robinson, it is about thirteen miles long, and in part six wide ; that is, as long as, and rather wider, I believe, than Windermere. But the atmosphere makes it look much smaller.   You never, from the west side, see it quite from end to end, without the promontory under which Tiberias stands cutting off the southern, as that over the plain of Gennesareth the northern, extremity ; so that it generally has the appearance of an oval.   The hills on the east side are, I think, what gives it its peculiar aspect, partaking, as they do, of that horizontal wall-like outline which marks, as I have so often said, the whole eastern barrier of the Jordan valley.   At first sight, and in the evening when I first saw them, they appeared to descend on the lake almost precipitously.   This, however, is not the case ; they are broken by grassy slopes with rocky faces, as far as I could judge, from north to south, . and most clearly so at the southern extremity, where must have been the scene of the rushing in of the swine ; and it must be, therefore, one of those rocky slopes and not a high

precipice which is there intended.   And also, at the north
end, it must have been on one of these wide grassy uplands
that the feeding of the five thousand took place.   In the full
daylight, when the lights and shades fell on the eastern hills,
I could with a glass make out these points with tolerable
certainty, though I bitterly longed for another day to see
them from a nearer position.

So much for the eastern or opposite side.   On the south,
which I reached within half an hour's walk, I saw the green
line of vegetation at the end, and the wide open valley
beyond ; it clearly marked the exit of the Jordan on its
rapid fall into the Dead Sea.   On the north, which I also
approached within two hours, I saw in like manner the
green plain, with the high eastern wall continuing far north
as the eye could reach, the green table-lands, already described, on its summits which mark the entrance of the
Jordan, where two solitary palms stood on the shore to
welcome it.

And now for the western shore, which we descended.
First we came down upon Tiberias, now a ruined though
still venerable village, built on the wide and scattered
foundations of the city which in our Lord's time had but
just been finished, and must have shone with its white
temples and palaces along the shore like the villas on the
banks of Como.   What remains is partly of this, partly of
that later Jewish University which arose in Tiberias, and
which caused it to become the burial-place of many illustrious Jews in later times, amongst others of their greatest
divine, Maimonides.   It does not appear from the Gospels
that our Lord was ever here, though there is a church on
the spot where He is supposed to have landed from the
storm, and the altar stone on which He stood when He ' gave
the keys ' to Peter (an event which really took place, as you
will hear, far away), and on it Peter laid the ' pesce di San

Pietro' for the tribute money. Beyond are the warm sul-
phureous baths, which, with the black stones which strew
the hills, are the signs that this, as well as the Dead Sea, is
in part the result of volcanic action.

But Tiberias is the least interesting part of the lake.
We encamped there, and the next day rode along the shores
as far as Khan Minyeh, which you will see on Robinson's
map. This brought us through the most affecting region
of the whole lake—shall I say of the world?—the plain of
Gennesareth. The western sides of the sea for the most
part consist of hills, grassy and rocky alternately, like those
on the eastern shore, though with a more varied outline ;
and as you stand on their tops, before descending, there is
Tabor, and the Mount of the Beatitudes behind, and the
exceedingly tangled and jagged mass of Safed, ' the city
that is set on a hill,' mingling with the view of the lake itself.
But they nowhere descend precipitously on the water ; they
always leave a thin line of beach, which you see running
like a white line under their dark base from south to north,
almost the whole way. Near Tiberias it is rough and
shingly, of white and black stone, the volcanic fragments of
which I spoke. But farther north the hills recede and leave
between themselves and the lake a small rich plain of waving
corn, fringed as it reaches the water-side with a jungle of
feathery reeds, of acacia, and above all of flowering oleanders, but not rhododendrons.

> All through the summer night,
> Those blossoms red and bright
> Spread their soft breasts. . . .

I saw them first at Tiberias, eagerly looking out for them,
and could not contain a shout of delight, ' There they are ! '
as I saw them. But on the shore of the plain of Gennesareth they grew and flowered in profusion, and, mingled with
the other vegetation, gave an appearance of richness such as

I have not seen since the Nile.   This is partly owing to the deep depression of the lake and its shores, but partly also to the streams which along this whole coast, and far up the valley even to the sources of the Jordan, seem the peculiar privilege of the region—clear crystal fountains pouring forth rivers of water to run for a few miles or less, fertilising all that they touch.

It was this rich plain, which Josephus describes as the most populous part of Palestine, which sent forth its fisher-men by hundreds over the lake, and turned the whole basin into a focus of life and animation.   Here were those towns and villages of immortal fame, Magdala, Bethsaida, Chora-zin, Capernaum ; and here for three years was the chief scene of the works and words of Christ.

Every sign of man has now passed away.   The Dead Sea itself can hardly be more dead than this region once teeming with life.   That house, so far more sacred than the house of Loretto, be it ever so genuine, the home of our Lord, not in His unconscious infancy or mature youth, but in the fullness of His labours, has so utterly passed away that even the site of Capernaum is lost.   The woe pro-nounced against the three towns, though I do not suppose this was its original or chief meaning, has been so literally fulfilled that not one of them is left even in name ; yet, in spite of all this, the interest is unspeakable.

The exact sites are gone; Bethsaida, the birthplace of the four Apostles, and Capernaum, the home of Christ, can only be conjectured.   Still you know within a very narrow compass where they must have been.   You see the plain, the cornfields, the flowers that He saw ; you see the beach, here of soft sand and shells, where He appeared to Peter and John after the resurrection.

Magdala too, the birthplace of Mary Magdalene, re-mains with its name almost unchanged, a wretched ruin

now, but still marked by its being the only village left
except Tiberias, standing on the south corner of the little
plain, and dignified by the high rocks which overhang it,
perforated with caves, like that in Correggio's picture, and
with a deep ravine behind it, at the end of which rises
majestically the Mount of the Beatitudes.   It was from
the hill above Khan Minych, which, after all that can be
said, is the most probable site of Capernaum, that I drank
in most fully that long-expected and now never to be
forgotten scene.   Oh! for two more hours to have passed
quite to the northern end, and so have trodden with
absolute certainty, somewhere or other, the traces of those
vanished cities!

I passed on to yet one other eminence to overlook the
ruins of Tell Hûm, the other chief claimant, and to see more
distinctly the close of the lake; and then we rode away,
with wider, because more distant, views of the waters,
Tabor, and the Jordan valley far away, and it was not till
late in the afternoon that we lost sight of it.   Keble's lines,
which I read that night, dearest mother, and dearest C.
in your little book, are extremely good.   The only expression which I should omit is ' *mossy* stone.'   There is a
bareness about all the rocks which forbids it.   ' Tabor's
peak ' is also, as you will have perceived, inapplicable.
From the west side you cannot see Sirion (Hermon), but
from the east side, where he rightly places the scene, you
can.   Ever yours,

A. P. STANLEY.

Q

LIX.

A. P. S. to Mary Stanley.

DAMASCUS.

Damascus : April 10.

I proceed, dearest, to describe Damascus, and, first, the interior which we first inspected.

In external architecture the streets are not to be named with Cairo. In fact they have no architecture at all ; they are nothing but mud walls, the streets themselves being gutters which run between two high *trottoirs* of rude pavement, on which, before the victories of Ibrahim Pacha over Syrian prejudices, none but Mussulmans were allowed to walk, all others (see *Eothen*) walking in the gutter. But in three respects they excel Cairo and any other Oriental city I have seen.

First, the bazaars are much more extensive—that is to say, the streets with stalls are much longer ; and, being mostly covered with wooden roofing, something like the arcades of Swiss bridges, it is like passing through vast galleries, and this effect is strengthened when you ride through them after sunset, when the great shutters are let down over the stalls, so that you seem to be riding through an endless array of cupboards. And their greater length, combined with the circumstance that each trade has a street of its own, presents an appearance, which, if it existed, I failed to observe at Cairo, of a perpetual multiplication of the same object. Thus you enter the street of shoemakers, and your eye wanders, as far as it can reach, through a vista of festoons of shoes, or rather slippers, almost all brilliant red. Or you pass into the street of tinkers, and instantly, from end to end, the ordinary hum of the stalls is borne down by the long succession of clinking tools.

Secondly, besides these narrow covered streets, there are—not squares, but—wide, irregular, rambling ways, with magnificent ashes and sycamores growing out of and into the houses, each forming a central point for loungers or business. Also there are cafés along and above the rushing waters of the Barada, very rude and rough, yet still having an appearance of primitive luxury worthy of this most ancient of cities.

Thirdly, the interior of the greater houses is a remarkable contrast to the deadness of their exterior, in this respect, as in almost all others, reminding one of the Alhambra. There are just the same marble courts with fountains and gardens, the same double alcoves, the same coloured tiles, the same high vaults.

For the rest there is nothing to see. The great mosque, which, like that of S. Sophia, is the old cathedral turned to that purpose, is inaccessible, except so far as you see it from the roofs of the adjacent houses. It is really the Church of St. John of Damascus; but the Turks believe it to be of St. John the Baptist, whom they revere as a prophet, and hence its extreme sanctity.

One peculiarity of Eastern life which you encounter in the interior of the houses is the presentation of coffee Thrice in the afternoon of yesterday did we have it offered. Another is the total absence of carriages. At Cairo they are, as you know, rare exceptions; but here there is but one exception, that of the Governor, and it cannot drive in the streets. Almost every one walks.

And now for the exterior, which, after all, is its great and enduring charm—that which it must have had from the days when it was the solitary seat of civilisation in Syria, and which it will have as long as the world lasts. One of the strongest impressions which you carry away from the East is the connection, obvious enough, perhaps, in itself, but certainly not thought of in Europe, between verdure and running water. The Nile, the Jordan valley, the plain of Gennesareth, are all witnesses to it. But the greatest of all is Damascus. Both are equally remarkable, the burst of fresh streams through every quarter of the town and every field in the neighbourhood, and the wide mass of green—walnuts and apricots above, and corn and grass below—which encompasses the city like a lake. This you see best from the heights above the town on the west, the sacred heights where the Prophet is said to have stood—if at all, it must have been when he was still a camel-driver from Mecca—and, after gazing on the scene below, to have turned away from the city without entering it. 'Man,' he said, 'can have but one Paradise, and my Paradise is above.'

To an Arab from the desert it must indeed have seemed a Paradise. To any one it is one of the great views of the world, ranking with Granada, and Athens, and Salzburg. There is the wide plain before you, the horizon bare, its lines of surrounding hills bare, as you look far away on the road to Palmyra and Bagdad ; and in the midst of the plain at your feet lies this vast lake or island of rich deep foliage, and in the midst of this foliage, striking out its white arms hither and thither, and its white minarets rising above the trees which embosom it, the city of Damascus. One thing only is wanted to the view—the sight of the snowy range of Hermon, which is hidden by the hills on which we stood, but which must be visible from those on the other side of the plain.

One view there is, however, from the eastern side, though nearer at hand and only from the level ground, which I did see, and which, with that view of Mahomet's from the

western side, is the most remarkable that even this world-
old city has presented to mortal eyes.   Through the gardens
on the eastern side runs the great road from Jerusalem, and,
a quarter of an hour from the walls of the city, the Christian
burial-ground and a heap of conglomerate stone mark
what at any rate must have been near the scene of the
Conversion of St. Paul.   We were there soon after morning.   There was the cloudless blue overhead ; close in front
the city walls—in part still ancient ; around it the green
mass of groves and orchards ; and beyond them the bare
hills of Salahiyeh, now studded with the sacred places of
Mahometanism, then probably presenting nothing but their
own rocky face.   Such was St. Paul's view when the light
became darkness before him, and he heard the voice which
turned the fortunes of mankind.

.   .   .   .

Such, perhaps, I ought rather to say, taking up my pen
after five days' consideration, is the traditional scene of St.
Paul's view.   Determined to ascertain what was the real
tradition on the spot, I broke into the Franciscan convent,
and, to my great delight, found a very intelligent monk,
speaking French—in fact a Frenchman from St. Gaudet in
the Pyrenees, which he was charmed to find that I had seen.
He assured me that this, and this only, was the place, and
that the Christians had chosen it as their burial-ground
from its being the site of the old church built on the
supposed scene of the Conversion, and, in fact, when I went
in the morning, I observed the foundations of the ancient
building.   However, on this, as on many other points, I
must withhold my judgment till my return.

But now I must return once more to the view of
Damascus.   I wrote of it before I saw the real and grand
view, which we should have seen in approaching Damascus,
but which we only saw in leaving it.   Damascus, like Petra,

should be approached only one way, and that is from the west. The traveller who comes from that quarter passes over the great chain of Anti-Libanus, and, on passing the watershed, he arrives at the head of a little stream flowing through a richly cultivated valley. This stream is the Barada, the ancient Abana, or Pharpar, it is not known which. It flows on, and the cultivation, which, at its rise, spreads far and wide along its banks, nourished by the rills which feed it, gradually is contracted within the limits of its single channel. The mountains rise round it, absolutely bare ; the river winds through them, everywhere visible by the mass of vegetation—willow-poplars like those of Spain, hawthorn, walnut-trees, hanging over a rushing volume of crystal water, forming as complete a picture of refreshment as you can imagine, and yet doubly striking from the contrast of the naked desert in which it is found. Never, not even in the close juxtaposition of the Nile valley and the sands of Africa, have I seen so wonderful a witness to the life-giving power of water. You advance, and the contrast becomes more and more forcible, the mountains more bare, the green of the river-bed more deep and rich.

At last a cleft opens in the mountains between two precipitous cliffs. Up the side of one of these cliffs the road winds. On the summit of the cliff is a ruined chapel. Through the arches of that chapel you look down at once on the plain of Damascus. I need not repeat what that is ; but it is here seen in its widest and fullest perfection, and you have here, what you have nowhere else, the visible explanation of the whole. You look below and see the river rushing through the cleft, and you see it scattering over the whole plain the same verdure which had hitherto been confined to its single channel. It is like the bursting of a shell, the eruption of a volcano, but an eruption not of death but of life. Here too alone, you have on your right the snowy top of Hermon overlooking the whole scene : here also alone, you have behind you the sterile limestone mountains, so that you literally stand between the dead and the living ; and here alone you have those ruined arches which serve as a centre and framework to the prospect and the retrospect, and which still preserve the memory of that magnificent story, whether truth or fiction ; for this, so far as I can make out, is the very spot on which the Prophet stood, when he made the choice which I have before described, and turned back from the earthly Paradise which lay before him to the barren mountains he had crossed. You will therefore understand this as correcting all that I have said before.

This view of Damascus is one of the very few views of the world that have every element of grandeur. Whilst in Damascus, I confess that I sighed for one drop of the water of Jordan amidst all the rivers of Abana and Pharpar. But the beauty of this view almost, if not altogether, compensated for what I had lost in Palestine.

Ever yours,

A. P. STANLEY.

LX.

A. P. S. to Mary Stanley.

BAALBEC ; TRADITIONAL SCENE OF THE MURDER OF ABEL : THE TOMBS OF SETH AND NOAH.

[Baalbec, the city of the Sun-god Baal, made a Roman colony by Julius Cæsar, was called by the Greeks Heliopolis. The Great Temple, built by Antoninus Pius (138–161), contained, it is said, a golden image of the Sun-god, which on festival-days was carried in procession through the streets of the city. South-east of the Great Temple stands a smaller temple dedicated to Jupiter. South-east of these two temples stands a third, the Circular Temple, dedicated, it is supposed, to Venus or Hedone. Successively plundered by the Arabs, Tartars, and Turks from the eighth to the fifteenth centuries, the city dwindled to a wretched village. The buildings, which its conquerors had not wholly levelled to the ground, were still further shattered by the earthquake of 1759.

Mahomet, to whom reference is made in the letter, was Stanley's courier. See ' Life,' vol. i. p. 448.]

Beyrout: April 14, 1853.

To-morrow, dearest mother, is your birthday. God grant all that He has to give, and, amongst all other gifts, that I may be never away from you upon it again.

This letter, dearest, must give you an account of the passage of Anti-Libanus and of Baalbec. I have described the first part of the passage in my last letter. We encamped at Zebedani just under the highest ridge, which we crossed the next morning. The descent on the other side was far less interesting ; indeed, I think I never saw scenery, I will not say so beautiful, but so remarkable as that contrast of the Barada and the mountains. On the western side there was nothing but a perpetual undulation of hills like those of Judæa, till you finally looked down on the vast green and red valley—green from its cornfields, red from its vineyards not yet verdant—which divides the Libanus and the Anti-Libanus ranges, the two ranges both, of course, rising over it, the Libanus range reaching its highest point in the snowy crest of Mount Libanus, behind which grow the cedars, the Anti-Libanus in the still more snowy crest of Hermon. The height, therefore, you will observe, is in the one at the north, in the other at the south, of the valley which they bound.

The view of this great valley was chiefly remarkable as being so exactly to the eye what it is on maps. It has no beauty except that of fertility, and Libanus is too long and straggling a range to be grand. Through a screen of low hills the Leontes breaks down the southern end of

the plain.   There is, I believe, something similar at the
northern end ; but that was too remote to be visible.

It is in the centre of this plain—on no commanding
position, and therefore with no great distant view—that
you find the ruins of Baalbec.   They are certainly very
fine, though to me not very interesting.   They consist of
two great Roman temples of Corinthian architecture, built
apparently on enormous foundations of unknown antiquity,
the whole turned in some later time into a Saracenic
fortress, and now, all alike, gone to neglect and ruin.
Long rows of high Corinthian columns still remain, on
their lofty platforms, amidst a mass of broken shafts and
capitals, of which I can give you the best notion by asking
you to imagine that one vast fragment of the Temple of
the Sun in the Colonna Gardens multiplied a thousand
times and scattered and piled over a space as large as the
Forum.   The stones in the great walls of the enclosure are
the largest in the world—that is to say, three of them are,
each being at least sixty feet long—that excellent measure
of Alderley Church steeple.   Their length was best seen by
the sight of a fourth, which was left in a quarry hard by,
and which really does look exactly like that dear old tower
laid on its face.   But about all these stones and every
other part of the temple, except the latest, there is the
unsatisfactory feeling that nothing is, or can be, known.
Not only is there no record, but the whole place has been
so pulled to pieces and put together again, that it is almost
useless to conjecture for what and when each part was
built.

So I leave Baalbec, and descend the plain between the
two ranges, and encamp last night (the 13th) on the slope
of Libanus.

And now I must make two remarks about Anti-
Libanus and this valley.   First, the general cultivation of

the ground, the lanes, the walls, and, above all, the *gates*, and also the evidently industrious and respectable character of the people are very striking. All notions of robbers &c. vanished the moment we entered the mountains. In this respect it is so different from other countries, where the plain is the secure, and the hilly region the insecure. It was as great a transition as from Italy to England.

Secondly—for what reason I cannot tell—the whole of this district, including Damascus, is fixed upon by the Mahometan, perhaps by the Christian inhabitants, as the scene of the primeval history of the world. Adam indeed has his grave at Hebron, and his head, strange to say, in the Church of the Sepulchre. But Nimrod's tomb is shown on the slope of Hermon, as we passed it from Banias ; the red earth, which you see in all parts of the fields of Damascus that are not clothed with verdure, is that of which Adam was made ; the high hill, which rises from the plain on the north, is that on which Cain killed Abel. So much I learn from books ; from the people I could learn but little. But as you mount the valley of the Barada in the bare mountains that I have described before, you come to a deep gorge, through which the river rushes, and over it rises a high rocky eminence, distinguished from all near it by large trees growing on its top. Hear now its story as told by a peasant of Zebedani through Mahomet : ' After the murder of his brother, Cain knew not what to do with the body, and carried it on his back for 500 years till, coming to this hill, he saw two birds fighting. One killed the other, washed it, and then buried it. Cain accordingly did the like, and to mark the spot planted his staff, which grew up into the seven oaks which still remain.'

But the greater wonders are yet to come. Many travellers visit Baalbec ; but few, I think, know that on either side of that wide valley, one on the Libanus, the

other on the Anti-Libanus range, sleep the two great
patriarchs of the human race, Seth and Noah. So said
our Zebedani guide, and Mahomet's devout Mahometan
feelings, quickened, as you may suppose, by one of the
party who had long cherished the hope of seeing these two
strange places, excited him to take us to each. The grave
of Seth we saw as we descended on Baalbec ; the grave of
Noah as we left it. They are almost exactly similar : a
rude mosque, attached to a still ruder building, into which
you look through a grating and see a long gallery, covering
a long coffin, decked out, as usual, with shawls and rough
drapery. But the coffin is, in the case of Seth, more than
70—in the case of Noah, more than 100—feet long ! The
difference arises from the belief that Seth, having been
killed by the Pagan inhabitants of the country in his
attempt to convert them, was buried with his legs doubled
under his knees, so that the coffin covers his body only
so far ; whereas Noah, dying peaceably, lies at his full
length.

Perhaps the most remarkable part of the sight was the
devotion of Mahomet. The moment he looked in at the
grating, he began with a ' Peace be with thee ' to the
dead patriarch, and then followed what corresponds to the
Lord's Prayer, repeated thrice—once for all Mahometans,
once for his friends, and once for himself and all the world.
And this without the least doubt that the enormous coffins
were the graves of the patriarchs, although he had never
heard of Seth before, and had never visited either before.
But it is one of the strange features of—shall I say
Mahomet's character or of Mahometanism itself ?—that
nothing seems too incredible for them. There was a
question one day about where the tomb of a Caliph was—
one being shown at Cairo, another at Baalbec. ' But,
master, perhaps he has two.' ' How ? ' ' Why, don't you

know ? there are some prophets have forty tombs, because
God Almighty has given them forty figures.'

Ever yours,

A. P. STANLEY.

LXI.

A. P. S. to Mary Stanley.

EPHESUS ; THE SEVEN SLEEPERS, THE THEATRE,
AND THE TOMB OF ST. JOHN.

[It must be remembered that Stanley paid his visit to
Ephesus in 1853, ten years before the excavations made
by Mr. J. T. Wood in 1863, and twenty-four years before
the publication of his 'Discoveries at Ephesus.' The
famous legend of the Seven Sleepers is given in the Koran
and elsewhere. They were fugitives from the Decian per-
secution in 250, and they are supposed to have awakened
in the reign of Theodosius, about 380. The legend, especially with its addition of Edward the Confessor's dream
that he saw them turn from right to left, and of the evils
which the change of position portended, was a favourite
one with Stanley. It is employed by Tennyson in
' Harold.'

> Woe, woe to England ! I have had a vision ;
> The seven sleepers in the cave of Ephesus
> Have turned from right to left.

Stanley refers to various traditions of the life of St.
John ; that he refused to enter the public baths at Ephesus
with the heretic Cerinthus ; that he won back to repentance
the robber chief whom in former days he baptised ; that,
when too old to teach, he repeated, without change or
variation, the words ' Little children, love one another ; '
that, after his interment, as Augustine relates, strange
movements of the earth which covered him showed that he
yet lived ; and that, when the tomb was opened, it was
found to be empty.]

The Dardanelles : May 19.

I wonder whether you will exclaim at hearing what I
have done, or whether it conveys no alarm away from the

spot. When I found that, by taking one more day at Smyrna, there would just be time to go to Ephesus and back, it seemed to me so great a pity to lose the sight of the place whence the First Epistle was sent to Corinth, not to speak of the grave of St. John, and the Third Council, and the Temple of Diana, that I determined, if possible, to go. And Theodore Walrond most kindly (I say so because it could not have been the same interest to him as it was to me) at once agreed.

The difficulties were twofold. First, the unhealthiness of Ephesus; this, however, was to be surmounted by sleeping four hours off. Secondly, the famous robbers who have for the last two years infested the whole region of Ephesus and Smyrna, and, curiously enough, in the very same way as they did in the time of St. John—not so much by plunder or attack as by carrying off people into the mountains and then demanding enormous ransoms. To such an extent was this pursued that the merchants of Smyrna have been obliged to leave their country-houses and retire into the town. The difficulty of dealing with these robbers was the greater because they made a kind of social or socialist war of the poor against the rich. Jani Kettargi, the chief, was a Robin Hood in his way, and they were supported in all the villages. However, two months before our arrival, a new governor, who was once Turkish Ambassador in England, had adopted vigorous measures, and Jani had fled to the remoter mountains. Therefore it was at least worth considering whether it was prudent to go.

Mr. Lemmi rather advised it: the consul dissuaded. On inquiry it was pronounced so decidedly that, if we went with no money, we should be quite safe, that we resolved to go. We started accordingly, with a servant from the inn as dragoman; a blanket, a plaid, a pillow, a toothbrush, a comb, and a pair of goloshes, were my whole stock.

We started at 11 A.M. on Monday, and rode, on Turkish saddles, till 10 P.M., with two hours for rest in the middle of the day ; again at 5 A.M. the next morning, and, with the same exception, were on horseback till 9.30 P.M. The next day, from 5 A.M. till 1 P.M., brought us back to Smyrna.

It was hard work, but the only fatiguing part was the night work—I mean after reaching our sleeping-places. These were coffee-houses, of which there was one at about every hour's or two hours' distance—a house with a shed attached, and usually a large plane-tree and fountain. Underneath this shed a mat was spread for us, with the blanket, plaid, and pillow. It was romantic, and would have been comfortable but for the fleas and mosquitoes. The first night I could not sleep one wink. This was the only drawback. It was almost worth the misery of the night to have the refreshment of the simple mode of bathing, which now superseded indiarubber tub and everything else. We stood by the fountain ' as if ' (to use the expression in ' Murray's Handbook ') ' we were going into a shower-bath,' and the dragoman, taking a large pitcher of water, poured it over us again and again, sweeping away fleas innumerable and cooling countless bites.

Of robbers there was not a thought ; strange to say, no one objected to our travelling long after dark, which was very agreeable in the moonlight. Nor was the heat excessive, which I had feared.

There was nothing to see till just before arriving at Ephesus, when we found ourselves in a precipitous gorge —the gorge of the Cayster—which at last opened into the Ephesian plain. There is nothing in the situation of Ephesus very striking ; but for that reason it is the more difficult to form a conception of it from descriptions. The plain is formed of the two parallel ridges of Coressus and Gallesus, opening to the sea on the west, and closed by low hills on the east. But the sea has now retired so far as to be hardly visible, and the whole plain is very much like a Scotch carse with low hills rising out of it, like those which rise out of the Carse of Stirling. One of these is just at the entrance of the Cayster into the plain. Another forms the centre of the modern village. Each of these hills contains a cave, which claims to be that of the Seven Sleepers. If they were to come yet again, what another change would they see! The modern village is itself in ruins; a ruined castle on the hill; ruined baths, possibly of the Roman times, possibly those of St. John and Cerinthus; ruined churches turned into mosques, themselves ruined; the cranes of Cayster standing on their green grassy roofs in every direction. Beyond these is a third and larger hill, Mount Prion, round whose sides are gathered almost all that exists of interest from the old Ephesus.

I was quite surprised, after the depreciating remarks of books and dragomans, to see the vast extent of ruins. It took us four hours of incessant riding to see those which I am describing. These are on the ridge of Coressus; we did not see all except from the plain. They are mostly vast masses of walls, broken pillars, &c., difficult to name. But one there was absolutely indisputable. On the eastern side of Mount Prion, facing the sea, which then must have been much nearer, is to be seen the deep scoop of the theatre, its terraces of seats still to be traced in the hillside, and the ruins marking clearly the site of the stage below. On that steep ascent were piled, tier above tier, the vast multitude who for two hours shouted, 'Great is Diana of the Ephesians.' On the stage below stood, or came forward in rapid succession, to address the crowd above, Demetrius, Paul, Alexander, and the town-clerk.   Like all Greek theatres, it had commanding views of the plain, of the sea, of the harbour, of the two ridges ; and between it and the sea, in full face of the exasperated populace, rose the magnificent Temple. Whether the very massive ruins which remain there are part of it, it is difficult to say.   I should think they must be.   At any rate, the whole scene is before you, and I am sure you will feel with me the new pleasure I shall henceforward find in reading the nineteenth chapter of the Acts.

High up on the ridge of Coressus, I saw in the distance the tomb of the Virgin Mary, who, according to the General Council of Ephesus, is buried here and not at Jerusalem, though the guides here say (I suppose to prevent a conflict with the now received tradition) that it is another 'Panhagia,' not the 'Theotokos.'   It was a strange feeling to hear from the mouth of an illiterate Greek the very word on the spot where it was first invented or adopted.

One other sacred locality there is—if genuine, the most sacred of all.   I little thought, dearest, when I saw with you the supposed tombs of St. Peter and St. Paul, that I should actually stand in the tomb of St. John.   Alone of all those graves, it remains, if it be the same, unaltered. No marble, no altar, no sign of any sanctity whatever, except the remains of a few candles brought by the Greeks when they come here on the day of his festival, mark the tomb of the beloved disciple.   Whatever else it may be, it is a genuine ancient sepulchre, hewn out of the rock in the side of Mount Prion, wild flowers growing round its entrance, wild shrubs overhanging it, the grave itself —sunk in the rock—now empty and half filled with water. I think that the Greek belief is that the body itself was translated, and therefore the vacancy of the tomb would be no surprise to them. On the other hand, being in the rock, I am afraid that it can hardly be that where St. Augustine imagined that he saw the *dust* heaving over the lips of the still-living body beneath. I am not sure whether it was in the Christian congregation or in the market-place of Ephesus where the last words of the Apostle, ' Little children, love one another,' are said to have been uttered. If the latter, I saw the probable site below the theatre. Ruins exist of a church called by his name.

This was my Whit-Tuesday. I hope you will think it was well spent.

Ever yours,

A. P. STANLEY.

LXII.

A. P. S. to Mary Stanley.

CONSTANTINOPLE.

[The visit to Nicæa, of which the letter speaks, is described in the ' Life of Stanley,' vol. i. pp. 462–3.

Constantinople was taken by Mahomet II. on May 29, 1453. Constantine Palæologus, the last of the Greek emperors, died in the breach. Gibbon applies to him the noble lines of Dryden :

> As to Sebastian, let them search the field,
> And, where they find a mountain of the slain,
> Send one to climb, and, looking down beneath,
> There they will find him at his manly length,
> With his face up to heaven, in that red monument
> Which his good sword had digg'd.

S. Sophia was built by the Emperor Justinian as a Christian church. Dedicated in 537, it was partially destroyed by an earthquake in 558. The architect originally devised one or two lights above the altar ; but the emperor could not decide. Then an angel of the Lord,

R

like the emperor, with royal robes and red shoes, appeared
to the craftsman, and said : ' I will that there be a triple
light, and that the conch be made with three windows, in
the name of the Father, the Son, and the Holy Ghost.'
In the splendid monograph on S. Sophia by Mr. Lethaby
and Mr. Swainson (London, 1894), full descriptions of the
original building are quoted from contemporary writers.
The last Christian service celebrated in the church was
that of vespers on May 28, 1453, when the emperor, according to Gibbon, ' devoutly received, with tears and prayers,
the sacrament of the Holy Communion.'

Stanley arrived at Constantinople' on the eve of the
Crimean War, and he so timed his visit as to be present on
May 29, 1853, the 400th anniversary of the capture of the
city.]

Constantinople : Trinity Sunday [1853].

At 4.30 we were on deck. The sky was overcast, and
the Bithynian Olympus veiled. But on the horizon was
the long line of domes and minarets, rising sheer out of
the sea.

The first comparison that occurred to me, and has in
detail occurred ever since, was Venice. It is Venice from
the sea on an infinitely grander scale, and this will give
also the only point in which my expectations were disappointed. I had imagined a background of mountains,
as at Genoa. There is none such ; it rises at once from
the waters against the sky. But then it rises on its own
seven hills—a long line of seven hills succeeding one
another, and each distinctly marked, and almost every one
crowned by a dome and minarets as magnificent as S.
Mark's, ending in a mass of foliage surrounding the
seraglio at the extreme point. This was what gradually
unfolded itself as we drew nearer, and the nearer we
approached the more stately and magnificent the whole
scene became.

Yet, beautiful as it was thus seen, the beauty was far
increased when, on turning the Seraglio Point, we found

ourselves within the Golden Horn, with the Bosphorus in front. It has all the effect of the confluence of two splendid rivers just before their issue into the sea, and the suburbs of Galata and Pera which rise on the other side of the Golden Horn, and of Scutari and Chalcedon which rise on the other side of the Bosphorus—each on high sloping hills intermixed with masses of cypress and plane—unite the whole in one great city, each itself a situation as fine as the city of Lisbon, yet each thrown into shade by the long and magnificent sweep of the seven-hilled city itself. No! there is no doubt that for situation Constantinople is absolutely unrivalled. No view of any city that I have ever seen can compare with it for beauty and grandeur combined—not Venice, not Genoa, not Edinburgh, not Prague, not Florence. And I mention these two last because, in addition to what I may call the sea and river view, there are also land views from the cypress groves of Galata, which, with the steep declivities, the bridges over the Horn, and the masses of verdure, and the stately city rising over against you, combine with those other elements the finest features of the glorious views from St. Miniato or the Hradschin.

We landed, breakfasted, and instantly ascended the tower of Galata. It is a high and massive watch-tower, itself an object of never-failing beauty, and thence you look over the whole of the opposite city. From the tower we proceeded to the palace, the new palace of the Sultan, to see him pass in state to the mosque close by, it being Friday. We arrived just in time. Every sound was hushed as he approached. First came the four great ministers; then in a simple European dress, a long blue cloak and a red fez, Sultan Abdul-Mejîd. Nothing could be more weak or ordinary than his pale and haggard countenance; yet still there was something dignified in the absolute immovability with which, statue-like, he rode through the silent crowd, the heir of all the great recollections of the East and West, the successor of the last of the Cæsars, and the last of the Caliphs, the supreme head of the Mahometan Church. Not a sound was uttered as he went, nor, for we stayed for this also, as he returned. Only, when he was once more enclosed within the dead walls of the palace, a cheer broke out from the officers and soldiers.

Having ridden through the tiresome labyrinth of modern Constantinople, we arrived at the Seven Towers— that is, the State prison which forms part of the old Byzantine fortifications. We passed through the gates and found ourselves outside the ancient walls of the city. All our suspended admiration returned in a moment. I have tracked the walls of Norwich, York, Rome, Jerusalem— always interesting and beautiful—but never did I see walls so beautiful as those of Constantinople. They are ruined, but still nowhere destroyed, and, being a quadruple wall, the ruin is complicated and picturesque far beyond what any simpler fortification could be, overgrown with beautiful creepers, and with nothing on the outside to hinder the view of them—green turf, and cypress forests, interminable as the pine-forests of Ravenna, coming close up to them.

Two or three points, too, of great interest they included : the golden gate, now walled up, through which the emperors used to enter in triumph ; the breach, still unrepaired, through which the Turks entered ; the gate where Palæologus fell. In a Greek convent outside a strange legend embodies the famous story that it was not till the third day that the capture of the city was realised by the inhabitants. A priest of the convent was frying fish ; the messengers burst in with the fatal news. ' I would as soon believe,' he said, ' that these fish would leap out of the frying-pan into the pool whence they came.' There were seven in the pan.

They leaped out into the pool, where they have remained ever since, with their stomachs fried, their upper parts fresh. Two of them have been lost. One of them was good enough to appear to me.

Of the mosques I was glad to find that there is not the least doubt of the superiority of S. Sophia to all the rest. Of the others there is nothing to say. There are the same monotony and bareness as at Cairo ; they are rather larger, and all of them well kept. But S. Sophia you see at once has been intended for something else. Its great peculiarity as a Christian church must have been the enormous marble gallery for women, but now deserted. There are the eight green columns from the Temple of Ephesus, the eight porphyry columns from that of Baalbec. You see the three windows, placed over the altar at the command, it is said, of an angel to commemorate the Trinity. But what most rivets the attention is that, in order to accommodate the church to Mahometanism and Mecca, all the mats and niches for prayer are turned aslant in total defiance of the architecture, so that the whole building seems to have received a twist.

And now I hope that you will not be disappointed if, finding that by delaying till the Austrian steamer of Monday I should just have time to see Nicæa, I think I must do so. It would be such a satisfaction to have seen all the four general councils that I think I can hardly resist. The country too is quite safe and healthy.

Ever yours,

A. P. STANLEY.

LXIII

A. P. S. to Mrs. Arnold.

'SINAI AND PALESTINE;' ITS DEBT TO DR. ARNOLD;
ITS SUPPOSED PANTHEISM.

['Sinai and Palestine' was published in 1856.]

Canterbury: February 20, 1856.

My dear Mrs. Arnold,—Many thanks for your letter, so welcome in all its parts. It *is* a great pleasure to feel that anything which I write must come home to you and yours with usury, if it has anything worth reading, knowing, as you do, how large a portion of it is owing to the same source from which I have received so much. Not only does almost every page contain some turn of expression which else I should not have had; but the framework of the book is the result of that sense of the connection of history and geography which I have never ceased to enjoy since it was first imparted at Rugby.

I cannot help suspecting that my kind critic whom you quote must be W. Conybeare. At least he combines great kindness towards me with a horror of Pantheism which makes him see it in every bush.

I merely meant to say that the argument so often adduced in favour of the traditional localities of the New Testament—viz. that it is inconsistent with human nature to suffer local recollections of famous scenes to expire—will not hold universally. The very feelings which in ordinary circumstances fix our attention on time and place are submerged in moments of great excitement. I remember that in the 'Life' I dwelt on the fact 'that it was naturally impossible for those who are present to adjust their recollec-

tions of what passed with exactness of time and place'
(vol. ii. 330) on June 12, 1842,[2] because it seemed to me
so apt and instructive an illustration of the variations of
time which occur in the Gospel narratives of the Crucifixion.
What I there said of *time*, in this book I meant of *place*, by
the illustration from the death of Mahomet, and I certainly
think it most important to show that there is a link between
the great events of Christianity and the deepest and most
stirring feelings of our common humanity; and it would
be the denial, not the assertion, of this truth, that I should
be inclined (if I ever thought it right to use these hard,
misleading names) to call ' Pantheism.' That Mahomet
should have been a centre, not only of personal, but of
religious reverence only makes the case more apposite.

The passage, however, is open to a more serious objection—viz. that Lieutenant Burton's reasons for doubting
the identity of Mahomet's tomb appear to me, on second
thoughts, hardly of sufficient weight to deserve serious
mention.

So I answer—and you may make what use of my reply
you may think fit.

Ever yours,

A. P. STANLEY.

LXIV.

A. P. S. to Rev. Hugh Pearson.

CHILDHOOD OF BENJAMIN JOWETT—
PARIS IN MARCH 1856.

[After his return from Palestine in June 1853, Stanley
was absorbed in his duties as Canon of Canterbury, and in
the preparation of his ' Memorials of Canterbury ' (1854),
his ' Commentary on the Epistles to the Corinthians'(1855),

---

[2] The date of Dr. Arnold's death.

and his 'Sinai and Palestine' (1856). In his 'Memorials of Canterbury' was republished his essay on the Murder of Becket, which originally appeared in the 'Quarterly Review' for September 1853. In the early spring of the latter year he and his mother passed several weeks at Paris. During this visit the Crimean War was brought to an end by the peace of Paris (March 30, 1856), and the late Prince Imperial was born (March 16, 1856). 'Melchizedek' was Stanley's nickname for Jowett, whose parents were living at St. Germains.

Four distinguished Frenchmen are mentioned in the letter. François Abel Villemain is perhaps best known for his course of lectures on mediæval and eighteenth-century literature, delivered at the Faculté des Lettres (1827–30). Felicien J. C. de Saulcy was distinguished as a numismatist. He had also travelled in the Holy Land, where he discovered, as he thought, the ruins of Sodom and Gomorrah. His 'Voyage autour de la Mer Morte' was published in 1853. Alexis de Tocqueville brought out his 'Démocratie en Amérique' in 1835. Retiring from political life in 1851, he devoted himself to the studies of which his 'Ancien Régime et la Révolution' (1856) was the fruit. Guizot's political career practically closed with the fall of Louis Philippe and the establishment of the Empire. In the consistory of the Protestant Church in Paris he was a prominent figure, as well as in the Académie Française, and the Académies des Sciences morales et politiques, and des Inscriptions et Belles-lettres. In this concluding period of his life his literary activity was great. Not only did he complete his studies on the 'Great Rebellion in England,' but he published several other works on historical, political, literary, theological, and ethical subjects.

Stanley never fulfilled his purpose of writing a description of the great scene of the 'Restoration at Canterbury' in May 1660.]

Maison Valin, Champs-Elysées, Paris : March 11, 1856.

My dear H. P.,—On Saturday last I went to St. Germains, and saw—the parents of Melchizedek! a truly antique and venerable pair, each bearing a slight resemblance to the son, each with some of the qualities in him concentrated ; very kind and rapt in interest concerning him, relating

singular stories of his childhood—how deeply historical he
then was, studying Rollin's Ancient History, well versed in
Assyrian dynasties, standing long in silent contemplation
of a 'Stream of Time' suspended in his little bedroom.
This historical phase passed away into the philosophical
on his going to school, and has never returned. Deeply
musical also, he listens with pleasure to Beethoven played
by his sister, while at work, and even proposes corrections.
I went with the aged father to visit the tomb of James II.,
which I doubt whether he had seen before. 'Regis cineri
regia pietas'—*i.e.* to James II. by George IV. What an
esprit de corps there is in royalty! How they all cling
together!

The imperial programme is, I am told, thought ridiculous, and the nomination of 'Gouvernante pour les enfants
de France' an absurd aping of the ancient dynasty. The
Rue Vivienne was inaccessibly blocked with a crowd
extending the whole street's length, to see the baby's
clothes. I stepped into an adjacent shop for a bun. 'C'est
le petit empereur qui vient,' said the bun woman ; 'on ne
sait pas si ce sera prince ou princesse, et on a fait des
coiffures pour toutes sortes de sexes.' The Empress
expects the confinement on the 20th, and is terribly
alarmed.

Villemain and De Saulcy called together yesterday ;
the one filled with admiration at 'Becket,' and the other at
'Sinai and Palestine.' Tocqueville has also crossed the
scene. All these persons, I repeat, more agreeable than
their English parallels. The two great topics of discourse
are the appearance of a certain Ristori as Medea, and the
late reception of the Duc de Broglie into the Academy.
You saw the speech of the emperor to him : 'I trust that
the same justice which you have rendered to the 18 Bru-
maire will be rendered by your grandson to the 2 December.'

To which the Duke, without addition of ' Sire ' or the like, replied, ' L'histoire prononcera.'   In the address he drew an elaborate likeness of the emperor under the character of Mazarin which drew forth a shriek of applause from the audience. ' Il y avait là toute l'aristocratie de race et toute l'aristocratie d'intelligence,' and all opposed to your Beloved One.

The great Guizot has presented me with ' Richard Cromwell.' Do read Mazarin's letters on the death of Oliver, plunged in the deepest affliction. It appears that the great scene of the Restoration on May 25–28 was at Canterbury.   I shall certainly describe it some day.

The aforesaid Guizot I heard the other day make a speech for the Bible Society, certainly powerful, and delivered under the shadow of a crucifix, which would, I suppose, in the eyes of our Evangelicals, have destroyed its whole efficacy.

Ever yours,
A. P. STANLEY.

LXV.

A. P. S. to Mrs. Stanley.

GLENCOE.

[Stanley, his mother, and his sister Mary started in August 1856 on a tour through Scotland. Mrs. Stanley did not go with her son and daughter to Skye and Glencoe, but rejoined them at a later stage of the tour.

By an accident the Macdonalds of Glencoe gave in their submission to King William III. a few days too late to claim the proffered pardon.

On January 16, 1692, King William signed an order, ending: ' If McEan of Glencoe and that trybe can be well separated from the rest, it will be a proper vindication of the public justice to extirpate that sect of thieves.' The massacre was carried out by Campbell of Glenlyon in the early morning of February 13, 1692.]

Fort William : August 28, 1856.

My dearest Mother,—Mary will have told you generally of our journey thus far. It has been perfectly successful, though I wish H. P. had been here for the third place. I was curious to see Glencoe, after Macaulay's account. I cannot quite call to mind how far he gives the details. But it strikes me that it is capable of a much better description than he has given of it.

Taking it from the western end, there is first the peaceful smiling valley, the Coe tumbling through in gentle waterfalls, grass fields and pine-trees down to the edge of the sea-inlet of Loch Leven. In this salt lake is a group of islands, on the largest of which is an old chapel in the midst of the burial-ground of the MacDonalds, whose bodies were always brought to the island, to be safe from the wolves which then infested all the mainland. Close by the water-edge, called from its situation 'Invercoe' (the Coe's mouth), is the ruin of the summer residence of the Chief of Glencoe. This flat part of the valley is the only portion now inhabited, but then there were settlements high up in the hills on each side.

The valley divides at the end into two recesses. The northern recess contains a lake or tarn, where one of the chiefs was led out to be killed, and escaped by throwing his plaid over the men's faces and rushing away. And still farther up is a tarn, high in the hills, called the 'thieves' correy,' or ' MacDonald's storehouse,' where the clans used to drive their stolen cattle. It is curious as being exactly like one belonging to the Johnstone clan at the head of Annandale, which (for the same reason) is called 'the beef-tub.'

In the southern recess was the winter residence of the old chief himself, who was there at the time of the massacre, and was there killed. All this we heard, partly from a woman whose grandfather had been a boy at the time, partly from a Captain Sutherland, who lives all the year round in a modern house at Invercoe, attending on a sister, partially deranged, whom we also met in the valley. One story too the woman told us, which I never heard before. A solitary tree in the lower part of the valley marks the place where one of the soldiers, anxious to save his hosts, but fearing to break his oath of secrecy, said to a STONE, on the eve of the massacre, 'If I were this stone, I would not stay here to-night.' If I were a Scotsman, what a beautiful subject the history of Scotland would be!

I shall calculate on finding you at Inverary on Friday morning. I think it just possible that, as H. P.'s joining us now seems very doubtful, we may not stay beyond Tuesday, and in that case I should be ready to be at Inverary on Thursday night, but any way on Friday.

Ever yours,
A. P. STANLEY.

LXVI.

A. P. S. to the Hon. Louisa Stanley.

SKYE; THE BURIAL-PLACE OF THE M'NABS; DUNNOTTAR CASTLE.

[Louisa Dorothea Stanley was the daughter of Sir John Stanley, Bart., first Lord Stanley of Alderley, and Arthur Stanley's first cousin. Although his senior by fifteen years, her sprightliness, wit, enthusiasm, and keenness of interest made her a delightful and stimulating companion. Whenever Stanley had met with any unusual experience or seen anything that was peculiarly striking, he made a point of describing it by letter or word of mouth to his cousin Louisa. An excellent Spanish scholar, she translated Cervantes' romance 'Persiles and Sigismunda' into English. (See LXXVIII.) In the park at Alderley was an old deer-house, with four turrets overlooking the park, the mere, and the wood. To these turrets the Stanley sisters used to retire to read, and indulge in the sentimental meditations of those days. Her hours of retirement were put by Louisa Stanley to such good use that the poet Rogers said she was better read in English poetry than any of his friends or acquaintances. Into Stanley's theological life she did not enter ; but with all his other interests and pursuits she keenly sympathised.

Scott's description of Coruisk will be found in the 'Lord of the Isles' (Canto III. stanzas 12–15).

> For rarely human eye has known
> A scene so stern as that dread lake,
>   With its dark ledge of barren stone.
> Seems that primeval earthquake's sway
> Hath rent a strange and shatter'd way
>   Through the rude bosom of the hill,
> And that each naked precipice,
> Sable ravine, and dark abyss,
>   Tells of the outrage still.

Stanley's new interest in the Trinity House arose from the fact that he had just preached the annual sermon before the Elder Brethren on Trinity Sunday.

Killin, at the junction of the Lochay and the Dochart, the two principal feeders of Loch Tay, is sometimes derived from Kil Fin—*i.e.* the cell of Fingal—who, as Stanley says, is traditionally buried there. At the western end of Glen Dochart, where it runs into Strath Fillan, is 'St. Fillan's blessed well,' celebrated for its supposed cure of epilepsy.

Dunnottar Castle, near Stonehaven in Kincardineshire, is the place where Scott met Robert Paterson, the original of 'Old Mortality.' In 1685, when Argyle had landed on the coast of Scotland, and Monmouth meditated an invasion of the west of England, the Privy Council of Scotland arrested more than 200 persons in the western and southern provinces, who might, it was feared, prove hostile to the Government from their religious principles. Driven northwards like a herd of bullocks, they were confined in the 'Whigs' vault' at Dunnottar Castle. Their sufferings on the way and in prison are described in Wodrow's 'History of the Sufferings of the Church of Scotland' (book iii. c. ix.).

The Regalia of Scotland were deposited here in 1641.

Ten years later, when the Castle was closely besieged by the English Army under General Lambert, they were removed by Mrs. Granger, the wife of a neighbouring minister, and hidden either in the manse or under the pulpit. In 1660 they were restored to the Government.]

September 14, 1856.

My dear Louisa,—What that very witty king James VI. (of this country) said of Fife may be said of Skye, that it is a 'grey suit with a gilt fringe,' only that in Skye the fringe is made, not of grand castles but of strange rocks. And moreover the fringe is so tattered and worn away that it is only at the extremities of N.W. and S.E., Quiraing and Coruisk, that you see anything to repay you for the long wanderings over flat bog and moor in the interior of the island. Quiraing is or was a 'beef-tub' (you know what a 'beef-tub' is in the language of the borderers?) on an immense scale. Coruisk—that is, 'the kettle' (corry) 'of water' (*uisk*, for 'whisky,' is only the Gaelic for 'water')—is awfully desolate, though not so absolutely sterile as Walter Scott described. That sterility can be seen only at Mount Sinai. The rocks which surround it are black in colour, and fantastic in shape, and are 'hypersthene,' a barbarous word, which is used to express the most primitive of all primeval formations, and of which Skye is the only specimen in the United Kingdom. This made me regard them with a peculiar veneration.

Let us now leave Skye and fly past the barren points of Ardnamurchan, on which a lighthouse has been lately erected by the Trinity House, on whose works I now look with new interest. An old Highland woman, who had lost her way amongst these desert hills and was benighted, saw through the darkness a celestial splendour such as she had never seen before. She approached, found a tower, and a winding staircase, up which she toiled, believing that she had found the way to heaven. This impression was fully confirmed when, at the summit, she suddenly found herself amidst the dazzling blaze of reflectors, amongst which was a man, whom, taking to be an angel, she asked in Gaelic whether this was indeed 'the Island of the Brave' (this is the Gaelic for Heaven). A torrent of Gaelic oaths convinced her that she was mistaken.

On coming over Glencroe, I saw with pleasure the stone inscribed ' Rest and be thankful.' It is the motto which I wish to be adopted by the Church of England, or any place where we may rest in peace without fighting with our neighbours.

Now look at your map of Scotland, and you will see the river Dochart flowing gently from west to east through a somewhat tame, prosaic valley. Suddenly, just before it reaches the river Lochay, and at the point where they both fall into Loch Tay, the scene changes as if by magic. The smooth stream breaks down a succession of crystal rapids ; deep woods fringe the hillsides ; high mountains shoot up beyond. This is Kil Lin, ' the cell of the waterfall.' It is the same kind of beautiful metamorphosis that the Nile undergoes at Philæ, and, like Philæ, it has, doubtless in consequence, become, as its name implies, an ancient sanctuary, the burial-place of ancient chiefs as far back as history extends. Here (not Osiris but) Fingal lies buried somewhere, lulled to rest by these rushing waters. And under the walls of old Finlarig Castle, by the side of the Lochay, are pushed into the pigeon-holes of a miserable funeral upper-storied vault the Breadalbanes, Marquis and Marchioness, all above ground, yet still in a green beautiful spot, approached by a long avenue of beeches, such as seem the glory of this country—most glorious in the ghostlike avenue planted by Gillespie Grummoch at Inverary.

But the true charm of Killin belongs to the burial-place

of the McNabs. They lie in an island in the midst of the
Dochart rapids, firs and beeches and birches all embowering
the cemetery. An aged female guides you to it, whose
every word is poetical. The avenue to the tombs overarches
a green carpet of moss. 'The high folk from London,' she
said, 'tell me that I should gather it up in a basket, and
give it to the Queen for the carpet of her house.' Inside
a rude chapel lie in one division 'the lower gentry,' in
another 'the high chiefs;' the chief himself is always laid
under a rude stone slab, carved with the figure of a warrior.
'Many a time have I seen it lifted,' she said. 'It was found
by the chief, years ago, on the top of Ben Lawers, and he
put it on his shoulders and carried it down here, and underneath it from that time the chiefs have been laid.' A head-
stone hard by contains the arms of the McNabs.[3] 'Look!'
she said, pointing to the several parts; 'in old times, when
there were no coaches rinning along the roads, the McNabs
in Kinnell Castle on Loch Tay had all their provisions
brought from Perth for New Year's Day. But there was a
robber who lived on an island in Loch Earn, who came out
and stopped the carts. So one New Year's Eve the Lady
at Kinnell said, "Now let us see whether the laird is lord."
They understood what she meant, and the chief carried a *boat*
(you see the boat) to Loch Earn, and it was by moonlight
(and that's the meaning of the moon), and he put the helmet
on his head (there it is), for he did not know what weapon
the robber might have. And he landed on the island and
knocked at the gate, and the robber answered from within,
"Wha's there?" and he said, "Wha should it be but John
McNab?" The robber was taken, and McNab cut off his
head (there you see it!), and brought it home to the lady,
and the meaning of the words above that they took from
that is, "Don't be afraid!"'

> [3] Here the MS. contains a rough sketch of the McNab arms.

'Well,' I said, as I went down the mossy avenue, 'I had rather be buried here than with the Breadalbanes.' 'Yes, she said, 'here it is all natural. It is a natural island. You see the water of Dochart and the water of Lochay meeting round it natural and no fause work. The Scripture says, "Dust we are, and to dust we shall return," and it is better to be laid here in dust and earth, all natural-like, than in yon holes there that they put men into.'

St. Fillan's was a combination of all the peculiar beauties of Scotland. Dark mountains, rushing brown streams, masses of rock and heather, crowned by pines, embowered in birch, all grouping round an exquisitely broken hill, where, beside his healing water, that ancient Saint had his cell.

September 23.

Perhaps you heard of my rising at break of day to visit from Stonehaven the ruins of Dunnottar Castle, a place which for many years I have desired to see, and which latterly in this tour had acquired a new interest in my eyes. For at Dumfries I fell in with one of the gravestones of the Covenanters, and have ever since been possessed with the passion of 'Old Mortality:' and at Dunnottar many of them were shut up. I had to rouse the guide from his slumbers, which shocked me when I found that he was an aged creature of eighty-six; but I was consoled by finding that he walked three miles every day to take up his abode in the castle for the sake of visitors, and so was this day spared by the ride in my dog-cart. It is an amphibious castle, as its name indicates, 'the hill of the otter,' running out into the sea, and all but parted from the mainland by a ravine, up and down which I and my venerable guide had to scramble. Wallace, the Regalia, the Covenanters, were the ghosts which I saw in these tattered walls. The solitary gravestone of the prisoners 'whose names,' says the

S

epitaph, 'we have not gotten,' is that where Walter Scott met the real 'Old Mortality.'

Affectionately yours,

A. P. STANLEY.

LXVII.

A. P. S. to Rev. Hugh Pearson.

SPURGEON AS A PREACHER.

[In December 1856 Stanley was appointed Regius Professor of Ecclesiastical History at Oxford. He did not, however, resign his Canonry at Canterbury till 1858. His three introductory lectures were delivered in February 1857. (See 'Life,' vol. i. ch. xv.) Spurgeon was at this time preaching in the New Park Street Chapel. The Metropolitan Tabernacle was not built till 1859–61.]

6 Grosvenor Crescent, London :
March 31, 1857.

My dear H. P.,—I have intended day after day to write to you of Spurgeon. On reflection I think it less good than when I heard it ; but briefly.

The congregation was magnificent—10,000—and although secular and unattractive before the service began exceedingly devout and decorous as soon as Spurgeon appeared, joining in the hymn with great and general fervour.

His exposition of a chapter in Isaiah, and of his own doctrine consequent therefrom, I thought very meagre, with a few coarse and irreverent expressions. The discourse was on 'Wist ye not that I *must* be about my Father's business ? ' divided into three parts. Firstly, the Life of Christ, as Example, Establishment, Expiation, not particularly good, but not offensive ; a slight attempt to act the Crucifixion was the only theatrical part. Secondly, application of it to us ; ' Tell me why Christianity has failed

to do its work in the world.   Mahomet the Impostor in
the street of Mecca in a few years collected disciples ; at
the end of a century, a million scimitars flashed from
their scabbards at the command of the Caliphs. . . . You,
my friend in the gallery, have your business in town, a
small farm in the country, a snug investment for old age,
which you leave to your bailiff.   The world is your shop ;
your religion is that little farm.   Not that I wish to see a
man bring out his religion always.   *I hate cant.*   I hate to
see a man bring out his tracts on his counter.   Some
minister came to me the other day, and said : " Brother,
let us pray together."   I said, " I like to do my praying
alone." '

' When I was converted, I was full of fervour ; that is
all passed away ; I wish it might return.   We must dedicate
ourselves entirely.   Once a slanderous report arose against
my character.   I fell on my knees and said, What! lose
that which I most value, my reputation !   Yes, this too I
sacrifice.

Some one says : ' I have no talents.'   Turning to one
side of the building : ' Brother, have you a child ?   That
is your opportunity.'   Turning to the other side : ' Sister,
have you a husband who ill-treats you ?   He is your opportunity of usefulness.'   To another side : ' You say, " I am
very ill ; I have not left my bed till to-day."   That is your
opportunity.'

These are, I think, the best points.   He is not to be
compared for real ability or effect to Evans ; no pathos ;
a commonplace countenance ; a very powerful but not
unpleasing voice.   Still a useful, humorous, sagacious
discourse.

I hope to go to Canterbury on Monday for a fortnight.   Ever yours,

                                A. P. STANLEY.

LXVIII.

A. P. S. to Mrs. Arnold.

HIS WORK AS REGIUS PROFESSOR AT OXFORD.

[In October 1856 Stanley was appointed Examining
Chaplain to the new Bishop of London, Dr. Tait. It is to
the examination of candidates for Holy Orders that he
refers in the opening sentence of the following letter.
His colleague was the Rev. G. E. L. Cotton, formerly an
Assistant Master at Rugby, at this time Head-master of
Marlborough, and subsequently Bishop of Calcutta.

Stanley had begun his lectures at Oxford as Regius
Professor of Ecclesiastical History in February 1857.
During term he lodged at 115 High Street, in the rooms
which Dr. Arnold had occupied before his marriage, as
Fellow of Oriel College. Matthew Arnold, the eldest sòn
of Dr. Arnold, was elected Professor of Poetry at Oxford
in 1857.

The two inscriptions in Whippingham Church to
William Arnold and his son the Rev. M. Arnold, the father
and brother of Dr. Arnold, run as follows:

'Sacred to the Memory of Wᵐ Arnold, Esq., late Collector of His Majesty's Customs in the Port of Cowes, Isle
of Wight,—a man, who by his amiable as well as his faithful discharge of his Duty in his public Station and in his
private Character, justly entitled himself to the warmest
Respect, Esteem and Affection by all who were occasionally or permanently connected with him in Business,
Society, or domestic Ties. The Public, his Friends and
his Family feel and deplore the Loss sustained by his
Death on the 3ʳᵈ March, 1801, aged 55.'

'Sacred to the Memory of the Revᵈ. Matthew Arnold,
B.D., second son of Wᵐ. Arnold, Esq. (late of Slatwoods),
Chaplain to His Majesty's Forces at Gosport, and Fellow
of Corpus Christi College, Oxford, who was unfortunately
drowned in Stokes Bay, Thursday, May 18ᵗʰ, 1820, aged 35.'

In August 1857 the Divorce and Matrimonial Causes
Bill, by which the Divorce Court was established, was
for the third time introduced as a Government measure.

Dr. Tait voted for the Bill. (See ' Life of Archbishop Tait,' vol. i. 210–14.)

' Tom Brown's Schooldays' was published in 1856.]

June 10, 1857:
6 Grosvenor Crescent, London.

My dear Mrs. Arnold,—I was so busy when your letter arrived, in the midst of the London Examinations, that I could not answer at once ; and now you have my letter, I hope, on the day that always brings us together in thought.

You would, I knew, be interested by my Oxford lectures ; it was quite as pleasant as I could have expected. There is, as you know, a distracted and irresponsive atmosphere in Oxford that prevents any work there from being absolutely satisfactory, and at the present time the air is choked with the dust flying about from the sweepings of the recent changes, like the Interpreter's house in the ' Pilgrim's Progress.' Still it was very agreeable once more to speak to young men, and also to have the opportunity of putting my own thoughts in order.

Matt's election was an unmixed pleasure, and will be so to him. You heard, I dare say, that he spent two days with me in my lodgings at Wyatt's, I occupying the very rooms which you knew so well. Wyatt retained a most grateful recollection of the name, and was quite delighted to welcome Matt for his father's sake. One letter from him he had, on the occasion of old Mrs. Wyatt's death. By the way, I think I never told you that, being by accident in the Isle of Wight for a day or two at Easter, I went to Whippingham Church and saw the tablets put up to old Mr. Arnold and Matthew A., a strange kind of unconsciousness about them, like Dr. Clarke's account of Sebastopol and Balaclava before they had become famous.

From Oxford I came up to London, after my month's

lectures, for my week's examination.   Cotton, as perhaps you know, is now my colleague, and lightened my labour considerably.   As at the Christmas ordination, so now, I was much struck by the power of the Bishop's addresses to the candidates.   And again, chiefly no doubt from the pleasure of finding such almost complete harmony, I found the work very pleasant and most interesting.   I am greatly impressed with the importance of the situation when Bishop and Chaplain can work heartily together.

I fully go along with the Bishop in his speeches on the Divorce Bill.   There have been some points where he must seem to have erred in his dealings with the High Church party.   But on the whole he has shown great toleration and judgment, and I cannot but think that these are qualities which increase of years in office will render more easy.

Of course you have read ' Tom Browne ' (*sic*).   I have just finished it.   The special phase of life described is one of which I remember or knew but little ; and I think that here and there a dash of Kingsleyism comes in, not akin to the general simplicity of the book or the subject.   But the descriptions of what I do remember strike me as wonderfully, startlingly accurate, and how remarkable is the account of the reception of the news of the death !   In this, as in so many other parts, so exactly my own feelings reproduced in a quarter so wholly new and different.   What a testimony to the character which could produce an impression so precisely alike in characters so wholly unlike !   Ever yours,

A. P. STANLEY.

On June 19 I hope to go to Canterbury, and on July 15 to Moscow.

LXIX.

A. P. S. to Mrs. Stanley.

STOCKHOLM AND UPSALA.

[One of the courses of lectures which Stanley proposed to deliver at Oxford as Professor of Ecclesiastical History was on the Eastern Church. In order to study the Greek Church he determined to visit Russia, passing through Sweden on his way to St. Petersburg. He left England in July 1857, accompanied by 'young Arthur Butler' (now the Rev. A. G. Butler, of Oriel College, Oxford). The three following letters were written on this tour. (See 'Life,' vol. i. ch. xv.)

A brief chronology of Swedish History may be useful as a key to Stanley's descriptions.

Sweden, in the earliest stages of its history, recognised as its ruler the priest-king of the great temple of Woden at Sigtuna. It accepted Christianity in the reign of St. Eric (IX.), 1150-60.

By the union of Calmar (1397) Sweden was united to the crown of Denmark. But the Swedes were in constant revolt against their rulers, and, after a struggle of 130 years, under the leadership of Gustavus Vasa expelled the Danes from the country. Gustavus Vasa was crowned King of Sweden in 1523, and the throne, hitherto elective, was declared hereditary in his family. He was succeeded in 1560 by his son Eric XIV., who, eight years later, was deposed by his brother, John III. Sigismund (1592), the son of John, was deposed in 1600 by his uncle, Charles IX., and the Protestant party. Gustavus Adolphus, son of Charles IX., and grandson of Gustavus Vasa (1611–32), headed the German Protestants against the Catholic League, and was killed at Lützen (November 6, 1632). His daughter and successor, Christina, resigned the throne to her cousin, Charles X., in 1654. The grandson of the latter sovereign, Charles XII., was killed at Fredrikshall in 1718, while invading Norway.

Ulfilas, the Arian missionary bishop (311–81), carried on his labours among the Goths in Lower Mœsia at the foot of the Balkan range. The Upsala manuscript of his version of portions of the New Testament is called the

Codex Argenteus, from the silver letters in which it was written. It was purchased at the death of Vossius, to whom it belonged, and presented to Upsala by the Swedish Chancellor about 1670.   Ulfilas has been called 'the father of Teutonic literature,' and his translation is the earliest written example of the Mœso-Gothic language.]

Stockholm: July 20, 1857.

My dearest Mother,—We got this morning the first good view we have had of the place, from a height above the town, called (it is supposed from its Pisgah view) the 'Hill of Moses.' It is an entirely different situation to what I had expected. It is in no sense a maritime town. I had conceived it like Venice, planted on a group of islands in the open sea. On the contrary, the sea is far away, out of sight.

Stockholm, the original 'holm,' or island, to which its founder was guided by the 'stock,' or log, which floated before him, was a granite rock, dividing the great inland Malar lake from the long winding fiord which advances to meet the lake from the distant Baltic. This granite rock, or rocks—for there are two—contained, till within the last two hundred years, the whole capital, and is still called 'the City,' as in the parallel case of London, and still retains the palace and public buildings. It is thus like a city in the midst of a very large river, by whichever side it is approached, the Malar lake and the inlet from the Baltic being about the same size, and lined, each of them, with low hills covered with wood of stunted oak and birch. Its resemblance therefore to Venice is very slight ; and it would be like Constantinople, if only Constantinople, instead of being where it is on the opening of the Bosphorus into the Sea of Marmora, were on an island high up in the middle of the Bosphorus. Here the beauty consists in the two long approaches, as up wide green avenues.

Gradually the town extended itself, first on the south, and then on the north side of the deep channel in which it lies, and it is from these that the best view is had of the whole situation. As elsewhere in Sweden, the granite rock is everywhere seen rising to the surface. Even in the midst of the streets it appears as the foundation of the houses, and it is from their being so built that the streets are often extremely steep, the sharp declivities only just concealed by the bad pavement.

I have no wish to stay here, and shall be as glad as Queen Christina when we are fairly out of Sweden. Gustavus Vasa, Gustavus Adolphus, and Charles XII. have every possible change rung upon them. There are curious relics of Charles XII.—his swinging cradle as a child ; the blue coat which he wore, exactly like what appears in his pictures, long-waisted and stiff ; and the greatcoat which he wore at Fredrikshall, besprinkled with the mud of the fall when he received his death-wound. He, with most of the Swedish kings, is buried in what is far the most interesting building in Stockholm—the Ritterholm Church—a kind of St. George's Chapel of the Order of the Seraphim—the Swedish Order of the Garter, of which the collar is made of alternate crosses and seraphs' faces. One of the transepts is devoted to Gustavus Adolphus, the other to Charles XII. The sarcophagus of each lies under a thick canopy of banners, won by each in their respective wars. Gustavus Vasa's tomb we shall see at Upsala. On the tombstones of some of the lesser persons in the church are some of the strange emblems carved on the Iona gravestones—*scissors,* just the same, and equally without any known explanation.

Yesterday we went to the Diet. The three Lower Houses sit in the three stories of a large building adjoining the House of Lords. We passed about ten minutes in each. Each House was occupied with the same question—nothing of supreme importance, but enough apparently to command a full attendance.

It was a very curious sight to pass thus rapidly in review the four stages of the society of a whole nation, occupied in precisely the same act each in its own way. First were the clergy. They were in black, and wore bands ; but otherwise had no official dress. A bishop, in the absence of the Archbishop, presided. They sate motionless, listened attentively, looked respectable, and those who spoke, spoke deliberately, and, as seems to be the case with the Swedish clergy, very distinctly. They might, but for their torpidity, have passed for the Lower House of Convocation. Next, the citizens, the middle class. This was the most animated. A Swedish Roebuck was holding forth somewhat energetically ; one or two were talking earnestly to their neighbours, evidently feeling themselves to be of some importance. Thirdly, the peasants. These were the most interesting—farmers or labourers, rustic in dress, appearance, beards, faces, speech, slowly dragging out their thoughts. Fourthly, the nobles or gentry. They sate in a splendid hall, covered with coats-of-arms. It struck me that the professional jealousies must be a great hindrance to legislation.

This morning (Sunday) we went to one of the large churches. It was a Sacrament Sunday, and accordingly the clergyman was in full costume—a crimson velvet cope embroidered with a silver cross behind—standing right in front of the altar. Everything else was purely Protestant, hymns and sermon occupying the greater part. But the few liturgical prayers that were read struck me as very impressive, and they were admirably read. The abrupt beginning—'Holy, Holy, Holy, Lord God Almighty!' —had a grand effect. The church was crowded, and I could not help thinking that any attempt to break up the attachment to such a worship would be extremely hazardous.

July 30.—Since I began this letter we have been perpetually on the move.

1. *Gripsholm.*—It is a fortress, built by Gustavus Vasa on the property of a rich old merchant, Bo Jonsson Grip, who crosses our path from time to time—most remarkably in the Ritterholm Church, where he caught an adversary, who had fled to the altar and held so fast to it that he could only be torn away by breaking the altar, and then Grip hewed him into twelve pieces, in commemoration of which double fracture the pavement remains broken to this day. But to return to Gripsholm. It stands about forty miles from Stockholm, on the shore of the everlasting Malar lake, which is the heart of Swedish history, and whose arteries run in and out of the country in such a way that you can never leave Stockholm except by one of them. Two of the Swedish kings were imprisoned in it—Gustavus Vasa's two eccentric sons. First John, who was imprisoned by Eric in a very pleasant apartment, in one corner of which John's son Sigismund was born; then Eric, who was imprisoned by John in a dismal dungeon, surrounded by a gallery, from which he was constantly surveyed by the guards, a curious monument of family quarrels multiplying with themselves.

Eric was one of Elizabeth's suitors, and she had to refuse him in English, French, and Latin before she could make him understand that his suit was hopeless. John was the Charles I. of the Swedish Church—a Laudian, Puseyite king, who tried to bring it halfway back to Rome—and his son Sigismund was its James II., abdicating because he became a complete Roman Catholic.

The rest of the castle is filled with historical portraits— the whole Swedish history—a little Versailles. The three great kings, Gustavus Vasa, Gustavus Adolphus, and Charles XII., I now know perfectly.   Another remarkable group was a succession of four archbishops of Upsala in the same family, a father and three sons.   One room was occupied entirely by the contemporary sovereigns of Gustavus Vasa, Henry VIII., Elizabeth, Charles V., and all the German Landgraves and Electors of the Reformation. The practice has been followed since in the other Swedish palaces, the present king having one of the same kind, including Victoria Regina.   But in the case of Gustavus Vasa it brings before one what one is always tempted to forget, that, being as he is almost the founder of the Swedish nation, and as much involved in wild escapes and strange vicissitudes as Alfred or Wallace, he is yet quite a modern sovereign, so that, as you will presently hear, his recollections and monuments are all authentic as of yesterday.

2. *Upsala.*—Again up another branch of the Malar lake. On the way we passed Sigtuna, the old capital of Sweden, whence the ' Stock ' was set afloat which brought them to Stockholm.   Nothing remains but an old square tower of unknown antiquity.   It is said to be the 'town' of 'Sig,' another name of Odin.   Next was the castle of the Brahe family.   Finally, through a long canal, we reached Upsala.

Upsala, the real old Upsala, bears the same relation to the present Upsala that old Sarum bears to Salisbury.   It is three miles distant   Let us go there first.   It is a wide, dreary plain, broken by a low line of hillocks.   Under these hillocks is all that remains of Old Upsala, the sacred city of Odin, the scene of the most ancient pagan worship of Sweden.   The hills of which I spoke assume a more definite shape as they approach this point.   Three, perhaps more, are evidently huge barrows, and are called the graves of Thor, Freya, and Odin.   We stood upon the grave of Odin. Close underneath is an old square tower, now attached to the village church, but, like that of Sigtuna, said to belong to the times of remote antiquity ; if so, the old pagan temple. It contains inside a rude wooden image, said to be the god Thor. Groups of trees, here alone in the bare plain, clustered round the hill, relics, or at least memorials, of the ancient sacred grove, and, by a curious coincidence, most of them ash trees, the old sacred tree of Scandinavia, ' Yg-drasil.' Wide and vast lay the plain all round, broken here and there, as everywhere in Sweden, by masses of grey granite, like the bones of the Scandinavian giant from whose limbs the earth was made.

It was a dark stormy evening, and looming through the mist on the only other height that rose above the level view were visible the castle and cathedral of the Upsala of Christian and historical times. It is a most interesting spot, the more than St. Martin's hill of a hardly less striking Canterbury.

To this we will now proceed. In fact, we saw it first. The town itself is perfectly devoid of interest—straight streets and roads running through it, without a vestige of architectural ornament. The three attractions are seen in almost every view of it.

First, the castle—built by Gustavus Vasa after the type of all his castles—massive red brick, with four round towers. It stands on a commanding height, overhanging the cathedral—type of the royal supremacy which Gustavus established over the Swedish Church.

Secondly, on a lower stage, the University Library. It has no outward charm. Its great treasure is the MS. of the translation of the Bible by the Arian Gothic Bishop, Ulfilas, for the Gothic tribes, the oldest fragment of the German language now existing in the world. Its presence in the Upsala Library is accidental ; but there could not be a place more fitted to receive the instrument of the first conversion of the Gothic tribes than the metropolitical city of 'the kingdom of the Swedes, Goths, and Vandals.'

Thirdly, on a lower stage again, the cathedral and its precincts. Externally the cathedral is rather strange than beautiful—of the usual red brick, though with stone porches, and its towers of purple copper, as, again, most of the Swedish towers, from the copper mines of Dalecarlia. But it is very large, and, standing in a wide open space, has an imposing appearance. There are trees about it, like the Close at Norwich. A little daughter or really mother church, of greater age, stands near, and the whole is encompassed by what were the canonical houses, but now occupied by the University. In one of them is a complete succession of portraits of the Swedish kings; in another, of the archbishops of Upsala from 1600 downwards. The interior of the cathedral, though whitewashed, according to the Swedish taste which is now what it was in England fifty years ago, is both grand and curious. It is a remarkable mixture of English, Genevan, and Roman Catholic. On the one hand, a magnificent crucifix stands right over the altar; on the other hand the Archbishop has no throne—merely a seat in a common pew.

There are many lesser monuments of interest; but the four chief are: *S. Eric,* still preserved in his silver shrine, on the north of the altar; *John III.,* the half Roman-Catholic king, a beautiful Italian monument, with his recumbent figure, the sceptre which he held in his hand broken off by Gustavus III. to restore to his brother Eric, on whose tomb we shall see it; *Gustavus Vasa,* a magnificent tomb, in the Lady Chapel—the walls painted with frescoes of his life, the tomb with all the emblems of the various provinces of Sweden, he himself lying between his two wives.

In the sacristy were the splendid vestments and mitre

of the Archbishop. Our guide was greatly surprised to hear that the English bishops wore no mitres;—'*Ja so!*' the universal Swedish expression, used, with every variety of intonation, to indicate astonishment, grief, indignation, incredulity, satisfaction, &c. &c.

I had left Stockholm with a bad headache; but it was completely cured by the interest of Upsala. I went on with the round from 2 to 6; then drove three miles to Old Upsala; then, leaving the companions, drove alone, seven miles, to the *Mora Stan*, 'the Stone of the moor,' where the old kings of Sweden were crowned. Except the wild *moor* in which the fragments lay, there was nothing of special interest. But it was curious to see the counterpart of Kingstone upon Thames, and the Stone of Scone. It has no connection with the Vasa dynasty. When Gustavus addressed the people of Upsala, in behalf of the Reformation, it was from the far grander position of the grove of Odin.

This was, unquestionably, the most important day of the tour. Ever yours,

A. P. S.

LXX.

A. P. S. to Mrs. Stanley.

THE METROPOLITAN OF MOSCOW; THE FAIR AT NIJNI NOVGOROD.

Nijni Novgorod : Aug. 20 (N.S.).

Here we are at the furthest point of our journey—at the furthest point eastward that I have ever reached, except in Palestine—and not very far short of Jerusalem. It was a wearisome journey, though done as comfortably as it could be under the circumstances. We had an extra-

diligence, containing two outside and two inside places, so
that there was every opportunity for change. We left Moscow at 6 P.M. on Monday and arrived at noon on Wednesday.

The only point of interest on the road was Vladimir,
one of the old capitals of Russia. Whilst they were dining
I flew in a droshky to see the silver tombs of three of the
Grand Princes of Vladimir.

The town of Nijni Novgorod (it is Lower Novgorod—
exactly 'Newcastle-under-Lyne') is stretched along a high
hill above the river Oka, and the farthest point of this hill,
crowned by its Kremlin, overlooks the confluence with the
immense Volga, the largest of European rivers, rolling
steadily on towards the Caspian Sea. Beyond it lies a
boundless plain of corn and forest. There is a striking
contrast between the profound stillness of the Volga, and
the animation of the Oka crammed with shipping, and
its banks covered with the booths and streets of the great
fair.

We had a letter from Mouravieff, the historian, to his
brother, the Governor, who lives in a house above the
bazaars to keep order during the fair. He is a thoroughly
honest, straightforward old soldier, with a benevolent old
wife of the same kind. Like most Russian laymen that I
have seen, he entered with far more zeal than ordinary laymen, either in France or England, into religious questions,
and entirely baffled me (or rather would have done so,
had I not caught a glimpse of something concerning it in
a collection of documents on the Swedish Church that I
borrowed at Stockholm) by asking me questions about the
'New Jerusalem' in England—*i.e.*, as it appeared, the
Swedenborgians.

The main characteristics of the country, which probably
is the same in these 260 miles as anywhere else, are—first,
the broad straight road—broad as a river, straight as an

arrow—over every undulation for miles and miles, without a turn ; secondly, scattered along the side, from time to time, wooden houses, like Swiss *chalets* without their picturesqueness.   Along this road, by the side of these houses, come in their carts, or sit with their wives and children, the Russian peasants.   Nothing can be simpler, or more easily described, than their costume—a bright crimson shirt, pulled out from under their waistcoats (if they have one) over their trousers, which again are stuffed into their large boots. This, with a good flaxen head of hair and a red beard, is almost universal.

I shall now go back to Moscow, and will at once proceed to my interview with the Metropolitan.   I must just give you first a sketch of his office and character.

There have been three stages in the see of Moscow. First he was, after the removal of the primacy from Kieff to Moscow, the Primate—the Archbishop of Canterbury. Next, after the fall of the Constantinopolitan Empire, he became the Patriarch of Moscow, and this was the time of his chief grandeur.   Thirdly, the Patriarchate was suppressed by Peter the Great as too independent a power in the State, and the Metropolitan of Moscow has since then been only one among the four Metropolitans, though always regarded with reverence as inheritor of the Patriarchal See.

Now for Philaret himself.   This is said to have been the history of his elevation. He was Bishop of some remote diocese, and was invited by the Governor of the Province to dine with him.   The Governor and his aides-de-camp were very free in their remarks on religion.   Philaret remained silent.   At last the Governor, irritated, turned to him and said, 'Why do you not say something in defence of the Scriptures?'   Philaret answered, 'I have learned from the Scriptures not to cast pearls before swine.'   The Governor, enraged, struck him on the face and said, ' What

T

do the Scriptures say to that?' Philaret replied, 'They say, "Whosoever shall smite thee on the one cheek turn to him the other also."' He then rose from the table, and, turning to the sacred picture, which, as is the case in every official residence, was hanging in the Governor's room, crossed himself, and said, ' For these and all other Thy blessings, good Lord, make me truly thankful!' and immediately left the room. A report of the story reached St. Petersburg, and the Emperor sent to know the truth from the Bishop. He for a long time steadily refused to touch upon it, saying that whatever had occurred was forgotten and forgiven. When at last the Emperor insisted on the punishment of the Governor, he endeavoured to beg him off, saying that he could not bear to be the cause of the ruin of an innocent family.

This affair first brought him into notice, and he at last became what he now is, the Metropolitan of Moscow. Properly speaking, the Metropolitan of Kieff is the first by the rank of his see, and the Metropolitan of St. Petersburg by rank of creation. But Philaret was so much reverenced for his virtues that he was chosen for the Imperial Coronation, and the Metropolitan of St. Petersburg died of vexation two months afterwards.

General Bashkirtseff had gone to Philaret and secured the hour on Monday for the interview. On Sunday evening he drove me out to a villa in the suburbs. In a small cottage adjoining was living Mouravieff, the brother of the hero of Kars, and author of a history of the Russian Church, of which I had carefully read the English translation. He is an immense man, an immense talker, and an immense controversialist. He was just the man, however, whose acquaintance I wished to make, and we had a great deal of most instructive conversation, walking backwards and forwards in the grounds, and gradually collecting other friends, till, by the time we returned to tea, we were quite a large party. They were all laymen, and it was curious to see with what interest they entered into theological subjects.

Meanwhile, for I am wandering away from the Metropolitan, a difficulty was gathering. On our journey, the General had said to me, 'Don't let Mouravieff know that you are going to Philaret on Monday, or he will endeavour to be present, and he talks so much that it will embarrass the Metropolitan and spoil the interview.' Accordingly I kept my counsel. But when the arrangements for my sight-seeing were being made, Mouravieff kept calling out, 'But when is he to see the Metropolitan? He must see the Metropolitan,' &c. &c. I remained silent; the General retired to the balcony outside. At last Prince Urusoff inadvertently said, 'Is it not to-morrow?' 'To-morrow!' exclaimed Mouravieff; 'why, I was with the Metropolitan to-day, and he said nothing about it.' Then, calling out to the General in Russ, 'Alexis, son of Nicholas!' (this is the invariable mode of address amongst the higher classes in Russia, when at all intimate) 'Alexis Nicolavitch!' the General still turning a deaf ear, 'what is this?' At last an explanation took place in voluminous Russ, and Mouravieff returned, somewhat agitated, but satisfied.

As soon as we got into the carriage again, I said to the General, 'You see that I kept the secret as long as I could.' 'Oh!' he said, 'I have settled it; but you observed that old Philaret, though he had had Mouravieff to tea with him this morning, had not opened his mouth on the subject.'

On Monday morning I went to join the General at his own house, whence we started for Philaret, who lives outside the town. I had dressed entirely *en ecclésiastique.* 'Vous avez très bien fait,' said the General. 'And now,' he continued, 'let us arrange the subjects of conversation.'

I said that I understood that the Metropolitan had paid
special attention to the subject of the Old Testament, and
I was anxious to hear what he had to say upon it.   It was
agreed that we should begin upon the bas-reliefs of the
new church (St. Saviour) building in commemoration of
the deliverance of 1812, which represent some of the most
striking scenes from the Old Testament.   It was also settled that the General should then put to him a difficulty
which he started with me—the apparently fierce and vin-
dictive character of the God of the Hebrews.

We were ushered through a suite of empty rooms, and,
in a few minutes, Philaret appeared.   He was dressed, like
all the Metropolitans, in flowing black robes—his special
dignity marked by a long white cowl, which, from the fourteenth century, the Metropolitans have worn as a kind of
indication of their derivation from the White (or married)
clergy, as their black robes indicate their derivation from
the Black (or monastic) clergy.   He was short, but very
dignified, with deep-sunk expressive eyes.   What chiefly
struck me was the almost supernatural sweetness of his
voice—a low, gentle murmur, hardly rising above a
whisper.

The General kissed his hand, having before warned me
to do the same.   I attempted it : but the old man reso-
lutely withheld the hand, using it to guide me to a seat.   We
then began, the General interpreting in French.   There
was nothing of great importance.   He explained at some
length the distinction which the Greek Church draws
between statues and pictures, and was anxious to know
the different impression produced upon me by the Gothic
and Russian styles, also by the modern and the ancient
Russian styles.   I expressed my preference of the Gothic
on the one hand, and the ancient Russian on the other,
and my admiration of the interior of the Cathedral of the

Assumption. He went through an elaborate elucidation, which charmed the General, of the pictures therein.

Then the General stated his difficulty. The old man replied with considerable animation, and the General was delighted, as indeed was I, to find that the Metropolitan quoted the very same chapter and verse of the Epistle to the Hebrews that I had done in answer to him before— (the verse, chapter, and Epistle were, I fear, wholly new to Alexis Nicolavitch)—'God who in sundry times and divers manners,' and this he enlarged upon very properly.

We then turned off to the English Church. I explained to him that I came, not from the Moscow, but from the Kieff of England, and told him the name of our Metropolitan, and that I was going home to meet him at his Visitation. Of two English divines the names had reached Russia—'Beveriga'[4] and Bingham.

Presently the Governor of Moscow (successor of Rostopchin), a tall, portly officer, was announced ; and so we parted. I insisted on kissing the reluctant hand this time, and the old man whispered softly in Latin, 'God bless you and your Church' ('Deus benedicat tibi et Ecclesiæ vestræ').

The General was much pleased with the interview, and asked me whether I was not struck with the contrast between the refined intelligence of the old Metropolitan and the rough, coarse appearance of the Governor. 'L'esprit et la matière,' said I, alluding to the distinctions which Philaret had drawn.

---

[4] Bishop Beveridge's principal work was his *Synodicon* (1672), a collection of the Apostolic Canons, and of the Decrees of the Councils received by the Greek Church. His best-known English works are his *Sermons*, his *Private Thoughts on Religion*, and his *Expositions of the Catechism and the Thirty-nine Articles*. He died in 1708.

The Rev. Joseph Bingham (1668–1723) published his *Origines Ecclesiasticæ; or, the Antiquities of the Christian Church*, in ten volumes between the years 1708 and 1722.

Well ! I have seen the fair at Nijni Novgorod, and come to the conclusion, which I had half anticipated, that it is not worth this long journey to come and see. It is undoubtedly a curious sight to see such an immense concourse of people—300,000, increasing by 5,000 a day—assembled in the little temporary town which covers the flat plain formed in the triangle between the two rivers ; and the Russian, Persian, and Tartar costumes, each of which is marked by a different head-dress, give it a barbaric appearance. But there is no variety beyond this, and the articles for sale, with the exception of sacred pictures, are such as might be found anywhere. Indeed, many of the booths are entirely furnished from London and Paris. To a merchant, the piles of goods of all kinds must be very interesting. Chests of tea are ranged by hundreds along the shores of the Volga, which have travelled from China to supply the immense demands of the Russian Empire, peasant and prince alike.

It has all the accompaniments too of a world-wide fair. The Governor descends from the Kremlin of the old town to live in a spacious mansion close to the bazaars. A mounted Cossack with his long lance keeps guard by day and night on the wooden bridge. I observed to the Governor's sister how picturesque an object the Cossack was with his lance. 'Il y a une raison morale pour la lance,' she said ; 'he cannot go into a tavern with it, and he cannot leave it outside if he does go in.'

Three conspicuous buildings tower high above the streets of the fair. The central one is the Cathedral of St. Macarius, to whom the fair was anciently dedicated. 'Malheureusement,' said the same good old lady, 'nous sommes sous la protection pas de notre Seigneur mais d'un Saint.' However, there he is—the old Egyptian saint standing in the picture outside with Alexander Nevsky. The building on the south is the Armenian Church for that race of traders, the Quakers of the East. The building on the north, with the crescent on the top, and the gallery round the tower, is the mosque for the Tartars. To-day being Friday, I went there to see, what I was never able to see in the East, their full service. It was strange once more to see the familiar sight of worshippers, seated on their haunches, passing through the mechanical forms of prostration, outstretched hands, hands behind the ears. Finally the Khan recited the Koran, and then, rising up, repeated what I could dimly perceive to be the prayer for all the members of the Imperial family.

All these various features do, after all, give the place a peculiar physiognomy, and when you add to this the everlasting clatter of wheels, the ceaseless thoroughfare of man and beast—not greater in London than in this remote corner of Europe—when you add besides, its magnificent geographical position, and the near chance which it had of being chosen as Peter's capital instead of St. Petersburg, it is a spot which I shall not regret to have seen.

I am almost ashamed to mention one of the things that have most interested me here—a puppet-show, on a very large scale, of the Coronation, divided into four acts. It gave me a far better notion of it than I could have had otherwise.   Ever yours,

A. P. STANLEY.

LXXI.

A. P. S. to Mr. (now Sir George) Grove.

THE ORIENTAL CHARACTER OF THE RUSSIAN PEOPLE.

September 20 (1857): The Baltic.

My dear Grove,—You asked me to think of you in my northern flight, and I will try to give you a proof (a proof sheet) of it on my voyage home.

I have been deeply interested, much in Sweden, more in St. Petersburg, most of all in Moscow. Russia fully answered my expectations in the flood of light which I derived from my sight of those two great cities. If one had wished to bring out the dramatic effect of Russian history, it could not be better done than by the contrast between Moscow and Petersburg—the great Eastern nation striving to become Western, or, rather, the nation, half Eastern, half Western, dragged against its will by one gigantic genius, literally dragged by the hands, and kicked by the boots, of the giant Peter into contact with the European world. It is Rome deserted for Constantinople ; and indeed Petersburg is to Constantinople, and Moscow to Rome, what Russia is to the Roman Empire—immensely inferior, yet still an empire of vast destinies, with the two capitals representing its ancient and its modern tendencies.

What were of special interest to me, and would also have been so to you, were the many signs of true Oriental character in the Russian people. Let me enumerate a few, some great, some small, but all delightful to me, as making me feel once more in the ancient East.

(1) The dress : *shirt, kaftan,* and *beard.* The nobles were compelled, by a tremendous effort of Peter, to abandon these things ; but even he did not venture to take them from the clergy and the peasants. Even for what he did he has never been forgiven by the old Russian Dissenters. They retain their allegiance to the old Tsar, as they knew him in his patriarchal dress and beard ; they will not recognise the new Emperor, in uniform and with smooth chin.

(2) The sacredness of *corners.* Every picture in a room —and what room in Russia is without a picture ?—is in the *corner.* The tombs of the four great Primates of Moscow are in the four *corners* of the Cathedral. The throne of the

Tsar in the Kremlin is in the *corner* of the Coronation
Hall. Just so, in the East, the corner of the Divan and of
the Mosque is always the place of honour.

(3) The women, till the time of Peter, lived almost as
secluded a life as the Orientals. The daughters of the
Tsars, from the difficulty of finding royal husbands for
them, most of them went into convents. To this day, in
the old Dissenting churches, the women worship apart from
the men.

(4) On the head of the red staircase of the Kremlin, at
the entrance of the Coronation Hall, there was till very
recently a picture of Joshua taking off his shoes before the
Angel, to indicate that the nobles were there to take off
their shoes before entering the presence of the Tsar. The
same picture, too, for the same reason doubtless, often
appears at the entrance of churches, and even now the
habit of wearing and taking off caloshes at the doors of
houses is very common in the upper classes, far beyond
what is required by the weather.

(5) The veneration for *hermits* continues, so far as I
know, here only in Christendom. The hermitages of the
Thebaid are exactly imitated in the frozen deserts of North
Russia. Men live secluded for the whole year, fakir-like,
except on Easter Sunday, when they come to receive the
Sacrament, and then again disappear. One such, after
having lived such a life for twenty years, allowed himself
to be consulted as an oracle, and was so, with immense
effect, by all classes, till his death, which took place a few
years ago.

(6) The abhorrence of *statues*, though certainly compensated by their veneration for pictures, must, I think, be
a relic of the old Oriental Judaic repudiation of graven
images. It is curious to see how slowly and clandestinely
the statues are creeping in, bas-reliefs, not figures, outside

not inside churches, and always as something heterodox and unauthorised.

(7) There is hardly such a thing as a surname in Russia in popular usage. The peasants have none, and the nobles always call each other by their Christian names, and the name of their fathers. I cannot describe to you the pleasing, patriarchal, family impression which this produces. It prevails everywhere, from the Emperor 'Alexander, son of Nicholas,' down to us poor English. Here they are somewhat puzzled by our unrecognised Occidental names. But they take the nearest approach. 'George' is happily common to both Churches. But 'Edward' is uniformly 'Demetrius;' 'William' is 'Basil;' 'Henry' is 'Andrew;' 'Robert' is 'Romanus.'

(8) There is the same absence of any attempt at effect in their worship or architecture. Hence its great poverty to those who, like myself on first coming, know nothing of its intention. Hence its great richness to those who, like myself after three weeks' instruction, become alive to what is meant. I do not imagine that the common people enter fully into what is represented ; but they certainly do to a great extent. Often I have seen groups standing before the outside pictures of the Kremlin churches, explaining and discussing them. On the other hand, there is no Raphael, no Handel, no Christopher Wren, no Michael Angelo.

I trust that you have had, and have, no dear friends in India. Except W. Arnold, and one or two more, I am thankful to say that I have none that I know of.[5]

Ever yours,
A. P. STANLEY.

---

[5] The outbreak at Meerut and the proclamation of the Mogul Empire took place in May 1857.

LXXII.

A. P. S. to the Hon. Louisa Stanley.

THE ISLAND OF RÜGEN.

[In the fortieth chapter of the 'Germania' Tacitus describes the worship of Hertha, or, as the more correct reading gives it, Nerthus, whom he identifies with the Earth-Mother. He speaks also of the sacred grove ('castum nemus'), and of the lake where the car, and clothes, and the person of the deity are washed (' vehiculum et vestes, et, si credere velis, numen ipsum secreto lacu abluitur').

The cliff described by Stanley is the Stuben-Kammer, at the top of which is the Königsstuhl. It, as well as the sacred grove and lake of Hertha or Nerthus, is on the peninsula of Jasmund.

Arkona is in the peninsula of Wittow. Within its earth fortress was the shrine of the four-headed god Svantevit, whose worship was suppressed by Waldemar I. (1157–81), when he added the island of Rügen to the dominions of Denmark.

Odoacer, by the capture of Pavia in 476, overthrew the western Roman empire. He ruled Italy till 490, when the Emperor Zeno, alarmed at his growing power, persuaded Theodoric the Ostrogoth to invade the country. Odoacer, thrice defeated, shut himself up in Ravenna. After a siege which lasted more than three years, famine compelled him to capitulate in 493. He was treacherously assassinated by Theodoric himself. Modern scholars would perhaps dispute the origin which Stanley here assigns to Odoacer.]

Rügen : Sept. 24 [1857].

My dear Louisa,—One more letter, more homogeneous with my first than with my second—the Isle of Rügen. It had long been one of my dreams to visit this Mona of Germany ; and now on returning from Russia, and finding myself close to it, and two days to spare before joining the dear travellers, as I hope, at Berlin, I threw myself out of the Russian steamer at the mouth of the Oder, and embarked on one taking flight for Rügen. . . .

It has been a fitting conclusion to the tour, for in it all ends have met. Its huge white cliffs remind me that I am drawing near to the shores of my own Kent; the granite boulders that are scattered over it carry me back to Sweden, whence, say they, these blocks were transported years ago on the shoulders of glaciers. But the great interest to me has always been, and now more than ever, that Rügen was the ancient heathen sanctuary of both the great races of Europe; the first, which I have so long known, and whereof we ourselves are part, the German; the second, with which I now for the first time have made acquaintance, the Sclavonic. How and in what order they succeeded each other, or accompanied each other, I know not; but I shall now describe to you the visit to their respective temples.

1. Behold me, then, approaching the sanctuary of the ancient German tribes, specially of that to which belonged Odoacer, the first victor of the Roman empire. Here, no doubt, as secure in this remote island, the holiest place of their worship was fixed, and its exact conformity with the description given by Tacitus enables us precisely to identify it.

On the south-east horn of a vast bay are combined two remarkable features, which I do not remember ever to have seen united before, a snow-white cliff overhanging the sea, rising like an alp or a ghost out of a mass of green forest. This cliff is called the King's Seat, from an old tradition that here the kings of Rügen used to receive the homage of their subjects, having won it by the impossible performance of climbing up the perpendicular face of the rock; and the story is even bold enough to go on to say that the last king who so won the prize was my old friend Charles XII., in his long blue coat and yellow breeches.

However, it is a very beautiful sight, and may well have attracted any roving tribes into the depths of the forest from which it springs. The forest is a *beech wood*. *Beech wood!*[6]—what a world of recollections, to us more ancient than the Pyramids, does that word call up! and how inferior all beech woods are to that one! I never yet have seen its like; the nearest approach to it (but that was an avenue only, not a wood) was the cathedral-like nave of beeches at Inverary. . . .

This German beech wood has no merit, except its vastness and thickness. Its trees are almost all of that puny paltry growth which characterises continental as distinguished from English trees. But it is dark and wide, and the ground rises and falls, with the peculiar colour which the beeches give it, much as we see it at home. In the midst of this forest is a deep oval hollow, thickly set with these trees, the sanctuary of the goddess Hertha. It is identified, first by the high earthen rampart which still surrounds it, and secondly by the pathway leading through the rampart to the little Hertha lake, where, says Tacitus, the goddess, her attendants, her waggon, her oxen, and her clothes used to wash. It is undoubtedly a mysterious spot. Hard by are two of the granite rocks before mentioned. One of these is called the 'stone of sacrifice,' and has, unquestionably, a small stone basin at its foot to receive the something which has left a mark as of long running over the side. The other is called 'the stone of trial,' and contains two footprints—one of a full-grown person, the other as of a little child.

The Sclavonic sanctuary is at the opposite horn of the bay, and at so great a distance that I hesitated to go. But the landlord wisely said, 'You will never be here again. By all means do not omit to see it.' So I went,

---

[6] The reference is to the wood at Alderley.

and, leaving the carriage, toiled away on foot along the
edge of the cliffs : now passing by innumerable ploughers ;
now by a small chapel, erected in the midst of the hills to
combine work and worship in harvest time ; now by a
fishing village, recalling, as all fishing villages, the abode
of Steenie Muckle-backit. At last I reached the extreme
point of the promontory—which is also the northernmost
point—'the Land's End'—of Germany. Sheer on the right
and the left went down the white cliffs into the sea. But
the very point itself was walled off, as it were, by an immense earthen rampart, rising almost in towers of grassy
mounds, with one deep entrance into what is now a mere
open space ending on the edge of the cliffs, but which once
contained the sanctuary of Arkona, the westernmost refuge
of the old Sclavonians, who remained here, unconquered
and unconverted, till, in the twelfth century, the temple and
fortress of their god *Svante-vit* were stormed and destroyed
on St. Vitus's day.

The huge rampart that I have described is all that
remains. But it was very interesting to see so vast and
incontestable a record of the last struggles of the Sclavonic
race and of heathenism in the centre of Europe ; and it is
important as adding authenticity to the very similar wall
round the sanctuary of Hertha. From the top of the
highest mound I enjoyed a splendid view—sea and bays
all round—a fragment of Denmark on the horizon. Here
might I long have moralised on the many sacred islands I
have seen—Anglesey, our own Anglesey, not unlike to
this in its featureless interest, and its beautiful fringe of
rocks ; Thanet, like in its boundless fertility and its
grand historic bay ; Iona, Philæ, Skye. Here many
thoughts too might crowd in, of the subsequent fates of
the two mighty races, who in this island met in close
quarters, as two obscure heathen tribes, parting, not to

meet again, till they met as Christian kingdoms and mighty empires — Bohemia, Poland, Russia — Germany, France, England—Western Europe and Northern America. But at length I descended. . . .

In casting up the pleasant recollections of our tour with my companions before we parted, we all agreed that the name of ' Louisa,' the Finnish bathing-place, held a primary position. I informed them that I had a relative of the same name, and of corresponding qualities, and that I would take the first opportunity of introducing her to them. So that, if Mr. Butler recognises you as an old acquaintance, you will know why.

Ever yours,
A. P. STANLEY.

LXXIII.

A. P. S. to the Hon. Louisa Stanley.

THE HEAD OF OLIVER CROMWELL.

[Oliver Cromwell was buried in Henry VII.'s Chapel on November 23, 1658. On the eve of January 30, 1661, the bodies of Cromwell, Ireton, and Bradshaw were dug up, and on the following day dragged to Tyburn, hanged with their faces turned to Whitehall, decapitated and buried beneath the gallows in what is now Connaught Square. The heads were fixed on spikes at Westminster Hall, Bradshaw's being placed in the centre, because he had presided at the trial of Charles I.

'The traditions,' says Stanley, in his ' Memorials of Westminster Abbey,' ' of the fate of Cromwell's skull are too intricate to be here described.' A writer in the ' Gentleman's Magazine' for May 1881 gives an elaborate account of the fortunes of this skull. He traces it into the hands of Samuel Russel, who appears to have sold it in April 1787 to Mr. Cox, the proprietor of a Museum in Spring Gardens. On the dispersal of this Museum, the skull was sold for 230*l.* to three joint-purchasers, who exhibited it in 1799 at Mead's Court, Bond Street. Through these persons it eventually passed to Mr. Wilkinson, by whose son it was shown to Stanley.]

Canterbury : Dec. 30, 1857.

My dear Louisa,—I waited till your anxieties were a little abated to write an account of my singular visit to, or rather from, Addington.   So long ago as October last, the Archbishop's [7] chaplain, Thomas, had excited my curiosity by mentioning that in the house of a gentleman in their neighbourhood was found no less a marvel than the *head of Oliver Cromwell.*   He had never seen it, but believed it to exist, and twice expressly urged my coming to Addington to inspect it.   Twice I was obliged to decline ; but, having a day to spare from Fulham and Canterbury, I seized the opportunity, was pressingly received by that very gracious and good personage, our Primate, and on the following day was driven in the archiepiscopal barouche, containing Thomas, Dr. Morier (brother of ' Hadji Baba '), and myself, over Kent and Surrey hills for five miles, to the rural abode of Dr. Wilkinson, late M.P. for Lambeth. He, with an accomplished daughter, who kindly filled up the blanks of her father's memory, had been prepared, and received us with all attention, first reciting to us the history from ancient newspapers and then showing us the relic itself.

Let me give you the story in due order.   The Protector, as doubtless you know, was embalmed after his death in 1658 in royal state, and buried in Henry VII.'s Chapel in Westminster Abbey.   There he lay till January 30, 1661, when (as states Mercurius Politicus), to consecrate the ' foul and bloody tragedy of that day,' there were dragged, out from Westminster in their coffins ' the carcases of his cursed highness, his son-in-law, Ireton, and the monster

[7] Dr. Longley.

Bradshaw (if indeed it be right to rail at the devil),' and dragged to Tyburn. There they were hanged at the three corners of the triple tree till sunset, then cut down, their heads struck off by the executioner, the trunks buried under the gallows, and their heads stuck up on Westminster Hall, the scene of the trial of the king : Bradshaw as judge in the centre, Ireton and Cromwell on each side. So far we trace our head in history, having, as you will perceive, undergone these three vicissitudes, unparalleled in the history even of royal heads—embalmment, decapitation, and transfixment on a spike.

Now comes in tradition. Twenty-five years afterwards, when Ireton's head and Bradshaw's had wasted away by wear and tear of weather, Cromwell's—preserved from its embalmment—still remained, and was blown down in a stormy night, picked up by a sentry, and by him sold to an obscure family of Russel, twice, however, connected by marriage with Henry Cromwell. With them it abode till the end of last century, when it passed from a spendthrift, Samuel Russel, into the hands of one Boxer, from whom, again, to three gentlemen, admirers of the Protector, who all died sudden deaths, when it fell into the hands of the daughter of the survivor, ward of Mr. Wilkinson, father of the present owner.

Now for the head itself. Out of two strong boxes and many wrappings its present owner produced it, and it is its own best witness. An *embalmed* head like a mummy, with the marks of *two strokes of the axe* on the neck, and the ancient oak staff and iron spike running through its skull. The hair still remains, so that you see the moustache, beard, and *eyebrows meeting*. There is a mark of the mole on the right eyebrow. The nose is slightly turned to the left. The under-jaw *is short, as was his*. A very awful apparition, and I myself believe it can be no one's but

U

Cromwell's own. Did you ever hear of it before ? There is a strange story of Charles I. having been by Cromwell's desire substituted for him in his coffin, and he buried at Hanley ; but this has been found fabulous by the discovery of Charles I. at Windsor.

We all returned quite convinced, and I sent to Dr. Wilkinson in repayment a copy of 'Canterbury Memorials.'

We are all here in a train of Christmas festivities, driving in and out almost every day. Many happy Christmas days and New Year's days yet. But *here* I cannot hope for many more.   Ever yours,

A. P. STANLEY.

LXXIV.

A. P. S. to Mrs. Stanley.

SIR JOHN HERSCHEL AND DR. WHEWELL AT CANTERBURY.

[The foreboding expressed by Stanley in the last paragraph of the previous letter was speedily realised. In February 1858 a canonry fell vacant at Christ Church, Oxford. The stall belonged to Stanley as Regius Professor of Ecclesiastical History, and he at once prepared to leave Canterbury.

The following letter describes one of his last parties at Canterbury. Sir John Herschel, whose great astronomical work at the Cape was completed in 1847 by the publication of his ' Astronomical Observations,' died in 1871, and was buried by the side of Newton in Westminster Abbey, Stanley, as Dean, performing the service. He was Senior Wrangler and First Smith's Prizeman at Cambridge in 1813, and it was probably during his undergraduate career that he heard Edward Daniel Clarke lecture on mineralogy. Several specimens of his translations into English verse will be found at the end of his volume of ' Essays and Addresses' (1857). His translation of the ' Iliad ' into English hexameters was published in 1866. Whewell, the Master of Trinity, Cambridge, was a man of encyclopædic

knowledge. Sydney Smith said of him that 'science is his
forte and omniscience his foible.' Friedrich Max Müller,
already known to Europe by his philological learning, was
at this time engaged, at the request of the East India
Company, in publishing his edition of the Rig-Veda.
In 1854 he had been appointed Taylorian Professor of
Modern Languages and Literature in the University of
Oxford. He became one of Stanley's most intimate
friends.]

Canterbury: Jan. 26, 1858.

My dearest Mother,—At 2 P.M. I went to the station,
and there received the whole party—Whewell, the Herschels
with one daughter, Mr. and Mrs. O'Callaghan—he a great
antiquary with an immense collection of autographs at his
house in Yorkshire near Bolton Abbey—she first married
to one of the Marshalls, whose three children were thus
adopted into the second family—one son, just married to
one of the Herschels, and the other two daughters with
them now. It was some time before I could make out all
his relationships. . . . The Master had never met Max
Müller before and was delighted to find him. Herschel
has so great a turn for philology, that he considers that
and not astronomy to be his proper vocation, and had met
Max before at Bunsen's. Nothing could be more excellent
than their behaviour. I cut short all apologies by saying
that I had only one condition to make, which was that
they must submit entirely to my orders—and this they did
to the letter. . . . After luncheon we went the round of
St. Augustine's, St. Martin's, and the Dane John. Sir John
Herschel was very feeble, and required some management
to prevent his overtiring himself. O'Callaghan was delighted with the Roman remains in St. Martin's, and
actually identified portions incontestably ancient, which
no one had ever pointed out to me before. Also he and
the Master came to the conclusion that the lower part of
Ethelbert's font was genuine.

Perhaps the most useful member of the party was the Master. I never saw him to such advantage. He talked on every subject, radiant with delight at everything, his knowledge truly surprising, addressing himself to everybody, and at the end of the whole visit, when I said that I hoped he had enjoyed himself, he answered with much feeling, ' Yes, indeed I have. I look back on these two days as the happiest that during these last few years have fallen to my lot.' The only *contretemps* of the visit occurred to him, and he took it so good-humouredly that it did not matter. The doctor, a very rough man, but to whom I knew that the sight of those two giants of science would be like a glimpse of heaven, caught Whewell at the end of the evening, and very abruptly asked him, ' What is your opinion as to the best slope of the sails of windmills ? ' Surprised to find that Whewell had not made up his mind —'Oh! I thought you had written a book upon it. I thought you had written a book upon everything.' I believe it was mere simplicity ; but the bystanders tell me that it had the most ludicrous effect.

Herschel warmed up after dinner, and there was a very lively conversation—first about Huc's travels, and then about Clarke. Herschel described the enthusiasm with which he (Clarke) lectured at Cambridge—holding up a particle of crystal which no one could see, but expatiating upon its marvels with such tenderness and admiration that the tears were streaming down his face. On Sunday breakfast was at nine. I preached on ' Be not overcome of evil, but overcome evil with good,' a school sermon, partly for the Canterbury schools, partly addressed to the reassembled schools. Luncheon, and then over the Cathedral between the services. There again all went off admirably, the Master expounding architecturally in the intervals of my historical expositions. I went at 3 P.M. to preach

another sermon for the schools at St. Paul's, the Herschels
going with me, the rest again to the cathedral ; then, at
4.30 P.M., a walk by St. Thomas's Hill and Harbledon.
This was perhaps a little too late and too long, and I had to
send some of them back ; but the Master, the three young
ladies, and the two young men went the whole round. At
6 P.M. I left them for the hospital service, and came back
to dinner at 7 P.M. Rost[8] was the only stranger—which
made twelve. A brilliant display of Whewell and Müller
after dinner, on the Nibelungen Lied, Ossian, and Homer,
Herschel occasionally joining in with great effect. He said
that he had read the ' Iliad ' again lately, as he would a novel,
reading it straight through in a day and a half, and that he
was greatly struck with the way in which the one redeeming feature in the savage character of Achilles was his
sense of justice. He also said (I think that it was in
speaking of the way in which Macpherson, in spite of himself, had been impressed with the poetical stories of the
Highland songs), ' I am convinced that, if a sinner were
shut up in Paradise two days in the year, he could not but
be the better for it ! ' It was contrary to the usual view of
the matter ; but it struck me as an instructive remark. In
the evening Lady H. produced an album with poems by
Sir W. Hamilton and others, and also 'Latin Hexameters '
written by Herschel after he came home from his walk on
Saturday, translations from the ' Elegant Extracts ' which
he took up to his room from the table in the hall. He
burst out with rapturous admiration of Müller, when he
(M.) retired. They were also much pleased with Rost's
modesty and learning combined, and with the cordial
brotherlike meeting of the two German scholars.

[8] Dr. Reinhold Rost was at this time Oriental Lecturer at St. Augustine's
College, Canterbury. He continued to hold this appointment after he became, in 1863, Secretary to the Royal Asiatic Society. He resigned his post
of Librarian to the India Office in 1893.

In parting I told them that I had found it a custom in the Russian monasteries to present pictures of the church to all pilgrims, and accordingly presented each person or party with a large view of the cathedral, ordered from Russell's betimes in the morning. Meanwhile the glories of the farewell were enhanced by the following remarkable scene. The Archdeacon's [9] scruples about the opening of the cathedral had given way, and, accordingly, immediately after the morning service, the whole building, nave, chapels, and cloisters, was swarming with hundreds and hundreds of people, giving the place an appearance of life and animation that was quite refreshing to see. The Master, Müller, O'Callaghan, and I walked amongst them, examining their numbers, and I at all odd moments explaining to the mob. I was rather sorry not to be able to give the latter my undivided attention. But perhaps it was as well that the whole interest and credit of the thing should fall to the share of the Archdeacon (the Dean being away) who was there, and who, in spite of his fears, must, I should think, have been pleased.

There were 9,000 people in the cathedral yesterday.

Ever yours,

A. P. S.

LXXV.

A. P. S. to Mrs. Arnold.

HIS PLEASANT POSITION AT OXFORD ;
THE AUTHOR OF 'TOM BROWN'S SCHOOLDAYS.'

Christ Church, Oxford : June 11, 1860.

My dear Mrs. Arnold,—Again the well-known day comes round, and you will be expecting your tribute from

[9] Benjamin Harrison, to whom Stanley's *Memorials of Canterbury* are dedicated.

me. How strange it seems to find myself approaching the age at which he, who seemed so full of years and labours, was taken from us! How much I still long to do or to see done before the time comes to me also! For one thing I feel daily more thankful, and that is my position here. It has, with all its necessary drawbacks, so many charms and so much independence that I should be perfectly satisfied to remain here always. Indeed, herein consists its chief charm—that I can do and say what I like, or think right, and can lose nothing that I care to have.

How much Mrs. Fletcher, if she were alive, would rejoice in Garibaldi's successes, and I think we may all fairly do so!

At the coming Commemoration I expect T. Hughes and his wife. Have you seen him of late? I hardly knew him before 'Tom Brown' appeared, but have renewed my acquaintance. He is a noble character, full of the most excellent recollections of the past, and giving me the best and most cheering hopes for the future.

I very much enjoyed Matt's visit here, and so, I think, did he. What a capital wife she is to him!

Farewell! and take my best thoughts for to-morrow. No changes or chances of life can ever take from us what that day has left with us.

Ever yours,
A. P. STANLEY.

LXXVI.

A. P. S. to the Hon. Louisa Stanley.

[In August 1861 Stanley and his sister Mary started on a tour through Hungary and the Carpathians to Constantinople, and thence to Mount Athos (see ' Life,' vol. ii.

ch. xvii.).   The three following letters were written during this tour.

The Fourth General Council was held in 451, in the church of St. Euphemia, which stands on a hill above the Thracian Bosphorus. 'The boundless prospect of the land and sea,' says Gibbon, 'might have raised the mind of a sectary to the contemplation of the God of the universe.' The Fathers attributed their success against the heresy of Eutyches to the prayers of St. Euphemia, who suffered martyrdom at Chalcedon in 307.

The garden of Haidar Pasha contained the spring which was once famous as the fountain of Hermagoras.]

Therapia : September 4, 1861.

My dear Louisa,—I gave you a day at Cairo.   Let me give you a day at Constantinople.   It will tell you how full of unexpected surprises and acquaintances our life here has been.

We start in the steamer from this beautiful Therapia at 9 A.M.   At 10 we land [that is, Lord Hobart, Mr. Foster, and A. P. S.] under the ruined castle of Kmeli Nissa, and toil up the hill.   There, in a red wood cottage, adjoining the ruins, lives Henry's friend, Achmet Effendi. He received us very cordially, laughed very heartily at his own jokes, and entered into many controversies, which at last we were obliged to cut short in order to catch the steamer again at 11 P.M. (*sic*).   For at noon I had made an appointment on the bridge at Pera with a man whom I had never seen, and who had never seen me ; and there-fore our only chance of meeting was strict punctuality. On the bridge we landed, but no Mr. Curtis was visible. Suddenly a Frenchman accosts me : 'Are you from Therapia ?   Do you wish to go to Kadikoi ? '   ' Yes,' says A. P. S.   'I am Major Gordon's dragoman ; and Mr. Curtis has sent me here to meet you, in case he cannot come himself.'   So to the care of Charles Lombardi, whom I had never heard of before, to go to Major Gordon, with whom I had not the slightest acquaintance, I entered in a caïque, my object being to hunt for the church of St. Euphemia, where the Council of Chalcedon was held. We fly across the Bosphorus, disembark at Kadikoi, the small village which lies on the site of old Chalcedon, and up the cliff and into Major Gordon's house. Here I find a very pleasing major and his wife, and apologise for my intrusion. 'On the contrary,' they say, 'your arrival has solved a great mystery.' By a singular coincidence, Major Gordon had fallen in with a Mr. Stanley, neither H. J. S. nor A. P. S., and had seen him go off two days before in the Austrian steamer; and when Mr. Curtis, the clergyman, had spoken of my going to Kadikoi, he mentioned that it was impossible, because he had seen him go that very day to Trieste. So when the question of my identity, or rather dis-identity, was settled, we set off in search of the church, *i.e.* Major Gordon, A. P. S., Lombardi the dragoman, and Dionysius the cook, who, being a native of Chalcedon, was sure that he could find the place.

When we arrived at the church, I felt certain that this was not the proper situation—no hill, no spring, nothing that suited. Dionysius being now at fault, the next thing was to find the priest. Dionysius accordingly undertook to hunt him out, and at last found him in a coffee-house. Into the coffee-house we went, and there sat down in the garden—the major, the professor, the dragoman, the cook, and the priest. 'Now, Dionysius, ask him where the holy Synod was.' D.: 'He says that it is sitting now at Phanar.'[1] A. P. S.: 'No! not the Synod that is now, but the Synod long ago, of Chalcedon.' D.: 'Chalcedon was here, more ancient than Stamboul, mother of everything.' A. P. S.: 'Yes, that is right—this is Chalcedon. Now ask him what was the Synod of Chalcedon.' D.: 'He

---

[1] The residence of the Patriarch of Constantinople.

says that there was a quarrel between Greeks and Armenians which was the best religion ; and they wrote figures, and put them on the body of St. Euphemia, and, three days after, they open the coffin, and find the Greek figures in her hands and the Armenian figures at her feet —and so the Greeks are right.' (This was a wonderful advance even on the legend in the 'Acta Sanctorum,' but I felt now that I was on the right track.) ' Now ask him where all this took place.' So, after a good deal of confabulation, Dionysius said, ' I know,' and off we set after him.

There was a spring in the beautiful gardens of Haidar Pasha ; this was in the vaults of the church, and the church itself was on the hill above, close to the English cemetery. Gibbon says that it is surprising that the magnificent view did not awaken the minds of the bishops to a sense of the universal love of the Creator ; and so it is. A glorious view, indeed, of city and islands and Sea of Marmora, and, now hard by, the tall pillar supported by angels, over the graves of the English officers and soldiers.

And so at the cemetery I parted with the major and the cook, and started in a caïque with Lombardi. As we passed by the little tower on the rock, which is called Leander's Tower, from a foolish confusion of the Bosphorus and the Hellespont, I thought that it would be curious to hear Lombardi's version of the story : ' Pourquoi cette tour s'appelle-t-elle la tour de Léandre ? ' ' Je vous dirai : Le Roi Constantin ou Bélisaire avait une fille Léandre—c'est à dire, Léonore. La princesse Léonore était enfermée dans cette tour, parce qu'elle devait être piquée par un serpent. Le serpent est apporté dans des raisins, et elle est morte là-dedans.'

On returning by the Bosphorus, I halted at the house of the Black Theodore, at the marriage of whose daughter

by the Bishop of Pera I had assisted the day before, and
there had an hour's eloquent discourse, on the hopes of the
Greeks and the decline of the Turks, from her beautiful
sister Smaragda, the wife of Spiridion Baltazzi.

Arrived at home for dinner, and there met an intelli-
gent Turk, Ali Bey, who thought Berlin the greatest of
European capitals, because every one there was called
' Doctor,' and because there he had found a German wife.
In the evening, a pleasant party at the Embassy, including
Philip and Madame Baltazzi, uncle and aunt of Smaragda.
And so ends a day at Therapia—a good preparation for
the solitude of Mount Athos. We have indeed had a
charming week.　　　　　　　　Ever yours,

　　　　　　　　　　　　　　　A. P. STANLEY.

LXXVII.

A. P. S. to Mrs. Stanley.

MOUNT ATHOS.

[At Constantinople Stanley parted with his sister, who
went on to Sebastopol, while he, with Professor Clark,
visited Mount Athos. The monasteries in the south-west
corner of the peninsula were left unseen ; but, after
accompanying Professor Clark to Salonica, Stanley returned with the English Consul, and saw the remaining
four. (' Life,' vol. ii. pp. 56–60.)

The most recent description of the monasteries will be
found in ' Athos ; or, the Mountain of the Monks,' by
Athelstan Riley, London, 1887.]

　　　　　　　　　　　September 17, 1861 :
　　　　On the rock of Simopetra overlooking the sea hundreds
　　　　　　of feet below, and the peak of Athos towering
　　　　　　immediately above.

My dearest Mother,—This—probably the most romantic spot in Athos—you would like to see.　But you would

never reach it : so rough the approach by land, so steep the ascent from the sea.

But I will reserve what I have to say on this till I have given you a general idea of the mountain and our tour.

The peninsula of Athos is, as you see on the map, one of the three prongs which run out from Macedonia into the Ægean Sea. The two others, Pallene and Sithonia, had cities upon them, famous in Greek history. But Athos had none of the slightest importance, and the mountain itself has no connection with Grecian mythology. It remained standing for thousands of years unoccupied by history or religion, till the monastic system and the troubles of the Byzantine Empire fastened upon it as a refuge from the storms which physically and morally raged round it.

The peninsula at large is a high ridge of hills, not unlike, I fancy, to the two others. They are covered with arbutus, holly, oak, beech, ivy, cypress, and, as mere specimens of forest, are amongst the most beautiful I ever saw. But what gives them a beauty far beyond this is that from almost every point, towering above these lower hills, is the unearthly vision of the pyramidal peak of Athos, to which the other two ranges have nothing to correspond ; sometimes it just peeps above the woods in the distance, sometimes it appears almost at its full height, and usually in the view of it is mingled the sight of the creeks of the blue sea running up into the green hillsides or under the white limestone or marble rocks.

And now the beauty is increased by the appearance at constant intervals of the various monasteries and their dependencies. Few of the monasteries themselves are architecturally grand, but they are all picturesque. They have all something of the appearance of a castle or ancient manor-house, with walls and a high tower, and inside some of them are almost like little towns—two or three or twelve churches, gardens, immense galleries and outhouses, huge cypresses standing in the courts. There are twenty in all, with several inferior establishments dependent upon them, all independent of each other, but all under a common government held at a town in the centre of the peninsula. In this respect, as in many others, there are only two institutions in the world with which, as far as I know, they can be at all compared, and that is the two English Universities—the colleges being like the monasteries, the University Council like the government.

To many people it might be tedious to go the whole round of the monasteries, but to me it was certainly not so. It became a matter of curiosity to see the difference of each from each, how we should be received, &c., what varieties of intelligence or of government there were, what element of the different races of the Eastern Church prevailed in each. There was one great drawback—the language. Clarke could talk some Greek, Georgio could interpret, and I could follow enough to guess what was said. But to have been able to converse would have made an immense difference, as they were extremely communicative.

I will first go through our personal 'narrative.' We landed, as the Russian steamer was in duty bound, at the Russian monastery (Russico), and immediately took mules and rode on to that where we were to sleep—the Xeropotamou (Dry River). Thence we plunged into the interior to the capital—the seat of the Council—Caryes ('The Heads' or 'The Nuts,' it is uncertain which it means), to present our credentials from the Patriarch and receive counter-credentials from the Council to all the monasteries.

There we were successively entertained by the Vice-Chancellor, as he would be—the President of the Council—the Council assembled, and the Khaimakham, or Turkish

Governor, who has to live there apart from his wife, and even from his mare, to preserve order. By a most glorious passage through the forests, with the peak of the mountain shooting up into the evening sky out of the luxuriant vegetation of arbutus, myrtle, holly, ivy, vines, pines, aloes, olives, we reached Simopetra (Simon's Rock).

This, as I anticipated in the beginning of this letter, is, with one exception, the most beautiful, certainly the most curious of all.

The hermit Simon lived in a cave hard by, 'and there,' said the porter of the monastery, 'the Virgin appeared to him as distinctly as I now see you'—('In a dream when he was asleep,' added the more cautious or more enlightened monk who was standing by, in a parenthesis, which, as it seemed to me, was the true addition to be made to the accounts of hundreds of apparitions in Mount Athos or out of it)—'and pointed out to him the high rock opposite where he was to build the monastery.' On this accordingly the monastery stands, the rock protruding through the floors of at least four stories, and the topmost story where we slept, surrounded by an open gallery overhanging the sea and looking up to the mountain.

Thence (by a change which is constantly occurring and which relieves the journey at once from fatigue and monotony) we went on in a boat skirting the shore and landing at the two small monasteries founded by the two hermits, Gregory and Dionysius, or rather suggested by the hermits and founded by some Servian or Byzantine or Bulgarian prince. St. Gregory's was exactly the kind of society which Tennyson would have described, a race of rough boorish monks, ruled by a gentle courteous abbot, who seemed quite unequal to the uncongenial task he had undertaken. That evening we reached St. Paul's, which, by the curious fatality that seems to wait on that name, is specially the English

monastery, being peopled entirely by monks of the Ionian
Islands, who therefore claim to be English subjects, and
receive English visitors with peculiar ardour.

Whether from this, or because being from the Ionian
Islands, they really are more intelligent, it struck me that
there were far more force and animation here than anywhere. The abbot had a considerable amount of classical
lore on Philippi, Amphipolis, &c. &c., which he poured
forth with immense volubility, and laboured hard, and I
dare say successfully, to prove that St. Paul's stood on the
site of the chief of the ancient cities which had once been
planted on the peninsula. Whilst in the full flow of his
discourse, he was suddenly stopped by not being able to
remember the name of one of these towns which was
identical with that of the wife of one of the Antiochuses.
'Who was she? what was her name?' None of the
monks could answer ; we could not answer. The old man,
much vexed, racked his memory in vain, and we parted to
go round the monastery. As evening was drawing on, and
as we were returning to our rooms, we were told that the
abbot wished to see us again in his own room. We entered,
and he immediately exclaimed, ' Stratonice—I have remembered the name.'

St. Paul's lies immediately under the south side of the
peak of Athos : and on the following morning was to be
made the tour of the peak, and, if clear, its ascent.

The two first pieces of intelligence in the morning
were that Clark and Georgio were both ill. *Georgio :* ' I
very sick, my heart sweats very much inside.' Whatever
might be meant by this symptom, I gave him quinine,
which restored him a little, and took some myself. Clark
announced that he felt so ill that he must have a day of
complete rest, and proposed that I should go on alone.
However, whilst we were debating this, he got up, and

manfully determined to go on, and we had a five hours' ride up the worst track that mule ever climbed, but also round the most noble mountain that ever sprang straight out of the sea.

Fortunately, though the day was beautiful, the horizon was so hazy that an ascent to the summit, irrespectively of the condition of my two companions, was out of the question. We crept round the cliffs, looked down on the sea immediately below us, saw groups of little monasteries planted here and there in almost inaccessible clefts and ridges, and midway reached a small wooden cottage, immediately under the summit, containing fifteen monks, who thus form the highest monastery or hermitage in Athos. They live on bread and water all the year round, and employ themselves chiefly in painting and carving. We climbed into the loft where these primitive artists were at work. 'This,' I said to Clark, 'must be the most elevated studio in the world.' 'Yes,' he replied, 'it is very *high art.*'

The extreme rudeness and isolation of these monks (one of whom, as if to vary the monotony of their life, was slightly insane) gave their remarks a curious kind of interest. Here, as elsewhere on the mountain, I was pleased with the simplicity with which they disclaimed any wonders to which they think they have no real claim.

On the top of the mountain is a chapel dedicated to the Transfiguration, of which the Light was in the fourteenth century believed to have revealed itself to the monks of Athos.

'Why is the chapel called the Transfiguration?' 'Only because it is a high mountain.'

There is a legend that the vision of the Temptation, and the vision of the Kingdoms of the World, were on the peak of Athos. A splendid legend, for the peak must command a greater number of celebrated spots in the classical world than any other that could be selected. 'Was this so?' 'Oh! no! no! no! nothing of the kind.'

'Some people say that Constantinople can be seen from the top: is this so?'

'No: certainly not.'

'What can you see from the top?'

They *might* have answered with perfect truth, the Dardanelles, Philippi, Thessalonica, Samothrace, Thasos, Lemnos, Eubœa, Olympus, Ossa, Pelion. They *did* answer (like how many of their betters who, however wide the horizon and however glorious and famous the view, see only the most commonplace and most familiar object), '*We can see Sykia.*' (Sykia is a village on the next promontory, where probably some of the monasteries have farms.)

From Kerasia we descended to the northern side, where, corresponding to the situation of St. Paul's on the southern side, is the vast and ancient monastery which ranks first in dignity, and is called alone by the name of *The Convent*, The Laura—the Christ Church, the Trinity, of the Holy Mountain. It is a very impressive pile of buildings, and there is a venerable antiquity spread over its courts and fountains and cypresses which is hardly to be seen elsewhere. But its estates were chiefly in Greece, and were confiscated after the declaration of independence, so that it is now very poor and in a state of decay.

To save our invalids we left the Laura in a boat. The ride by land from thence is said to be very beautiful, but it can hardly be more so than the passage by sea, creeping immediately under the fold upon fold of green drapery, surmounted by the peak, silvery and rosy according to the time of day. It was in a blaze of red as we reached Caracalla, so called from the Moldavian monk its founder.

X

By this time Clark consented to take quinine, and the result, or at any rate the sequence, was that the next day he was almost entirely well.

Three more monasteries—the Iveron (or Georgian), the Stauroniketa (or Cross Conqueror), the Pantocratoros (or the Almighty)—brought us to the end of the second group of convents.

In each of these the mountain peak still occupied the chief feature in every view. From this point the scenery became more tame, the mountain more distant. We reached that evening the largest and richest of all the monasteries, with an income, it is supposed, of 20,000*l.* a year—Batopedion (' The Boy and the Bush '). The boy was Arcadius, son of Theodosius, who, being shipwrecked on the coast, was found by some men—or some angels—under a blackberry bush. ' Who are you ? ' they said. ' I am the son of the Emperor,' he answered. News was sent to Theodosius, and accordingly he and Arcadius founded the monastery. Honorius sent four granite columns, and our old Ravenna friend, Galla Placidia, his sister, helped forward the building of it, and was hastening into the church to see how the work went on, when a picture of the Virgin at the entrance of the choir bade her pause, and a gallery which exists here alone in the monasteries was built for her to overlook the interior. It is believed that the same voice forbade the entrance of Lady Stratford !

The interior of the church, whether built by Galla Placidia or not, is the oldest in the peninsula. It has some venerable mosaics and some curious relics. One is the head of Gregory Nazianzen ; another is the girdle of the Virgin given by her to St. Thomas, who doubted a second time, to convince him of the Assumption. We arrived on the eve of the Festival of the Girdle, and, in consequence, the monastery was crowded with pilgrims, and therefore, instead of the magnificent apartments we had anticipated in this the greatest of the monasteries, we had the very worst and smallest that we had in the whole circuit.

There was service in the church all night, part of which I attended, but without a Michael Sukatin to explain ; it was useless, and it had, besides, this inconvenient result : that the whole efficient staff of the monastery was asleep the next day till 2 P.M., so that we had much difficulty in finding any one to show us about. Amongst other objects was the exiled Bishop of Philippopolis, whom, as you remember, the Patriarch had desired us to see. ' He is gone to Caryes this very morning' was the answer, so that we were obliged to content ourselves with an outward survey of his rooms, which certainly had not the appearance of a dungeon, but were, on the contrary, a charming turret commanding extensive views, and opposite to another occupied by the exiled Bishop of Varna. In fact, all the bishops on Mount Athos are exiled bishops, except the ex-Patriarch Anthoinus, who lives here for pleasure.

It was not till a week afterwards that I heard through the servant of Philippopolis, who met Georgio on the steamer, that the expedition to Caryes was all a fiction, that the Bishop had been asleep with the rest of the monastery after the vigil of the preceding night, and had told his servant to refuse admission to any one, and had been much vexed on waking to hear that two English gentlemen had asked to see him, and that he had lost the opportunity. The muleteers and peasants belonging to the monastery were all drunk from the festival, so that we started with a drunken Bulgarian and an obstinate mule, who between them tore one of our bags—I think the only misfortune our luggage has sustained.

From the confusion and grandeur of the 'Boy in the Bush,' we found a charming retreat in the little Convent of

Esphigmenou, ' the Squeezed,' squeezed between three hills, but opening immediately on the sea shore, the waves dashing audibly through the night against the walls, the view opening full on Samothrace.

The Abbot paid us a long visit, and chatted familiarly on things great and small. In this monastery was the ex-Patriarch Anthoinus, to whom we had a special letter of introduction from his relative, Philip Baltazzi. His chief conversation turned on Reschid Pasha and Lord Stratford, whom he described as the physician always feeling the pulse of the sick man.

At Chiliandari, the monastery of the thousand men, we closed the third group of monasteries. There still remained the four in the south-west corner, which I left unseen, reluctantly, but not liking to leave Clark, who was forced to press onwards by land to Thessalonica, and also wishing to see the canal of Xerxes, I determined to advance. Chiliandari was a beautiful inland monastery, with a large vine growing out of the tomb of its Servian founder, of which the grapes have a large circulation throughout the empire for insuring heirs to a family.

With regrets I turned away from the last of the hospitable portals. Nothing could have been more friendly, with the single exception of Batopedion, nor more luxurious than our reception. The cleanliness of the rooms and beds was a constant surprise to us.

Far different was the scene when from this world of shades we emerged once more into the world of life : but this for another letter.   Ever yours,

A. P. STANLEY.

LXXVIII

A. P. S. to Mrs. Stanley.

THE CANAL OF XERXES.

[On leaving Mount Athos, Stanley and Professor Clark travelled to Salonica, passing on the way the canal of Xerxes. The deep dyke which still remains forms the boundary of the Holy Mountain. The word 'Provlaka' is stated by Mr. Tozer ('The Highlands of Turkey,' vol. i. ch. vi.) to be a corruption of προαύλαξ—*i.e.* 'the furrow in front of Mount Athos.'

Stagira, the birthplace of Aristotle, was identified by Leake with Stavros; but the local tradition of Macedonia claims the honour for Isboros.]

Salonica : September 23 [1861].

My dearest Mother,—The descent from the Holy Mountain was very gradual. It took, I think, five hours to disentangle ourselves from its long skirts. We then followed the isthmus which connects it with the mainland of Macedonia. Through this isthmus somewhere we were to look for the remains of Xerxes' canal. Our muleteer from Chiliandari had been charged by the monks there to point it out to us, by the name which, through a slight corruption, it still bears of Provlaka, 'the Hollow.' He was a Bulgarian, and could not speak a word of Greek, so that no questions could be asked him. It was therefore somewhat tantalising when, on arriving at the isthmus, we found that it was not a single plain, but a succession of elevations and depressions, each of which might be the canal. At each successive ascent we exclaimed, ' The next will be the one ; ' at each successive descent we exclaimed, 'The next will be the one.' Clark, who was more eager about the canal than about all the monasteries put together, became quite nervous. We had begun to make up our

minds that we must have passed it, when, just as the
isthmus seemed about to end, we dropped down on one
remaining plain. It was only a mile or so across. It was
nearly flat. There was a complete opening to the sea on
each side. We both exclaimed, ' This is the canal,' and at
the same moment the Bulgarian at last broke silence, and
said one word, ' Provlaka.' It certainly was interesting to
see the traces marked by a visible hollow running across
from sea to sea, of that great and fatal attempt to sur-
mount the difficulties thrown out by Athos in the way
of the Persian king.

The sun was setting as we climbed the opposite hill,
and every feature lay clear before us—Athos himself in the
distance, the vast wooded promontory intervening, the
narrow tempting neck of land, the course of the canal
tracked by a continuous line of trees from the eastern to
the western side. The sun set and the young moon rose,
and we entered the village of Acanthus, and climbed up
into the wretched loft of a Greek cottage, such as I had
not seen since 1839. How all the past came back! the
same clatter and delay, and darkness and filth, and old
recollections faded and strange. It was, however, far
worse than anything I recollect before. Such an army of
fleas and sandflies, that I had at one time really the
thought of returning to my beloved mountain, and leaving
Clark to finish his journey alone. But after a night,
sleepless as it was, in which I felt for the sufferings of H. P.,
I determined to go on. A somewhat wearisome day and
a ten hours' ride. We halted at Isboros, the site of the
birthplace of Aristotle, passing through the remains of the
mines of Thucydides—woods and lanes like an English
park—and at last reached a second sleeping-place hardly
better than the first. The third day was a magnificent
ride. It was along the ridge of a wooded range, which on

the north looked down upon the plains and lakes of
Macedonia, on the south over the three peninsular promontories, on the east rose the now familiar peak of Athos, and
just as we lost sight of it by crossing over the hills to the
west, burst into sight the many-headed range of Olympus,
with its little satellite Ossa beneath—Athos, Olympus, and
to them we must add Samothrace, the three great sacred
mountains of this recess of the old Grecian world. Samothrace, the island, rugged, bare, jagged, the seat of the old
Pelasgic worship, no one knows what, or by whom ; Olympus
on the mainland, its long sweep of many tops, the natural
seat of the many gods of Polytheism, the great basin
enclosed within its sweep, the scene of their council, and
the curved crags above it, the throne of Jupiter ; and
behind these two, entirely unappropriated by any pagan
tradition or mythology, rises the solitary peak of Athos.

The third night we had a tolerably good resting-place.
The fourth day was over a wilderness, broken at noon by
an oasis, in which we halted under a plane tree by a well.
Our caravan is increased by a merchant from Athos, a
little maid going into service at Salonica, two Jews, and a
monk from a neighbouring convent of the Anastasis (the
Resurrection). As we lay there, I could not help thinking
how like it was to a scene in 'Persiles and Sigismunda,' [2]
and indeed we had on the two preceding days passed over
the scene of two singular tragedies which might easily have
been worked into a romance.

With these stories the time was whiled away, and we
reached the desolate plain of Salonica. Two Turkish
baths, at some distance from the town, indicate the origin
of its old name Therma, 'the hot springs.' The plain is
covered with funeral mounds just like those on the plain of

---

[2] A romance by Cervantes, which had been recently translated by the Hon.
Louisa Stanley.

Troy.   Had there been a Macedonian instead of a Chiote Homer, this and not Troy might have been the scene of the ' Iliad.' We proceeded at once to the Consulate.   Clark was to embark the next day for the Dardanelles, and so here we parted.   He was an agreeable companion, full of information and interest on all classical subjects, but for the monasteries caring but little.

The curtailment of my tour of the monasteries had left me open to any distribution of the remaining week.   As soon as I saw the Consul, he said, ' I am going to Mount Athos for three days—to-morrow—will you not come too ? ' I at once consented ; the results in my next letter.

Ever yours,

A. P. S.

LXXIX.

A. P. S. to Mrs. Stanley.

THE TWO AUGURS.

[The seven theological essays collected in ' Essays and Reviews ' were published in February 1860.   The volume was severely criticised in the ' Quarterly Review ' (Jan. 1861), in an article which was at the time attributed to Bishop Wilberforce.   Stanley, in a powerful article in the ' Edinburgh Review ' for April 1861, insisted on the injustice with which the writers had been treated.

The death of the Prince Consort (December 14, 1861), to which the remainder of the letter refers, deeply affected Stanley, who was one of the late Prince's chaplains. (See ' Life,' vol. ii. p. 60.)]

January 12, 1862.

My dearest Mother,—I missed H. P. yesterday.   I think that I must dine with Price, and return early. Labuan[3] wants me to dine with him on Friday ; he appeared

---

[3] Bishop McDougall.

at Cuddesdon last night; the rest of the party were mostly
domestic. The curate had been two years chaplain to the
Embassy at Constantinople, and told me some curious
things about Lord Stratford.

S. O. had a bad cold. Whether from this or any other
cause, he was much more subdued than usual, and we had
actually some *reasonable* talk, a *tête-à-tête*, about 'Essays
and Reviews.' I will tell you about it when we meet. I
defended Wilson, and asked him to name the objectionable
passages. 'I am not so well up in his essay,' he said, 'as
I was a year ago.' 'Neither am I,' said I, 'for a similar
reason.' He burst out laughing and said, 'The two Augurs
have at last met.'

Max Müller has been here to-day; he told me a few
more details about the Prince and the Queen : that the
Queen said to the Duchess of Sutherland, as they looked
together at the dead face, 'Will they do him justice now ?'

I walked with Mark Pattison to-day. He took the most
serious view of the death, of any one that I have seen, saying
that he could not have believed it possible beforehand that
the loss of one man could have made such a difference in
his thoughts, and that, whenever he began to think of public
or Church affairs, he felt a blank.

I shall, if I can, sleep at Sonning to-morrow night, and
come on Tuesday.   Ever yours,

A. P. STANLEY.

LXXX.

A. P. S. to Mrs. Stanley.

PRINCESS HOHENLOHE AND THE PRINCE CONSORT.

[Victoire Marie Louise, the youngest sister of the Duke
of Coburg and aunt of the Prince Consort, married in 1803
Prince Emich Charles of Leiningen. At his death she

was left a widow with one son and one daughter, Anna
Feodora, who afterwards married the Prince of Hohenlohe-
Langenburg. In July 1818 the widowed Princess Leiningen
married the Duke of Kent. Her daughter, born on the
24th of May, 1819, is Queen Victoria. The Princess
Hohenlohe was, therefore, not only first cousin to the Prince
Consort, but half-sister to the Queen. She died in Sep-
tember 1872. It was during Stanley's visit to Osborne
that he was asked to go with the Prince of Wales on his
Eastern Tour.]

Osborne: Jan. 17, 1862.

My dearest Mother,—The Prince of Wales and Prince
Louis called me out to walk. We went to the farm and
the Swiss Cottage. The different objects in the museum
were very interesting, collected by himself or by Prince
Alfred from the different countries where they had been.

We parted in order that I might return to see the
Princess Hohenlohe. She is a charming person. She
began by asking about Athanasius—where there was a
good life of him. Strangely enough, there was really none
that I could recommend except in the great Church His-
tories. I promised her that I would send her a volume.
From him we passed on to Luther's Translation of the Bible,
Bunsen, the controversies in England and Germany, the
disputes about the Eucharist, on which she spoke most
admirably, describing the hopelessness of explaining to
children the differences between the various views, and the
necessity of resting at last in the thoughts inspired by the
original institution.

Then she said : 'What a loss we have had !' and proceeded to talk of the Prince. What she said confirmed
everything we had heard from the best authorities, but in
the highest sense. He had often said to the Queen herself
that he had no clinging to life—that he knew, in case of a
dangerous illness, he should fall before it, because he could
not resist it. It was partly, she said, the actual burden of

life, partly the strong feeling of an ideal that he could never realise or see realised here. He also was inclined to take a dark view of the various questions that came before him, much more so than the Queen; who, 'happily,' the Princess said, 'has always taken a hopeful view.' Then he never spared himself, but, to spare her, took everything on himself first. I spoke of the support which the Queen must derive from the universal sympathy. 'It may be so afterwards,' she said, 'but it is not so now. The Queen says : "They cannot tell what *I* have lost." The much greater support was the doing all that he would have wished, and the feeling that he was constantly with her still in spirit, and happier than he could be on earth.' I said how wonderful a proof this kind of consolation was of another life. The Princess quite agreed with this, and indeed had felt it herself in the sorrows she had herself gone through. But 'no sorrow that I have ever had,' she said, 'has been equal to this. It is so hard to see a life crushed and to be without the power of alleviating its suffering. I had always regarded their happiness as too perfect to last ; but at the same time I could not bear to think of anything so dreadful as his death. Those poor children ! He was with them so like a child.' And then she said : 'It may be a small thing to speak of; but it was something to have so noble a spirit in so noble a form.' A cast was taken after death, from which an excellent bust has been made. I said how he was a king in all but in name. 'Yes,' she said, 'that was exactly the case, and that was what he was felt to be in foreign countries.'

She then rose, and I took my leave. They say that she is the main support of the Queen. Prince Louis impressed me very favourably. A long talk with Lady Augusta Bruce.   Ever yours,

A. P. STANLEY.

Note by the Queen, June 1895 : 'A most true account.'

LXXXI.

A. P. S. to Mrs. Arnold.

INVITATION TO ACCOMPANY THE PRINCE OF WALES
ON HIS EASTERN TOUR.

[Slatwoods, near East Cowes, in the Isle of Wight, was the early home of Dr. Arnold, whose father was Collector of Customs at Cowes (see LXVIII.).]

Osborne: January 20, 1862.

Dear Mrs. Arnold,—Your letter reached me—you see where. You will perhaps guess what I am about to tell you. The Queen desired that I would come here, to fulfil a wish of the Prince Consort that I should discuss the Syrian tour with the Prince of Wales. I came ; and after being here two days, General Bruce communicated to me that it had been the wish of the Prince, and was still the wish of the Queen, and was now the wish of the Prince of Wales, that I should accompany them to Palestine. You will suppose that such an offer so suddenly made, and involving difficulties so great of all kinds, and a separation from my dear mother for so long an interval of time and space, could not be accepted at once. But, after weighing all that can be said, and considering the urgency of the opportunity, I have determined that it would be wrong to decline an offer coming under such circumstances. I shall, I believe, join them at Alexandria.]

I am sure that I shall have your good wishes and more than wishes in this undertaking.

What the interest of my stay here has been you can imagine better than I can describe.

But I must not forget to tell you that one of our walks was to Slatwoods, which I had never seen before. The willow tree has now withered to a stump, but still remains.

The house is about to be sold. To see it from this place did indeed seem to bind the past and the future and the present together. One of the equerries of the Prince of Wales who went with me told me that he had seen a volume of the sermons in the Prince's library, with an inscription in it from his father and mother commending it to his special attention.

God grant that in these months which lie before me I may have something of the spirit and power which I first learned to know from that source !

Ever yours,

A. P. STANLEY.

LXXXII.

A. P. S. to Mrs. Stanley.

[The two following letters were written in February 1862, when Stanley, accompanied by his servant, Waters, was on his way to Alexandria to join the Prince of Wales on his Eastern tour. At Madame Mohl's house in the Rue du Bac he was a frequent guest, both before and after his marriage. There he first met his future wife, and there she was struck down by the illness from which she never recovered. For Madame Mohl's life see ' Julius and Mary Mohl,' by M. C. M. Simpson (London, 1887), and ' Madame Mohl ; her Salon and Friends,' by K. O'Meara (London, 1885). The Comte de Circourt and his wife in the Rue des Saussaies were among Stanley's chief friends in Paris. Madame de Circourt was the daughter of Simon de Klustine and the Countess Vera Tolstoi. After 1855 her life was one of great suffering, owing to an accident, but her *salon* was the meeting-place of the most distinguished men and women from all countries. Her life was told by Colonel Huber-Saladin in ' Le Comte de Circourt, son temps, ses écrits ; Madame de Circourt, son salon, ses cor-respondances ' (Paris, 1881). The letters of Count Cavour to Madame de Circourt have been recently edited by Count Nigra (London, 1894).]

Marseilles: February 15, [1862].

My dearest Mother,—Nothing can have been more prosperous thus far. A pleasant passage and journey, and reached Paris at 6.10 ; drove at once to the Rue du Bac, found the Mohls delighted to receive us. The party were Renan, Tourguénieff, Circourt, Prévost-Paradol, and two others whose names I did not catch. I devoted myself chiefly to Renan, who was what Madame Mohl called 'very nourishing.' He showed a curious mixture of interest and want of interest ; had not been to Damascus, because there were no monuments there ; was disappointed in Jerusalem, because there were so few monuments ; had made every effort, with special recommendations, to enter the Mosque of Hebron, but found it totally impracticable, unless by storming the town. On the other hand, he gave most valuable information about the various races, the ruins in Galilee and Phœnicia, and the Maronites.

Circourt spoke with the greatest interest about my going, saying that it gave such satisfaction to the Russians and Greeks, that the Prince of Wales should have some one with him who would not prejudice him against them.

A long sleep the next day, and did not go out till the afternoon. Then to Madame de Circourt. I sate with her alone for more than an hour, and never had seen so much of her before. She was quite delighted with 'the Crimea,' which I had sent to her the night before; 'so masterly, so completely placing one in the hospitals without a word to say how much your sister had performed there.' She asked a great deal about the Prince of Wales and the Queen, what books I took with me, &c. I also had much talk with her about her conversion from the Greek to the Roman

Catholic Church ; partly, she said, from the great discomfort of not belonging to the Church of the country
and family into which she had married, partly from the
inefficacy of Confession in the one and the efficacy in the
other.

Grant Duff, who was in Paris, had given her 'a new
Prayer Book' which she had not seen before. She begged
me to look at it on the table.   It was 'The Christian Year.'
She had been enchanted with it, and had only found out
that it was not by a Roman Catholic from the omission of
a hymn for the Fête-Dieu.   I opened it for her at 'Wish
not, dear friends, my pain away.'⁴   'Oh, yes! I know that
well.   I have read it many times.'   She had read Faber's
book with great pleasure and thought it showed a wonderful knowledge of human nature : it was like St. François
de Sales, not like Fénelon, whom she found quite useless.
I asked what parts of the Bible she found most con-
soling.   'Job and Tobit.   Not the Psalms : they are too
jubilant.'

I then, after calling on De Saulcy who was out, went
back to the hotel and there found M. Carvalho, the
President, I think, of the Jewish Consistory in Paris.   As
I was in the midst of packing, or rather directing Waters to
pack, taking my last cup of tea, paying the bill, &c., the
presence of this visitor was at first rather troublesome.   But
I found him so willing to be interrupted, and his conversation so curious, that I encouraged him to go on talking in
the lucid intervals of my preparations.

The curiosity was this.   Though a Jew, he professed
the greatest desire, not for conversion, but for reunion with
Christendom.   He said that the old feeling of the Jews
against our Lord had entirely passed away, and that they

⁴ The Sixteenth Sunday after Trinity.   They were the favourite' lines of
his nurse, Sarah Burgess.

regarded Him as the greatest of their Prophets, not, however, as *their* Messiah, but as the Messiah of the Gentiles.
'And whom do you expect as your Messiah?' 'There is
much difference of opinion. Some think that civilisation
is the Messiah : others the coming epoch, &c. &c.' 'What
is the opinion of modern Jews about the authorship of
the Pentateuch?' Great differences as to the date of its
composition, but unanimous belief that Moses wrote only
a small portion of it. 'What about the miracles of the Old
Testament?' Very free answers indeed. 'But are these
opinions general among the Jews of France?' Not merely
general but universal, amongst all classes, amongst all ages.
'But are the French Protestants with whom you converse
aware of this?' 'Yes.' It was remarkable that he did not
seem to be aware that there was any likelihood that they
would be shocked by it.

He was a Portuguese Jew, and thirteen of his family in
former times had been burnt by the Inquisition. I asked
him to what he attributed the great change of sentiment
among the Jews towards our Lord. 'Undoubtedly to the
change of feeling of the Christians towards us. Our change
dates from the great French Revolution when the per-
secutions of the Jewish nation ceased.'

Whilst holding these Germanising opinions on miracles,
&c., he was firmly convinced of the restoration of the Jews,
and the rehabitation of Palestine, and thought that steam-
engines were predicted in Ezekiel i., railroads in Isaiah xl.,
and telegraphic messages in Isaiah ii.

At 8 P.M. we started from the station, well wrapt up,
and with warm tins for the feet, slept tolerably well, and at
daybreak were at Lyons. It was literally like passing
through the iron gates of winter and the north into the
land of summer and the south.

We embark to-night. And so I start in perfectly good

heart. I feel that this journey is for me what that to Koulaka was to Mary—our part in history, whether we fail or whether we succeed.[5]   Ever yours,

A. P. STANLEY.

I asked my haircutter here whether the Emperor had ever been to Corsica. ' Not since he became Emperor ; nor will he ever. When once a man has reached the point that he has reached, he must not go back to those he has known under other circumstances.'

Farewell, but only for a week. Then you will hear again from me, and I from you.

LXXXIII.

A. P. S. to Mrs. Stanley.

AARON BURR.

Feb. 21 : Between Malta and Alexandria.

My dearest Mother,—' And when neither sun nor stars in many days appeared . . . and when it was day they knew not the land . . . and when they were escaped, then they knew that the island was called Melita.' For ' many days ' read ' many hours,' and this describes our misfortunes at Malta. The fog thickened so much before we reached the island that we had to go at a foot's pace in the night, and in the morning not an object of any kind could be seen in the harbour. Such a fog, they said, had never been known within the memory of man, and it was thought to forebode an earthquake. However, after keeping us there the whole day and half the night, it cleared off, and I was waked at

---

[5] This refers to Miss Mary Stanley's organisation of a band of hospital nurses and her expedition to Koulaka during the Crimean War. (See *Life,* vol. i. pp. 490-1.)

midnight by the delightful sound of moving paddles and rushing water, and we are now steaming away, with no hindrances, I trust, till we reach our destination.

I hope that, whilst Calypso from her island was thus employed, in a manner suited to her name, in detaining Mentor, Telemachus, who was to have been on the same day at Phæacia, was equally or more agreeably kept back by Alcinous in the shape of Sir Harry Storks.

Our crew has become somewhat more varied. To our Arab pilgrims are now added, on deck, a flight of Carmelite monks, and to our dinner-table a high ecclesiastical dignitary, Bishop at least, who, however, speaks nothing but Italian.

I have been going through all the Egyptian books again. They once more fill me with the thought how completely Egypt is the parent of all civilisation. Whatever may be the details of the interpretation of the hieroglyphics, I feel certain that the names and reigns of the great kings, and the general character of the people, are known beyond possibility of mistake.

Did you ever hear of Aaron Burr? He was the grandson of the great Calvinist minister, Jonathan Edwards, was early left an orphan, and was brought up at the college of Princeton in America. He was a boy of great abilities and firmness, and powers of persuasion, but wonderfully ambitious and unprincipled. A revival took place in the college, and the head of the college talked to him seriously and apparently made a deep impression. Aaron Burr retired to his room, walked to and fro in great agitation, and then said : ' I have made my resolve : I will never think of religion again as long as I live.'

Accordingly he devoted himself to his political career ; was all but elected President ; was elected Vice-President, and only failed of the other by the influence of Alexander Hamilton, a man of high character, and, from his being the sole survivor of the family of Washington, exceedingly popular in the United States. Aaron vowed revenge and challenged Hamilton to a duel. Hamilton reluctantly accepted the challenge, and made it known that he would not fire at Burr. Aaron meantime practised till he was sure of his aim. Hamilton fired in the air. Aaron shot him through the heart, and returned home to take his bath.

A howl of execration rose against him, and he was to be tried for murder as soon as his Vice-Presidentship was over. But such was the persuasiveness of his eloquence that the Senate, who hated him, were melted into tears at his farewell address, and under cover of this and a momentary excitement he escaped to France. He sent up his card to Talleyrand, who was Minister of Foreign Affairs. Talleyrand sent down the message: 'The Minister of Foreign Affairs will be glad to see the Vice-President of the United States; but M. Talleyrand begs to inform Mr. Aaron Burr that he has always the picture of Alexander Hamilton hung in his room.'

Burr returned at last to America. There was only one person for whom he cared in the world—his only daughter. He sent to implore her to come and see him. She embarked for Maryland. He went down to the shore every day to meet her. The ship was never heard of, and he died of a broken heart, and was buried no one knows where. A monument was raised to him by a lady whom he had deceived. He figures in 'The Minister's Wooing,' and he appears to be the acknowledged villain and genius of American history.

One of the passengers is a Professor of Physiology, going out at the expense of the French Academy to investigate the fishes of the Nile. He is full of the praises of

Aristotle—the wonderful observation and classification shown in his Natural History, particularly, as I have heard Professor Owen say, of fishes. The special points in which my friend is interested are the voices of fishes and submarine acoustics. They have, it seems, nothing corresponding to our voices ; but they have a kind of musical instrument in their intestines, on which they play, and of which the sounds sometimes penetrate to fishermen, and by which they communicate with each other. The Professor anticipates a time when, by further knowledge of these points, we shall be able to summon together shoals of fishes, as we now whistle for flocks of birds. He said of Lord Bacon this, which struck me a good deal : ' He was the first man who urged the study of secondary causes. That one dictum opened the door to the whole of modern science.'

This, I think, must be the eve of our landing at Alexandria.

A 'coloured child' stays away from an American ' Sabbath School.' One of the teachers—one of our fellow-passengers—goes to look after him, and finds him sitting on a stool demurely in the middle of the room. 'Why was he not at school ?' His mother answers : ' He went into a Methodist chapel, and there he *got religion*, and I was afraid that he would lose it again if he went out ; so I have kept him in the house ever since.'

Feb. 24.—The white cliffs of Barbary, and now the first headland of Egypt. We shall arrive too late to land.

Ever yours,

A. P. STANLEY.

LXXXIV.

Rev. B. Jowett to A. P. S.

THE DEATH OF MRS. STANLEY.

[Mrs. Stanley died on Ash Wednesday (March 5), 1862. The news of her death reached Stanley at Cairo on his return from the expedition up the Nile with the Prince of Wales. Stanley's answer to the following letter will be found in the ' Life,' vol. ii. pp. 75–6. In losing his mother he lost, to quote his own words, ' the guardian genius that nursed his very mind and heart.' He has left a touching record of his mother's life in his ' Memoirs of Edward and Catherine Stanley,' 1879.]

Balliol College, Oxford : March 9, 1862.

My dearest Friend,—The greatest trial that you could ever have in this world has come at last ; I wish I could be with you ; it grieves me to think of what you must suffer when you receive this packet. May you have strength to bear it !

I have no faith in words being able to do anything to alleviate such a blow. But the remembrance of the strong inextinguishable affection of many friends may be of some value even in this great trouble. Let me assure you how many care for you as though you were a relative, and what a sense there is (as a person said to me) of the noble and useful life you have been leading, and how unceasing this has been since your return to Oxford. Indeed, though the blank and the chasm are great, other ties are beginning to weave themselves for your support. Don't let yourself wither in sorrow like one without hope, but embrace the ever-increasing field of duties that is opening before you.

I know that she was father, mother, brothers, and friends to you all in one   Considering her extraordinary ability and intense affection, it was most natural. And now, perhaps, there is only one thing that she would have cared for on earth, or does care for, if the spirits of the departed retain the memories of such things — that the end of your life should answer to the beginning of it, and be consecrated, not without the thought of her, to the service of God and of mankind. I can hardly conceal from myself that life must be for years painful to you ; but things may be done in it far beyond, and of another sort from, the dreams of youthful ambition.

Please write to me, if you are able, and tell me whether there is anything you would like me to do for you. I called in Grosvenor Crescent on Friday and saw your sisters : they were quite well and took their great sorrow quite naturally ; they were full of kindness and thought about others. You need have no anxiety about them ; they are sure to do exactly what you would wish. All that I heard from them and from Lady Stanley would have given you comfort, if accidents could give comfort in such an overwhelming trouble.

Write to me for another reason, which is, perhaps, a selfish one, that life is very dark with me at present. I can't bear to think that I shall never more see that dear kind smile which used to greet me at Christ Church—that I have lost a friend who will never be replaced, who always greatly over-estimated me for your sake.

I trust that you will have strength to continue your journey and fulfil the great trust which you have undertaken. Don't allow yourself to think of any other alternative ; indeed, it would be wrong. It was her last request, and I hope you will not think me hard for saying that you ought to show yourself able to fulfil such a request and be worthy of such a mother. They told me that she never for a moment regretted your absence. She was glad of it, and said that 'she had thought much of its being better as it is.' What should you come back for? To leave a duty and do nothing, for nothing can be done? All her arrangements, as I heard of them from Lady Stanley, were as good and wise as possible, and such as might have been expected from her.

Rest assured, my dear friend, that there is a divine love as well as a human love which encompasses us, the dead and the living together, which leads us through deserts and solitudes for a time, to make us extend the sphere of our affections, beyond living relatives, to other men, to Himself, and to the unseen world. I am most afraid of your being stunned by the first news, not at all of your failing in the duty which you have undertaken, if you could reflect for a moment.

Let us remind you that your sermon at Oxford was one of the last, if not the very last sermon that she could have heard—with what happiness and pride! Will you think that I make a singular request if I ask you to read over the last chapters of St. John when you receive this news?　　　Ever affectionately yours,

B. JOWETT.

I shall often talk to you about her, when you come home, if the subject is not too sad a one.

LXXXV.

A. P. S. to Mary Stanley.

CARMEL; ACRE; THE HILLS OF GALILEE.

[This letter describes Stanley's ride through the hills of Galilee, a part of the Holy Land which he had missed on his first visit in 1853.

Josephus defended Jotapata against Vespasian (A.D. 67)

for nearly seven weeks.   The modern village Jefât between
the Bay of Acre and the Lake of Gennesareth seems to be
the site of the ancient fortress.]

Good Friday, Nazareth :
April 18, 1862.

My dearest Child,—After Nablous, we came by the old
route to Jenîn—the same view over the plain of Esdraelon
—and, the next day, along the plain by a corner of it which I
had not before traversed, and which to me was deeply instructive—the actual plain of Megiddo, the precise scene of the
victory of Barak and the defeat of Josiah.   Often as I had
thought of it, and earnestly as I had gazed on it before
from a distance, there were still points which this nearer
view brought out.   First there was the gradual drawing
together of the two armies, the one from Mount Tabor,
the other from Taanach ; then the waters of Megiddo—
the many rivulets streaming down from that angle of the
hills into the Kishon below, and in the flood occasioned by
Sisera's tempest turning the plain into a vast swamp in
which the horses and chariots would plunge and struggle in
vain ; then the great caravan road running from Damascus
to Egypt, by which Pharaoh Necho would approach, and
on which the Damascus merchants would have the shrine
of Hadad Rimmon.

All this I thought—and how our dearest mother on
that her birthday (April 15) would have rejoiced to think
of my gaining any new touches for my lectures.

To the rest of the party also a fresh interest sprang up.
For the first time since we entered Palestine there was a
chance of sport.   A gazelle appeared—not wholly without
interest even to me—in the sight of Mount Gilboa, on which
David laments for Saul, ' The gazelle of Israel is slain on
thy high places.'   The gazelle itself escaped.   But there
were quails &c., and in this way, riding through the deep

corn, the scattered party at last reached the easternmost point of Carmel, immediately beneath the scene of Elijah's sacrifice, which in my former journey I had reached along the ridge of the hill.

Our tents were pitched on the plain below. There were still two hours before dark, and it was proposed to go up and catch the sunset from that glorious spot. The ascent of the mountain, its rocky dells, its glades of honey-suckle and clematis, its fine old olives and ilexes, seemed to me lovelier than ever, and the view from the summit—birds again meeting every requirement of the historical scene—was fitted to a sunset just sufficiently tinged with western clouds, as the little cloud of Elijah's servant, to indicate the approach of the tempest in which I am now writing. The rest of the party were enchanted, and we descended just before nightfall.

There was no rain, as had been expected, on the 16th, and we went, still over new ground to me, across the plain of Acre, crossing the Kishon, and through the palms and gardens of the town, suddenly coming in sight of the sea breaking on the shore, pouring a flood of sea breezes through the hot noonday, and the little promontory of fortified walls, so inseparably united with the story of England from the Crusades downwards. It was a very striking moment. On the curve of the shore stood the troops drawn out to receive us. The Governor of Acre was with our party. The drums beat, and the Prince rode at the head of the cavalcade—the first heir to the English throne who had done so since Edward I.—through the old gateway and was conducted round the walls. We lunched in some beautiful Alhambra-like gardens, and then advanced three hours on the way to Nazareth.

The next day it was arranged that the party should halt and devote themselves to the pursuit of the gazelles,

and that the photographer should come on here.   I added
my request to do the same, by which means I should see
Cana of Galilee and Jotapata.   All gladly agreed, and at
10 A.M. Waters and I, with a native guide, who did not
speak a word of English, set out alone on our travels.

It was all new to me.   For the first time I made a
thorough acquaintance with the hills of Galilee—so far
exceeding in beauty those of Judæa—a continuous park,
lawns, glades, occasional cornfields of the richest green,
here and there a gipsy encampment.   Our solitary guide,
our only protector, was a curious satire on the band of fifty
spearmen, who, with their red pennants flying, add so much
to the picturesqueness of the royal cavalcade.   Even he
failed at last ; for, although he had been chosen for the
express purpose of taking us to the places I wanted to see,
he knew hardly a step of the road.   But when on emerging
from the hills we descended on the plain of Seffûrieh,
I knew from the map exactly the point to make for,
and so, disregarding his entreaties, started off across the
plain with Waters, leaving the poor guide transfixed with
bewilderment.   ' Behind that point,' I said to Waters, ' we
shall come to a ruined village, which is Cana.'   On we
went ; we turned the point ; for a moment I thought I was
wrong, but in the next the ruins appeared.   It is a village
absolutely deserted, on the side of a hill overlooking a vast
expanse of plain.   I carried off from it a beautiful hyacinth,
a branch of a fig tree (' When thou wast under the fig tree,'
in Cana of Galilee, ' I saw thee '), and two reeds or canes,
probably the seed wafted from a neighbouring marsh, and
I have little doubt the origin of the name—the same in
Hebrew.

Having thus secured Cana, I insisted on Jotapata, the
fortress where Josephus was taken prisoner.   By this time
the guide had rejoined us, and fortified by our success and

by the information of two or three peasants, he became
tractable and went on with us. We mounted a glen, at the
mouth of which Cana stands, the most beautiful I have seen
in Palestine, more like those of Mount Athos, filled with
the most luxuriant vegetation of various trees, creepers, and
flowers. At the head of this is the huge hill with its abrupt
sides, which Josephus, with much precision and some exag-
gerations, describes so as to leave no doubt of its identity.
Riding above the defile which forms its eastern defence,
descended again into the plain, and we, passing by Seffûrieh, the alleged residence of Joachim and Anna, reached
Nazareth, or rather the hill above it, at sunset.

I was thoroughly rejoiced with my day's work, and
went to bed at 8 P.M. After I was in bed, I received a
long visit from the Protestant missionary in the town, Mr.
Zeller, and then fell asleep, to be waked by the most violent
storm of wind and rain, which lasted all night, and to-day
(Good Friday) is still raging, and, I am almost afraid, will
detain the shooting party. I walked down into the town
and looked into the three churches, Greek, Latin, and
English, each with its little sprinkling of Arab con-
verts. But the true interest, as heretofore, is the secluded
basin in which those thirty years were passed.

I do not think I told you our adventures on the return
from the Jordan to Jerusalem. First, there were some
Russian pilgrims, and amongst them an old Russian lady
carried in a litter. At a certain point in the road, not far
from where the thieves are supposed to have attacked the
traveller in the parable of the Good Samaritan, some Arabs
leaped out of the rocks, and plundered this poor old lady,
carrying away her parcels and off into the hills. At this
moment our luggage mules appeared, with our dragoman
Hadji Ali. He immediately drew a long sword which he
always wears, and capered about on the rocks, and so

terrified the robbers that they dropped their plunder and
ran away.   The next adventure was that we passed a poor
horse, wounded in several places but not dead, standing
where its master had been shot by these Arabs some days
before.   They had left the horse in this sad state, not
thinking it right to interfere with the will of Heaven about
it.   When the Prince came up, he took a more merciful
view of it, and it was determined to put the poor beast out
of its misery.

And now farewell.   Ever yours,

A. P. STANLEY.

LXXXVI.

THE BEAR OF BLUDÂN.

[These lines were written on a bear-hunt in the Libanus,
in May 1862.   In the sixth stanza Stanley mentions the
names of several of the attendants on the Prince of Wales.
By a metrical licence 'Kanné' (the courier) becomes
'Kanne.'   See 'Life,' vol. ii. p. 87.]

WHO is it from yonder dark cave that looks out,
With a visage so brown, and a long hairy snout?
O Yusuf! come tell us, I pray, if you can.
''Tis the famous old bear of the hills of Bludân!'

He lives like a hermit, he never tastes meat,
But the juice of the grape is his favourite treat,
And back in the morning, like a guest from the Khan,
Comes the merry brown bear from the vines of Bludân.

There is not a temple, or column, or ruin,
That is not well known to this learned old Bruin.
In the fragments of pillars he makes his divan,
And looks scornfully down on the world of Bludân.

There's no one enjoys a more excellent view
Of Mount Hermon so white and the Hauran so blue ;
The Palestine hills, from Beersheba to Dan,
Can almost be seen by the bear of Bludân.

Up, up, Colonel Fraser, and leave on your shelves
The Blue-books and 'Times' to take care of themselves.
You must lay out to-day your most politic plan,
For the game you must play is the game of Bludân.

Ho ! General, Equerries, Diplomatists both,
Professor and Doctor, come on, nothing loath !
Crosse, Downie, Macdonald, and Waters and Kanne !
The Prince hunts to-day on the hills of Bludân.

Ho ! Sheykh of Sarouza ! Ho ! Sheykh of Zebdâny !
Ho ! beaters and peasants !—if you can find any,
You all will be put under terrible ban
Unless you beat up the great bear of Bludân.

Look out for his footmarks, you see where he goes,
On the muddy soft earth, on the drifted white snows ;
See here where he clambered, look there where he ran,
O give us one shot at the bear of Bludân !

But the day is too short and the sport is too long,
And the horses are beat, and the beaters go wrong :
We must mount on the wings of those eagles to scan
The course of this wily old beast of Bludân.

Now the sun is gone down, and the tents are in sight ;
Come down, my good huntsmen, while yet there is light ;
You have had the best views to be looked at by man,
Tho' you have not set eyes on the bear of Bludân.

Climb up, never tire, tho' the mountain be steep,
Slide down, never fear, tho' the valley be deep.
There are chasms in life that are harder to span,
And pathways more rough than the rocks of Bludân.

LXXXVII.

A. P. S. to the Hon. Louisa Stanley.

MONTE CASSINO.

[In September 1863 Stanley went to Italy with his sister Mary and Hugh Pearson. During his absence from England he made up his mind to propose to Lady Augusta Brûce and to accept the Deanery of Westminster.

The two new points of interest on this tour were Canosa and Monte Cassino. The first is described in a letter to the Hon. Louisa Stanley, printed in the 'Life' (vol. ii. pp. 137-8). The following letter describes Monte Cassino.

The monastery at Monte Cassino was founded by St. Benedict about 529, and there, fourteen years later, the founder died. Florentius, the priest who by his slanders drove Benedict from Subiaco, was killed by the fall of a building while the saint was yet on his way to Cassino. From the sixteenth century onwards the abbot of Monte Cassino was the official head of all the abbots of the Benedictine Order. The present church was built in the eighteenth century on the site of the church consecrated, as Stanley says, by Alexander II. (1061–73), to take the place of the building destroyed by the Normans. Hildebrand, when Gregory VII., found a refuge at Monte Cassino before he retired to Salerno, where he died in 1085. The monastery was dissolved in 1866, but survives as an educational establishment and historical monument.

The best accounts of Monte Cassino are those of Tosti, 'Storia della Badia di Monte Cassino' (1843) and 'Archivio Cassinese' (1847). The letters by Mr. Gladstone to which Stanley alludes are 'Two Letters to the Earl of Aberdeen on the State Prosecutions of the Neapolitan Government' (1851).

September 30, 1863.

My dear Louisa,—I think that you heard of us from Florence. Since then we have seen two magnificent cathedrals, Siena and Orvieto. Orvieto, the refuge of two and thirty popes, we entered at dusk, in a whirlwind of thunder and lightning. Our four horses tore at full gallop through the streets, to outstrip, if possible, the approaching deluge. The lightning was one vast red blaze, and as we rushed into the hotel a thunderclap shook the whole place at the very moment that Hohl's [6] face glowed bright in the ruddy lightning flash. This was the close of a storm of twenty-four hours, which finally broke up the long drought. By Viterbo we finally reached Rome, and after one night came on to Monte Cassino. This, you know, with Orvieto and Siena, had been the main object of my journey. I had seen so many great conventual sanctuaries—the Grande Chartreuse, Sinai, Athos—that this always seemed to be wanting. When St. Benedict was driven away from Subiaco by the temptations of the wicked people in the neighbourhood (too near to the capital), he found a refuge in this lonely corner. There had been the old town of Casinum, by that time probably in ruins, as it is now ; and high above it towers the mountain on which the palace-like convent stands.

Mary (not being allowed to sleep within the walls) remained with Hohl in the village of St. Germano below ; H. P. and I took with us a ' vettura ' (not, as you might suppose, a ' voiture,' but—so they called the gentle beast— a donkey) to carry our bags. H. P. in his bag took with him his whole wardrobe, I only a change for the night : the consequence was that the ' vettura,' being unequally balanced, was always being overturned. Mark the result. When we reached our rooms at the convent, I found H. P.

---

[6] The courier.

sitting in despair over his bag, out of which he had hoped
to extract his little luxuries, and, behold, it had sustained
some vital injury, which made it impossible to be opened
till the carpenter of the convent appeared and rent it
asunder by main force.

When we reached the convent the learned Padre Tosti,
well known to the Dean [Milman], had come out to receive
us, excited by three letters of introduction which I had
brought from Gladstone, Odo Russell, and Lacaita. We soon
plunged into an animated conversation, or rather a flow of
eloquence from him, interrupted and guided here and there
by a question from A. P. S., on all the main topics of interest—Pope, Church, King, Italy, Naples, Temporal Power,
Martin Luther, Ernest Renan. He went on without inter-
mission in bad French (I am sorry to say out of compassion
to my infirmities), rather than in his own beautiful Italian.
I thought him exceedingly intelligent. He had a wonderful admiration and appreciation of England, so much so
that I could not forbear to ask him how he had acquired it.
' Was it by reading English novels ?' The keeper of the
archives, another very pleasant Benedictine, who was
sitting by, broke in with the suggestion that it might be
' David Copperfield'—startling sound in that remote corner
of the world. ' No,' said Tosti, ' I have not read it, but I
have a kind of inspiration. I feel myself more than half a
poet, and a small hint, the sight of little Mary Gladstone
(he had known the Gladstones at Naples at the time of
Mr. G.'s famous letter), is enough to give me *une dilatation
d'esprit.*' I begged him to take advantage of this poetic
inspiration, and predict to me the future fortunes of the
papacy and of Italy. ' Ha, ha ! What do you ask of me ?
Chi sa ? ' But I would not let him off, and the upshot
(delivered, I must say, with a vast amount of fine thoughts
and words) was that he felt sure that sooner or later the

geological crust of the Temporal Power would fall off, and a new formation would be upheaved in its place ; that the how and the when were quite beyond his imagination to conceive, but that he did not doubt some means would be found at the right time, and that some Pope for the emergency would be found, as unlike as Paul III. had been to Leo X., as Leo X. to Gregory VII., as Gregory VII. to St. Peter.

By this time dinner was prepared, at which we three fell to, and after a hearty meal retired ; H. P. and I to two spacious apartments, from the windows of which we overlooked a moonlight view of the whole valley and mountains far and wide around.   In the morning we were shown by our kind friends all over the curiosities of the place. Almost every vestige of the original habitation of Benedict has disappeared, and over his rocky cell have been raised a palace and church of princely splendour.   The antiquities of the place consisted chiefly of the archives, some of which were very curious.   There was the original deed of the consecration of the church, attested by the signature of Alexander II., the Pope who consecrated it : ' Ego Alexander Episcopus Catholicæ Ecclesiæ,' followed immediately by ' Ego Ildebrandus, qualiscunque, archidiaconus Romanæ ecclesiæ, Ego Petrus Peccator Episcopus Ostiensis.'   You see, or will see by referring to the Dean,[7] who these two last are.   The first, the mighty Hildebrand, not yet Pope, and with his curious affectation of humility—*qualiscunque* (as if he said, ' Whoever I may be—Nobody '), and the second, Peter Damiani, Bishop of Ostia, descending still lower in the scale of self-humiliation—' Poor sinner that I am.'   After a parting meal, at which Padre Tosti devoured a pile of macaroni with a celerity absolutely inconceivable, we descended and fled away to Naples.

[7] Dean Milman's *History of Latin Christianity.*

Naples pleased me very much. I had forgotten much and saw many things new. The whole public mind there is occupied with the question of the brigands. ' How wrong of the Pope not to discourage them! How weak must be Victor Emanuel not to be able to suppress them!' The Abbot of Monte Cassino (a truly dignified personage whom I forgot to mention) had issued a pastoral letter against them, but in vain. A party had been seized between Sorrento and Castellamare just before we arrived, and it was only by encountering some risk that we went to Amalfi. Then, having seen on the way the vast Cyclopean remains of Aletri, and I having explored a singular pit called the Pit of St. Tullus (caused, say the peasants, by a judgment which fell on some farmers who were threshing on a threshing-floor on St. James's Day, and were all in consequence swallowed up), we reached Rome again last night in the pitchy darkness of one of the thunderstorms which have now become habitual to us.

Ever yours affectionately,

A. P. STANLEY.

LXXXVIII.

A. P. S. to Mrs. Arnold.

ENGAGEMENT TO LADY AUGUSTA BRUCE
AND ACCEPTANCE OF THE DEANERY OF WESTMINSTER.

[Lady Augusta Bruce, the fifth daughter of the seventh Earl of Elgin, was married to Stanley in December 1863. Their life together was singularly happy, ' rich,' as he said, ' in incidents of extraordinary interest and happiness.'

Stanley was installed as Dean of Westminster on January 10, 1864.]

6 Grosvenor Crescent, London : Nov. 7, 1863.

My dear Mrs. Arnold,—From no one else must you hear

(1) That the marriage so long talked of without foun-

dation is to be. Lady Augusta consented yesterday to become my wife.

(2) That to-day I hear, on authority which I cannot doubt, that I am to have the Deanery of Westminster.

Oh, my dear friend of blessed days gone by, give your blessing to me in the great crisis of my life. It is my comfort to believe that my dearest mother would have given it her entire sanction.

Yours ever,
A. P. STANLEY,

LXXXIX.

A. P. S. to Mrs. Arnold.

DEATH OF BISHOP COTTON.

[In the autumn of 1866 Stanley and his wife left England for a foreign tour, which made Rome its extreme point. For references to G. E. L. Cotton, Bishop of Calcutta, see XXV. and LXVIII. The Bishop was drowned in India while endeavouring to cross a plank leading from the shore to a steamer. Stanley wrote an obituary notice of his friend in the 'Times' for November 3, 1866. (See 'Life,' vol. ii. pp. 252-3.)

The journals to which Stanley refers are those of Dr. Arnold. The description of the view from Monte Mario is quoted in Appendix D of the 'Life of Dr. Arnold.'

The result of the temporary withdrawal of the French troops was the attack of Garibaldi on the Papal States, and his defeat at Mentana in November 1867.]

Address : Deanery, Westminster.

Rome : Oct. 23, 1866.

My dear Mrs. Arnold,—I promised to write to you from hence, but I should not have written so soon had it not been that you have been so much in my thoughts since I heard of the sad news from Calcutta. You will feel with me how in our dear and faithful friend—faithful beyond what in this changing world we have any right to expect— a long tradition of past times is snapt asunder. I have always thought that there was no one in whom the recollections of what he had learnt at Rugby were so vivid and unbroken as they were in him. He had received those influences with all his heart at the age when he was most able to appreciate them, and he had never since received any others with anything like the same force. Living so much within their atmosphere, they were less disturbed in him than in any of his contemporaries, and he worked upon them and lived upon them to the end. I am sure that in the general mourning of his friends, and of those who know what he was in India, you may hear a reverberation of the same grief that overwhelmed us all in 1842.

We heard this sad tidings at Florence. Thence we came on here by Perugia and Terni. At Terni we drove up beyond the falls to Pic de Lago, which I had long wished to see on account of that beautiful description in the journals, and truly it deserves all that is said of it. Last night we were on the Monte Mario ; and there, again under a glorious evening, which blended the purple shadows with the golden lights of the city, and the Tiber, and the hills, and the sealike Campagna, we read the account of it from the journals of the first visit to Rome. The interest and expectation of what will take place when the last French troops are withdrawn on December 11 is intense, but no one knows.   Ever yours,
                                   A. P. STANLEY.

XC.

A. P. S. to Mrs. Arnold.

ANNIVERSARY OF DR. ARNOLD'S DEATH ;
THE RUBRIC COMMISSION.

[For a note on Mr. Hull see XXV. The Royal Commission to inquire into the varying interpretations put upon the Rubrics &c. contained in the Book of Common Prayer was appointed on June 3, 1867. The first sitting of the Commissioners was held on June 17 in the Jerusalem Chamber.

The Commission which sate for the revision of the Liturgy in the Jerusalem Chamber from October 3 to November 18, 1689, made, says Stanley, 'the last attempt to improve the Liturgy and reconcile Nonconformists to the National Church.' ('Memorials of Westminster Abbey,' ch. vi. p. 468.) The result of their labours was not printed till 1854.]

Deanery, Westminster : June 11, 1867.

Dear Mrs. Arnold,—How, as this day comes round there is always some fresh incident or recollection to recall the past! On Whit-Sunday, as I was administering the Communion in the Abbey, I felt myself standing in front of a well-known, unexpected face, which seemed to me hardly altered since I had first seen him, although his hand shook, and when he rose he seemed infirm and old. It was Mr. Hull. I have been to call upon him to-day, but did not see him. There was something peculiarly touching in the sight of him at this moment, when, after all this lapse of years, I am placed on the very Royal Commission, of which he used to talk so much in those old days, for the revision of the Rubrics. A great desire of his had always been that such a Commission, if ever it was called together, might sit in the Jerusalem Chamber, where sate the Commission which both Mr. Hull and he, through whom I first took an interest in those things, so much admired, in 1689. And it was as much from the thought of the pleasure that it would give him as the fitness of the thing in itself, that I have made an offer of the chamber to the Archbishop of Canterbury. Very likely he will not accept it, but it was a gratification to have had the power of proposing it. You will think of us all in the approaching Rugby Tercentenary on the 26th.

God bless you. Ever yours,

A. P. STANLEY.

A. P. S. to the Hon. Louisa Stanley.

CLERMONT AND LE PUY.

[The Council of Clermont was convoked by Pope Urban II. in 1095. The vast multitude, assembled on the open space behind Notre-Dame de Port, answered the Pope's appeal with the cry 'Dieu le volt,' and the red cloaks of the nobles were torn to shreds to supply the crosses laid on the breasts of those who took the vow.

Gergovia was defended by Vercingetorix at the head of the Gallic tribe of the Arverni who have given their name to Auvergne. The campaign is described in the Emperor Napoleon's 'Histoire de Jules César,' livre iii. ch. 10. The mediæval tower, standing on La Roche Blanche, and called the 'Tour de César,' is supposed to mark the spot which was seized by the Roman legions in the hope of cutting off the water supply of the Gauls.

Sidonius Apollinaris (b. 431, d. 489) was Bishop of Clermont ; his nine books of letters are in verse.

Puy is described by George Sand in 'Le Marquis de Villemer.' 'Rien ne peut donner l'idée de la beauté pittoresque de ce bassin du Puy, et je ne connais point de site dont le caractère soit plus difficile à décrire. Ce n'est pas la Suisse, c'est moins terrible ; ce n'est pas l'Italie, c'est plus beau ; c'est la France centrale avec tous ces Vésuves éteints, et revêtus d'une splendide végétation.'

The two peaks described by Stanley are called the 'Rocher de Corneille' and the 'Rocher de St. Michel,' also called 'L'Aiguille de St. Michel.' St. Michael is traditionally supposed to have appeared to Laurentius, Bishop of Siponto, in 491, and admonished him to build a church to his honour on the top of Monte Gargano in the Capitanata which juts out into the Adriatic and forms the 'spur' of Italy. The shrine of the Monte Sant-Angelo is a favourite place of pilgrimage.]

The Peak, or Pew, or Le Puy : October 26, 1867.

My dear Louisa,—I think it so very improbable that the course of our short tour will bring me to a stranger

place than this, that, according to my wont, I shall select
this as the point from which to address my accustomed
letter to you.   It is a spot I have long desired to see, but
have always hitherto hurried past it on my way to more
important objects.   Now we have wound ourselves towards
it through Auvergne.   Seventeen years ago we were at
Clermont, with the dear mother, Mary, and E. Penrhyn.
I had almost forgotten, at any rate I had not remembered,
how magnificently the city rose on its hill out of the rich
plain, backed by the long line of extinct volcanoes, and
how fit a theatre it formed for the bursting forth of that
moral volcano, the first Crusade.

In that first visit I climbed one of those old monsters,
and so this time turned my feet in another direction.   From
a reading-room in the town I borrowed 'Cæsar's Commen-
taries,' the works of Sidonius Apollinaris, first Bishop of
Auvergne, and five pamphlets on the site of Gergovia, for
it was this ancient fortress of the Gauls, which alone held
out against Cæsar, that we sought.   It is a vast oblong
plateau, running out from among the volcanoes into the
level plain, with sides in part precipitous, in part broken
into terraces, on which the various Gaulish tribes were
arranged round their chief, Vercingetorix, who was termed
by our prosaic driver 'Vierge historique,' and by a poetic
little shepherd-boy on the height, guarding his single goat,
'St. Victorix.'   With the help of these two guides, of
Cæsar, and of the five French Antiquaries, we contrived
to identify the scene of the siege, the false attack, the real
attack, and the walls of the ancient city.   The little shepherd did what he could to illustrate Cæsar, by pointing
out to us a mediæval tower, in which the Romans had fired
pistols up the chimney, and a breach in the wall, by which
a woman had indicated an entrance by showing them a pig
eating corn on the steps.   The commanding position, the

immense horizon, make this as fine a stage for the glory of St. Victorix as Clermont is for Pope Urban and the Hermit.

The letters of the first bishop seemed to me the feeblest I had ever read. If I were to imitate them on the present occasion, I should write thus : ' I might tell you that I am going to Rome. But you shall not find here an account of Garibaldi's occupation of Viterbo, nor of the movements of the troops at Toulon, nor of the Pan-Anglican Synod,' &c. &c. &c. But, taking warning by Sidonius's example, I shall proceed at once to our arrival at Puy, or *Le Puy*, the Peak, or, as some say, the Pew (Podium, or Pulpit), of Auvergne. Well may it be called so, for it is a city of a peak or pulpit—nay, of two—quite exceeding any other, on which any town was ever built. Both are volcanic or basaltic cones, remnants, they say, of a huge volcanic bed, from around which the intervening earth has been washed away, and these left erect ; and indeed there are others in the neighbourhood, though none equal to these two. One is dedicated to Our Lady of France, who has taken possession of it in various forms : once by a Miraculous Dedication, performed by herself like St. Peter at Westminster : then by a black image, brought by St. Louis from Cairo : now by a colossal statue, made of Sebastopol cannons, into whose shoulder you climb. She and her peak are framed round by a girdle of convents and by an extraordinary cathedral, of which the nave runs out from the hill into open space, supported by a vast portico and flight of steps, at the top of which in former times, and now, but for the stupidity of French architects, the high altar could be seen from far off in the heart of the city. On the top of this flight of stairs is a venerable old stone, called the ' Stone of Fevers,' probably descended from Druidic times, and used for 1,200 years for the cure of fevers. The old women stamped hard upon it, as they passed over it, as if to contract some of its healing virtues.

The other peak, or Needle as they call it, is a chapel of St. Michael—one of that long series of the Archangel's shrines which, beginning from his apparition to the Hermit on Mount Garganus in Apulia, on September 29, in the fifth century, have crossed from height to height through Europe, ending in our own St. Michael's Mount in Cornwall. There was a good old creature who had the charge of this chapel, and spoke with some little irritation at the secondary part which she and her chapel played, in comparison with the prouder peak and grander image which overtopped her and hers from the other side of the town ; though, on the other hand, nothing could be more contemptuous than the manner in which the male guardian of the Virgin's statue spoke of the convents and the clergy which were under its protection. But indeed they are both so beautiful that neither need murmur at the other, even although 'Michael has been robbed to pay Mary.'

Another most interesting point in the neighbourhood is the rock, also an old basaltic rock, in shape like the Athenian Acropolis, on which stands the ancient castle of Polignac, seat of the Polignac family, though now in total ruins ever since the Revolution of 1789. The peasant woman who showed us over it had belonged to the retainers of the house, who had been themselves unchanged for 350 years, as the Polignacs had been for 1,200. They had been left unmolested whilst the castle was torn to pieces by the Revolutionists : only their food was weighed lest they should be feeding, unknown to the Government, a Polignac prince. Poor woman'! she turned over with the most touching simplicity Augusta's locket, and said : 'You are in mourning for some near relation ; this must be the lock of hair which belonged to your lost one. How often I have lamented that I did not preserve a lock of my sister's hair when she died! And when my husband died, and some time afterwards the Princess of Polignac came with her husband, I said to myself, "Had I been rich, I might have saved my husband's life ; " but it was not long before I heard that the Prince of Polignac was dead, and then I knew that death could not be averted by riches any more than by poverty.' She assured us (and so do many old antiquaries) that the castle was an old oracle of Apollo, and that the Polignacs are descendants of the Apollinares, the priests of Apollo, whence springs our old friend the Bishop, Sidonius Apollinaris, the writer of the Gaulish letters. But the wise ones say that this is all moonshine. Farewell.　　　　　　　　　　　Ever yours,

　　　　　　　　　　　　　　　　　A. P. STANLEY.

XCII.

A. P. S. to Mrs. Arnold.

ANNIVERSARY OF DR. ARNOLD'S DEATH.

[The second volume of the 'Lectures on the History of the Jewish Church' had appeared in the autumn of 1865. In December 1867 Stanley published his 'Memorials of Westminster Abbey.' But the third volume of the 'Lectures on the Jewish Church' was not published till 1876, owing to his interest in the Irish Church question ('The Three Irish Churches,' 1869), his increasing work at Westminster, his 'Lectures on the History of the Church of Scotland,' and especially to the illness and death of his wife. The summer tour of 1868 was chiefly spent in a study of the Irish Church Question in Ireland.

The passage in Moultrie's poem of the 'Three Sons,' from which Stanley quotes, runs as follows :

' I have a son, a third sweet son ; his age I cannot tell,
　For they reckon not by years and months where he is
　　gone to dwell.

To us, for fourteen anxious months, his infant smiles
    were given,
And then he bade farewell to Earth, and went to live
    in Heaven.']

Deanery, Westminster : June 12, 1868.

My dear Mrs. Arnold,—Here comes your accustomed
letter. Two of your dear children were with us last night,
and I had a word with them in the hurlyburly which, as
you know, is always part of our London gatherings. How
vividly has the remembrance of all that we learnt (now
nearly thirty years ago) sprung up afresh this year! The
whole question of Church and State, the Irish Church, the
admission of Dissenters to the Universities—how completely fortified I feel at all points by the long familiarity
with the solution of these questions which almost all
reasonable people have acknowledged to be the best!

Last week I went to preside at the opening of a church
at Herne Bay, which led me again to read the poem of
Moultrie on the ' Three Sons,' and I fell again on a line
which had struck me much in 1842 :

They do not count by months and years where he is
    gone to dwell.

It is quite the feeling which grows with the lapse of time.
But another thought is added which is the result of the
increasing weight that is given by months and years to
the life and work of the departed. We have now counted
by months and years, and find that his influence has grown
and spread, and that the rock of his example is firmer than
ever. May you, dear Mrs. Arnold, still be spared to see
many months and years to witness and to be a witness of
what he was and is to us all.

Ever yours sincerely,

A. P. STANLEY.

XCIII.

$\left.{}^{\mathrm{O}}_{\mathrm{E}}X\right\}$ON.

[These lines were written to the Dean of Windsor
(Gerald Wellesley) in 1869, when Samuel Wilberforce,
Bishop of Oxford, was promoted to the See of Winchester,
and Dr. Temple, Head Master of Rugby, to the See of
Exeter.]

A MIGHTY difference seems to be
'Twixt Oxon's O and Exon's E.
In Oxon's O I seem to know
The mouth rotund, the world's round O,
The mystic sign that meaneth aught,
But yet may be an empty naught.
In Exon's E I seem to see
The simple, flashing, upward e'e,
The good beginning, broad and high,
Of Eager, Earnest Energy.
But still there is a likeness clear
'Twixt Oxon's and Exon's career.
On is the cry, to each the same,
Which closes either honour'd name !
On, *Oxon*, on ! from See to See !
Win*ton* ! wind *on* thy mystic dree !
On, Exon, on ! until thou stand
Where *ends* at last our earthly *Land*.
The boundless ocean's mighty force
Alone shall check thy onward course !
On ! Oxon ! on !   On ! Exon ! on !
Till each his destin'd goal has won !
And bid the Church that lags behind
Life in your *on*ward movements find.
And if, to analyse them better,
You wish to search out every letter,

There still remains, our minds to vex,
In each the common central X.
Perhaps a quantity unknown
Which makes two warring symbols one.
Perhaps a sign more sacred still,
Which moves the heart and bows the will ;
And marks the gold amidst the dross
In Winton's *crozier*, Exon's *cross*.

XCIV.

DIES IRÆ.

[The following translation of the ' Dies Iræ ' was originally published in 1864 in Mr. Portal's ' Hymns for the Use of the Parish of Albury.' It is here reprinted in the form in which, with the prefatory note, it appeared in ' Macmillan's Magazine ' for December 1868. It may be added that the accepted author of the Hymn is Thomas de Celano, a Franciscan of the thirteenth century. The best authorities are now agreed that neither Gregory the Great nor St. Bernard, to whom the whole hymn has been at various times ascribed, lived at a time when they could have composed a poem of its structure and metrical character. In Daniel's *Thesaurus Hymnologicus* (vol. ii. p. 123) the verse attributed to St. Bernard is thus given :

Cum recordor moriturus
Quid post mortem sim futurus,
Terror terret me venturus,
Quem exspecto non securus.

Terret dies me terroris,
Dies iræ ac furoris,
Dies luctus ac mæroris,
Dies ultrix peccatoris,
Dies iræ, dies illa.]

THE accompanying lines do not pretend to add another new version to those already existing of this famous hymn. But it has sometimes occurred to the writer that the supposed necessity of forcing all translations into triplets

corresponding to the Latin has produced an artificial stiffness, which fails to represent the spirit in the attempt to
preserve the form of the original.

The only exception to this is Sir Walter Scott's—in
the 'Lay of the Last Minstrel'—and this accordingly has
alone achieved a permanent and universal place in our
English Hymnody.

The following is an experiment of a version which has
endeavoured to compress only where compression was
needed by the sense, and to enlarge where the sense could
only be conveyed by enlargement.

Some stanzas have been omitted ; as, indeed, in the
hymn used in the Missal one-third of the original poem is
left out.

Lines from Scott's version, as well as from those of
Archbishop Trench and Dr. Irons, have been freely used,
where they represented the sense better than any other
form of words that could be found.   Into the original itself
have been doubtless interwoven other earlier fragments :
one is the opening line, taken directly from the Vulgate
of Zephaniah i. 15 ; another is the stanza ascribed to
St. Bernard.   A. P. S.

Day of wrath, O dreadful day,
When this world shall pass away,
And the heavens together roll,
Shrivelling like a parched scroll,
Long foretold by saint and sage,
David's harp, and Sibyl's page.

Day of terror, day of doom,
When the Judge at last shall come ;
Thro' the deep and silent gloom,
Shrouding every human tomb,
Shall the Archangel's trumpet-tone
Summon all before the Throne.

Then shall Nature stand aghast,
Death himself be overcast ;

Then at her Creator's call,
Near and distant, great and small,
Shall the whole creation rise
Waiting for the Great Assize.

Then the writing shall be read,
Which shall judge the quick and dead :
Then the Lord of all our race
Shall appoint to each his place ;
Every wrong shall be set right,
Every secret brought to light.

Then in that tremendous day,
When heaven and earth shall pass away,
What shall I the sinner say ?
' What shall be the sinner's stay ? '
When the righteous shrinks for fear,
How shall my frail soul appear?

King of kings, enthron'd on high,
In Thine awful Majesty,
Thou who of Thy mercy free
Savest those who sav'd shall be—
In Thy boundless charity,
Fount of Pity, save Thou me.

O remember, Saviour dear,
What the cause that brought Thee here ;
All Thy long and perilous way
Was for me who went astray.
When that day at last is come,
Call, O call the wanderer home.

Thou in search of me didst sit
Weary with the noonday heat,

Thou to save my soul hast borne
Cross and grief, and hate and scorn,
O may all that toil and pain
Not be wholly spent in vain!

O just Judge, to whom belongs
Vengeance for all earthly wrongs,
Grant forgiveness, Lord, at last,
Ere the dread account be past.
Lo! my sighs, my guilt, my shame!
Spare me for Thine own great Name!

Thou who bad'st the sinner cease
From her tears, and go in peace—
Thou who to the dying thief
Spakest pardon and relief;—
Thou, O Lord, to me hast given,
Even to me, the hope of Heaven!

XCV.

A. P. S. to the Hon. Louisa Stanley.

THE ROMAN WALL.

[Bede was born in the neighbourhood of Monkwearmouth about 673, and was educated in the Benedictine Abbey of the same place. In an offshoot of the same monastery at Jarrow he lived, laboured, and died (May 26, 735).

St. Cuthbert, whose mind, as he herded his flock on the heights of Lauderdale, was turned towards a monastic life by a vision of angels bearing to heaven the body of St. Aidan, the Bishop of Lindisfarne, was born about 635. Eventually he became prior of the monastery of Lindisfarne. But, eager to lead a life of greater austerity, he became an anchorite in a hut which he built with his own hands on one of the Farne Islands. There, after a brief

tenure of the bishopric of Lindisfarne, he died in 687.
His body was removed successively to Lindisfarne, Chester-
le-Street, and Ripon, and found its final resting-place at
Durham.

Dr. Bruce, who accompanied Stanley on this expedition along the Roman Wall, was the Rev. John Colling-
wood Bruce. His history of ' The Roman Wall,' published
in 1851, is dedicated to ' John Clayton, Esquire, the proprietor of the most splendid remains of the Roman barrier
in Northumberland, whose antiquarian intelligence and
classical learning have been most profusely and kindly
afforded to the author.'

The wall ran from Newcastle (Wallsend) to Bowness,
on the Solway Firth. Cilurnum, Borcovicus, and Vindolana
are three of the stations on its course.]

Chesters : August 17, 1869.

My dear Louisa,—This letter ought to have been begun
at Chesters ; but you must take the will for the deed. I
chose this locality because I think you may have heard of
it from Albert, and he, I know, will be much pleased at
our having been there. You may have heard that we
determined to vary our northward journey by exploring
Durham and Northumberland, which we did under the
guidance of young Victor Williamson, brother of Sir Hed-
worth Williamson, at whose house (Whitburn) we stayed,
or rather slept, for four nights, making long expeditions
each day to the haunts of the Venerable Bede, and the
curious, though not very venerable, Cuthbert.

These, however interesting, I omit, and pass on to
our fourth day, when we rose early and journeyed by
Newcastle and Hexham, under the charge of Dr. Bruce,
(Presbyterian) clergyman of Newcastle, who, in 1848, had
meditated a journey to Rome. The Revolution of that
troubled year interrupted him, and he accordingly determined to make acquaintance with Rome nearer home. He
turned to the Roman Wall, which from that time he has

A A

taken under his special care, more to him than Canterbury Cathedral or Westminster Abbey have been to me. In 1849 he took a pilgrimage of twenty-five friends along the whole route, guiding them with a staff cut from the oaken piles of the old Roman bridge at Newcastle, walking from point to point, and at times assisted by a long waggon drawn by two horses, called Romulus and Remus. As they advanced, their numbers swelled to two hundred, and they spent a good week in passing from sea to sea.

This charming old likeness of Monkbarns only needed Sir Arthur Wardour to make up the comparison, and him we found in our host at Chesters, Mr. Clayton, an ancient Northumbrian, who, by industrious and frugal living, had amassed, they say, a fortune equal to that of the Duke of Northumberland, and whose only luxury is the Roman wall, which he has taken under his special protection, living, as the name of his abode, 'Chesters,' explains, in a Roman camp or fortress on the wall, which they identify with Cilurnum. These two old antiquaries, differing from their prototypes only by never quarrelling, undertook to be our guides. There was, however, a third member of the party who must not be overlooked—Miss Clayton, the sister. She was attired in a sort of man's jacket, drawn over her robe, and we had not been in the house ten minutes before she produced her coins, with which she was as conversant as if she had lived in the court of Hadrian or Severus.

The first day, of course, of our arrival was devoted to the remains of Cilurnum immediately round the house, where we were shown the traces of the different epochs in fortress, wall, and bridge, and finally led, as by 'the Interpreter,' not to the 'House Beautiful,' but to what they call Antiquity House, filled with statues and inscriptions from the neighbourhood. One of these, as the 'Spectator' would

say, ' pleased me very much.'   It was an altar, dedicated
by some soldier, tired, doubtless, and vexed by the constant changes of religion, ' Divis veteribus '—' To the Old
Gods '—as if determined that they should not be forgotten
in the medley of new beliefs.   Another was by a soldier of
a very comprehensive turn of mind : ' To Jupiter, and to
all the rest of the Immortal Gods,' and then, remembering
that he had forgotten some one, ' To the Genius of the
Camp.'   The party in the evening consisted of the family,
including a nephew, heir of the place, corresponding to
' Hector of the Phoca.'

The next morning we were commanded by the stern
Claytona to breakfast punctually at 8.30 A.M.; and at
10 A.M. we three (Victor Williamson and our two selves),
with the two antiquaries, started along ' the Military,' as
General Wade's road is called, to the fortress of Borcovicus.
Most poetic and interesting was the sight of the wall,
holding its straight course over hill and dale, availing itself
of rock, morass, and height, wherever it could, but always
with its earthenwork towards England, and its foss towards
Scotland ; and at every mile its guard-house, and at every
six miles its station, and every station inhabited by the
same legion from century to century ; Spaniards from the
Asturias in one, Dutch in another, Belgians in another.
What a romance of ancient days might be woven from
the tidings of the distant world they had left, floating up to them in their remote fortresses, disturbed at
times by the naked savages from north or south breaking in upon the thin line of civilised life which runs
between !

Then we explored every hole and corner of Borcovicus,
including the trough, which is close by one of the gates.
Antony Place, an old labourer of eighty-one, who has long
lived on the spot, on being asked his opinion of the use

of the trough, expressed his belief that it was where ' the Romans washed their Scottish prisoners.'

We returned to dine at 7 P.M., and were again regaled with coins and legends of the ancient time, and started away the next morning, full of agreeable recollections, and indulging the hope that, in the rise and fall of Northumbrian nobles, our host and his nephew and his nephew's son might become the Duke of Cilurnum, Marquis of Borcovicus, and Earl of Vindolana.

Ever yours affectionately,

A. P. STANLEY.

XCVI.

LINES ON LORD HATHERLEY.

[William Page Wood, Baron Hatherley, was born November 1801, and died July 1881. Solicitor-General to Lord J. Russell's Government 1851–52, raised to the judicial bench as Vice-Chancellor in 1853, appointed a Lord Justice of Appeal in 1868, he became Lord Chancellor in Mr. Gladstone's Government from 1868 to 1872. In the latter year he retired owing to his failing eyesight. For many years of a busy life he never failed to attend the early week-day services in Westminster Abbey, and as a resident in Westminster he took a prominent part in every useful scheme of practical benevolence. Archdeacon Jennings was at this time Rector of St. John-the-Evangelist, Westminster.]

In remembrance of St. John's Schoolroom, March 16, 1870 :

A SPEECH OF LORD HATHERLEY.

A rolling stone gathers no moss.

I TRAVELL'D down the vale of years,
The path of mingled smiles and tears ;
For shelter from the rude wind's shock
I sate beside a tall grey rock ·

Long had it stood, from year to year
Unchang'd, whilst all was changing near.

Thro' summer dews, thro' winter snows,
Still deepening in its calm repose ;
The storms that from the mountain roar'd,
The floods that thro' the valley pour'd,
Fix'd yet more firm its ancient place,
Gave brighter hues and fresher grace.

Beneath its base the wild flowers sprung,
The feathery fern around it hung ;
Its head the hoary lichen crown'd,
Its sides the mantling ivy bound ;
The spreading shrub, the towering tree,
That flung their branches far and free,
And scattered wide their flowers and fruit,
Deep in its heart of hearts struck root.

So in life's wanderings have I seen
A good old age, so richly green,
Around whose form, beneath whose feet,
Bright children play, kind neighbours meet ;
Within whose deep and open heart
From each soft place and tender part
Sweet thoughts their fragrant odours shoot,
Good deeds their firmest fibres root.

Not so the restless crags that leap
From stream to stream, from steep to steep,
Smooth, slippery, solid as they glide,
But harder than the hard wayside ;
Along whose bright and burnish'd mass
Can creep no blade of living grass ;

Within whose stark unyielding breast
No seed or blossom finds its rest,
But from the stern intruder shrinks
To calmer nooks and humbler chinks.

No—let some cold congenial fate
Plant in the marbled halls of state
The rolling stone that day by day,
Continuing in no constant stay,
Spurns without heed or sense of loss
The softening touch of kindly moss.
Give me the rock that stands unmoved
By long familiar contact proved ;
The good grey head which all men know,
The tower that stands four-square to all the
    winds that blow ;
The hand across whose steadfast grasp
The thousand tendrils of a home can clasp ;
The heart that gathers sure and fast
The flowers of times to come, the lichens of
    the past.

XCVII.

A. P. S. to Mrs. Arnold.

ANNIVERSARY OF DR. ARNOLD'S DEATH.

[William Edward Forster, 1818–86, afterwards Secretary
of State for Ireland, married in 1850 Jane Martha, the
eldest daughter of Dr. and Mrs. Arnold.]

Deanery, Westminster: June 11, 1870.

My dear Mrs. Arnold,—Here again comes round this
well-known day, and again finds you blessed more and
more with the fruits of the past.   How thankfully you must
feel that dear Matthew's increasing influence and fame are
growing so worthy of his father, that, with all the differences

of character and taste, there is still the same element at work! I so rejoice in the prospect of his honours at Oxford. How thankfully, too, you must rejoice in the thought that, of all the rising statesmen, the one on whom all seem to rely with the utmost confidence is your excellent William Forster—such a true stay as he has been to you and yours!

You will sympathise with me in the great pleasure which I have just received in the almost certain assurance of Jowett's election to the Mastership of Balliol—so good for Oxford—so good, even more, for himself.

We are toiling on, as you saw us. I do very much hope now that I shall be able to return to my lectures on the Jewish, perhaps also on the English, Church. You can understand how the desire to accomplish what I have begun increases as the years in which it is to be done begin to be counted almost on one's fingers. But how constantly those words of this day return—'Not anxious that it should be done by me rather than by others, if God disapproves of my doing it.'[8]

This is the very day of the week, Saturday, June 11, which, whenever it so comes round, seems to bring the whole of that and the following week more clearly before me.

Accept our joint hopes and wishes for you and your dear daughters—for both are, I trust, with you.

Ever yours,
A. P. STANLEY.

XCVIII.

A. P. S. to the Hon. Louisa Stanley.

THE CELTIC CHURCH IN SCOTLAND.

[John Stuart, LL.D., was secretary of the Spalding Club throughout its existence, and was also secretary for many

***

[8] Quoted from Dr. Arnold's diary.

years to the Society of Antiquaries of Scotland. His best known work is 'The Sculptured Stones of Scotland.' He died in 1877.

Ninian preceded Columba in his missionary labours by nearly 150 years. He died on September 16, 432, at Whithorn, and was buried in the church which, says Alban Butler, he had dedicated to St. Martin. The gate-post of the deserted churchyard of Kirk Madreen, in Galloway, bears on it the name of Mathurinus, who was a disciple of St. Martin of Tours, and with whom, according to Bede, St. Ninian spent some time on his return from Rome. The more usual name of the churchyard is Kirkmaiden, as in the line

'From Maiden-Kirk to John o' Groat's.'

This inscription, says Stanley, is 'the first authentic trace of Christian civilisation in these islands.' ('Lectures on the History of the Church of Scotland,' p. 25.)

The story of the Wigton Martyrs, who were tied to stakes and drowned by the rising tide in 1685, is told by Wodrow in his 'Sufferings of the Church of Scotland,' Book iii. ch. ix. sect. 6. The truth of the story is doubted by Mark Napier in the appendix to his 'Memorials of Claverhouse, Viscount Dundee;' but according to the late Principal Tulloch ('Macmillan's Magazine,' December 1862), the tradition rests on a basis of fact, though the Government must probably be exonerated from the guilt of the murder.]

Newton Stewart, Galloway [1871].

You must have a few words before we return from this dear land of Walter Scott and my Scottish wife. Last year we left 'half seen' this remote corner, partly from the ignorance of hosts, partly from an impenetrable mist which veiled all its essential features. So this year we tried again. Our headquarters were with some old friends of Augusta—the Maxwells of Monreith, in Wigtonshire. They kindly asked to meet us the chief antiquary of Scotland, Dr. Stuart. Under his auspices, we devoted ourselves for two whole days to the exploration of St. Ninian and his contemporaries.

St. Ninian, you must know, is the oldest British missionary in existence.   He was a disciple, some say a kinsman, of
St. Martin of Tours, and long before Augustine, long even
before Columba, he took advantage of a Roman fortress,
of which traces still exist, to build himself a 'White House'
at Whithorn, which grew into a vast priory, frequented by
pilgrims of all degrees.   Of this there are two traces left:
one, the remains of the ancient priory church where he was
buried; the other, a wild island or rather peninsula where
he is supposed to have lived.   There was also, deep down
by the water's edge, a cave called by his name, on the
walls of which Dr. Stuart discovered what had never been
observed before—a rude cross carved, showing evidently
that it had been a sacred place.   This was on the peninsula of Wigton.

The next day he and I started alone on a journey of
discovery into the next peninsula, the Rinns of Galloway.
We were in search of two objects: one, a stone of the
fourth century having an inscription of one of Ninian's
companions, St. Mathurinus; the other, a cave-chapel of the
eighth century, whence an Irish saint, Medan, embarked on
a stone to cross the neighbouring bay.   No one exactly
knew where either of these sacred places was, and we,
therefore, had to depend on the chance information of the
manses on the road.   The manses of the Established Church
were mostly in the interior, so that we had to descend to
the manses of the Free Church, which lay along the coast.
At the first of these we interrupted the minister at his
dinner.   He was a man of very few words, and when I
apologised to him for the untimely intrusion, he replied, ' I'm
through.'   Being ' *through* ' this important meal, he was
able to go with us, and there, on a bleak hill, serving as the
gate-post of a deserted graveyard, was this earliest authentic monument of Christian antiquity (unless it be our Sarco-

phagus at Westminster) to be found in Great Britain. The name of Mathurinus is still distinct in its original characters, and confirms by its presence there the whole substance of the tradition of Ninian.

When we parted from our Free Church friend, he gave us a list of three friends, a minister, a farmer, and a schoolmaster, in the next village, to help us to the next object of our search, adding that he was sure that the name of the ' Dean of Westminster ' would secure us at least the loan of a pony, and that for himself it was sufficient reward to have had this half-hour's interview with us.

When we arrived at the appointed village, the minister was out, but his wife, an active, sprightly little woman, came to our assistance, and at once said, ' You must come to the doctor of the village ; he is an antiquary ; he is the only one who knows anything about it.' Thither we went, and found a bronzed and black-moustached little practitioner, who (as it turned out) had never been in London, but had been in both East and West Indies, and fought under the Princes of Oude during the Mutiny till India became too hot to hold him. He undertook to be our guide. The next thing was to get a vehicle, for our own horses had to rest after their long drive. For this the minister's wife and I went to the farmer. He, too, was out, but his wife, too, was at home, and she offered her services. ' There was the pony, but he was in the field. Peter should go out to catch him, but sometimes he took two hours to catch, and when he was caught there was no one to drive him, and the harness was lent to Mr. Hamilton.' However, in half an hour the pony was caught, the harness brought, and the doctor undertook to drive us. We drove on four miles over a waste country, almost to the very Land's End of Scotland ; left the pony with another farmer, mighty in cheeses, which we inspected for his (not

our) gratification ; and then scrambled down a huge precipice to the seashore, where, opening through rents in the
rocks on the wide, stormy bay, was Medan's cave, faced
with the rude masonry of which there is only one other
example in Scotland, and probably of the eighth century.
By the time that the doctor had driven us back (his tongue
by this time having got full play, and pouring forth the
most trenchant and amusing reflections on all things,
sacred and profane), and that the minister's wife had given
us tea and shown us Walter Scott's autograph in her
album (for her mother had been a friend of Willie Laid-
law, and had the inkstand from which 'Marmion' was
written), it was already 6 P.M.; and we started on our way
back to Monreith, which we had left at 10 A.M., and did
not reach till 1.30 A.M., having made a journey of seventy-
four miles. Often did I think of Guy Mannering's midnight travels in those parts, in the never-failing hope of
reaching Kippletringan.

Along with these memorials of ancient date are the
gravestones of the celebrated Wigton Martyrs of the
Covenant, Margaret Maclauchlan and Margaret Wilson,
concerning whom so fierce a controversy has been stirred
up by Mark Napier, and the scene of whose drowning we
explored this morning, almost at the risk of being ourselves
drowned in the pitiless torrents of a Galloway storm.

This morning we have plunged into the hills where
Robert the Bruce defended himself. To-morrow we hope
to see 'the dark made light, and the wrong made right'
on Ellangowan's height, and on Saturday to be in Westminster for a few days. We return rather more hurriedly
than we intended, I having been much pressed to preach
a sermon on Sunday in Spitalfields in memory of Charles
Buxton, whom, as you know, I highly valued and deeply
regret.   Ever yours,

A. P. STANLEY.

XCIX.

A. P. S. to the Hon. Louisa Stanley.

THE CHURCH OF BROU—LAMARTINE'S HOME.

[In September 1872 Stanley attended the Old Catholic Congress at Cologne. He gives his impression of the meeting and its work in two letters to the 'Times,' headed 'From an occasional Correspondent' (September 27 and October 2, 1872).

The Church of Notre-Dame de Brou was built, as narrated by Stanley, between the years 1506 and 1536. The motto of Margaret of Austria, 'Fortune—infortune—forte une,' is generally interpreted, 'Against good or evil fortune one woman is strong.' Matthew Arnold, in his beautiful poem 'The Church of Brou,' describes the scenery incorrectly, and, it may be added, tells the story wrongly. The church is not in the mountain solitude, surrounded by pines, among mountain streams, but within a quarter of a mile of an important town, and in the midst of a level plain.

Stanley, as a previous letter shows (XXXIX.), was an ardent admirer of Lamartine in 1848. The home of the poet's childhood is at Milly, six miles from Mâcon. In his 'Harmonies' (livre 3, 'Milly, ou la Terre natale') Lamartine has described the house and the surrounding country. He was, however, obliged to sell it to pay his debts.]

Mâcon [1872].

My dear L.,—Our tour has this year been so restricted in its limits, partly by our long detention at Baden, in consequence of the death of the Princess Hohenlohe, and partly by the singularly wet weather which drove us altogether from our projects in Switzerland and the south of France, that I almost feared we might return without giving you my usual letter—not that the earlier part was not exceedingly interesting.

Two places we saw in our first week that I had long wished to visit: (1) Varennes, whither we followed over hill and vale, and along the endless lines of poplars, the unfortunate Louis XVI., into the miserable little town of Varennes, where we explored every hole and corner of the scene of the arrest, with Carlyle in our hands, who has made not one mistake. (2) Tolbiac (now Zulpich), where Clovis was converted, a very ancient little church, which we were shown by a very intelligent parish priest, the 'rural dean' of his neighbourhood.

Of Cologne and of Baden I will say nothing, trusting that you may have detected my authorship of the two letters in the 'Times' of September 27 and October 2. Then, Geneva. Here began our rainy days, but I found the society so very engaging that I could willingly have stayed much longer. I always imagine that it still retains something of the flavour of those good old days when my dear godfather and your dear father travelled here in the days of their youthful enthusiasm for Rousseau, of whose works I always read something when I am on the spot.

Old Merle d'Aubigné I saw with much pleasure, and we talked much of the massacre of St. Bartholomew, little thinking that in ten days from that time the good old man would have passed away to a better world.

Then Aix and Annecy, birthplace of St. Francis of Sales, and then Grenoble, and then an unsuccessful attempt to reach the Cevennes; then Valence, Lyons, and a pilgrimage to a French Sonning,[9] of which I shall write to H. P.; and now here at Mâcon, whence to-day we made an excursion, which I shall describe.

It was to the Church of Brou, at Bourg-en-Bresse. Margaret of Bourbon made a vow to build a church in consequence of her husband's recovery from an accident. She died, and bequeathed the vow to her son, Philibert the Handsome, Duke of Savoy. He married Margaret of

---

[9] Ars, where lived the Curé d'Ars.

Austria, aunt of Charles V., and left her a widow after she had been married three years. For the twenty-seven years of her widowhood she devoted herself to fulfilling her mother-in-law's vow, and recording her love for her lost Philibert. The result is this beautiful church; it is contemporary with our Henry VII.'s Chapel, and in some respects reminds me of it; but the monuments are the most beautiful, I think, that I ever saw. They lie side by side; first the mother-in-law, the elder Margaret, her tomb festooned with clusters of marble daisies (marguerites), little nuns and geniuses weeping alternately, the nuns of the Middle Age, the geniuses of the coming Renaissance. Then in the middle, Philibert, his marble corpse below, his marble form, as in life, above, with his hands turned to his mother and his face to his wife. She, the younger Margaret, in like manner, both in death and life lies next to him. On her dead foot is a deep mark in the marble, said to indicate the manner of her death, from thrusting her foot into a slipper into which her lady-in-waiting had dropped a piece of glass. All over her tomb, and indeed all over the church, are engraved the words of her motto, ' Fortune—infortune— forte une.' much disputed as to its meaning. In the chapel close by is the corner, with a fireplace, where she assisted at the service. The windows are all of the time, repeating herself and her husband again and again. The architect, Andrew Columban, has perpetuated himself by beautiful figures of St. Andrew wherever he could get him in.

After Margaret's death her nephew did not care for a monument in this far-away corner of the world, and did no more for it than was absolutely needed. It was a marvel that all this delicate work should have escaped the Revolution, but the people of the Bressais knew its value, and for years it was stuffed with hay, which by concealing preserved it. How charming is a little fragment of history like this, crystallising the very thoughts and words and signs of the times in forms which deserve to be, and which one hopes may now, even in this destructive country, be imperishable.

To-morrow we hope to explore all that remains of the great Abbey of Cluny, and then to Paris (120 Rue du Bac) for a few days before we return.

You know that this is the birthplace of Lamartine. I forget whether you shared my temporary enthusiasm about him, which I still think was in some degree merited, when he was in power in 1848. I found some verses of his about his own neighbourhood here, which seem to me, in spite of his sentimentalism, to be really true—at least I always feel it in thinking of Alderley. Next to the great and famous places I have seen, or rather on a level with them, though a level of another kind, seem to me to stand out from all the past the rectory, the church, the village, the mill, the beechwood, the park, the mere.

> c'est là qu'est mon cœur !
> Ce sont là les séjours, les sites, les rivages
> Dont mon âme attendrie évoque les images,
> Et dont, pendant les nuits, mes songes les plus beaux
> Pour enchanter mes yeux composent leurs tableaux !
> Là mon cœur en tout lieu se retrouve lui-même !
> Tout s'y souvient de moi, tout m'y connaît, tout m'aime !
> Mon œil trouve un ami dans tout cet horizon ;
> Chaque arbre a son histoire, et chaque pierre un nom.
> Ce site où la pensée a rattaché sa trame,
> Ces lieux encor tout pleins des fastes de notre âme,
> Sont aussi grands pour moi que ces champs du destin
> Où naquit ou tomba quelque empire incertain.

And now, with affectionate love from both of us to our two excellent cousins,   Believe me,

Ever yours affectionately,

A. P. STANLEY.

C.

THE TRAVELLER'S HYMN FOR ALL SAINTS' DAY.

Being an adaptation of Arndt's Poem :
' Was ist des Deutschen Vaterland ? '

[Reprinted from 'Macmillan's Magazine' for November
1872.]

WHERE is the Christian's Fatherland ?
Is it the Holy Hebrew Land ?
In Nazareth's vale, on Zion's steep,
Or by the Galilean deep ?
Where pilgrim hosts have rush'd to lave
Their stains of sin in Jordan's wave,
Or sought to win by brand and blade
The tomb wherein their Lord was laid ?

Where is the Christian's Fatherland ?
Is it the haunted Grecian strand,
Where Apostolic wanderers first
The yoke of Jewish bondage burst ?
Or where, on many a mystic page,
Byzantine prelate, Coptic sage,
Fondly essay'd to intertwine
Earth's shadows with the Light Divine ?

Or is the Christian's Fatherland
Where, with crown'd head and crozier'd hand,
The Ghost of Empire proudly flits,
And on the grave of Cæsar sits ?
O by those world-embracing walls,
O in those vast and pictur'd halls,
O underneath that soaring dome,
Shall this not be the Christian's home ?

Where is the Christian's Fatherland ?—
He still looks on from land to land—
Is it where German conscience woke,
When Luther's lips of thunder spoke ?
Or where by Zurich's shore was heard
The calm Helvetian's earnest word ?
Or where, beside the rushing Rhone,
Stern Calvin rear'd his unseen throne ?
Or where from Sweden's snows came forth
The stainless hero of the North ?

Or is there yet a closer band—
Our own, our native Fatherland ?
Where Law and Freedom side by side
In Heaven's behalf have gladly vied ?
Where prayer and praise for years have rung
In Shakespeare's accents, Milton's tongue,
Blessing with cadence sweet and grave
The fireside nook, the ocean wave,
And o'er the broad Atlantic hurl'd,
Wakening to life another world ?

No, Christian ! no !—not even here,
By Christmas hearth or churchyard dear ;
Nor yet on distant shores brought nigh
By martyr's blood or prophet's cry—
Nor Western pontiff's lordly name,
Nor Eastern Patriarch's hoary fame—
Nor e'en where shone sweet Bethlehem's star :
Thy Fatherland is wider far.

Thy native home is wheresoe'er
Christ's Spirit breathes a holier air ;
Where Christ-like Faith is keen to seek
What Truth or Conscience freely speak—

B B

Where Christ-like Love delights to span
The rents that sever man from man—
Where round God's throne His just ones stand—
There, Christian, is thy FATHERLAND.]

COLOGNE : *Sept.* 20, 1872.

CI.

HYMN FOR ADVENT

[Stanley's Hymns for Good Friday, for Ascension Day, and on the Transfiguration, will be found in the 'Life,' vol. ii. pp. 417–421. The first six stanzas of the following Hymn were first published in 'Macmillan's Magazine' for December 1872.]

THE Lord is come ! On Syrian soil,
The Child of poverty and toil—
The Man of Sorrows, born to know
Each varying shade of human woe :
His joy, His glory to fulfil,
In earth and heav'n, His Father's will ;
On lonely mount, by festive board,
On bitter cross, despis'd, ador'd.

The Lord is come ! Dull hearts to wake,
He speaks, as never man yet spake,
The Truth which makes His servants free,
The Royal Law of Liberty.
Though heav'n and earth shall pass away,
His living words our spirits stay,
And from His treasures, new and old,
Th' eternal mysteries unfold.

The Lord is come ! With joy behold
The gracious signs, declar'd of old ;
The ear that hears, the eye that sees,
The sick restored to health and ease ;

The poor, that from their low estate
Are rous'd to seek a nobler fate ;
The minds with doubt and dread possess'd,
That find in Him their perfect rest.

The Lord is come ! The world's great stage
Begins a better, brighter age :
The old gives place unto the new ;
The false retires before the true ;
A progress that shall never tire,
A central heat of sacred fire,
A hope that soars beyond the tomb,
Reveal that Christ has truly come.

The Lord is come ! In Him we trace
The fullness of God's Truth and Grace ;
Throughout those words and acts divine
Gleams of th' Eternal splendour shine ;
And from His inmost Spirit flow,
As from a height of sunlit snow,
The rivers of perennial life
To heal and sweeten Nature's strife.

The Lord is come ! In ev'ry heart,
Where Truth and Mercy claim a part ;
In every land where Right is Might,
And deeds of darkness shun the light ;
In every church, where Faith and Love
Lift earthward thoughts to things above ;
In every holy, happy home,
We bless Thee, Lord, that Thou hast come !

The Lord shall come ! Where'er the day
Bids earthly shadows flee away—

Where'er across the listening sky
The lightning of God's Truth shall fly—
Where'er the gathering eagles sweep
Around corruption's mouldering heap,
There twice, and thrice, and yet again
We hear and see the Son of Man.

The Lord shall come ! His still, small voice
Bids every human heart rejoice ;
By each clos'd door He stands and knocks,
O turn for Him those rusted locks ;
Clear from each home the dust of sin,
That He may freely pass within ;
Give ample verge, give ready room,
For He to be thy guest shall come.

The Lord shall come ! In that great day,
When Heaven and Earth shall pass away
May we, in armour pure and bright,
Flash back His own Eternal Light,
And join at last the white-rob'd band,
Whose spirits round their Saviour stand ;
Where, when this weary world is o'er,
He comes with them to part no more.

CII.

HYMN FOR WHITSUNDAY.

[The following Hymn, with the accompanying note, is
  reprinted from 'Macmillan's Magazine' for June 1873.]

THE *Veni Sancte Spiritus*, the most beautiful of all Latin
hymns, ascribed to Robert the Pious, King of France, in
the eleventh century, is appointed in the Roman Church
for Whitsuntide, and in Luther's 'Form of Ordination'
(Daniel's 'Thesaurus Hymnologicus,' ii. 36, v. 69–71). In

the accompanying translation the attempt has been made,
whilst preserving as far as possible a verbal and rhythmical
likeness to the original, to bring out the deeper meaning
which belongs to the words, when considered as describing
the purely spiritual aspect of Christianity.

> Come, Holy Spirit, from above,
> And from the realms of light and love
>   Thine own bright rays impart.
> Come, Father of the fatherless,
> Come, Giver of all happiness,
>   Come, Lamp of every heart.
>
> O Thou, of comforters the best,
> O Thou, the soul's most welcome guest,
>   O Thou, our sweet repose,
> Our resting place from life's long care,
> Our shadow from the world's fierce glare,
>   Our solace in all woes.
>
> O Light divine, all light excelling,
> Fill with Thyself the inmost dwelling
>   Of souls sincere and lowly :
> Without Thy pure divinity,
> Nothing in all humanity,
>   Nothing is strong or holy.
>
> Wash out each dark and sordid stain—
> Water each dry and arid plain,
>   Raise up the bruised reed.
> Enkindle what is cold and chill,
> Relax the stiff and stubborn will,
>   Guide those that guidance need.
>
> Give to the good, who find in Thee
> The Spirit's perfect liberty,
>   Thy sevenfold power and love.

Give virtue strength its crown to win,
Give struggling souls their rest from sin,
Give endless peace above.

CIII.

HYMN ON THE ACCESSION (JUNE 20):
FOR NATIONAL BLESSINGS.

An Accommodation of Milton's Version of the 136th Psalm.

[This Hymn is reprinted from ' Macmillan's Magazine '
for June 1873.]

LET us with a gladsome mind
Praise the Lord, for He is kind !
Long our island throne has stood,
Planted on the ocean flood ;
Crown'd with rock, and girt with sea,
Home and refuge of the free :
For His mercies aye endure,
Ever faithful, ever sure.

Let us with a gladsome mind
Praise the Lord, for He is kind !
On that island throne have sate
Alfred's goodness, Edward's state ;
Princely strength and queenly grace,
Lengthened line of royal race :
For His mercies aye endure,
Ever faithful, ever sure.

Let us with a gladsome mind
Praise the Lord, for He is kind !
Round that throne have stood of old
Seers and statesmen, firm and bold ;

Burleigh's wisdom, Hampden's fire,
Chatham's force in son and sire :
For His mercies aye endure,
Ever faithful, ever sure.

Let us with a gladsome mind
Praise the Lord, for He is kind!
Him, in homely English tongue,
Epic lay and lyric song,
Shakespeare's myriad-minded verse,
Milton's heavenward strains, rehearse :
For His mercies aye endure,
Ever faithful, ever sure.

Let us with a gladsome mind
Praise the Lord, for He is kind!
Soldiers tried in every clime,
Sailors famous through all time—
Hands of iron, hearts of oak,
Fresh from their Creator's stroke—
These His gifts for aye endure,
Ever faithful, ever sure.

Let us with a gladsome mind
Praise the Lord, for He is kind!
Science, with her thousand eyes,
Sunless mine and starlit skies
Probes and pierces far and near,
Man's estate to guide and cheer :
For His mercies aye endure,
Ever faithful, ever sure.

Let us with a gladsome mind
Praise the Lord, for He is kind!

Hither, in our heathen night,
Came of yore the Gospel light ;
By the Saviour's sacred story
' Angles ' turned to angels' glory :
For His mercies aye endure,
Ever faithful, ever sure.

Let us with a gladsome mind
Praise the Lord, for He is kind !
Rustic churchyard, lordly pile,
Studious cloister, crowded aisle,
Lady chapel, gorgeous shrine,
All proclaim with voice divine
That Thy mercies still endure,
Ever faithful, ever sure.

Let us with a gladsome mind
Praise the Lord, for He is kind !
Breaking with a gracious hand
Ancient error's subtle band ;
Opening wide the sacred page,
Kindling hope in saint and sage :
For His mercies aye endure,
Ever faithful, ever sure.

Let us with a gladsome mind
Praise the Lord, for He is kind !
Give us homes serene and pure,
Settled freedom, laws secure ;
Truthful lips and minds sincere,
Faith and love that cast out fear :
For Thy mercies aye endure,
Ever faithful, ever sure.

Let us with a gladsome mind
Praise the Lord, for He is kind !
Grant that Light and Life divine
Long on England's shores may shine ;
Grant that People, Church, and Throne
May in all good deeds be one :
For Thy mercies aye endure,
Ever faithful, ever sure.

CIV.

A. P. S. to Mary Stanley.

THE VIEW FROM MONTE GENEROSO.

[In the autumn of 1873, Stanley spent a brief holiday
in Italy. His tour was shortened in order that he might
be free to obey the Queen's request, and perform the English
ceremony at St. Petersburg on the occasion of the Duke of
Edinburgh's marriage in January 1874.

Stanley refers to Milton's ' Paradise Lost,' Book V.
lines 185–94 :

Ye Mists and Exhalations that now rise
From hill or steaming lake, dusky or gray,
Till the sun paint your fleecy skirts with gold,
In honour to the world's great Author rise,

.   .   .   .

. . . . . and wave your tops, ye Pines,
With every plant, in sign of worship wave.]

Monte Generoso : October 1, 1873.

My dearest Child,—This beautiful place is just what I
expected—a large, very simple hotel overlooking the plains
of Lombardy, and then, within ten minutes' walk, the Lake
of Lugano and the range of the Monte Rosa, and, at an
hour and a half farther, the top of the mountain commanding the whole Alpine range from Monte Viso to the
Engadine, Lugano, Como with the Bellaggio promontory,

Maggiore—all visible, near or far, the vast sealike plain, the Apennines, Milan, the ridge of the Superga at Turin.

We have been twice to this mountain-top, once at sunset. On each occasion, the higher mountains rose out of a sea of clouds, which, from time to time, rolled up, enveloped us and then opened out, disclosing new glimpses of lake or peak. I have never seen anything of its kind so complete. The Monte Rosa, which I have not seen since our Zermatt days, brooded over the whole; above her shoulder rose with its irregular shape distinctly visible, the Matterhorn; then, after a number of nameless peaks, the Bernese Alps, Jungfrau, Monk, and the pyramid of the Finster-Aarhorn; then, far away, the snowy line of the Bernina. On the other side, springing up quite alone in the midst of the sky, the solitary Monte Viso.

What a vision as of another world, ethereal as air, yet solid with the solidity of eternity—as of the Isles of the Blessed floating over the shifting clouds of this troubled world—as of the everlasting principles of Truth and Goodness dominating alike over lake and plain and hill, on this side the mountains and on that, Cismontane and Ultramontane in all senses of the word! The setting sun struck here and there on each of the features of the view with different effects, as Heavenly Light strikes with different effects on each character and doctrine. Then comes the solemn moment of deathlike pallor when the sun itself vanishes 'in a moment, in the twinkling of an eye,' and the whole scene is changed—yet with a departing smile.

We saw a large part of the view also at sunrise from a nearer point this morning. There was the deep, dark shade resting on the Lake of Lugano and its mountains, just varied and veiled with a floating fleecy veil of mist, and the heavens from the East gradually brightening with the dawn. Then the great range, which up to that moment had stood out clear with a blank, ghastly whiteness against the dark sky, becoming more and more suffused with the advancing blush of morning, suddenly lighted up into splendour. We had found at the hotel a volume containing Milton's Hymn at Sunrise in the 'Paradise Lost.' It struck me for the first time that the five lines, which speak of the 'steaming lake' and their 'mists and exhalations' whose 'fleecy skirts' are touched with gold, as also the invocation of the pine forest which immediately follows, must have been his recollection of these very Swiss or Italian lakes. English or Scottish lakes he had never seen. These he must have passed in his early journey to Italy, and never forgotten through years of controversy, civil war, desolation, and blindness.

One very singular experience we had twice over—the refraction of ourselves in the mist, as in the spectre of the Brocken. Without a word beyond the truth, we might have described the 'Apparition of the Monte Generoso' as a colossal figure, standing in the clouds, with a halo round its head, encircled by a glorious rainbow, gazing at us till suddenly it vanished into thin air. It was the reflection just of the one person who was immediately in front of it.

No papers but the Swiss 'Times.'

Ever yours,
A. P. STANLEY.

CV.

A. P. S. to Mary Stanley.

THE COMTE DE CHAMBORD
AND THE CRADLE OF THE BOURBON FAMILY.

[During the year 1873, Stanley had lost several of his oldest friends—Dr. Lushington, Professor Sedgwick, Mrs. Arnold—and now, as this letter records, Sir Henry Holland.

In August 1873, the Comte de Paris had paid a visit to

the Comte de Chambord at Frohsdorf, and, by formally recognising the claims of the elder branch of the House of Bourbon, reunited the Royalist party in France. It was confidently expected in October 1873, as Stanley here describes, that the Comte de Chambord would be called to the throne. These hopes were frustrated by his refusal to sacrifice the 'drapeau blanc' to the tricolor. (See the Comte de Falloux, 'Mémoires d'un Royaliste.')

Paray-le-Monial owes its celebrity as a place of pilgrimage to the visions of Marguerite Marie Alacoque (1647–90).

Henri de Montmorency was executed in 1632 by Richelieu for an alleged conspiracy against Louis XIII. The monument to his memory was erected by his widow, Maria Orsini, in what was then the chapel of the Convent of the Visitation, founded by Madame de Chantal, at Moulins.

Moulins was the capital of the Duchy of Bourbon, which in 1523 was forfeited to the French Crown by the treason of the Constable of Bourbon. In the magnificent Cluniac church of Souvigny are several monuments belonging to the family, and at Bourbon l'Archambault are the ruins of a castle which still belongs to the Duc d'Aumale.]

Rue du Bac, Paris : November 1, 1873.

My dearest Child,—Here we arrived last night, and the first news we found was in Frank Holland's [1] letter. Being completely out of the reach of English newspapers, we had seen nothing since we left Rome. It is a great pleasure to have seen dear Sir Henry for that one evening at Rome ; he left all sorts of messages for us on his passage through on his return from Naples, when we were absent at Subiaco. He was a most faithful friend, and did truly rejoice in all our joys, and mourn in all our sorrows. When Dr. Lushington died, he said to me with tears in his eyes that that was just the end which he should desire for himself. It is singular that on this journey I should have lost the two oldest friends. How well I remember Sir Henry,

---

[1] The Rev. Francis Holland, Canon of Canterbury.

Dr. Holland as he then was, coming across the way in Brook Street to ask what we had heard of Arnold's death when the news came in 1842. I have written to Frank. To-day and to-morrow are indeed the days of the dead.

You heard of our hurry in leaving Rome. Besides the uncertainties that made us hesitate about the return by Cannes, there came the urgent reason that we should, by coming the shortest way, arrive in time for the proclamation of the French monarchy, as it was then thought, in the Assembly on October 28. The 'Times' Correspondent at Rome, the French Ambassador, Monseigneur Howard, were all persuaded of it. So interesting an occasion we thought was not to be lost. So we left Rome by the night train on the 23rd, arrived at Turin on the 24th, crossed the Mont Cenis on the 25th, and in the railroad heard that the Assembly was put off till the 5th. It was then too late to change; so we came that night to Geneva, where we spent the Sunday, saw Hyacinthe [2] installed in the church, saw the new-born babe, which had come on the previous Sunday, saw Madame de Staël at Coppet, and left by the express the next day for Mâcon, where we slept, and then came on to Moulins, where we had always intended to sleep, to see the cathedral, and a very interesting monument of the Duke of Montmorency. On the way the train stopped for an hour at Paray le Monial, and we accordingly walked up to the town to try if possible to see the interior of the convent. We asked a curé, whom we overtook on the road, whether it was possible. 'Quite impossible,' he said, 'unless you have the permission of the bishop. But it so happens that the Bishops of Autun and Moulins are both here to-day with the Nuncio.' We found them; the curé mentioned our wish, and the Bishop of Autun gave

---

[2] Père Hyacinthe Loyson was married in September 1872. (See *Life*, vol. ii. p. 411.)

his permission, and we walked round ; not much to be
seen, but still it was curious.

When we returned to the train, we found that the
Nuncio and the Bishop of Moulins were going back to
Moulins. So we sent into their carriage a letter which
Monseigneur Howard had given us for ' Monseigneur· de
Moulins.' When we arrived at Moulins, he came to us on
the platform, and begged that we would come to him at
the palace instead of going to the inn. We hesitated
for a moment ; but he so graciously insisted that we
consented, and it ended by our staying there two nights.
It was exceedingly interesting. The bishop belongs to one
of the old French families, the son of the Grand Master of
Ceremonies at the Court of Louis XVI., and grandson of
General de Castries, singularly gentlemanlike and attentive.
In honour of the Nuncio—an ecclesiastic of quite another
sort, an Italian diplomat, but distinctly agreeable—there
was given each night a dinner to all the high lay and
church functionaries of the town ; so that we saw the
whole world of Moulins. The intervening day the bishop
planned an excursion for us. We started at 8 and returned at 6.30, going to Souvigny, St. Menoux, and
Bourbon, the cradle of the Bourbon family—exceedingly
interesting in itself and particularly so at this time—and
the next day, before we left, he sent us all round the
town in his carriage to see the different churches.

We then slept at Nevers, and saw what there was to
be seen, and came on here by the next day, to arrive at
6 P.M. Every conversation and every French newspaper
have of course during the whole week been full of the
coming event, and speculation as to the result of the
Assembly ; and now, when we arrive, we find that all
is virtually over, owing to the sudden disclaimer by
the Comte de Chambord of all the concessions which

down to yesterday he had allowed to be circulated as having obtained his sanction. I cannot conceive anything more mortifying to the Orleans Princes, or indeed to the whole of the monarchical party, because there is now no time to organise any new plan. He has made his own return impossible, and has ruined the chances of the monarchy also. It does seem the height of weakness, or of folly, or of double dealing. However, we shall probably go to the Assembly to see what happens, and come here by the end of the week.

All are quite well, and the Mohls particularly—their house all new painted and in beautiful order.

The moment we passed through the tunnel we emerged from summer into winter, and bitterly cold it has been ever since.   Ever yours,

A. P. STANLEY.

CVI.

A. P. S. to her Majesty the Queen.

[The five following letters were written by Stanley to the Queen, and give an account of the marriage of the Duke of Edinburgh at St. Petersburg in January 1874. Further details of the wedding are given in the ' Life,' vol. ii. ch. xxvi.]

January 6/18 [1874] : Winter Palace.

The Dean of Westminster presents his humble duty to your Majesty. He thinks the Queen may expect to hear from him some of the details of this extraordinary visit, which in interest and splendour—he must also add, if your Majesty will allow him to descend to such matters, in *comfort* and in *warmth*—far exceeds his expectations.

From the moment that the Russian frontier was crossed, the attention was never failing. The arrival at the station was a sample which may suffice. There were servants dressed in a kind of Venetian costume, red cloaks and white ruffs of fur, who escorted us, amidst a thick fall of snow, to the three Imperial carriages, of which one took each of us separately to the Palace.

Lord Augustus Loftus had already arranged for the Dean to have an audience with the Emperor, preliminary to which he had a very interesting conversation with Prince Gortschakoff. The Emperor received the Dean alone, and carried on the conversation in the most kindly and gracious manner, partly in French, partly in English. The Dean spoke of the auspicious occasion which had brought him to St. Petersburg, and it was impossible not to be affected by the visible emotion of the Emperor at the prospect of losing his daughter. 'The two countries,' the Dean ventured to observe, 'the two Chambers, the two young persons themselves, are all rejoicing. It is only the parents that suffer.' The Emperor's eyes filled with tears, and he said : ' Yes. It is true. She has been the constant joy of our lives. But so it must be. I trust that God will bless the marriage.' Although so much moved, he seemed to be quite satisfied, and spoke only with the natural grief of a father losing a beloved child.

The Emperor also spoke of the former visit of the Dean to Russia, and of the coming festival of the Epiphany. This took place to-day, and occupied the whole morning. The service was in the Imperial Chapel—the same where the Russian marriage will take place—about the size of the nave of St. George's Chapel at Windsor. The Emperor and all the Princes of the Imperial family, even down to the youngest son of the Grand Duke Constantine, were all present. It would have been a fine service had it not been for the constant repetitions. The singing (no instrumental music is allowed) even to the Dean seemed magnificent, particularly the Creed and the Lord's Prayer. The latter the Dean had never heard chanted before, except by the American negroes, whom he thinks that your Majesty heard, and, strange to say, the effect of the voices was very much alike.

After the service came the blessing of the waters of the Neva. The Epiphany in the Eastern Church is supposed to commemorate our Saviour's baptism, and the Neva for the time is made to represent the Jordan. The Emperor and all the Princes were bareheaded on the platform on the river, and the whole quay below was filled with a vast multitude of people, all bareheaded, and all looking upwards, and crossing themselves when the cannon from the fortress across the river (where Peter the Great and the successive sovereigns since his time are buried) announced that the benediction was completed. The mixture of popular devotion with vast imperial pomp was very striking. The only drawback to the sight, as indeed to the visit generally, is the dark, dismal thaw, which reduces everything to a state of disagreeable twilight and slough, very unlike to the brilliant sunshine and sparkling snow that had been promised.

In the afternoon, there was the service at the English church, which holds about 500 persons. The Prince and Princess of Wales, the Duke of Edinburgh and Prince Arthur, with their suites, were present, and a large number of English residents, and several gentlemen and ladies of the Russian Court. The Dean preached on the marriage of Cana in Galilee, which, by a singular coincidence, occurred in the services of the day, both according to the Old and the New Style. It was, in fact, the same sermon which the Dean had preached before in Whitehall Chapel, on the Sunday following the marriage of the Prince of Wales, but. with many alterations to suit the present circumstances. He hopes that it gave satisfaction to the Russians, who were feeling so much the loss of their Princess, and that it would also, in part, reconcile the English to the English marriage not being in their chapel.

The Dean has seen the Hall where the English service will be celebrated. It is very well suited for the purpose. It is twice the size of the English chapel. It is close to the Imperial Chapel, so that the procession will pass immediately from one to the other. Even the pictures in it are not inappropriate, being of Alexander I., who was, if the Dean remembers right, your Majesty's godfather, and of the battles fought under him in alliance with the English. It has been arranged that the musical parts of the service —the Psalms and anthems—shall be sung by the Russian choir.

CVII.

A. P. S. to her Majesty the Queen.

The Dean of Westminster presents his humble duty to your Majesty. The marriage is happily completed, and the Dean trusts that the blessings which certainly may be anticipated from it will be accomplished.

The Dean, with the two English clergymen, went at 12 to his place in the Imperial Chapel. It was immediately outside the chancel rails, the whole of the interior of the chancel being occupied by the Russian clergy and the Imperial family. The clergy, of course, were there long before the service began, which was not till the entrance of the bridal procession. The Dean found himself with the other 'Églises étrangères,' *i.e.* the authorities of the Polish Roman Catholic Church and the German and Danish Lutherans. They are all under a special minister, who came to look after us. The clergy of the Russian Church were extremely friendly, and the old chaplain, Bashanoff, who speaks a few words of German, managed, by repeating a sentence several times over, to convey his assurance that love and fidelity were a very good basis for union everywhere.

The bouquet which your Majesty desired to be presented to the bride was, with the Prayer-book, held by an officer of the Court, deputed for this purpose, till the proper moment arrived. He came to speak to me, as having once stayed for a week with the Dean at Oxford, and was very much interested in learning that the lady to whom he was to surrender the bouquet was the Dean's wife, and that the myrtle had come from Osborne. He begged, if there was a twig left from the rest, he might have it as a remembrance of the day, and the Dean ventured to assure him that your Majesty would be glad to think that it was so well bestowed. The bouquet itself was one of the two that had been made up for the purpose. The Queen will be amused to know that one of them was procured late yesterday evening by Sir Howard Elphinstone and the Dean, who went out in a sledge to a flower shop to see if any white roses were to be found. It was with the utmost difficulty that they could make the shopkeeper understand what they wanted, as he spoke nothing whatever except Russ. At last the brilliant thought occurred to him of calling in his next-door neighbour, a barber, who spoke French and negotiated the business with the utmost intelligence and alacrity. Thus your Majesty's wishes were accomplished.

To return to the ceremony. The Dean need not repeat the details which the newspapers will doubtless give. He followed it throughout in a French translation. The tedious repetitions were shortened, and the interesting portions of it were thus brought out more clearly. There is much in it which is doubtless very ancient. The crowning is evidently a relic of the old practice of placing garlands on the heads of conquerors and of guests. They were held over the heads of the bride and bridegroom, not by the priest, but by the four 'best men,' Prince Arthur and the three Grand Dukes, each taking it in turn, and they were thus, as it were, suspended for many minutes. Another striking part is where they walked three times round the altar, followed, or rather accompanied, by the Princes holding the crowns aloft. This probably is the likeness of the wedding dance, and it was explained to us by a very intelligent Russian priest that this is one reason why the bishops are not allowed to perform the marriage, it being thought not quite decorous for these high dignitaries to take part in what is in fact dancing. Certainly it had a very pretty effect, and gave a more dramatic appearance to the ceremony than anything either in Protestant or Roman Catholic marriages.

What added to the beauty of the scene was that the sunlight, which after a dark, dull morning had gradually crept into the dome of the chapel, descended by this time upon the groups below, and lighted them up with a bright auspicious gleam.

The Dean was obliged to leave before the close, in order to take his place in the Alexander Hall, which meanwhile had been transformed by the drawing down of all the curtains and the lighting of all the candles. The Dean stood, with the two clergy on each side ; and, of the Russian clergy, five of the chief were behind him. The Hall was entirely filled, and the Dean endeavoured to reach the whole space with his voice. Your Majesty can understand that it was very affecting to him when he came to address each of them by their Christian names, and to receive their responses, which they gave most distinctly and firmly. The Dean felt, as he looked full in their faces, that he should never see them again as he saw them then, and he could not but trace in both of them the signs of deep emotion and earnest attention. They both had with them the Prayer-books which had just been received from your Majesty, and held them open till the moment came for the Dean to clasp their hands together. The Russian music was perfect, and the only regret was that the Lord's Prayer had not been sung with that wonderful effect which the Dean has before described.

At the close of the service the Dean bowed to the Emperor and Empress, and the whole assembly dissolved. The register was signed immediately afterwards in one of the adjoining apartments, and the Queen will be much interested in seeing the roll of names. The Dean could not help thinking, both in the chapel and at the subsequent banquet, how singularly different in character and expression were the four heirs who were there present— the Prince of Wales, the Prince of Prussia, the Cesarewich, and the Prince of Denmark.

The Dean was so much relieved by the termination, in all respects so gratifying, of this long-expected day, that he feels no fatigue.

CVIII.

A. P. S. to her Majesty the Queen.

Winter Palace, St. Petersburg :
Jan. 21 (Feb. 2), 1874.

The Dean of Westminster presents his humble duty to your Majesty. He will first answer the questions in the Queen's last letter.

His first sermon will be printed in St. Petersburg for the sake of the English readers here ; but he will send home, as soon as it is finished, a number of copies for your Majesty, and he proposes to add at the end the

Marriage Service exactly as it was performed, both with additions and *omissions*, thus, he hopes, fulfilling the Queen's wishes.

The Dean had during the Russian Marriage Service the French translation, which is, he thinks, the same as that which your Majesty showed to him, and it seemed to him faithfully rendered, *so far as he could judge* of a language which he does not understand. There were also in this several parts omitted, in order to avoid the repetitions. He will bring home the German translation caused to be made by the Grand Duchess Helen.

By this time, the Dean trusts that there has been a correction of the mistake made in the newspapers by the statement that the Duke of Edinburgh 'took the Communion three times in the Russian marriage.' The mistake was a not unnatural inference from seeing him three times drink of the cup, which is symbolical of the husband and wife loving, throughout their future course, to drink of the same cup of love and sorrow. In the Russian service, there is a different word for this cup and the sacramental chalice, and moreover, in the Greek Church, the bread and wine in the Sacrament are not given separately, but are mixed together in a spoon. It is curious that, as far as the Dean has seen, there has been no comment on the supposed Communion, which, until the correction appears, the English public probably believes to have really taken place.

There were one or two other questions which the Queen desired the Dean to ascertain about the marriage, which he will here answer.

One is as to the choice of the day. *Monday* is unlucky for some unknown reason. *Tuesday* afternoon was impossible because it is the eve, or rather the beginning, of Wednesday (the day being counted in the Russian

Church according to the old Hebrew method, beginning
with the afternoon of the previous day : ' the evening and
the morning were the first day '). *Wednesday* afternoon
could not be taken because it was the anniversary of the
death of the Grand Duchess Helen. *Thursday* afternoon
could not be taken because it is the eve, or beginning, of
Friday. (*Wednesday* is excluded as being the day of our
Lord's Betrayal, and *Friday* the day of His Crucifixion.)
Saturday afternoon is a general repose, being kept something like a Jewish Sabbath. On that evening the most
religious never go to balls or plays. Therefore *Friday
afternoon* was the only one that remained.

Another question was as to the day of receiving the
Sacrament. They receive it usually only on the first
Saturday in Lent (as a preparation for Lent, and after the
preparation of the first week in Lent), or in the *week after
Easter*.

The Dean on Sunday was invited by the Prince of
Oldenburg, an excellent old man who has the charge of
the beneficent institutions in St. Petersburg, to have a
short service in the small Lutheran chapel in his Palace.
This the Dean thought that he might safely do, feeling
assured of the full concurrence of your Majesty and of the
sympathy of the English community. The Prince had
asked about fifty boys of some of the schools under his
direction, who speak English, and their English-speaking
teachers. To these were added a few of the Imperial
family—the Grand Duchess Marie, the Princess Helen and
her brothers, his daughter-in-law, the daughter of the Grand
Duchess Marie. The Crown Prince and Princess of Prussia
were also present. It was very interesting. The Dean
made a selection of the best prayers from the Prayer-book,
and also of what he ventures to think the two most perfect
passages of the New Testament—the Beatitudes and the

description of Charity from the Epistles—and he preached for about ten minutes from the latter of these.

The Prince afterwards took them to a splendid institution for girls, widows, and what he called 'old maiden girls.' It was founded by the Empress Elizabeth, and much increased by his grandmother, the Empress Marie, wife of the Emperor Paul.

In the evening the Dean and Lady Augusta dined with the Emperor, a dinner of 200 people, which only lasted an hour. Afterwards the Crown Princess had the choir from the Imperial Chapel to sing sacred music. The Dean must here observe how considerately (and he presumes in consequence of the Duke of Edinburgh's representations after his conversation with the Dean in London) the Russian Court have avoided any uncongenial festivities on Sunday.

On Friday in last week, the Dean had a long interview on Church affairs with the Grand Duke Constantine. It was exceedingly interesting. The Grand Duke brought the Dean into his study, and made him sit down exactly opposite to him, so that neither could avoid looking the other full in the face, and thus, for half an hour or more, with the utmost precision, the Grand Duke went over the main topics of the Old Catholics, the condition of the Russian Church, &c., and ended by expressing an earnest wish that the Dean should be present at a meeting of an association on these subjects of which he is the head. The conversation was more remarkable because, as the Dean afterwards heard, the Grand Duke was suffering from a violent sick headache. It was, perhaps, somewhat difficult to interrupt him; but still it was just possible at the close of each part of his argument to introduce the expression of some contrary or modifying opinion.

The visit that the Dean paid to-day to a monastery about seven miles from St. Petersburg, going in a sledge drawn like lightning by three horses, was very curious.   It revealed such a strange state of feeling and belief.   The conversation ran almost entirely on the stories told by the Archimandrite, or Abbot, about the hermits who still exist in the forests of Russia, not clergymen, but peasants or shopkeepers, who retire into perfect solitude, and become oracles for counsel, and also workers of wonders quite as extraordinary as any in the Roman Catholic Church.   It is a very interesting subject to discuss these with the educated religious Russians, for, unlike the Roman Catholics, they talk about such matters quite freely.

CIX.

A. P. S. to her Majesty the Queen.

Moscow : February 5, [18]74.

The Dean of Westminster presents his humble duty to your Majesty.   He thinks that the Queen will wish to have a few lines from him, dated from this most interesting place, which he now revisits, by your Majesty's kindness, after an interval of sixteen years—almost the whole reign of the present Emperor.

In 1857 the Dean was here alone for a month, living entirely with the Russians, and studying the history of the Eastern Church, which he has since incorporated in his Lectures.   Of the friends that he then made, some have died ; others have risen high in the service of the State ; all who are still living, without exception he is glad to say, have retained him faithfully in their remembrance, and welcome him back as an old friend in these strangely altered circumstances.

The journey itself, performed before in the midst of the short nights and long days of the Russian summer, through an endless series of green forests and rolling rivers, was now accomplished through wild wastes of snow, every tree laden with icicles, and the courses of the rivers marked by the long line of lights along their dark banks. At every considerable station there was a crowd of peasants assembled to cheer the Emperor, joined sometimes with illuminations, sometimes with national songs. In this way Moscow was approached. It was long past midnight when the various suites found their apartments in the hotel which has been taken for them.

At eleven this morning took place at the Kremlin what is called here the 'sortie'—the 'coming out' of the Imperial family. The dignitaries of the Court and the different guests were assembled in one of the chief halls of the Kremlin. There was a sudden hush, and then the Emperor entered with the Princess of Wales, and the other Imperial and Royal persons followed, and marched straight on, with the whole assemblage behind them, through the magnificent halls—magnificent even after the Winter Palace—of St. Andrew, St. George, and St. Alexander ; then through a quaint corridor, on each side of which were arranged deputations of nobles, merchants, upwards from peasants in their peasants' dresses, holding their emblematical gifts in their hands, made up in the form of cakes, loaves of bread, &c. At last the procession reached a curious vaulted hall, the ' Hall of the Patriarchs,' very much corresponding to the Jerusalem Chamber in the approach to the Abbey ; and immediately afterwards, by a few steps through the open air, carefully guarded by canopy and curtain, we found ourselves in the Cathedral.

The Dean, as he looked round on its gilded and painted columns, walls and roof—gilded and painted so that not a spot is left bare—and recalled its eventful history as the scene of all the coronations since the time of Ivan the Terrible,

felt that he had nothing to add or take away since he
described it in his Lectures after his first visit. But what
was new on this occasion was the part of its history now
being enacted within its walls. Not only the clergy, with
their splendid robes and splendid voices, but the Emperor
and his children, were all there in their places, listening to
the *Te Deum* (one of the few parts of the services of the
West that are also used in the services of the East), and going
round to each of the sacred pictures that have become famous
in Russian history. The Grand Duchess went with the
Cesarevna. The English and German Princes remained
apart and were not expected to join, further than by their
respectful presence. To English and Protestant feelings it
is a strange mode of expressing devotion. But the Russians
do not, like the Roman Catholics, wish to impose this upon
others ; they only claim it as edifying for themselves.

The cathedral is very small ; and the procession from
the Palace nearly filled it. Still, there were others admitted,
and amongst them very humble men and women, who
gazed with all their eyes and seemed to feel it with all their
hearts. This also appeared to be the case with the higher
classes who were present. The procession then returned
the same way and dispersed.

Immediately afterwards there was a review in the
Riding School, one of the largest covered buildings in the
world. The Dean went to see this, thinking that the rest
of the Court would be there also. He was a little abashed
and confounded when he found that, in the immense hall
and amidst all this military pomp, he was the only person
present not a soldier. He sheltered himself as well as he
could behind a great stove. But when the review was over,
the Emperor, followed by all the Princes, stalked across the
hall, and said in his most gracious manner, ' We shall in
the end make you become a military man.' One curious

feature of this Riding School is that it contains a church for the troops.

The general view of the town is less striking than in the summer. It needs both the verdure of the grasses and gardens, interspersed with the houses, and the flashing sunlight on the gilded domes and towers, to bring out the salient features which are now almost lost in the dreary waste of snow, and the dark, cheerless horizon. But Moscow is a rare instance of an ancient and, one may say, deposed capital not having been deserted, and not exhibiting any signs of decay. It has, on the contrary, increased in later years, and the Dean thinks that, since he last saw it, there is far more appearance of stir and animation, even apart from the Imperial visit.

The Dean has been encouraged to write thus much by the Queen's kind remarks on his letters, and by the assurance that your Majesty has been able to read them.

CX.

A. P. S. to her Majesty the Queen.

St. Petersburg : February 13, [18]74.

The Dean of Westminster presents his humble duty to your Majesty. The interest of Moscow continued unabated to the very end. The splendour of the Palace, the quaint beauty of the three cathedrals, of the coronations, marriages, and funerals of the Czars, the mass of curious vestiges of old times—not old for Western Europe, but old for Russia, as everything before Peter is ancient, and everything after Peter is modern—the fortress convents in the neighbourhood, the delight of flying over hills and valleys of unbroken snow in sledges drawn by three prancing horses, the revival of old friendships of 1857, and the formation of new acquaintances which almost immediately ripened into friendships, the visits to charitable institutions founded by the singularly devout and generous merchants of Moscow, the extraordinary jealousy, mixed with disdain, of the old capital for the new—all these things made the six days spent there a delightful excrescence upon the Petersburg experiences

The Dean, on Sunday, after preaching at the English chapel in the morning, joined the Imperial family on their pilgrimage, for such it was, to Troitza, an hour and a half's journey from Moscow. It is the greatest convent in Russia, and has been the refuge of the national independence both through the Tartar and the Polish occupation. St. Sergius, the founder, a hermit of the fourteenth century, 'a joué un très grand rôle dans notre histoire ; c'est pourquoi nous avons beaucoup de confiance dans son secours,' said the Cesarevich. At every station there were crowds of peasants assembled to see the Emperor pass, and this, the Dean was told, was quite invariable during his journeys. On one occasion, on the way to the Crimea, a party of peasants came fifty miles in the middle of the night to catch a glimpse of the Imperial party at the station, and the Empress, although very ill at the time, was waked up, at her desire, to show herself to an institution of young girls who had thus come.

On arriving at the terminus there were a number of sledges waiting to convey the whole party to the convent. It was a scene never to be forgotten to see them dashing over the snow, while thousands of peasants were watching from the snow-clad banks, and to hear the great bell of the convent, the largest even in Russia, sounding far and near to welcome the approach. The Emperor and the family, with the various suites, immediately entered the church where St. Sergius is buried, and then began a series of prayers which ended in the salutation of the saint by the whole family. They then passed out to another church, where is the grave of Philaret, the old Metropolitan of Moscow, who exercised so important an influence during the reign of the Emperor Nicholas and still more of the present Emperor. The Dean had seen him in 1857, and had in that year spent a whole day at this convent, which is also a clerical seminary. When the Emperor saw the Dean enter this second church, he pointed out to him the tomb of Philaret, and said : ' Here are some old acquaintances,' and out came the Rector of the seminary and the aged Abbot, whom the Dean well remembered, and who also immediately recognised him and kissed him again and again, the Abbot repeating several times, ' Stanley ! Stanley ! ' The visit was too short for those who had not seen the place before to form a complete idea of the institution. But the general effect was very striking to all who were there.

The Imperial family returned to St. Petersburg that night. But the three days that remained for the Dean were full of interest, not the less because the apartments in the Kremlin which the Prince of Wales had vacated were given him for this interval.

There was a story told by some one who overheard it in the crowd, which will amuse the Queen. ' What is the reason,' said one peasant to another, ' why there are so many foreign Princes here ? ' ' Don't you know ? ' replied the other ; ' whenever there is a marriage of one of the Emperor's children, all the sovereigns of Europe come, with the exception of the sovereign of France. He never comes because one of his predecessors in the year 1812 occupied Moscow.'

Another fine story relating to that year, which the Dean never heard before, was this. There was a general belief that the chief Cathedral in the Kremlin had been mined by the French, and would explode whenever the sacred doors were opened which led from the chancel. After the retirement of the French, in spite of this apprehension, but in great awe, a vast congregation assembled, and the then Metropolitan of Moscow (Augustine), when the time came for opening the doors, issued forth from them and immediately pronounced the text, ' Let God arise, and let His enemies be scattered,' and preached upon it a most impressive sermon of triumph at their deliverance and thanksgiving for their safety.

It is exceedingly interesting to hear the description of what has been done in Russia during the reign of the present Emperor. The most striking change is, of course, the emancipation of the serfs. But it is said that an even more important change has been the reform of the judicial system, based partly on that of France, partly and chiefly on that of England, and that the effects of this on the education of the people are quite astonishing. Those who returned from Siberia, after thirty-three years of exile, say that they find all their highest wishes more than fulfilled. There is much still to be done ; but the success of these two experiments must be very encouraging.

CXI.

A. P. S. to the Hon. Louisa Stanley.

LA ROCHELLE.

[The fatal illness of Lady Augusta Stanley had already begun its course. She had been ordered by her doctor to take sea-baths, and the autumn of 1874 was therefore spent in following the line of the French coast from Dieppe to Rochelle.

Rochelle was the centre of the Huguenot cause in France

from 1562 to 1628. In it Jeanne d'Albret and the King of Navarre had for some time lived, and Henry IV. might call it, in a peculiar sense, his 'own Rochelle.' To it, as to a city of refuge, Protestants fled from all parts of the country. It was at Rochelle that Théodore de Bèze in 1571 presided over the Synod which drew up the Huguenot Confession of Faith.

It stood two famous sieges. The first was in 1573, when, after a siege of more than six months, the Catholics were obliged to retire from before its walls. The second began in August 1627, and ended in October 1628, when Guiton and the townsfolk capitulated to Richelieu.

The Hôpital Aufrédy still commemorates the generosity of Alexander Aufrédy and his wife.]

La Rochelle : September 27 [1874].

And thou, Rochelle, our own Rochelle, proud city of the
    waters,
Again let rapture light the eyes of all thy mourning
    daughters.

You remember, my dear Louisa, these lines from Macaulay's 'Battle of Ivry,' and therefore I have chosen this interesting place, this city of refuge for the Protestants of France, wherefrom to send my usual letter. Most tedious to reach. A long, long railway journey with perpetual stoppages, but nowhere long enough to rest, brought us at 11 P.M. to this extremity of Western France. The first hotel to which we drove was closed, the season of baths over ; at the second an old woman put forth her head, and, after a severe rebuke to us for having passed her hotel before, took us in, and we gradually scrambled into bed, not without bats and the like flying about. But we were quite rewarded on the morrow. We found ourselves on the shore of a beautiful bay, of which one end opened into the wide Atlantic, and the other closed in the town of La Rochelle, with its ancient towers at the entrance of its little port. All that was needed was a good guide to explain to us its two famous sieges—especially the second, the counterpart of the most interesting of all British sieges, that of Londonderry. It was Sunday morning ; we went to the Protestant Church, had a very good sermon from the pastor, and then introduced ourselves. Like many of these good people, he did not know much about Rochelle himself, but suddenly bethought him of one of his congregation, caught him, and sent him with us—the very man, the ' Archiviste ' of the place. He would have done dear Albert Way's heart good to see and hear ; so exact, so full, so deeply interested. With him we went all around to every spot, he explaining everything.

La Rochelle has two great names—one of benevolence, the other of heroism. The benevolent name is Aufrédy. He belongs to the time when the town was still occupied by the Templars, vestiges of whose churches still remain. He was a merchant, like Antonio, whose argosies, ten in number, had gone to the Levant and returned not home. He waited and waited in vain. He descended from the height of wealth to the depth of poverty,

> Deserted in his utmost need
> By those his former bounty fed,   .

—he and his wife Peronilla ; and he worked for his bread as a porter. Suddenly, after several years, five of his ships returned, loaded with the treasures of all the intervening time ; and then he, remembering all the miseries he had undergone and seen in his low estate, devoted all this wealth, and himself, and his wife Peronilla, to the service of the poor, and left a legacy to the town for a hospital, which continues still, and bears his name, and has this story over the entrance.

The other is Guiton. He is the hero. He was the Mayor of La Rochelle when Richelieu and Louis XIII.

D D

began the siege which was to reduce the ancient liberties
and the Protestant predominance of the city. You see the
staircase and the balcony where he addressed the people,
and showed them the dagger which he was to plunge into
the heart of any one who proposed surrender to him, or
they into his heart if he proposed it to them.

The siege lasted for fourteen months. The 'Digue'
which Richelieu caused to be constructed in front of the
bay (like the boom at Derry) is still visible at low water,
and against this the 'Duc de Bouquinquam' (our old friend
Steenie, Duke of Buckingham) strove in vain. Contrary
winds prevented him, and he returned, to be murdered by
Felton and buried in the Abbey. Then, after the death of
twelve thousand people, and the reduction of the garrison
to sixty-two Frenchmen and sixty-two Englishmen, the
town surrendered, on condition that Guiton should be continued Mayor, and that their religious liberties should be
respected. But it was the end of La Rochelle. Its walls
were destroyed, and then came the Revocation of the Edict
of Nantes, and Guiton's grave in the Protestant cemetery
was swept away. But his memory is still loved, even
amongst the Roman Catholic population in the town, and
the town has often, though in vain, endeavoured to obtain
from the Government the permission to erect a statue of
him in the public place.

Such is the story of La Rochelle. It was charming to
sit in the evening on the shores of the bay and see the
bathers leap into the waters, and the towers of the ancient
gates on one side, and the tower which marks the dyke of
Richelieu rising from the waves at the entrance, and the
unworthy commemoration of the triumph by a tall column
and statue of the Virgin which have lately been erected
at the place where the dyke touches the shore ; or still
more beautiful to see, in the depth of the night, the full

moon casting a silver brightness over the whole tranquil scene.

Thence we came on to Arcachon, dropping down the Garonne by steamer, as when, in 1828, I first saw foreign parts in that ever-memorable journey by the 'Leeds' steamer from Liverpool.   Ever yours affectionately,

A. P. STANLEY.

CXII.

'THIS DO IN REMEMBRANCE OF ME.'

[Reprinted, with the accompanying prefatory note, from 'Macmillan's Magazine' for November 1874.]

IT is intended in the following lines to furnish a Sacramental Hymn founded on the one common idea of commemoration which lies at the basis of all views of the Eucharist, whether material or spiritual, and to express this undoubted intention of the original institution apart from the metaphorical language by which the ordinance is often described.

When the Paschal evening fell
Deep on Kedron's hallowed dell,
When around the festal board
Sate the Apostles with their Lord,
Then His parting word He said,
Blessed the cup and broke the bread—
'This whene'er ye do or see,
Evermore remember Me.'

Years have past : in every clime,
Changing with the changing time,
Varying through a thousand forms,
Torn by factions, rock'd by storms,
Still the sacred table spread,
Flowing cup and broken bread,

With that parting word agree,
' Drink and eat—remember Me.'

When by treason, doubt, unrest,
Sinks the soul, dismay'd, opprest ;
When the shadows of the tomb
Close us round with deep'ning gloom ;
Then bethink us at that board
Of the sorrowing, suffering Lord,
Who, when tried and grieved as we,
Dying, said, ' Remember Me.'

When, thro' all the scenes of life,
Hearths of peace and fields of strife,
Friends or foes together meet,
Now to part and now to greet,
Let those holy tokens tell
Of that sweet and sad farewell,
And, in mingled grief or glee,
Whisper still, ' Remember Me.'

When diverging creeds shall learn
Towards their central Source to turn ;
When contending churches tire
Of the earthquake, wind, and fire ;
Here let strife and clamour cease
At that still, small voice of peace—
' May they all united be
In the Father and in Me.'

When, as rolls the sacred year,[2]
Each fresh note of love we hear ;

***

[2] This stanza has been lengthened in order to accommodate it to the successive seasons of the Christian year.—[A. P. S.]

When the Babe, the Youth, the Man,
Full of grace Divine we scan ;
When the mournful Way we tread,
Where for us His blood He shed ;
When on Easter morn we tell
How He conquer'd Death and Hell ;
When we watch His Spirit true
Heaven and earth transform anew ;
Then with quicken'd sense we see
Why He said ' Remember Me.'

When in this thanksgiving feast
We would give to God our best,
From the treasures of His might
Seeking life and love and light ;
Then, O Friend of humankind,
Make us true and firm of mind,
Pure of heart, in spirit free—
Thus may we remember Thee.

CXIII.

EASTER HYMN.

CHRIST is risen !   He is not here,
Chain'd within our earthly sphere ;
As in garb of flesh before,
Henceforth know we Him no more.

Christ is risen !   Cross and Tomb
Sink behind in passing gloom !
From those shadows drear and dim,
We must rise and live with Him.

Christ is risen !   Our lifelong sorrow
Fades before a brighter morrow.
For a time our courses sever,
Soon to be rejoin'd for ever.

Christ is risen !   The Truth that died
Mock'd and scourged and crucified,
Still unquestion'd mounts on high
Next to God's own Majesty.

Christ is risen !   Deep within
Every charnel-house of sin
Lives a spark which yet may shine
Radiant with the life divine.

Christ is risen !   The things of earth
Lose their power and change their worth,
As we soar to things above—
Cloudless Light and boundless Love.

Christ is risen!   Lo ! all is new.
Hail the coming Good and True !
From the old world's weight releas'd,
Therefore let us keep the Feast.

Keep the Feast with mind sincere,
Conscience as the noontide clear,
Heart untouch'd by falsehood's leaven,
Freeborn citizens of Heaven !

CXIV.

TO LORD STRATFORD DE REDCLIFFE
ON HIS 90TH BIRTHDAY, 1876.

WHAT art thou, whose eyes of fire
   Flash beneath the locks of snow—
Thou, whose look and mien inspire
   Words that breathe and thoughts that glow?
With thy fourscore years and ten,
Stout of heart, and bright of ken,
Fresh as with the good green youth
That attends immortal truth?

Statesman of the olden time,
   British patriot, Christian sage,
Read us, in thy latest prime,
   This our last historic page—
Like the aged seer who came
When the heaven-sent hand of flame
Wrote in Babel's midnight gloom
Words unknown of mystic doom.

Hearts that fail, and hopes that yearn,
   Fading crescent, tottering cross,
Still to seek thy counsel turn
   In their hour of shame and loss.
Still by upright word and deed
Hold the strife of race and creed.
As of old from force and wrong
Guard the weak and ward the strong.

Tell us, 'mid the lengthening shades,
　From thy sunset's deepening glory,
Something of the heavenly aids
　Which sustain life's wondrous story.
Teach us how to leave a name
Brighter even than it came—
How in calm and high repose
The long eventful day to close.

CXV.

A. P. S. to the Dean of Christ Church.

CHARACTERISTIC WORDS OF LADY A. STANLEY.

[Lady Augusta Stanley died on Ash Wednesday, 1876. At Stanley's request the Dean of Christ Church (Dr. Liddell) was preparing a funeral sermon to be preached in Westminster Abbey on the following Sunday.

The third volume of Stanley's 'Lectures on the History of the Jewish Church' appeared in September 1876. Written in great part by his wife's bedside, it contains a touching dedication to her 'beloved memory,' with the prayer that 'its aim might not be altogether unworthy of her sustaining love, her inspiring courage, and her never-failing faith in the enlargement of the Church and the triumph of all truth.' Stanley never entirely recovered from the shock of her death.]

Deanery, Westminster : March 10, 1876.

My dear Liddell,—On looking over the notes I made of her words during the last week, I find these two, which you might use indirectly, though not perhaps directly :

1. 'Work on ; work on and go to the very bottom of things, and leave work that shall be imperishable.'

2. And, in speaking of my forthcoming volume, which I said that I would dedicate to her, and though I felt it to be unworthy of her, yet would try to make it worthy, she said with great emphasis : 'make it . . . *perfect.*'

You will see in these the covert, gentle rebuke, or reminder, that I was too much inclined to be contented with what was superficial, and you will understand also how *I* feel that, in making these requirements, she was aiming too high and asking for impossibilities.

Still, taken as general expressions, they are very characteristic of her habitual aspirations for herself, for me, and for all that she loved.

A friend of ours said on our wedding-day (December 22), ' From this day your days will begin to lengthen,' and she always spoke of the day in that sense.

Ever yours sincerely,
A. P. STANLEY.

CXVI.

A. P. S. to Mrs. Drummond.

ANNIVERSARY OF HIS WEDDING-DAY.

[These lines were written on December 22, 1876, the first anniversary of his wedding-day after the death of Lady Augusta Stanley.

Mr. and Mrs. Drummond of Megginch, and their daughter Mary, were, after the death of Lady Augusta Stanley, in the habit of spending part of each year at the Deanery.]

Deanery, Westminster: December 22, 1876.

My dear Mrs. Drummond,—And so this day (I will not call it sad, for it gave me the best of blessings) is over.   I will try to think that the future may be less dreary than it seems to be—something like what I have scrawled on the opposite side.   Affectionately yours,

A. P. STANLEY.

Some one said to me in 1863 (December 22), ' Now
the days begin to lengthen ! '

WHEN first my life was crown'd
With bliss beyond all seeking,
Kind friends came crowding round,
Such words of comfort speaking—

' Henceforth the days will lengthen,
Henceforth the sky grow brighter,
Henceforth thy strength will strengthen,
Henceforth thy load be lighter.'

And now—that bliss has fled,
The joyous crowd has vanish'd,
Far, far amongst the dead,
My light, my love, is banish'd—

Yet still perchance this day
May give its former greeting,
Still point the heavenward way
To our eternal meeting.

Henceforth each flying year
The waiting shall diminish ;
The day of union draws more near,
These weary toils to finish.

Henceforth the length'ning hours
Shall gain a purer light,
And Heaven's far distant towers
Shine closer and more bright.

CXVII.

A. P. S. to Miss Arnold.

THREE ANNIVERSARIES.

[Mrs. Arnold died on September 30, 1873. From this time Stanley addressed his letters on the anniversary of Dr. Arnold's death to Miss Fanny Arnold.

Dr. Arnold died on June 12, 1842; Mrs. Stanley on Ash Wednesday 1863; Lady Augusta Stanley on Ash Wednesday 1876.

The beautiful bust of Lady Augusta by her niece, Miss Grant, was always placed in the Library at the Deanery by the desk at which Stanley worked.]

Deanery, Westminster: June 11, 1877.

My dear Fan,—I do not know where this will find you, and so write on the eve of the day on which the long-expected letter is due. How wonderfully all my life seems to hang on those three anniversaries—June 12 and the two Ash Wednesdays !

It was only last week that I received from Murray the new edition, the tenth, of the 'Life.' I feel that the track still blossoms. The old Slatwoods willow is not dead, but still living in root and branch. Would that I could do something of the same kind for those two others under whose shade I have grown up—for the memory of my dear mother and my dear Augusta ! My existence is now so overburdened, so different from the days in which I undertook your dear father's 'Life' with such an undivided, undistracted energy.

You have not, I think, passed through London since I had the bust of my dear wife in the Library here. You must see it as you pass through. The marble face expresses so much more than I could ever have expected ; and as I see it by sunshine and shadow, by moonlight and lamplight, it seems to live over again through the changes of this solitary state, and to encourage me to perseverance, ' *till death us do join.*'   Ever yours truly,

A. P. STANLEY.

CXVIII.

TO MRS. GROTE. ST. VALENTINE'S DAY, 1878.

HAS Valentine no gracious smile
    For aught but childhood's earliest stage ?
Is there no message to beguile
    The shadows of our later age ?

Though Turk has failed and Pope has died,
    Though war and faction round us lower,
Sweet memories with us still abide
    To gild and soothe our anxious hour.

Dear friend of long eventful years,
    What volumes of our tragic life
Have closed for us their hopes and fears,
    Their noble joys, their gallant strife !

In thee I see them all renewed,
    As in some monumental shrine,
The reflex of each changing mood,
    The impress of each grace divine.

In thee still lives the lofty soul
    Of him that weigh'd in balance just
Present and past, and parts and whole,
    Like finest grains of golden dust.

With thee I seem to see entwin'd,
    As by a kindred genius bound,
The grace of her whose ' porcelain mind '
    Shed its calm lustre far around.

With thee I catch the sunshine bright
    That dawn'd from her perennial love,
Who wrapt us in her own sweet light
    And drew us all to things above.

Thus thou in them I gladly view,
    But hail thee for thyself beside—
The kindly wise, the keenly true,
    The ever faithful friend, the never failing guide.

CXIX.

TRANSLATION OF A HYMN OF SAVONAROLA.

[Girolamo Savonarola (1454–98), the famous Florentine reformer, wrote hymns to counteract the evil influence of the ' Canti Carnescialeschi,' using the same metres in order that his spiritual songs might fit the popular tunes. The following is Stanley's translation of the first three stanzas of a hymn written in five stanzas by Savonarola in 1495. The original begins thus :

> Viva, viva in nostro core,
> Cristo re, duce e signore !
> Ciascun purghi l' intelletto,
> La memoria e volontade,
> Del terrestre e vano affetto.

Stanley's version was made in 1878.]

LIVE, let live in every heart
Jesus Christ, our Better Part.
With His mind our spirits fill ;
Cleanse the memory, thought, and will

From whate'er is foul and base.
Kindle for its lofty aim
Love, the soul's celestial flame,
Soaring towards its native place.

If ye would that Christ should reign
In your heart by truth and grace,
All fierce hate and harsh disdain
Must to sweetest love give place.
They who bid all rancour fly
And, instead, calm peace inthrone,
These alone shall Jesus own
Here below and there on high.

Lord ! how blest is he who scorns
This blind world's bewildering scene ;
Happy he who, though he mourns,
Keeps a heart of joy serene.
O ! how strange to see or hear
That for moil and toil unblest
Oft we lose our All, our Best—
Jesus Christ our Saviour dear.

CXX.

OUR FUTURE HOPE.

[Reprinted, with the prefatory note, from 'Macmillan's
Magazine' for May 1878.]

AN EASTER HYMN.

IT has been thought that there may be a place for some
expression, such as the following hymn or hymns endeavour to embody, of the prospect of another world, more
hopeful than the touching address of the Emperor Hadrian
to his soul, less vague and material than Pope's graceful
version of it in his well-known lines, 'Vital spark of
heavenly flame.'

PART I.

I.

O frail spirit—vital spark,
  Trembling, toiling, rising, sinking,
Flickering bright 'mid shadows dark,
  Spring of feeling, acting, thinking,
Central flame of smiles and tears,
Boundless hopes and wasting fears,
Whither wilt thou wend thy way,
When we close this mortal day?

II.

Shall the course of earthly joys
  Still repeat their round for ever,
Feasts and songs, and forms and toys,
  Endless throbs of this life's fever?
Or, beyond these weary woes,
Shall we find a deep repose,
And, like dove that seeks her nest,
Flee away and be at rest?

III.

Dimly, through those shades unknown,
  Gleams the fate that shall befall us;
Faintly, entering there alone,
  Can we hear what voices call us;
Yet our spirit's inmost breath,
As we near the gates of death,
In that purer, larger air,
Thus may shape a worthier prayer:—

IV.

' Maker of the human heart,
    Scorn not Thou Thine own creation,
Onward guide its nobler part,
    Train it for its high vocation :
From the long-infected grain
Cleanse and purge each sinful stain ;
Kindle with a kindred fire
Every good and great desire.

V.

' When in ruin and in gloom
    Falls to dust our earthly mansion,
Give us ample verge and room
    For the measureless expansion :
Clear our clouded mental sight
To endure Thy piercing light,
Open wide our narrow thought
To embrace Thee as we ought.

VI.

' When the shadows melt away,
    And the eternal day is breaking,
Judge Most Just, be Thou our stay
    In that strange and solemn waking ;
Thou to whom the heart sincere
Is Thy best of temples here,
May Thy Faithfulness and Love
Be our long last home above.'

PART II.

VII.

' Rise, my soul, and stretch thy wings,
   All thy better portion trace,
Rise from transitory things,
   Heavenward to thy native place.' '
Higher still and ever higher,
Let thy soaring flight aspire,
Toward the Perfectness Supreme,
Goal of saints' and sages' dream.

VIII.

There may we rejoicing meet,
   Loved and lost, our hearts' best treasures,
Not without surprises sweet
   Mount with them to loftier pleasures ;
Though the earthly bond be gone,
Yet the spirits still are one —
One in love, and hope, and faith ;
One in all that conquers death.

IX.

And, in those celestial spheres,
   Shall not then our keener vision
See, athwart the mist of years,
   Through the barriers of division,
Holy soul and noble mind,
From their baser dross refined,
Heroes of the better land
Whom below we scorn'd and bann'd ?

' These four lines are taken, with two slight alterations, from the fine Hymn of Robert Seagrave, 1748 —[A. P. S.]

X.

May we wisely, humbly scan,
　　Face to face at last beholding,
Glimpses of the Son of Man,
　　All His Grace and Truth unfolding ;
Through the ages still the same,
As of old on earth He came ;
May our hope in Him be sure,
To be pure as He is pure.

XI.

As we climb that steep ascent,
　　May the goodness and the glory,
Which to cheer our path were lent,
　　Seem but fragments of the story,
There to be unroll'd at length,
In its fulness and its strength,
Not with words that fade and die,
In the Book of God Most High.

XII.

Through our upward pilgrimage,
　　Larger, deeper, lessons learning,
May we boldly page on page
　　Of diviner lore be turning ;
May we still in labours blest
Never tire and never rest,
And with forces ever new
Serve the Holy and the True.

CXXI.

A. P. Stanley to Mary Stanley.

THE VOYAGE TO AMERICA.

[On September 6, 1878, Stanley, accompanied by Mr. (now Sir George) Grove and Mr. Gerald Harper, left England for a tour in America. In the winter of 1877–1878 he was himself prostrated by a severe illness. To recover from its effects he made the expedition on which this and the two following letters were written.

Dr. Church was at this time Dean of St. Paul's. The point of the message to Dr. Leighton, Warden of All Souls College, Oxford, and Canon of Westminster, is that he had recently broken one of his knee-caps. The lines with which the letter concludes are a continuation of Miss Fanshawe's enigma ''Twas whispered in Heaven.' For an account of the whole tour, see ' Life of Stanley,' vol. ii. ch. xxvii.]

'Siberia :' Sept. 15, 1878.

Three hundred miles from Boston ! At 8 A.M. to-morrow we hope to have the pilot, with the news of what has taken place during these ten days in which we have been buried from the world. After the first three or four days, which were very disagreeable—wind, rain, and fog—the weather cleared up, and has been very enjoyable, bright sun, fine moonlight, and the wide circle of the sea, from time to time piled with its tufts of snow-white foam on the dark blue waves.

The company consists of about fifty. The Bishop of Western New York and Mrs. Coxe—far the most conspicuous—an American Boston clergyman, a philosopher of the name of Spilsher, a clerk from the War Office, a young lad from Marlborough School, who has left all his clothes behind at Liverpool, a rough settler from Natal, seeing the world once for all before he returns—these are all that we know.

I have read through nearly all my books—'The Spy,' 'The Scarlet Letter,' 'The History of New England,' 'Tocqueville,' &c. &c. But the best of the journey has been endless conversations with the bishop on America. One has to make allowance for his point of view; but he is full of information and very agreeable.

Last Sunday I had a short service with a very scanty congregation. This Sunday he had a service, and, being fine, there were more than a hundred, and he preached an excellent sermon on 'There go the ships.' I send you an epigram on St. Paul's and the Abbey which he has made on the voyage. I helped him to the A. P. S. of the 2nd.

> Some say how frigid is St. Paul's,
>   Great London's crown and pride—
> Not they who go within its walls
>   And find a CHURCH inside.

> The Queen the Abbey walls surveys,
>   Deploring past mishaps,
> And 'mid its massive walls and bays
>   Adorns it with an APS (e).

He lives at Buffalo, and we are to see him on the way to Niagara.

I can now repeat the names of all the Presidents, and explain the meaning of Democrat and Republican. Democrat is Liberal, and Republican is Conservative, and, at the time of the war, Democrat was for slavery and Republican against it.

Give my particular regards to the Warden of All Souls, and tell him that a wild Westerner on board, describing his voyage across the Pacific, says: 'I was that sick that I almost brought up my knee-pans.'

September 16th, an exciting moment. The white sail

of the pilot is in sight—all on deck to see the arrival—a small boat descended, and he is brought up with the newspapers. Absolutely *not one* word of English news. We shall be in Boston before night.

Boston, September 17.—The approach was certainly very interesting—the bank of cloud which marked *Cape Cod*, the promontory which the pilgrim fathers first saw, and round which they were decoyed from their original settlement purpose by the jealousy of their Dutch pilot, and which takes its name from the cod on which they lived on their first landing. Then, in the depths of the bay, the opening of Plymouth, where they first drove ashore. Then on the north, Cape Anne, called after Anne of Denmark ; then all the English names in succession— Gloucester, Manchester, Beverley ; then all the villas of the Bostonians on the out-jutting intervals ; then the gilded dome of the State-House of Boston, so called from the Lincolnshire Boston, which first I learned when I went there with dear Cotton in 1858.

The near entrance is not imposing ; scraggy rocks and green islands with a house or two upon them ; little steamers come out with the gilded American eagle, and the stars and stripes ; custom-house officers, agents, &c. Finally, the landing : an immensely long affair, the silence, the gravity, the delays in the custom-house, and then the embarkation of our luggage and ourselves in a huge close coach—the portemanteaux tied on as in the old, old times of continental travelling, the vehicle itself almost as much behind Europe as those tumbledown carriages at Constantinople.

We reached the Brunswick Hotel at 6 P.M. and took a walk before dinner. It has a certain Dutch or French appearance in parts, but is otherwise neither continental nor English ; immensely broad streets, large gardens in

the midst, dead silence, except now and then the bells of
the passing railway.

In the hotel a troop of negro or mulatto waiters,
entering into a sort of soft, familiar, confidential, almost
whispering conversation.   Extremely comfortable ; a lift,
'elevator,' to our rooms at the top of the house, being
warned below ' that we need not fear as it was all fire-
proof.'   I expect to see Mr. Winthrop to-day, and Mr.
Phillips Brooks on Thursday.   Farewell.   I feel tolerably
well.   The two companions are very kind.

Ever yours,
A. P. STANLEY.

The enclosed is a continuation of Miss Fanshawe's
poem on the letter ' H,' which I have written on the
discovery that, amidst all the vulgarities of America, our
absurd pronunciation of omitting and inserting the letter
' h ' has never taken root here.

LETTER 'H' IN U.S.A.

But mark what a mystery seems to await,
On each side the ocean, its varying fate.
    In England, the home of good customs and manners,
Of poets and purists, and critics and scanners,
Where its presence is needed, it flies and lies hid,
Yet flaunts itself boldly, when sternly forbid.
With our Henries it loses its own proper throne ;
With our Edwards it grasps at a rank not its own.
To whichever the party it claims to belong
It is doomed to be always and hopelessly wrong,
In earth and in heaven, with humble and high,
A false life to live and a false death to die.
    But behold it when freed from its insular thrall,
When Westward, with Empire, its destinies call !

Like fair Arethusa, when troubled at home,
It crosses long leagues of the salt ocean foam,
And then, amidst forest and prairie and wild,
Springs up all afresh in its well undefiled ;
Unsullied it shines in its pure native grace,
Not pushing, nor bashful, but always in place :
From Huron and Homersville drawing new breath,
In Iowa's regions as silent as death ;
Untouched by the savour of Puritan twang,
Unsoiled by the torrent of wild western slang ;
Not 'carpet-bag,' 'Caucus,' nor 'Tammany ring '
Can stain the fair fame of the heaven-born thing ;
It shows what Old English may one day become
In the purified air of its New English home.

CXXII.

A. P. Stanley to Mary Stanley.

BOSTON AND THE SALEM ANNIVERSARY.

[The occasion on which Mr. Story's ode was delivered
was ' the anniversary of the fifth half-century of the landing
of Governor John Endicott.' Mr. Story, who was an intimate friend of Stanley and of Lady Augusta, lived at the
Barberini Palace at Rome. In a letter written to him
from Boston on September 18, 1878, Stanley describes the
reception of the poem. ' What was to me, as a stranger,'
he says, ' most thrilling, both in the poem itself and in its
reception, was the powerful, the almost terrible, denunciation
of the dangers of the country and the heart-stirring appeal
to its better spirit. I assure you that, as I listened, my
eyes filled with tears, not only because the impassioned
words brought before me days long past in the Barberini
Palace, never to return, but because they seemed to show
that in our English race the backbone of our strength was
not, as in my desponding moments I sometimes think,
either in our own country or yours, broken and shattered,

and that our own hopes were not altogether doomed to extinction.

'You know the somewhat self-gratulatory tone which pervades all meetings of this kind. And although there had been slight hints in previous speeches of the same warning notes, yet it was your poem which first gave them full and unmistakable utterance, and which called forth a response, that showed how the almost audacious courage of your rebuke was not misplaced or ill-timed. The whole audience seemed to me in a highly susceptible state, and every such allusion came with a double force.'

After describing the vices of political, social, and commercial life in the United States, Mr. Story urges his countrymen to save their great Republic, now fast

> 'sliding down the dire declivity
> Of ruin and of shame.'

He appealed to them to rouse from their selfish apathy :

> 'Awake! arise! cast off this lethargy!
> Your ancient faith renew,
>   And set your hands to do the task
> That freemen have to do ;
>   Cleanse the Augean stall of politics
>   Of its foul muck of crafts and wiles and tricks ;
> Break the base rings where commerce reeks and rots ;
> Purge speculation of its canker spots ;
> Drive off the cruel incubus that squats
>   Upon our sleeping country, till it rise
>   Renewed in strength, with upward-looking eyes,
>   And forward go upon the path
> Of its high destinies.']

September 19.—Three days in America. After all our misgivings everything has far exceeded all wishes and expectations. The hotel was very comfortable, and the first night after the voyage very refreshing. At breakfast the next morning a gentleman came up and introduced himself as the Governor of Massachusetts. I had once seen him in London. He offered his services for the day. Meanwhile Mr. Winthrop, an old friend and a great civic

dignitary in these parts, arrived, having heard of our landing, and joined us. We started in the Governor's carriage,
an open carriage, with two fine black horses, and saw, with
the very best guidance, all the principal places in Boston—
the Public Library (whose books are lent out promiscuously
to the whole population, and of a million in the year only
seventy lost) ; the scene of the ' Scarlet Letter ; ' the spot of
the first scene of the Revolution, the battle of Bunker's
Hill ; Faneuil Hall ; the old State House before the Revolution and the new State House afterwards ; the Art
Museum—all interesting, if not for themselves, yet for
the pictures and statues of the founders of the American
Republic, or for the stories which they told us.

Mr. Winthrop returned to his country house, and we
pursued our drive with the Governor to Cambridge, about
three miles off. It is far more like one of our English
Universities than any other that I have seen. Not colleges
exactly, but cottages scattered about amongst beautiful
trees and small garden plots, and a magnificent hall, equal
to Christ Church or Trinity, built in commemoration of the
students who perished in the Civil War. I saw Longfellow,
who received me with true affection and sympathy. The
Governor, who lives in our hotel in a charming suite of
rooms, dined with us.

The next morning (September 18) Phillips Brooks, the
clergyman of the chief church, arrived from New York, and
he, with the Governor and Mr. Winthrop, took us by train
to Salem to celebrate the 250th anniversary of its foundation. It was an extraordinary scene. It began in a tolerably large hall about noon—crowded with natives of Salem
—a chapter from the Bible—a prayer, a hymn, a long poem
by a local poet, a very striking oration from Judge Endicott,
one of the descendants of John Endicott the founder of
Salem—a very forcible poem, very well recited, by Story

the sculptor, a native of Salem—the 100th Psalm, and the Benediction.

Then, in another hall, a luncheon with speeches, including one from A. P. S. The only drawback was the immense length of the proceedings, which prevented my seeing Salem itself properly. But this itself was instructive as showing what a hold the anniversary had on the people. Hardly any one left either hall. It was very striking that there were present descendants of the same name of almost all the original settlers, and the two first Governors were represented by the two chief men present—Endicott and Winthrop. Almost all the speeches were good, had it not been for their extreme length and self-laudation. But the most impressive feature was that underneath the whole festivity there was an under-current of strong political feeling against the excesses of disorder and corruption in the State, especially occasioned by a tumult which had occurred at Worcester the day before, that caused the whole meeting to be like a smouldering volcano. Every allusion to the necessity of order and political purity was received with shouts of applause, and this reached its climax when Story's poem was recited. I thought it quite magnificent in its tone. It denounced the follies and corruptions of the United States with a vigour which I should have thought quite impossible to have been attempted, and which, even after having heard it, I can hardly think could have been attempted if he had been present. But these denunciations, instead of being received in silence or with disapproval, were heard with a profound attention even more significant than the bursts of enthusiasm. I have written to him to describe the scene, saying that when he wrote the poem he could not have thought that there would have been one listener able to give an account of it without any partiality. My own speech was very well received.

One remarkable circumstance was that whereas, when the health of the President of the United States was given with the American National air, the guests remained seated ; when 'Our Old Homes' was given with my name, and 'God save the Queen' was played, the whole audience rose. This, I was told, was always done. There were twenty minutes left between our leaving the hall and our departure, during which one of the clergy drove me round the remarkable places of the town. I came back with Mr. Winthrop to his charming country house, five miles from Boston, where I occupy the room occupied by Sir H. Holland, Père Hyacinthe, Lord Dufferin, and many others. Nothing can exceed his considerate attention. To-day we went into Boston to see a few sights omitted before.

We stay here till Tuesday. There has been absolutely no drawback. The weather is splendid—the brightest, clearest sky—the most exhilarating air—so that I really feel better and stronger than for a long time past.

There has been no attempt at 'interviews'—no undue pressure. I shall preach for Phillips Brooks, and for no one else till I come to New York. There is the liveliest interest in my coming, and I feel the liveliest interest in talking to every one. There is something very new in finding oneself in a foreign country with one's own language. The wonder—the amusement—the consternation, in all this refinement and civilisation, is to read the hideous state of things in the newspapers, hideous in itself and hideously expressed. The want of cabs in the streets would be very disagreeable, were it not alleviated by the intervention of the Governor's private carriage.

There has been no trouble whatever. The only absurd demand has been a score of letters asking for autographs. It strikes me that the society of Boston is very like that of Geneva, which I have always maintained to be the most civilised in Europe—the same uniform amount of intelligence and cultivation in all the families—all well-conditioned, and all intermarried with each other. The only difficulty is to resist the invitations to stay here, there, and everywhere.   Ever yours,

A. P. STANLEY.

CXXIII.

A. P. S. to Mary Stanley.

NIAGARA.

Niagara : October 13, [1878].

We left Albany at 3 P.M. and started straight for Niagara, passing by the absurd agglomeration of classical names—Attica, Syracuse, Rome. Finally, at 12.45, we arrived at the station of this famous name. When we reached the suspension-bridge, we left the omnibus to walk over it by ourselves. It was the brightest, clearest light of the full moon—the very full moon which, in making our plans while on the steamer, we had set apart for Niagara, and, but for my temporary indisposition, should have missed.

Before us were the two vast masses of water—the almost unbroken whiteness of the American Fall—and further off, with its depths of light and shade, the irregular gloom of the Canadian Fall, out of which, high in the moonlight air, twice as high as the fall itself, rose a column of ghostly mist, like a pillar of silver fire, into the clear sky ; all was still, except the roar of the vast amphitheatre of cataract, in which I recognised exactly what Frederick Bruce once said to me as, walking with him in the Birdcage Walk, we heard the distant rush of Piccadilly, ' This is the sound of Niagara.'

When we reached the hotel, the landlord said, ' You could not have come on a more glorious night,' and others have told us since that the column of spray is rarely seen as it was then. In the morning it had vanished, but it remains in my mind the first and transcendent impression of the great Niagara—the cloud of moonlight incense going up from the turmoil and confusion of earthly conflict.

A long sleep. The English Church in the morning, and then an exploration of some of the many points of view, which I will not describe in detail, but will give my impressions as a whole.

There is the immense mass of water. We have heard much of the Falls of Niagara, but far too little of the River of Niagara. It is an immense sealike stream, foaming and spreading above the Falls, and filling up the whole line of the horizon, and below it is a splendid volume of green waves like the Rhine at Bâle ; and then the Falls themselves, which are at least three—the Canadian and American Falls, and the Bridal Veil. They correspond to the Cascada, the Cascadella, and the Cascadellina at Tivoli ; and the place gives the same impression of a barrier of rock and earth saturated like a sponge, with springs and streams bursting forth in every direction. But on what a scale ! The two great Falls are no doubt deficient in height, but this is compensated by their enormous sweep. Each seems to contain a world of waterfalls in itself, with every variety of character ; the vast green sweep, the volumes of foam shooting through and through, and bursting into fountains of snow-white spray. There is a most impressive cleft in the midst of the Canadian Falls, exactly where the English and American boundaries are divided, out of which comes a chaos of confusion and conflict.

Besides these two great prodigies there are the rapids above and below—the rapids above spreading far and wide with white-crested waves—the rapids below tossed up with mountains of foam from the mere depths of the river, which is there as deep below the surface as the Falls are high above it.

There has been a great deal of encroachment of shops, houses, and mills, particularly on the American side. The town there had originally been called *Manchester*, with a view of using the water for manufacturing purposes. Now they have grown wiser, and call it *Niagara Falls*. But there is still a large amount of wild natural scenery— Goat Island especially, with rocks and broken trunks of trees. I was astonished at the size of the island—three miles long, I think, whereas I had imagined it a mere rock.

The incidents have been full of amusement. We determined to see the inside of the American Falls, and were equipped in waterproof hat, vest, trousers, stockings, shoes, and crept down a staircase into the first entrance beneath the Falls. The huge columns of water burst over our heads, but the spray was a driving rain. Presently I heard Harper's voice behind me shouting at its utmost pitch above the roar of the cataract, ' *You must not go on.*' It was not the danger of the rocks, but the prospect of spending half an hour in this drenched state ; with all the precautions, it was like passing through a river. So he dragged me back, and we ignominiously scrambled up again, none the worse.

October 14.—Detained here another day ; went down the river to see the Archdeacon of Niagara. On the way there was a splendid view over the Niagara river, with the original primeval pass through which the Falls must have been, and the opening into the Lake Ontario. This was also the scene of the last battle between the English and Americans in 1814, when the Americans invading Canada were driven down the heights into the river. A fine monument of General Broch, who was killed in the victory, crowns the height.

On our return, for Catherine's sake, we looked in for five minutes at Maria Rye's establishment, and saw forty blooming children.

On a little rock, such as I had imagined Goat Island to be, on the Canadian Falls, we met two Englishmen. One of them turned out to be a son [5] of Darwin, known both to Grove and Harper.

We have just heard that Goldwin Smith is not at Toronto—a great disappointment. We go on to catch Lord Dufferin at Montreal, and see his departure at Quebec on Saturday. Then return to the U.S.A. and slowly back to New York about October 30.

The only thing that has failed has been the autumnal tints. With the exception of a few blazing scarlet maples, like the Burning Bush, there has been an untowardness in the change of colour, owing to the long heats.

Let dear H. P. see this letter. I am thankful to hear of his amendment. This is the first place he would have enjoyed. It is a real hotel and a splendid situation, very comfortable, and the only natural object that he would have cared to see. As at Chamounix, we are the last in the hotel ; it is closed the day we leave it.

It seems so strange to have only received the response to my first letter.   Yours always,

A. P. STANLEY.

P.S.—You will want a few words on Americanisms. Well, ' I guess' I will ' go right away,' and ' start out in advertising ' you, lest you should ' reckon ' that I have been only ' fuss and feathers,' or ' a frizzle and a fraud.'

I trust you have not ' torn down ' St. Margaret's, and

[5] Mr. William Darwin of Southampton.

that you have 'picked up' all the seats. It seems 'way off' to Westminster. We hear that Dr. Farrar is 'a very lovely man.' We have 'gone ahead' every day, and our knowledge in this country is now 'pretty considerable.'

Harper is 'quite smart,' and Grove is 'mighty clever.'

We have tried to understand the politics of the States. We are not yet converted to Greenbackism, nor are we satisfied to become 'know-nothings' or 'small-a-ways.' It is very doubtful whether we are 'democrats or republicans.' If you had a good 'ticket' we think we could 'run' you for the next Presidential Election, but we question whether the 'planks of your platform' are quite sound. We are not ready to eat a 'boiled crow,' but you must have 'backers,' and then you will 'go in right and tight.'

We have been 'down South,' and lived amongst the rebels, but even in the North we have met with some 'Copperheads,' and we have heard a song which has taken our fancy, from the South to Maryland, when she was hesitating between the Union and the Confederates:

> She is not dead, nor deaf, nor dumb ;
> She longs to fight the Northern scum ;
> She breathes, she burns, she'll come, she'll come ;
> Maryland, my Maryland.

Everything has been 'handsome.' We have none of us yet got 'a complete suit of hair,' though often near to it. Now our appetites are 'sharp set for dinner,' so I must 'mail' this letter, and ask you to 'rush' its contents to Mrs. Drummond, &c.   Ever yours,

A. P. STANLEY.

CXXIV.

ABSENCE AND PRESENCE.

[The following lines were written after Stanley's return from
America, on the third anniversary of his wife's death.]

I FEEL her absence, as I move
   Stumbling in ways untried, unknown,
Without the word of warning love
   To guide my path, uncertain and alone.

I feel her presence, as there heaves
   Some noble thought or deed in view,
Thro' which her tone, her look inweaves
   Its own sweet harmony, its radiant hue.

I feel her absence, as I roam
   Where had she come, each strange abode
Would seem like some long-cherished home
   And with triumphal joy and wondering awe
      have glow'd.

I feel her presence, in each hand
   That presses mine with firmer hold,
Because her soul from land to land
   Has laid the magic touch which turns
      one's life to gold

Absent or present, far or near,
   Named or unnamed, the vacant space,
In ease or care, thro' smile or tear,
   Speaks with that silent voice, shines with
      that vanished face.

F F

CXXV.

MANZONI'S HYMN FOR WHITSUNDAY.

[The following lines are a translation of the last eight stanzas of Alessandro Manzoni's hymn, ' La Pentecoste.' The original poem, consisting of eighteen stanzas, was published in the first quarter of the present century. It thus begins :

> Madre dei Santi ; immagine
> de la città superna,
> del sangue incorruttibile
> Conservatrice eterna.

Stanley's version is reprinted, with the prefatory note, from ' Macmillan's Magazine' for May 1879.]

OF all the Sacred Hymns of Manzoni this is the one which breathes the most comprehensive spirit. The first part runs on the more mystical emblems of the Church. But the latter part, which alone is capable of general use, enters into the very heart of the doctrine of the spiritual nature of Christianity, and contains a meaning beyond the original force of the words, which was intended to be confined to the limits of the Roman Church. It is in this wider sense that the following paraphrase has been attempted.

I.

Spirit unseen, our spirit's home
Wheresoe'er o'er earth we roam,
Lost in depths of trackless wood,
Tost on ocean's desert flood,
By the Old World's sacred haunts,
Or the New World's soaring wants,
Peopled isle or coral shoal,
We through Thee are one in soul.

II.

Spirit of forgiving Love,
Come and shelter from above

Those who claim Thee as their own,
Or who follow Thee unknown ;
Come and fill with second life
Minds distraught with doubt and strife ;
Conquering with Thy bloodless sword
Be the conquer'd's great reward.

III.

Come, and through the languid thought
Of the burden'd soul o'erwrought,
Send, as on a gale of balm,
Whisperings sweet of gentlest calm ;
Come, as with a whirlwind's might,
When our pride is at its height,
Lay its surging billows low,
That the world her God may know.

IV.

Love Divine all love excelling,
Quell the passions' angry swelling ;
Lend us thoughts which shall abide
That last day when all is tried ;
Nourish with the grace of Heaven
All good gifts to mortals given,
As the sunshine seeks to feed
Brightest flower in dullest seed.

V.

Yea—the flower would fade and perish
Were there no kind warmth to cherish,
Never would its petals rise,
Clothed with their refulgent dyes,

Had no genial light been near,
Turning from its loftier sphere,
With unwearied care to nurse
Highest good 'mid darkest curse.

VI.

Led by Thee the poor man's eye
Looks towards his home on high,
As he thinks with joy of One
Deem'd like him a poor man's son :
Touch'd by Thee the rich man's store
From his open hand shall pour,
Lightened by the loving look
And the silent self-rebuke.

VII.

Breathe the speaking speechless grace
Of the infant's smiling face ;
Pass with swift unbidden rush
Through the maiden's crimson blush ;
Bless the solitary heart
Dwelling with its God apart ;
Consecrate to things above
Happy home and wedded love.

VIII.

When the pulse of youth beats high,
Be Thy still, small warning nigh ;
When for great resolves we yearn,
Towards the Cross our manhood turn ;

When our locks grow scant and hoary,
Light them with Thy crown of glory :
When at last we come to die,
Sparkle in the vacant eye,
Hope of Immortality.

CXXVI.

A. P. S. to Miss Arnold.

THE ANNIVERSARY OF DR. ARNOLD'S DEATH.

The Deanery, Westminster : June 11, '79. Eve of June 12.

My dear Fan,—Here is this day come round again—
and how much I should love to be able to tell your dear
mother of the experiences in America which told me how
'the Life' was, after all, the most abiding and universal
impression which I had left on the American people. And
how curious it was to see, as an instance of the effect of
your father's teaching on me, even in detail, that, going to
the United States in almost entire ignorance, the few places
and events which sounded familiarly in my ears are those
which I remember in the lessons at Rugby, and which even
then gave me a dim and dark impression that America
must be an interesting country.

How striking to me is the thought of the three characters
that stand out prominently in my memory beyond all
others—your father, my mother, and my dear Augusta !
All the other beloved memories circle round one or other
of these.   Ever yours affectionately,

A. P. STANLEY.

CXXVII.

[The two following poems are reprinted from 'Macmillan's Magazine' for March 1880.]

THE DIVINE LIFE.

'Who lived amongst men.' (In the original draft of the Nicene Creed— from the Creed of the Church of Palestine.)

WHERE shall we find the Lord?
Where seek His face adored?
Is it apart from men,
In deep sequestered den,
By Jordan's desert flood,
Or mountain solitude,
Or lonely mystic shrine,
That Heaven reveals the Life Divine?

Where shall we trace the Lord?
'Twas at the festal board,
Amidst the innocent mirth
And hallowed joys of earth,
Close neighbour, side by side,
With bridegroom and with bride,
Whilst flowed the cheering wine,
That first appeared the Life Divine.

What was the blest abode,
Where dwelt the Son of God?
Beside the busy shore,
Where thousands pressed the door,
Where town with hamlet vied,
Where eager traffic plied—
There with His calm design
Was wrought and taught the Life Divine.

What were the souls He sought ?
What moved His inmost thought ?
The friendless and the poor,
The woes none else could cure,
The grateful sinner's cry,
The heathen's heavenward sigh—
Each in their lot and line
Drew forth the Love and Life Divine.

Where did He rest the while
His most benignant smile ?
The little children's charms,
That nestled in His arms,
The flowers that round Him grew,
The birds that o'er Him flew,
Were nature's sacred sign
To breathe the spell of Life Divine.

Where shall the Lord repose,
When pressed by fears and foes ?
Amidst the friends He loves,
In Bethany's dear groves,
Or at the parting feast,
Where yearning host and guest
In converse sweet recline,
Is closed in peace the Life Divine.

O Thou who once didst come
In holy happy home,
Teaching and doing good,
To bless our daily food ;
Compassionating mind,
That grasped all human kind,
Even now amongst us shine,
True glory of the Life Divine.

CXXVIII.

THE PERFECT DEATH.

Disce mori.

WHERE shall we learn to die?
Go, gaze with steadfast eye
On dark Gethsemane,
Or darker Calvary,
Where, thro' each lingering hour,
The Lord of grace and power,
Most lowly and most High,
Has taught the Christian how to die.

When in the olive shade,
His long last prayer He prayed;
When on the Cross to heaven
His parting spirit was given,
He showed that to fulfil
The Father's gracious Will,
Not asking how or why,
Alone prepares the soul to die.

No word of angry strife,
No anxious cry for life;
By scoff and torture torn
He speaks not scorn for scorn;
Calmly forgiving those
Who deem themselves His foes,
In silent majesty
He points the way at peace to die.

Delighting to the last
In memories of the past;

Glad at the parting meal
In lowly tasks to kneel ;
Still yearning to the end
For mother and for friend ;
His great humility
Loves in such acts of love to die.

Beyond His depth of woes
A wider thought arose,
Along His path of gloom
Thought for His country's doom,
Athwart all pain and grief,
Thought for the contrite thief—
The far-stretched sympathy
Lives on when all beside shall die.

Bereft but not alone,
The world is still His own ;
The realm of deathless truth
Still breathes immortal youth ;
Sure, though in shudd'ring dread,
That all is finished,
With purpose fixed and high
The Friend of all mankind must die.

Oh ! by those weary hours
Of slowly ebbing powers,
By those deep lessons heard
In each expiring word ;
By that unfailing love
Lifting the soul above,
When our last end is nigh,
So teach us, Lord, with Thee to die !

CXXIX.

A. P. S. to Miss Arnold.

THE ANNIVERSARY OF DR. ARNOLD'S DEATH.

Deanery, Westminster : June 11, 1880.

My dear Fan,—I anticipate by one day the letter which I always wrote to your dear mother at this time, that you may get it in the midst of dear Matthew's home.

I am going to give an address to a school of Alice Lushington's on your father, and I shall make it, as at Rugby, on the two words whose meaning and hope Matthew told me that we had both learned from the same source— Religion and History.

How I seem to see him towering above the rest of the world, amidst all the changes that have happened since! How I trust to what he taught us and what he showed us!

.We are on a little island of memory, and all who share in that memory must hold together as long as life lasts.

Ever yours affectionately,

A. P. STANLEY.

CXXX.

Rev. B. Jowett to A. P. S.

THE LAST YEARS OF LIFE.

[For an account of the agitation against the erection of a monument to the Prince Imperial in Westminster Abbey, see 'Life,' vol. ii. pp. 324–330.]

Oxford : July 14, 1880.

My dear Arthur,—I hardly like to offer you advice, because it is intrusive, and because it is so difficult for one friend to judge of another's character or circumstances. And please not to suppose that in giving it I think myself your superior in any way ; the reverse is the truth.

It always seemed to me that the last ten years of life are the most important of all (and for myself I build my hopes entirely on what I can do in them). I sometimes fear that you are allowing yourself to be crushed by personal misfortunes—some very real, like the loss of dear Lady Augusta which I shall never cease to lament, but others partly fanciful, like this matter of the Prince Imperial, which really does not affect you in any important manner. Will you not shake this off and fix your mind exclusively on high things? I really believe that this ' expulsive power ' is necessary for your happiness. I am certain that your talents are as good as ever and your experience far greater. I am not flattering you when I say that you are the most distinguished clergyman in the Church of England, and could do more than any one towards the great work of placing religion on a rational basis. If you can accomplish this task you may effect more good and have a much more enduring fame than any Bishop or Archbishop of the English Church.

What you have done has been good and valuable ; but like other theological writings it has been transient, suited to our generation more than to another. But *this* work should be of a deeper kind—the last result of many theological thoughts and experiences, into which your whole soul and life might be thrown, all the better because the truths of which you speak had been realised by suffering.

It may be objected that such a book could not be written by a person holding a leading position in the Church. But if it were, it would win the battle of freedom for other clergymen, and to fight such a battle would be a great interest and a legacy to leave to the Church if gained. Few things will rouse the laity ; but that certainly would.

Such a labour would require you to withdraw a good deal from society, from Convocation, and from Church agitation of other sorts. But there would be nothing lost in this ; you have gained all that you can possibly gain from society, and as for Convocation, your friends regret your going to a place where they are rude to you ; and, whereas they do you harm, you can do these bigots no good, to say nothing of the whole affair being a great sham. You would return to the studies of your youth, the great religion of the world, the early Christian Church, its Gospels, the good in everything which is a mere vacant and unmeaning word, but may be made a power in the world. You would live among the thoughts which a wise and good man would wish to have familiarly haunting him during his last years. And you would be able to say after all, ' It is finished.'

Will you reflect upon the whole matter ? Forty years ago we all expected you to be the most distinguished man among us, and you must not disappoint us. I would like you to plan out a course of study and writing, and to place yourself in circumstances in which you can carry it out, and allow nothing to interrupt it. The more you come to Oxford for the search of quiet reading, the more I shall be the gainer. You shall talk to us about the work or *not*, as you think best. You and I, and our dear friend Hugh Pearson, and Rogers,[6] and some others are rather isolated in the world, and we must hold together as long as we can.

Farewell ; I shall not intrude upon you again in this way, but   Believe me, ever your affectionate

B. JOWETT.

I have good accounts of Rogers. I have no doubt he will recover, but it will be a slow business.

[6] The Rev. William Rogers.

Rev. B. Jowett to A. P. S.

THE DEATH OF GEORGE ELIOT.

[George Eliot died on December 22, 1880.]

West Malvern : December 29, 1880.

My dear Arthur,—Many thanks for your kind and sympathising letter ; I do feel greatly the death of Mrs. Cross, who is a friend never to be replaced. She was one of the few persons eminent in literature, whose conversation was equal, or even superior, to her writings. She made one great though excusable mistake in her own life. But with this exception she was a remarkably good woman, especially in all womanly qualities, absolutely free from vanity, jealousy, and every form of egoism, and her influence over young men was entirely good and pure.

I always sympathised with her marriage with Mr. Cross (who was her devoted admirer and quite worthy of her for his moral qualities), for it gave her six months of unalloyed happiness. The only real objection was disparity of age ; but he only thought of the 'high companionship' which will be the light of his future life.

I am very sorry for him : if you could call upon him (4 or 5 Cheyne Walk),[7] the attention would be greatly valued.

Dear Mrs. Cross was buried to-day in the Highgate cemetery. About this time last week she was first discovered to be dangerously ill : Doctor Andrew Clark came to see her, looked at her, and said to the general practitioner, 'Moritura.'

[7] 4 Cheyne Walk.

I do not wonder at your mind often returning to Lady Augusta : this is a death that she would have felt greatly. I do not think that Mrs. Cross's power of mind or writing was at all exhausted. On Friday, she was at the ' Agamemnon,' and had been explaining to her husband the lines,

$$\iota\grave{\omega} \; \beta\rho\acute{o}\tau\epsilon\iota\alpha \; \pi\rho\acute{\alpha}\gamma\mu\alpha\tau'. \; \epsilon\grave{\upsilon}\tau\upsilon\chi o\hat{\upsilon}\nu\tau\alpha \; \mu\grave{\epsilon}\nu$$
$$\sigma\kappa\iota\acute{\alpha} \; \tau\iota s \; \grave{\alpha}\nu \; \tau\rho\acute{\epsilon}\psi\epsilon\iota\epsilon\nu.^{8}$$

And Mr. Cross tells me that she had intended to write one more great work of fiction.

May you have a happy new year !

Ever yours affectionately,

B. JOWETT.

CXXXII.

A. P. S. to Mrs. Drummond.

HIS LAST LETTER.

[This unfinished letter was found at Stanley's death, and given to Mrs. Drummond of Megginch, who in July 1881 was travelling in Greece.

The Rev. Henry Montgomery, now Bishop of Tasmania, had been for several years a close and intimate friend. Stanley was to have performed the ceremony at his marriage with Miss Maud Farrar, the daughter of the present Dean of Canterbury.

President Garfield died on September 19, 1881, of the wound received on July 2, 1881.

On Saturday, June 18, 1881, Stanley had begun a course of weekly sermons on the Beatitudes. The course was never completed. His last words in Westminster Abbey were spoken on Saturday, July 9, 1881, on the text, ' Blessed are the merciful, for they shall obtain mercy. Blessed are the pure in heart, for they shall see God.'

He died on July 18, 1881.]

---

[8] With this reading, the meaning is, ' Alas for mortality ! By a mere shadow even a prosperous man may be overturned.' *Agamemnon*, 1298-9.

Deanery, Westminster.

My dearest F. D.,—I am delighted that you have seen
and enjoyed Athens, and that Mary was dragged, like
Hector, round the walls, not of Troy, but of Mycenæ.
What recollections that name suggests! I have not seen it
since 1840, and it then struck me as the most impressive
place, except Delphi, that I had ever seen.

You will come just in time for the Montgomery marriage—the 28th—. We shall receive you with open arms.
I have begun my sermons fairly well; they have reached
the fourth Beatitude. I found that I could not afford
to give them all separately, so I have taken two at a
time.

I am now quite well again. The assassination of
President Garfield throws us all into commotion. Beware
of the heat.   Ever yours,

A. P. STANLEY.

You will have heard of my effort to

INDEX

G G

PRINTED BY
SPOTTISWOODE AND CO., NEW-STREET SQUARE
LONDON